colloquium slavicum 4

vsevolod setchkarev

ivan goncharov
his life and his works

 jal-verlag · würzburg

colloquium slavicum

Beiträge zur Slavistik

Herausgeber
Heinrich Kunstmann, Universität München
Vsevolod Setchkarev, Harvard University

Band 4

jal-verlag · würzburg

Vsevolod Setchkarev

Ivan Goncharov

His Life and His Works

jal-verlag · würzburg
1974
ISBN 3 7778 0091 0

© jal-verlag, würzburg 1974
Composed by: Gerda Ruff, Würzburg
Printed by: repro-druck „Journalfranz" Arnulf Liebing, Würzburg
Printed in Germany
ISBN 3 7778 0091 0

Preface

In literary scholarship and among Russian readers Ivan Aleksandrovich Goncharov (1812–1891) is always being named as the fourth along with the three great Russian novelists of the XIXth century Tolstoj, Dostoevskij, and Turgenev.

At the same time only one of his three novels, *Oblomov,* is really known to the foreign public and secondary literature about him is rather scarce everywhere. In English only two monographs on him exist, both rather short: Janko Lavrin, *Goncharov,* New Haven, 1954, and Alexandra and Sverre Lyngstad, *Ivan Goncharov,* Twayne Publishers, New York, 1971. His great novel *The Precipice* was never translated into English in its entirety.

This study is an attempt to provide an introduction to the life and the work of this undeservedly neglected writer. I have used all available material in Russian and I have tried to analyze all of his relevant work. I have not tried to provide "a picture of the writer's time" and I have deliberately refrained from quoting extensively critical evaluations of his art, which take such an unduly large space in Soviet monographs. The concentration is exclusively on Goncharov, and certainly his personality and his great literary achievement are a rewarding topic.

I would like to thank Dr. Michael Henry Heim, who edited the parts of the text, which I wrote in English and translated long portions of it written in German, as well as most of the extensive Russian quotes. A great help were the publications of Anatolij Alekseev, providing a firm line of data concerning Goncharov's not too well known life. The interpretation of his work in literary scholarship is so erratic and mostly so little in conformity with the writer's own text that I had to try to find a path for myself. Where I am indebted to predecessors I have indicated this in the notes.

Belmont, Mass.
September 1973

V. Setchkarev

Note on Transliteration

The transliteration follows Chart III in *The Transliteration of Modern Russian for English-Language Publications* by J. Thomas Shaw (The University of Wisconsin Press, Madison, Milwaukee, and London, 1967), except for letters which would require diacritical marks (ch, sh, shch, zh), and for the Russian letter x rendered as kh.

Childhood and School

Ivan Goncharov came from a wealthy, well-established merchant family in Simbirsk (now Uljanovsk) on the Volga. Although his grandfather, also Ivan, tried his hand at a military career and worked his way up to the rank of captain, his father Aleksandr returned to trade and made a flourishing grain merchant.

In 1804, at the age of fifty, he married the nineteen-year-old Avdot'ja Matveevna Shakhtorina, also of merchant extraction. She was his second wife. Avdot'ja Matveevna bore him six children, of whom two died young.

Their second son, Ivan, was born on June 18, 1812. For the rest of his life he maintained relations with his older brother Nikolaj (born in 1808), his sisters Aleksandra and Anna (born in 1815 and 1818 respectively), and their families.

Goncharov père enjoyed a good reputation in Simbirsk and was several times elected to the office of mayor. His spacious stone house (large stone houses were somewhat of a rarity in those days) was located in the center of the city and boasted a large reception hall complete with chandelier. The countyard surrounding the house was large enough to support a bevy of buildings: servants' quarters, stables for cattle, poultry coops, storehouses, barns, and even a private bathhouse. Goncharov was fond of pointing out that the ensemble gave more the impression of an estate in the country than of a town dwelling.

Young Ivan scarcely knew his father; he died in 1819. Nothing certain is known of his character, but there are rumors that he suffered fits of depression. And it is a fact in any case that mild forms of mental illness tended to crop up now and then among various members of the family.

Avdot'ja Matveevna took charge of the children's upbringing. What she lacked in education, she made up for in energy and common sense. Goncharov describes her as "decidedly more intelligent than all women I know." [1] In later years he characterizes her as a woman who knew how to "love wisely", a strict and righteous mother, who watched over her children's development without sentimentality. [2]

After her husband's death she had to run his business and his large household in addition to bringing up her children. She was therefore doubtlessly grateful for the able assistance afforded her by the godfather of all her four children, Nikolaj Tregubov. Tregubov relieved her of the onus of seeing to her children's intellectual development.

There seems to have been a close relationship between the retired naval officer and the merchant's widow. Intimations of an old love gradually shading into friendship sound quite plausible.

Tregubov moved into the house and entered with great zeal upon the mission of educating his charges. His success was not surprising; he was well cut out for the task. He combined fine character with an education that was not, as might be expected from his profession, limited to mathematics and the sciences (in which he instructed the children); it included the humanities as well. For one thing he was a Freemason. And extensive readings seem to have broadened his intellectual horizons.

It goes without saying that he told the children many stories about his travels, thereby awakening in young Ivan, who appears to have been his favorite, a desire to travel, which may well have been a factor in his later decision to undertake a voyage around the world. Goncharov speaks with great affection of his godfather in his reminiscences (in which he refers to him as Jakubov). [3]

Ivan's early childhood was clearly a happy one. He was loved and sheltered, but not spoiled and surrounded by his beloved brother and sisters. The small provincial town in which he grew up was spared the effects of the Napoleonic Wars; they cannot have dealt the family any

---

1) Utevskij, p. 12.
2) VII, p. 235.
3) VII, pp. 233-254.

sort of psychological blow. Rather, it was the complete calm and lack of events that left the strongest imprint on the child.

With a view toward giving Ivan a more systematic education, his mother sent him at the age of eight to a private boarding school not far from town, in a village on the opposite bank of the Volga called Rep'evka. The school was run and owned by a priest, Fedor Troickij, a well-educated man and evidently a skillful pedagogue. His wife, a German who knew French well, laid the foundation for Goncharov's facility with foreign languages.

The priest had a small library which Goncharov (as he notes in an autobiographical sketch dated 1872) [1] read through with great zeal. To illustrate the chaos in his choice of reading material, Goncharov makes special mention of assorted travelogues, as Cook's, Krashennikov's trip to Kamchatka and Mungo Park's journey to Africa; histories by Millot, Karamzin and Golikov; and random works by Lomonosov, Derzhavin, Fonvizin, Zhukovskij, Nakhimov, Racine, Tasso, Voltaire, Rousseau, Sterne, Fénelon's *Télémaque,* Radcliffe; "The Saxonian Robber" an anonymous French novel, Malek-Adhel, the hero of Mme. Cottin's novel *Mathilde* (1805) and "suddenly" a little volume by Eckartshausen, not to speak of children's books.

In an earlier sketch of his life (1858/59) [2] he cites Ozerov, Kheraskov (whom he could never quite plow through), Genlis and again Cottin and Radcliffe, all three of them "in atrocious translations" as he expressly notes. He was also of course familiar with Russian folktales, and calls special attention to Eruslan Lazarevich and Bova Korolevich.

Ivan remained at the boarding school for two years, but his stay there was naturally broken by constant visits home. It is tempting to draw an analogy between Goncharov's life at the boarding school and Oblomov's life in the house of old Shtol'c. But Goncharov was neither indulged nor coddled at home. Indeed, the priest's boarding school was soon declared inadequate, and the ten-year-old Ivan, whose mother wished him to become a merchant, was sent to Moscow to the Commercial Academy (Kommercheskoe uchilishche). His brother had preceded him there, and it was expected that he would help Ivan learn the ropes.

---

1) VIII, pp. 228–230.
2) VIII, pp. 221–224.

His certificate of admission to the Academy shows him to be quite accomplished for a boy of his age: "He reads, and writes Russian, German, and French; is sufficiently acquainted with both parts of arithmetic; and has been introduced in the catechism, Bible history, Russian grammer, and the rudiments of geography." [1]

In none of the several *curricula vitae* he was obliged to write for one reason or another does Goncharov mention his school years, i.e. his eight-year stay at the Commercial Academy boarding school. In a letter to his brother Nikolaj dated December 29, 1867 he writes in connection with a *curriculum* he composed for the Simbirsk statistical records: "I also said nothing about the Academy in the biography because it's painful for me to think back on it, and if I had to, then I could only find bad things to say, and that I cannot do. So I'll say nothing at all. Because of the stupid and rigid authoritarian Tit Alekseevich (Kameneckij, the headmaster, V.S.) we moped away eight years there, eight of our best years, doing nothing. Yes, nothing at all. And if that were not enough, he kept me four years in the younger class, when I was the best of them all, only because I was too young, that is, too small. Yet I knew more of them all . . . . . No, forget your fine Academy!" [2]

According to the unanimous opinion of those pupils who later wrote about the Academy, instruction was unusually bad. Sergej Solov'ev, an important Russian historian and father of the celebrated philosopher Vladimir Solov'ev, stated pithily: "The quality of the teaching at the Commercial Academy was low, the teachers antediluvian." [3]

In the above mentioned letter to Nikolaj, Goncharov draws a devastating picture of the faculty members and their methods. He accuses them of stupidity, lack of interest, unwarranted rigor — which means blows — and drunkenness. He is especially biting in his criticism of the director, Tit Kameneckij, who is known to have placed spies among the students and who in general seems to have been an uneducated parvenu. Goncharov's animosity toward him was quite personal: Kameneckij, while admitting that Ivan "knew more than all the others", kept him back a grade

---

1) Alekseev, p. 14.
2) Utevskij, pp. 20–21.
3) *ibid.*,p. 20.

(the standard course consisted of four two-year grades) on the grounds that he was too young to be promoted.

Entries in the minutes of teachers meetings have by and large much good to say on Ivan's account. He was even awarded a prize at one point of his progress. It is nonetheless clear that he considered his hours in school sheer torture – in retrospect, at least – and he has his own mental agility to thank for having emerged as untainted as he did from such a deprived educational experience.

Naturally the young student spent all the long summer vacations at home where he must have once again come under Tregubov's tutelage. But in a letter he wrote as an adult to the editor Leonid Polonskij (dated May 20, 1880) we read that even during the school year he did a good deal of reading on the side: "My first straightforward teacher in humanistic studies – and in the moral sphere in general – was Karamzin. And as far as poetry is concerned, my fifteen and sixteen year old schoolmates and I had to get along with Derzhavin, Dmitriev, Ozerov, and even Kheraskov, who was also passed off on us at school as a poet. And all of a sudden along came Pushkin! I first knew him in *Onegin*, which was appearing serially, one chapter at a time. Good Lord! What a world, what enchanted vistas suddenly opened up before me, and what truths – of poetry, of life itself, contemporary life, a life I could grasp – gushed from this source, and with what brilliance in what harmonies! What a school of elegance and taste for someone of an impressionable nature!" [1]

Despite the little we know about the period Goncharov spent at school, one thing is clear: in one way or other he managed to acquire sufficient knowledge to qualify him nine years after he began for entrance into the University of Moscow.

By the time eighteen-year old Goncharov had completed the third grade, school had become too much of a burden to him; his love of literature was taking more and more of his time. His mother motivated her decision to withdraw him from the Academy before he had finished his studies there by pleading his brother's serious illness and her resultant shaky financial situation. These are obviously no more than excuses, though,

---

1) Cejtlin, p. 21.

because Goncharov later made a point of how grateful he was to his mother for not prescribing to him where to go. [1]

Apart from a note to the effect that he did not complete the entire curriculum, his school certificate (dated April 27, 1830) is quite satisfactory. He received a grade of Very Good in religion, "Russian, German and French syntax", English etymology, geography, history and Russian law; Good in penmanship and drawing; Fair in commercial arithmetic; and Weak in algebra, geometry and business. [2] To these subjects we must add Latin without which no Moscow University department would consider any candidate for admission. Since the dissatisfied schoolboy wished to enter the University as soon as possible, he must have learned the language somewhere along the way.

Nevertheless he was forced to wait. In the fall of 1830 Moscow University was closed because of a cholera epidemic. Industrious Goncharov spent his year at home preparing even more thoroughly for all entrance examinations. It turned out he really did need the time. For several months before the examination there was a new ruling that required Greek of all candidates wishing to study philology. Even although Goncharov took private lessons, he did not feel quite at home in the "language of the Hellenes" after only five months.

Before taking the examination, he had to be released from merchant standing by the local Simbirsk authorities, a formality still required at the time. Not until the request was granted would he be free to "enter the university and hence civil service or scholarly pursuits", as his birth certificate (issued in 1831) says. [3]

Finally in August 1831 he took the examination, which seemed very easy to the candidate. Even Greek (Xenophon's *Anabasis*) gave him no trouble. His reminiscences entitled "At the University" contain a very amusing account of the ordeal: "At this point he (Professor S. Ivashkovskij, V.S.) and I joined in a kind of battle: as I read, he corrected every word: my stress was all off. His ear couldn't bear it. 'No, no. That's wrong', he kept interrupting. But I couldn't care less about the

---

1) Utevskij, p. 12.
2) Alekseev, p. 17.
3) *ibid.,* pp. 17–18.

stress. I was casting about in the text for words I knew, as if for friends in a crowd." [1]

But everything turned out all right in the end; the professor had had word from above to go easy on "the Greeks" in consideration of the severely limited period the students were given to master the language.

At the University

Not too much is known about Goncharov's university career (September 1831 to July 1834, the normally prescribed three-year program). The above-mentioned reminiscences provide us with our most extensive source material. Probably, jotted down during the sixties and early seventies, they were reworked and published in 1887. They pertain strictly to the university and make no mention whatsoever of Goncharov's private life.

Yet we have every reason to believe that he was very much the student: quick, enthusiastic, and industrious. His long-nursed interest in languages and literature now blossomed forth. In addition to scrupulous, loving analyses of the required Russian authors — the Russian neoclassicists, chiefly — and "Indian epics and dramas, biblical poetry, Homer, Vergil, Tacitus, Dante, Cervantes, Shakespeare etc." [2] Goncharov kept up intensive outside reading. He expressly mentions Tasso's *Gerusalemme liberata,* Klopstock, Ossian, the Russian epic poets (with a critical attitude), and Walter Scott. To the latter he "devoted much careful study." [3]

Needless to say, he kept up with all the latest literature, both Russian and foreign. Pushkin was and remained his ideal: "The poetry of Pushkin in his freshest and most brilliant period of development made a keener and deeper impression on Goncharov than that of any other poet, and his admiration for him remained unswerving even after he later became

---

1) VII, p. 199.
2) Autobiographical sketch (1858/59) composed in the third person, VIII, p. 222.
3) *ibid.*

closely acquainted with the outstanding figures of French, German and English poetry." [1])

Besides the "coryphaei" Goncharov read now and again quite avidly French romans-feuilletons. The first work he ever published is a translation of two chapters from Eugène' Sue's novel *Atar Gull*. It appeared in Professor Nikolaj Nadezhdin's (professor at the university and editor at the same time) journal *"Teleskop"* (issues 15 and 16) in October 1832. [2])

The translation – the second and third chapters ("Les empoisonneurs" and "La veille des noces") of the fifth book – show young Goncharov not always precise, especially in his use of formal almost pompous vocabulary, completely not called for by the French. On the whole, however, it reads well and preserves the dynamic drive of the original.

We must certainly go along with André Mazon's hypothesis that the works M. Poulet recommends to Julija Tafaeva in *A Common Story* were also known to Goncharov: "Ce sont surtout 'les œuvres des écrivains français à la mode' (quote from Biographical Sketch, VIII, p. 225, V.S.), 'toute une littérature qui inondait alors la France et l'Europe' (quote from *A Common Story*, II, 3, V.S.): les fadasseries mystiques, si oubliées aujourd'hui, de Gustave Drouineau (*Ernest ou le travers du siècle; Le Manuscrit vert*, qui fit grand bruit en son temps; *Résignée; L'ironie; Les ombrages, contes spiritualistes*), les brillantes et absurdes pirateries d'Eugène Sue *(Atar Gull; Plik et Plok; La salamandre; La vigie de Koat-Ven)*, les sentimentales et prétentieuses nouvelles de Jules Janin *(L'âne mort et la femme guillotinée; La Confession; Barnave; Contes fantastiques et contes littéraires; Contes nouveaux)* et enfin les premiers chefs-d'œuvre

---

1) Autobiographical sketch (1858/59) composed in the third person, VIII, p. 222.

2) O. Demikhovskaja argues convincingly that even before starting work on Atar Gull Goncharov had translated Sue's novel Kernok le pirate (which first appeared in 1830 and was published again by the author the next year together with the novel El gitano under the collective title Plik et Plok). A fragment from the novel, entitled Gadan'e (Fortune-Telling), appeared in Nr. 4 (pp. 263–275) of the journal Severnaja Minerva (Northern Minerva) for 1832, signed Ippolit Glebov, very likely (note the initials!) a pseudonym for Ivan Goncharov. (Cf. Materijaly jubilejnoj goncharovskoj konferencii, Ul'janovsk, 1963, pp. 56–59).

d'Honoré de Balzac *(La physiologie du mariage; Contes drolatiques; La peau de chagrin; La femme de trente ans;* Eugénie Grandet, etc. [1])

In any case his skillful translation is proof that Goncharov was able to put his leisure to good use. And he was surely proud to see himself in print.

Goncharov's interest in literature went hand in hand with a delight in the theater. He saw great Moscow actors like Shchepkin, Mochalov, and Vasilij Zhivokini at the peak of their forces. He was introduced into the salon of the prima donna Marija L'vova–Sineckaja as an enthusiastic (and perhaps love–struck) admirer — by the prolific but not very proficient poet, writer, and publisher Fedor Koni, who was three years older than Goncharov and obviously a friend of his. And of course he was completely conversant with the repertory (mainly French and Russian neoclassicists).

Otherwise, however, his acquaintances during this period are pretty much a closed book. The fact that in a letter he mentions Dmitrij Min (later a translator known for his rendering of *The Divine Comedy)* and Efrem Baryshov (likewise a successful translator, known for his version of *Faust,* and also a less successful poet) indicate that he was totally taken up by "professional" interests and that he considered the university an institution for *learning* only. [2])

Such an impression is given by his remincences "At the University". Soviet scholarship does not find this very pleasant, assuming as it does that all great men must necessarily have been revolutionary and fought against absolutism at least in their youth. It especially likes to cast students in the role of revolutionaries and very often exaggerates their revolutionary activities. Only relatively small groups of students took an active part in such activities, and most of those who did were academically speaking far from the best. It would be difficult to agree with A. Cejtlin's claim that Goncharov idealized life at Moscow University in the thirties. [3]) The university was not bad at all at that time. Students who wished to learn could do so, and most of them paid scant attention to the measures taken against individual "politicians" with liberal sympathies.

---

1) Mazon, pp. 28–29.
2) Alekseev, p. 23; Cejtlin, pp. 441–442.
3) Cejtlin, p. 22.

In 1859 P. Prozorov wrote in an article about Belinskij and Moscow University: "1830, which was marked by a cholera epidemic may be called a transitional period in the life of Moscow University. From the highest administration to the instructors, all those grown too obsolete for scholarly pursuits gave way to newcomers with modern views and new goals." [1]

Goncharov cites approvingly Dean Mikhail Kachenovskij (Russian History), Nikolaj Nadezhdin (Theory of the Fine Arts), Stepan Shevyrev (Foreign Literatures), Mikhail Pogodin (General History), Ivan Davydov (Russian Literature) — all of whom left perceptible traces on the history of Russian culture. He speaks less positively of Semen Ivashkovskij (Greek), Ivan Snegirev (Latin), and the instructors in French and German. [2]

September 27, 1832 marked a great event in Goncharov's life: Pushkin visited the university. While still at school Goncharov had seen him from afar in church. Now here he was in Davydov's Russian Literature course accompanied by Sergej Uvarov, the Minister of Culture. "There you have the theory of art," said Uvarov to the students pointing to Davydov, "and here — art itself." During the following lecture, Kachenovskij's Russian History, an argument broke out between Pushkin and the professor concerning the famous *Lay of Igor's Campaign*. Kachenovskij argued that this curious work of Old Russian literature was a forgery of modern vintage (a view that still claims its adherents); Pushkin defended its authenticity. "I simply cannot express how great a delight we derived from seeing and hearing our idol." [3]

It is worth noting that the great poet Mikhail Lermontov was in the same class as Goncharov (though he soon abandoned his studies). Goncharov's fellow students, who later made names for themselves were Konstantin Aksakov (the Slavophile), Osip Bodjanskij (the dialectologist) and Nikolaj Stankevich, the inspiring nucleus, around whom congregated a group of students with an interest in philosophy. Though Goncharov showed no inclination toward German idealism that infused Stankevich's circle, he does note in retrospect that "literary circles (literaturnye kruzhki) were significant in his development." [4]

1) Utevskij, p. 26.
2) At the University, VII, pp. 208—220.
3) VII, p. 207.
4) Literaturno-kriticheskie stat'i, p. 338; cf. p.302.

In Simbirsk

In June 1834 Goncharov completed his studies at the university, and the following month he returned home to Simbirsk. Despite his mother's wish to see him married off and settled down, he stayed there only nine months. He was anxious to broaden his scope of activities in the capital. "Back Home" a sketch he wrote in 1887, gives a lively and perceptive picture of his stay in Simbirsk, though of course it does not hold entirely to the facts. The names of the characters have been changed, and the author's desire to provide the events with an entertaining veneer comes through almost too clearly. At any rate he thoroughly succeeds. [1]

Objectively speaking, however, the following can be said about his stay at home: the loving reception, which greeted the young man after he had successfully completed his studies and the endless attentions, which were lavished upon him by devoted housemates — the cook in particular — led him for a time to consider the possibility of remaining in Simbirsk forever. He even went so far as to accept the post of secretary in the office of the Simbirsk Governor Aleksandr Zagrjazhskij. The post proved less than ideal, however.

The governor — and we have mainly to rely on "Back Home" now — whom Goncharov calls Uglickij, was a parvenu with elegant manners, but no education to speak of and what is more, he cultivated a marked penchant for the ladies. He had apparently hired the inexperienced Goncharov as a front, the better to allow his predecessor, who had been compromised by accepting bribes but was still a clever operator, to finagle freely behind the scenes. Twenty-two-year old Goncharov soon caught on the goings-on around him, and so he was careful not to make any decisions involving any sort of responsibility. He turned instead to the attentions of the governor's wife and daughter, each of whom was charming in her own way.

Neither diplomacy nor administrative policy, nor politics as such, held any fascination for him whatever. In "Back Home" he pokes fun at Tregubov, his godfather, for trembling before every policeman that crossed his path, since the Decembrist Uprising (the Simbirsk police chief, E.I.

---

1) VII. pp. 224–315; cf. p. 315 sq.

Stogov — Goncharov calls him Sigov — was known for his severity), and at
the idealistic Freemasons (Prince M.P. Barataev, who founded the Keys of
Virtue Lodge — Simbirsk's first — under the name of Bravin he portrays as
a man without a firm political backbone). When it came to politics, says
Mazon in a witty mot, all Goncharov could muster was "a yawn or a jest." [1]
He maintained this attitude as long as he lived.

Zagrjazhskij's exploits — along with skirt chasing he was an expert at
feathering his own nest — finally went too far. It is said, for example, that
he sneaked into the house of a young lady whom he favored, disguised as
an old woman. In the end he was dismissed, apparently not without Stogov's assistance.

Even without these shenanigans Goncharov would soon have grown weary
of the provinces' narrow, fusty atmosphere. In April 1835 he and the ex-
governor left Simbirsk together for St. Petersburg. Zagrjazhskij's goal was
to see himself rehabilitated, Goncharov's to enter upon a career in the Civil
Service.

In Petersburg. The first literary steps as poet

Within a month Goncharov had secured himself a post at the Foreign
Trade Division of the Ministry of Finance. His main concern was translations
from English, French, and German. He remained at this position for seventeen years, slowly climbing the ladder of ranks, until in 1851 he became a
collegiate assessor (which approximately corresponds to the military rank
of major).

Though evidently conscientious in performing his duties, he was not
overzealous. Literature remained his principal interest, and he continued
reading widely. He also did translations from West European literatures

---

1) Mazon, p. 39.

"without any practical goal in mind, simply out of a *craving to write* . . ."[1]
and soon began to try his hand at original works in poetry and prose.

The circumstances under which he took these first steps were highly favorable. A superior of his in the service, Vladimir Solonicyn, who took great interest in literature and had even translated some Dickens, introduced him to the family of the painter Nikolaj Majkov in the summer of 1835. Goncharov's relationship to the Majkovs became a crucial factor in his further development.

Nikolaj Majkov, one of the period's most successful artists, and his wife Evgenija, a well-known poet and author of books for children, kept open house — a salon — for the Petersburg world of letters. They had four sons, all of whom eventually became involved with literature in one way or another. Goncharov was invited to act as private tutor to the older two ones: fourteen-year-old Apollon (who later became an acclaimed poet) and twelve-year-old Valerian (who became a literary critic). His job was to take over their Latin lessons and provide them with an introduction to rhetoric, poetics, and Russian literary history.

As a result of these new duties Goncharov visited the Majkov house daily. Moreover, he often stayed on after lessons to take part in the salon's literary conversations. There he met the poet Vladimir Benediktov, the writers and journalists Ivan Panaev, Stepan Dudyshkin, and Albert Starchevskij. In later years the salon was frequented by Ivan Turgenev, Fedor Dostoevskij, Dimitrij Grigorovich, Nikolaj Nekrasov and Jakov Polonskij, who all of them developed into great luminaries in the literature of the XIX century. The advantage of moving in this society is plain: at the very start of his career Goncharov established a number of valuable literary connections, some of which lasted the rest of his life.

Goncharov enjoyed of reminiscing about this juncture in his career: "The Majkov family bubbled over with life and with people, who provided them with an inexhaustible supply of material from the worlds of thought, science, and the arts. Young scholars, musicians, artists, and many writers and critics from the school of the thirties and forties would crowd into their neither spacious nor splendiforous, but comfortable and cozy rooms. Together with

---

1) Literaturno-kriticheskie stat'i, p. 337.

their hosts they comprised a sort of fraternal order or school." [1] Several sets of memoirs from this period are just as positive.

The witty, charming, and beautiful lady of the house knew how to make the most of the abundant possibilities surrounding her. She sponsored two handwritten "reviews" that "published" poems, stories, essays, and short plays by members of her family and habitués of her salon. Illustration — pen-and ink drawings and water colors — were provided by the master of the house. The highly attractive finished production was written in an excellent hand on quality paper and bound in Morocco leather. In harmony with the somewhat sentimental leanings of its founder, the first review was called "Snowdrop" (Podsnezhnik) and its follow-up, an almanac, "Moonlit Nights" (Lunnye nochi). It was in these reviews that Goncharov made his literary debut.

Issues Two, Three and Four (1835–1836) of *Snowdrop* contained four poems, the first of which was signed G and eight dots, the rest with G alone. Since no one else in the salon had a last name beginning with G and the eight dots correspond to the number of letters in the cyrillic spelling of Goncharov there is every reason to attribute the poems to him, even if they seem a strange sort of debut. The evidence in favor of Goncharov's authorship becomes overwhelming when we find that he parodies them in *A Common Story*.

The first poem "Fragment from a Letter to a Friend" (Otryvok iz pis'ma k drugu) follows romantic models. The poet exhorts his friend to abandon all attempts at consoling him. He has apparently been cruelly deceived in love (though he only hints at the reason for his plight). Time alone will heal the wound. And notwithstanding the depth of his despair, he acknowledges that all is not vain, that certain sempiternal values — friendship and love — still exist.

Despite a number of awkward, cliché-ridden passages, there are artistically impressive lines:

---

1) Cejtlin, p. 30; cf. his note I, 29, p. 443.

"Poprobuj v strashnoj buri chas
Bor'bu stikhij unjat' slovami
I zaglushit' gromovyj glas
Svoimi robkimi ustami!
Skazhi volnam nedvizhno lech',
Kogda ikh burnyj veter roet;
Kogda puchina diko voet
Veli vodam smirenno tech'."

(Try with words to calm the battle of the elements during a
terrible storm and smother its thunderous voice with your
timid lips. Tell the waves to lie motionless while a stormy
wind burrows them; while the ocean depths wail wildly,
command the waters to flow in peace).

The second poem "Grief and Joy" (Toska i radost') treats the two moods
in the title as enigmatic intruders that tend to take us by surprise and subject
us to their vagaries. The gloomy mood (which Gocharov develops much more
fully than its antithesis) gives rise to metaphysical meditations of life and
death. Even the rotation of the earth on its axis serves as a source of "mournful doubts":

"Kuda, zachem s tolpoj mirov
Ona tak pristal'no nesetsja,
I mnogo li eshche vekov
s ee gromadoj obernetsja?"

(Where and why, with a multitude of worlds, is it, so intently
rushing? And will it be for many more centuries that it will
still continue turning with all its bulk?)

The phrase "ona tak pristal'no nesetsja" ("is it so intently rushing") is
unusual, but very much to the point and convincing. The section devoted
to the joyous mood ends in a series of dots: it s a short dream and opens no
depths.

"Romance" (Romans), the third poem, is a plaint over lost youth. In its
diction it is reminiscent of Pushkin, and perhaps Goncharov actually did

intend to imitate him. If so, however, he did not succeed, for the poem has little merit, if one thinks at the model.

"Lost Tranquility" (Utrachennyj pokoj), the fourth poem, treats the same theme. Suddenly the usual feeling of strength and security of youth gives way. An inscrutable melancholy, the portent of death perhaps, refuses to be driven off by rosy dreams of a bright future. The poet uncovers an "abyss of agony" within himself. — These last two poems are quite weak; they are constructed almost entirely of poetic commonplaces. The first two, however, appear to be attempts at imitating the mannerisms of Vladimir Benediktov, a popular poet during his days, who was admired for his grandiloquent, almost bombastic use of lexicon. As such they do achieve a measure of success.

Goncharov chose his subject matter from among the standard themes of the somewhat saccharine, second-rate romantics, who were quite numerous in the thirties. Sentimental observations on the senselessness of earthly existence, the healing force of nature, the perturbations of true passions — such was the poetic order of the day. It was only natural for neophyte Goncharov to cut his teeth on this sort of material, without any personal involvement or feeling, of course. Clearly this lack of genuine involvement lies at the bottom of his caustic retrospective self-parody.[1]

Early Prose Works

At the same time Goncharov wrote an unsigned novella called "Nimfodora Ivanovna" as a supplement to the second issue of *Snowdrop* (1836). It was identified as a work from Goncharov's pen by Ol'ga Demikhovskaja[2] and first published in 1968 *Izvestija's* Sunday supplement.[3]

---

1) The poems were published for the first time by A. Rybasov in the periodical The Star (Zvezda) 1938, Nr. 5, pp. 243–245.
2) Cf. Russkaja literatura, 1960, Nr. 1, pp. 139–144.
3) Izvestija, 1968, Issues 1–4.

The subject matter may seem unusual for the Goncharov of *Oblomov* and *The Precipice*, but considering his infatuation with Eugène Sue at the time, his love for Gogol', and his own style at the beginning of his career, there can be little reason to doubt his authorship.

The story proceeds as follows. Seventeen-year-old Nimfodora Ivanovna lived with her aging father in Petersburg in shabby but decent circumstances. Sitting at the window with her needlework, she fell in love with a handsome young man who passed her house daily on his way to work in the Civil Service. He too noticed the pretty girl and before long paid a visit to her father, who — also a Civil Servant — was quite taken with him. In two and a half months Serebrov, for such was the young man's name, and Nimfodora were married. At first the marriage seemed a happy one, and in nine months Nimfodora gave birth to a son. But one December morning, about a year after the wedding, Serebrov set off to work never to return. As fate would have it, her father was struck dead by a heart attack on the very same day. The unfortunate Nimfodora did whatever she could to find her dearly beloved husband: she reported his disappearance to the police. Two days later she was summoned by the police and shown a hideously disfigured corpse dressed in her husband's suit with the briefcase she had made for him in the pocket. What is more, Nimfodora's wedding ring still adorned a finger of the corpse's mangled hand. There could be no doubt: Nimfodora was a widow.

Living of the interest of a small amount of capital, Nimfodora spent a winter of terrible affliction. Springtime saw her affliction steadily giving way to the desire to be loved. Then while walking along Nevskij Prospect one day she caught sight of her husband elegantly dressed and riding an elegant carriage. In her perplexity she nearly fainted, and before she could react, the carriage had disappeared. She began to look at the entire incident as a hallucination, though of course she could not forget it.

That summer the house she was living in burned down, and she and her child would have perished in the flames had it not been for a young official by the name of Astrov who risked his life to save them. He had long been secretly in love with her and was only too happy to take her in with him. Deprived of the very roof over her head, Nimfodora finally consented to be his lodger. And though Astrov took tender care of her, their relationship was entirely above reproach.

One day there was a gala military parade in Petersburg. Astrov and Nimfodora were among the large crowd of spectators. Not far from where they
stood Nimfodora again caught sight of her husband, and again he was
elegantly dressed. This time, however, she did not let him get away. Yet
her desperate adjurations were met with utter bewilderment. The man
claimed not to know what she wanted from him and never to have seen
her before. Nimfodora refused to leave him, and a crowd began to gather.
Then a police officer came along and the genuine passion of Nimfodora's
plead induced him to arrest Serebrov or Streleckij as he now called himself.

It turned out in the end that Serebrov had met a young woman, — the
wife of the decrepit Court Councillor Streleckij —, who had fallen in love
with him and persuaded him to murder her husband, mutilate his body,
and stuff it into his own suit. As a result he was pronounced dead, while
in fact he was living a life of ease as Court Councillor Streleckij, after a
cleverly accomplished change of apartment. He committed the fateful
error of not leaving Petersburg because his pleasure seeking "wife" would
hear nothing of it. In a highly dramatic scene in prison just before being
deported to Siberia for life he manages to strangle his former lover, whom
he now hates, and commits suicide. "Rumor has it," concludes the author,
"that Astrov took Nimfodora for his wife a year after this incident, but I
tend to doubt it; I know all the fervor of her first love. But then again,
who can explain the workings of a woman's heart?" The novella ends on
this ambiguous note.

Goncharov is very adroit in his treatment of the criminal case. He mixes
horror, humor, feeling, irony, realistic details and pathos. Though he does
occasionally parody cheap romanticism, Ol'ga Demikhovskaja is going too
far when she labels the work a "parody novella." [1] Goncharov does enjoy
joking, a trait that stays with him throughout his life, finds abundant expression in his works, and is certainly in evidence here; but basically he is
serious and pessimistic both as an individual and as a writer. He saw life as
a mixture of the horrible and the comical, a view that is clearly mirrored in
"Nimfodora Ivanovna." An author who always stands above the events he
describes, maintains the upper hand in his narration of those events, and

---

1) Materialy, p. 73.(Cf. p. 8.)

lets his reader know he is doing so — such an author is not necessarily parodizing; he is, however, making clear use of the devices of romantic irony.

His story begins *in medias res*. Desperate, alarmed, naive, and very attractive, Nimfodora goes to the police station, and the things Goncharov pauses to point out — "faces streaming with blood, broken arms and legs, corpses without a strip of clothing, or simply dirty clothing without corpses" — sets the tone for the entire narrative: a combination of horror and an aloof sort of irony.

For the most part the accent on horror may be attributed to Eugène Sue and the French *école frénétique*. Yet it is obviously filtered through Gogol's prism; his *Arabesques* with its "Nevskij *Prospect*" had appeared in 1835. The police official's long monologue on the peculiarity of Nimfodora's loss (he is accustomed to lost dogs, horses, cows, and stolen linen and answers her they can be found; but husbands . . .) is likewise Gogolesque, though probably closer to the *Evenings on a Farm near Dikanka* (1832) and *Mirgorod* (1835).

Not until after the visit to the police station does Goncharov recount the events leading up to it and describe how attractive Nimfodora is. She blossomed "like a violet, if you haven't grown tired of that simile," he says in a typical example of his frequent literary asides to the reader — and sometimes specifically to the female reader as when he tries to make horror acceptable to delicacy and fragility.

Immediately thereafter comes the body identification scene at the Police Department. Here the "female readers" are spared none of the gory details. They are first asked to imagine how they would feel if they had been walking through the tropics and "had suddenly seen some beautiful yellow and blue flowers peeping out of the thick grass, if they had stopped to pick them, stretched out a tiny white gloveless hand and then? . . . instead of the flowers had touched the head of a dead snake that had deceived their eyes with its multi-colored scales." After this brilliantly sinister introduction the dismally grisly reality of the story becomes that much more effective. The police official's cool matter-of-factness contrasts markedly with Nimfodora's desperation, which purposely hovers near the maudlin, but never crosses the border of good taste.

A digression, which deals with a certain Katerina Ignat'evna, a second cousin of the narrator who would be glad to be in Nimfodora's shoes because she would gladly have exchanged her first husband for a younger suitor — gives a clear hint as to the outcome and sounds very much like Gogol''s *Mirgorod*. But what can be done with a simpleton like Nimfodora who actually loves her husband, remains true to him, honors her father, and stands by other outmoded customs that are looked upon nowadays as suspicious.

The winter of Nimfodora's affliction comes alive in several effective nature descriptions designed to mirror her frame of mind. "Two birchtrees and an acacia bush stood by her window. The winter had dismantled them. At times the poor orphans bent under the onslaught of a terrible snowstorm; at times they stood motionless with naked skeleton-like branches." She is constantly visited with sad memories and horrorful nightmares, but only until spring and love awaken, for "many a wise man claims that the force that awakens nature is love," one of the many literary and philosophical references Goncharov so enjoys indulging in, — here he seems to be thinking of Plato.

Next comes Nimfodora's first encounter with her missing husband. Here is how Goncharov describes its effect on her: "Until now, novel and novella writers desiring to convey the shock produced on a person by something unexpected would resort to thunder and lightning, cannon shots and electric sparks. I authorize you to select any one of these comparisons because I do not feel like looking around for something new to describe Nimfodora's position." We learn immediately that she was not mistaken, only prejudiced by her own imagination. To substantiate this point, Goncharov abruptly launches into an anecdote from the life of Philip III of Spain which has nothing to do with the thesis to be proven (that imagination leads to error), but calls the reader's attention Lawrence Sterne-like, to the author's style and lays bare the device he is using. The narrator seems to feel a bit disconcerted about having gone astray: "Now let us put the wheel of our story back on the track it has slipped out of as a result of the coachman's lack of skill and the insane sprightliness of a group of horses only recently put into harness." (A charming hint of Goncharov at his being just a beginner in writing).

Goncharov describes the burning house in glowing colors, while at the same time gently parodying the usual treatment of this type of scene. The narrator enjoys comparing the unpretentious Nimfodora with classical gods and statues, often with comic effects, as is evidenced by his juxtaposition of the unusual name Nimfodora with the very common patronymic Ivanovna.

The Nimfodora-Astrov negotiations — first about his justification for rescuing her in her nightgown and then about the conditions governing their life together — is a perfect gem of humor. In the first case Goncharov allows his sense of humor such free rein that he raises some doubts as to the gentleness of Nimfodora's character. In the second he fares much better with a diplomatic treaty which regulates utter trifles in a solemn official tone and is clearly reminiscent of Gogol'. Here too he skillfully interpolates a literary reference: Chateaubriand has to suffer the brunt of demonstrating the dangers that may arise when two unmarried members of the opposite sex live under one roof.

After describing this harmless idyll, the narrator moves on to a description of the parade which centers around the impression it produced on the ladies. His irony with respect to the gentle sex and its reation to a soldier's black mustache doubtless reflects further traces of Gogol''s influence, especially when the enthusiasm for the moustache is put down to "patriotism."

The gripping and swiftly paced recognition scene finds Nimfodora plagued by disparaging remarks from the crowd which, except for one old gentleman, misses the entire point of what is going on, takes Nimfodora for a psychopath, and thereby heightens the tension. The tension is also dynamically heightened by the conversation with the police officer which leads to Serebrov's arrest and unmasking.

The following section, a long description of the state of the now conscience ridden Serebrov as he awaits transport in prison, provides effective contrast to the parade scene. Goncharov's tendency to incorporate general aperçus into his works of fiction can be plainly seen even in this early work ("ridicule is the most bitter aspect of misfortune," "a kind soul tends to be gullible," "friendship is good only in books," "love does not ask permission when it knocks at your heart," etc.). It culminates in a long excursus on happiness which the author perceives in an individual's complete and utter obsession by an emotion; he maintains that even if the emotion consists of

strong pangs of conscience, the individual will be happy provided it has
complete control over him. This somewhat peculiar theory may have ironic
overtones to it. "To live a full life, a human life, we must exercise our feelings and do so not by tickling them once over lightly. No! We must come
to grips with them at their mysterious depths, draw loud sounds from them,
– whether sounds of pleasure or of sorrow, – it does not matter –, but loud
sounds, sounds that will not let you forget yourself for a minute, that will
not let you forget that you are alive."

It is noteworthy that an Oblomov-like portrait serves as an example of an
unhappy person: a man who is fat, red-cheeked, and healthy sitting on a
cushion and peering out at the lives of people, with sleepy eyes, taking no
part, showing no emotions, no hate, no life, having no problems and no
joys.

The ending is short and effectively executed. Accompanied by Astrov
Nimfodora goes to the prison to see her husband one last time before his
deportation. She sees him at rollcall. He has changed notably; he is ugly,
almost benumbed. A moment later in comes his accomplice. The murder
and suicide are over in a flash, but not before the narrator sets forth all the
gory details. The above cited laconic and somewhat ambiguous sentence
closes the work.

In "Nimfodora Ivanovna" Goncharov does not quite hit upon a viable
balance of gravity and parody. The gruesome scenes have too genuine a ring
to them to work as parody, and it is only rarely that the exaggerations can
qualify as absurd. The characters of Nimfodora and Astrov have a clear
sense of unity to them and are quite convincing. Even the weak, stupid,
wicked – yet plucky and resourceful – Serebrov is believable. His lover remains a mere shaddow; we only hear about her pernicious influence, though
she does make an appearance in the last scene: "a dried out figure with a
yellow face and black eyes that flitted wildly and maliciously around the
room."

Despite some weaknesses, however, the flow of the narration in this novella is so swift and the sequence of scenes so skillfully handled that Goncharov manages to generate a real sense of suspense. The other important
redeeming factor is the work's humor, its comical turns of phrase. Here as
in later works humor is almost a trademark of the author.

Goncharov, like the Russian literary world in its entirety, was deeply shaken by Pushkin's death on January 29, 1837. For a personal account of Goncharov's relation to Pushkin and his reaction to Pushkin's death, let us turn to Anatolij Koni's description of a conversation he had with Goncharov in the summer of 1880: "And suddenly word came that he was killed, that he was no more ... I was at work. I went out into the hall and losing all control over myself I turned to the wall, covered my face with my hands, and began to cry bitterly ... Anguish pierced my heart like a knife, and even as my tears fell, I still refused to believe that he was no more, that Pushkin was no more! I could not grasp the fact that the poet I had worshipped lay lifeless. And I cried bitterly and inconsolably, like a man, who has just received news of the death of his beloved, — no, that's not correct, of the death of his mother, yes, his mother!" [1]

From now on there was never a hiatus in Goncharov's literary activity. The Majkov salon provided a constant incentive to writing and also promoted deep thinking. We have records of games that required great intelligence and knowledge from their players. One of them consisted of posing broad, far-ranging questions for the opponents to answer in writing. Someone e.g. asked Goncharov: "Which is stronger: the power of reason or the power of love?" Ivan Aleksandrovich replied: "Reason never governs all of man's actions the way love often does. We have no trouble recalling people, who have made fools of themselves or committed crimes for love, but try to recall a single one, who has destroyed love by force of reason. Only time and separation can heal love's wounds. That's the way people are put together!" When asked: "Which human failing is hardest to set right, in your opinion?", he answered: "Selfishness and avarice. These two failings are not only difficult, but impossible to set right. Their potency increases with age." [2] This prepossessing combination of scepticism, irony, humor, sagacity, and kindness characterizes Goncharov quite accurately.

The same tendency to make a game of writing is inherent in the "debate": "Is Life on Earth Good or Bad?", a humorous description of the Ekaterina

---

1) A.F. Koni, Na zhiznennom puti, II; 1913: pp. 491–492.
2) Cejtlin, p. 443.

Institute for Girls at which one of the Majkov's relatives, Natal'ja Majkova, held the position of inspectress. [1]

"Life is composed of two distinct halves: one is the practical, the other the ideal." This statement at the beginning has implications far beyond the "treatise" at hand; it contains the germ of the predominant position of boredom (skuka) in Goncharov's later writings: Boredom is the determining factor in man's practical everyday relationships with men, and how boring to live for others only! The other half alone, the ideal or aesthetic part of life enables man to concentrate on his inner being and deliver himself up to the dreams and universals. The "practically useful" half of life could drive man into suicide, but — (and at this point what was nearly a serious descussion falls into pure pleasantry), before taking this last step, the reader is requested to follow his author into the Ekaterina Institute, to get there force for life until the next attack of boredom sets in. No matter how much he jested, however, Goncharov never gave up the idea that life is either battle for existence or boredom, interrupted only by flashes of the ideal, by delight in nature, art, and love.

With good-natured irony he describes the Institute and its inhabitants, all of whom are perfect angels and find everything "just divine." Apparently this little work has been conceived as a kind of introductory letter for Vladimir Solonicyn and his nephew, whose name was also Vladimir Solonicyn, nicknamed Solik, to the "fairy castle," where they would find not only beauty, but also intelligence, which womankind is unrightfully reputed to lack. Goncharov gives them advice how to behave in this atmosphere of sheer beauty and adoration and tells them how and what to adore. Clearly, he makes fun of the sentimentally romantic ideas, traditionally governing the milieu of such Institutes.

It is interesting how Goncharov plays up indolence and even brings in his reputation as a sluggard. In the Majkov salon he was nicknamed the Prince de Legne (len' meaning 'indolence' in Russian). This indolence, however, seems to have been restricted to serious work, work meant for publication, for he himself stresses that he wrote copiously; what gave him trouble was deciding on the final form, putting an end to something flowing along of its own accord.

---

1) The original manuscript is in the archives of A.F.Koni. The work was first published by Ljackij, pp. 119–125, then by Cejtlin, pp. 445–449.

In 1843 and 1844, for example, he worked on a novel called *Old Men* (Stariki), in which he intended to show "how two men who had retired to the country made a great change for the better under the influence of their friendship." [1] Despite strenuous exhortations on the part of the older Solonicyn, he abandoned the novel. From Solonicyn's unsuccessful attempts at salvaging it in his letters to Goncharov, we can deduce the following: Goncharov felt he was too young and inexperienced, he argued that the work might force him to forgo the joys of youth, and he was afraid that there might be too blatant parallels with Gogol'. [2]

For a time, at least, the only works Goncharov completed were those for the Majkov's private periodicals. The qualities he demonstrated in the game — humor and a kind heart — come across amply and charmingly in the story "The Galloping Disease" (Likhaja bolest'), which first "appeared" in the twelfth issue of *Snowdrop* (1838), [3] signed I.A. (i.e. Ivan Aleksandrovich), an abbreviation frequently used by the Majkov's in their letters. In his 1858/59 autobiographical resumé, Goncharov writes the following about himself (in the third person): "Once accepted as a friend into the heart of the family of the artist N.A. Majkov (the father of the famous poet), Goncharov began taking part in their, so to say, household (i.e. not open to the public) literary occupations. Slowly and imperceptibly journals to which several of the Majkov's friends contributed, grew out of these endeavors. Goncharov was among those who participated, translating and adapting foreign-language articles on various topics, which were included in the journals anonymously. Within this circle of friends he also wrote stories, humorous stories that alluded to occurences or individuals connected with the group and were in no way remarkable." [4]

Such is "The Galloping Disease." The Majkov family very much enjoyed making excursions in and around St. Petersburg during the summer months. From this harmless propensity Goncharov cleverly develops an obsession, a contagious illness, the narrator himself only narrowly escapes.

---

1) Alekseev, p. 24.
2) *ibid.*
3) It remained unpublished until 1936, when it finally saw print in the journal Zvezda (No. 1, pp. 202–230).
4) VIII, p. 223.

The story's motto is a quote from a "scholarly paper" on the devastating consequences of the 1830 Moscow cholera epidemic, or rather its effect on hens. This detail sets the basic tone of the entire story: comic contents encouched in grave, sometimes anguished style. The medieval legend of the children, who inexorably gravitated toward Mont St. Michel serves as an example of the possibility of such an obsession. Its repetition in modern times is what the author wants to narrate now.

The afflicted belong to the "good, kind, well-bred" Zurov-family, whose leading representatives are being described with hilariously funny details, applying mainly to mother and father Majkov. The grandmother is also very successfully limned: a cripple confined to her armchair, she is always ready to pinch one or another of her withered members, in response to a request for weather report. "Snow, clear skies, a thaw, heavy frost," she jerks out fitfully, like an inspired sibyl — and never errs.

We learn that our guide through these sad happenings, Filipp Klimych by name, had been in the habit of visiting his uncle in the country during the summer and so knew nothing of his friends' obsession (they were completely normal in winter). He did not discover it until his uncle died of grief over a cattle epidemic ("he fell together with his last beloved cow") and he stayed in Petersburg an entire summer. It turns out that the Zurovs were infected by a peculiar retired State Councillor, Ivan Stepanovich Verenicyn (presumably Goncharov's superior Solonicyn in real life), whose eerie wanderlust Goncharov depicts with clear overtones of E.T.A. Hoffmann.

All this information has made its way to the narrator under the auspices of his school friend Nikon Ustinovich Tjazhelenko, in whom the editor of the first edition of the "Galloping Disease," B. Engel'gardt rightly sees the prototype of Oblomov. [1]

All he says in support of his thesis is well and good, but Tjazhelenko is also strongly reminiscent of Gogol's Ivan Nikiforovich from the "Report About How Ivan Ivanovich and Ivan Nikiforovich Quarreled" and Storchenko from "Ivan Fedorovich Shpon'ka and His Aunt." Tjazhelenko, an Ukrain-

---

1) Zvezda, 1936, No. 1, p. 233.

ian like Gogol' by the way, can only get excited over eating and sleeping, "activities" he praises in forcible tirades.

Soviet criticism constantly points out young Goncharov's "battle with romanticism," arguing that he treats romantic themes with devastating irony. If this is so, then Tjazhelenko's speeches might be said to reflect a "battle with materialism"; his praise of eating is as ironic as it can possibly be. In fact, however, young Goncharov's goodnatured irony is directed entirely against harmless human frailties, and it is quite senseless to interpret them in terms of a personal philosophy or outlook on life.

Tjazhelenko warns Filipp Klimych that Verenicyn is out to infect him too; thus forwarned he escapes the spell, by falling asleep on time and so not being able to hear the incantations.

Once his own immunity is ensured, he seeks to secure his friends'. His main offensive is a speech, which he compares to that of the anchorite Peter to the Crusaders (from Tasso's *Gerusalemme liberata)*, with the difference that Peter urged his audience on to action, while Filipp Klimych tries to talk his out of it. The speech has no effect.

In the end the family emigrates to America, where virgin nature offers them endless opportunities. Then one day they go off for a hike in the mountains and are never heard from again.

Goncharov had certainly no intention of picking a fight with romanticism. One of the principal targets for his irony, is excessive sentimentality. The main offenders among the Zurovs are Mme. Zurov and a cousin Zinaida, who gives the following response when asked what there was so wonderful to do in the country: "Gaze at the sky's azure expanse, inhale the flowers' perfume, look at one's reflection in the water's flow, wander through the grain of the field," and Mme. Zurov adds: "In short, revel in nature in the full sense of the word. In the country the air is purer, the flowers more fragrant. An unidentifiable extasy fills one's breast. The vault of heaven is never obscured by dust rising in clouds from stifling city walls and fetid streets. One's blood circulates more freely, one's thoughts are freer, one's soul is lighter, one's heart more pure. Man converses with nature in her temple, in the fields, he comes to know all the grandeur of . . . " – and so on, and so on adds the narrator. [1]

---

1) Ogonek, VII, p. 385.

Here an example of a concrete description of a "romantic" trip:

„Leaving them there, we set out on foot ourselves, and, as they say in
fairy tales, walked, walked and walked, and there was no end to our walking;
I will say only that we descended into five valleys, rounded seven lakes, climb-
ed three mountain ridges, sat for a while under seventy-one trees of the vast
dense forest, and stopped at all interesting spots.

'What a gloomy abyss!' said Mar'ja Aleksandrovna, after having glanced
into a ravine.

'Oh,' Zinaida Mikhajlovna added with a deep sigh, 'truly it has buried more
than one living creature within itself. Look, there in the shadows . . . bones
are showing white!'

And indeed, on the bottom were scattered about the skeletons of various
noble animals — cats, dogs, and among them was strolling Verenicyn, that
passionate lover of glancing into all ravines as was mentioned above. In another spot my unforgettable Feklusha found an opportunity to be captivated
by nature.

'Let's climb that magnificent knoll,' she said, pointing to a swell about
an arshin (yard/28") and a half high, from there there must be a lovely view.'

We clambered up and a fence presented itself to our views. It had once
served to delimit the bounds of a brick factory.

'Everywhere, everywhere there are people!' exclaimed Zinaida Mikhajlovna with annoyance." [1]

Clearly this attitude has nothing whatsoever in common with true Romanticism. Goncharov's criticism of romanticism (if such charmingly
ironical thrusts can be described as criticism at all) is directed at best against
the cheap epigones of the romantic movement.

The story's humor derives from the descriptions of the many misadven-
tures and sufferings to which "the obsessed" fall prey. Rain, heat, an over-
turned carriage, a surprise attack by a pack of hounds, or simply total ex-
haustion — the variations are very numerous and very witty. Another
source of humor is their grim determination to enjoy themselves in spite
of everything. "We had a wonderful time!" (My slavno poguljali!) is their
stubborn refrain, as they straggle back, half dead, from their expeditions.

---

1) *ibid.*, p. 393.

Besides its sometimes irresistible humor the story contains some quite original descriptive passages, this personification of spring, for instance: "April has come. The fiery rays of the sun have seen out the last winter day which exited with such a mournful grimace that the Neva cracked open with laughter and overflowed its boundaries, and rigorous Mother Earth smiled out through the snow." [1]

Many of the dialogues anticipate the verbal duels that characterize *A Common Story*. Tjazhelenko, for example, flies into a fury over the fact that some of the outings begin very early in the morning:

"... 'Sometimes in the dead of night when all are lying down, both rich and poor, and the animals, and ... the birds ... '. 'I believe birds don't lie down,' I remarked. 'Well ..., all right, it doesn't matter. I'm sorry for them. Why should nature deprive them of this innocent pleasure? Now what was I saying?' 'Birds,' you said. 'But you were just saying they don't lie down. Wait! What else lies down?' 'But couldn't you, dear Tjazhelenko, more directly, perhaps, come to the point? Otherwise you'll grow tired.' 'True, true. Thanks for reminding me. Let me rather just lie down for a bit, then I'll be more comfortable!" [2]

In contrast to these obviously Goncharovian touches, there are also passages that bear a distinctly Gogolian stamp. The description of the saloon in which "a bearded Ganymed" awaits his customers owes a great deal to Gogol''s style. Goncharov tops the passage off with a hint at Pushkin; his hero pretends to have too meager an acquaintance with such establishments to give a convincing portrayal of them: "For lack of observation and experience, I was unable to put together a sufficient number of facts and interpret them in greater detail. But there's no cause for despair; it is rumored that two prolific writers — on from Moscow and the other from St. Petersburg, O(rlov) and B(ulagarin) — are in possession of all necessary information, have made a practical study of the matter, and have long been preparing a major work on it." [3] Aleksandr Orlov and Faddej Bulgarin, two second rate writers, had shortly before been the target

---

1) Ogonek, VII, p. 373.
2) *ibid.*, pp. 380–381.
3) *ibid.*, p. 400.

of two extremely spirited and biting articles by Pushkin, which Goncharov must have known ("The Triumph of Friendship or the Vindicated Aleksandr Anfimovich Orlov" [Torzhestvo druzhby ili opravdannyj Aleksandr Anfimovich Orlov] and "Some Words about the Little Finger of Mr. Bulgarin and about Etcetera" [Neskol'ko slov o mizince g. Bulgarina i o prochem]).

"The Galloping Disease," which was actually nothing more than a humorous sketch, was followed by a longer more ambitious story "The Lucky Blunder" (Schastlivaja oshibka), which first came out in the handwritten *Moonlit Nights* in 1839. [1] Because it exhibits many of the earmarks of Goncharov's style in embryo, we will take a closer look at it.

The plot is quite straightforward. Egor Aduev, a rich young aristocrat, and the beautiful Elena Nejlejn, the eighteen-year-old daugther of a wealthy baron, are in love and as good as engaged, though no official mention has yet been made of it. One afternoon the infatuated and impetuous Egor visits his love and accuses her of coquetting. When she responds by laughing and teasing him he gets irritated; at last both get really angry and he storms off in the resolve never to see her again. Both immediately regret the quarrel. In an attempt to wipe it from his mind, Egor decides to go to a public ball scheduled for this very evening. His coachman takes him to a wrong address by mistake, however, and he winds up at an exclusive ball in the house of the Neapolitan ambassador. At first he is so distraught that he does not realize where he is, but then to his astonishment he catches sight of Elena (who would never attend a public ball). Far from playing the coquette, she is sitting alone, sad and lost in thought. It becomes clear to him that it is their quarrel and thoughts of him, what tortures her. He goes up to her, they make up and the engagement is announced the same evening.

That is all there is. But Goncharov relates it with obvious relish. He incorporates many details and digressions into the narrative and pays special attention to giving his main characters tenable psychological motivation for their actions.

---

1) It was first published in 1927 in the omnibus Nedra, No.10, pp. 243-287.

After the quarrel comes the question of whether Elena was actually guilty as charged. Goncharov shows that her character together with the conventions of her social set could not possibly have produced any other sort of behavior. On one level she did flirt with the men around her, but on another, deeper level she was actually drawing a magic circle around herself. The circle signifies her milieu's well-defined boundaries of purity and morality, the magic, the seductive means with which her beauty and upbringing supplied her. Even her love for Aduev could not make her renounce this magic. Why should it? The nucleus remains intact; indeed love has strengthened it.

Since Egor understands none of this, the question of whether he was not at fault also suggests itself. No, says Goncharov, he is not to blame either. Egor is basically an idealist, he explains, who has become a sceptic (much like Chackij, the hero of Aleksandr Griboedov's comedy *Woe from Wit,* and Onegin, the title hero of Pushkin's novel in verse *Eugene Onegin),* as a result of enjoying too many pleasures with too little effort. Scepticism had led him to reject all emotion as ingenuine.

When confronted with true love, however, his idealism rekindles. It focuses entirely on his beloved, in whom he sees his conception of the exemplary, a woman who will live for him alone. Coquettery clearly has no place in this ideal picture and could only bring about a strong reaction. No, Goncharov concludes, even though his "female readers" may take his hero for a tyrant, Egor is not to blame. Character and evironment account for all supposed faults.

Despite this impasse, love does conquer all — temporarily at least. It was pride that caused their separation; loving, they still would not give in. Moreover, it was only the coachman's "lucky blunder" that set everything right — or as right as possible under the circumstances. Goncharov is not one to delude himself; he is too clever. To the question of who is to blame he gives the following answer: "I don't think anyone is. If their fate had depended on me, I would have separated them once and for all and ended my story right there. But let's see what happens next." [1]

---

1) VII, p. 443.

This sceptical stance, a position that allows a certain distance, typifies the Goncharovian approach. Goncharov combines a clear understanding of his characters' emotions with a clear head. The former quality makes itself felt in his lively, believable characterizations, the latter in the irony of his incidental remarks. When Elena makes too many concessions during the reconciliation scene, Goncharov admonishes her to exercise a bit more self-control and accuses her of acting like a child. And when Egor cannot rid his mind of the insult he has had to suffer, Goncharov warns him not to be so sensitive. But — "their eyes gleamed with happiness. For a time they remained motionless. Then the invisible electric thread that stretched from one to the other began to shorten, they shut their eyes, and their lips met. He swooned, his heart stood still, and with a tremor he sank to his knees and covered her hands with fiery kisses." [1]

And so end the peripeties of the love of Egor and Elena — for the time being.

Psychological discussions — some of a general nature and others concerned with specific cases — always have a certain conversational quality to them. In this they resemble analoguous passages in the works of Vladimir Odoevskij, Russian literature's foremost propagator of German romanticism; Aleksandr Vel'tman, a contemporary novelist, who experimented in the romantic grotesque; and of course Gogol' (the two mottos of the story are taken from Gogol' and Griboedov).

The very first sentence provides a good example: "Once in winter at twilight . . . Yes, but please allow me to inquire first, whether you are partial to twilight." [2] Not until running through a two page excursus on twilight, — which sets the tone for the frequent digressions interspersed throughout the work —, does the narrator return to his story.

Though Goncharov's psychological analyses are in no way comic, his digressions bubble over with humor. The result is an inner tension that comes through clearly in many of his writings. He will carry on a paragraph-long polemic against the view that there is a type of suffering that deserves no sympathy because its motives are trivial, arguing that any suffering is

---

1) *ibid.*, p. 460.
2) *ibid.*, p. 427.

true suffering to the sufferer, — and follow it up with a description of Elena's boudoir; a description that culminates in an invitation to blow with the author on her gossamer dressing gown to prove it is light enough to fly away.

Another amusing passage gives a detailed analysis of the similarities between society ladies and the firmament, playing on a parallel passage from Gogol''s story "Nevskij Prospekt". Indeed, literary references appear again and again. By referring his reader to Pushkin's *Eugene Onegin* for example the author exonerates himself from the chore of describing the ball scenes.

Yet another humorous touch comes from the contrast between Aduev's behavior toward both his steward and his servant Elisej during his rage after the quarrel and his bliss after reconciliation. Elisej, the faithful old servant who keeps harping on his service to the young master's father during the campaign "against the Turk," may be seen as a successful preliminary study for Zakhar, Oblomov's man. The orders he gives his steward — first showing an almost inhuman disregard for his serfs and then the most tenderhearted sort of benevolence — are introduced merely to heighten the before-and-after effect, and as such they are quite overdone. Of course they can also give rise to deliberations of a strictly social bent, a point which has not gone unnoticed by Soviet scholarship. It seems quite risky, however, to draw conclusions about Goncharov's position vis-à-vis serfdom on the basis of one side of a pair of antitheses that has been postulated for purely formal, compositional ends.

Goncharov composed "A Lucky Blunder" of two main elements: sharp psychological analysis and a broad-minded, sympathetic humor. Apparently he had no intention of publishing it, however, for he never went back to it.

In 1842 Goncharov wrote a group of sketches (*ocherki*) under the title *Ivan Savich Podzhabrin*. It was not published until six years later — in the first issue of the journal *The Contemporary* (Sovremennik) — i.e. after the success of *A Common Story*.

Boredom *(skuka)*, the basic problem of Goncharov's philosophy of life, makes its appearance in the very first paragraph of this tragicomical work. Ivan Savich is a literary descendant of Onegin, but on a very low level. He is relatively well-to-do; he does not have to work for a living and his post in the Civil Service is pretty much fictitious. His mental facilities are no more than mediocre, though he is rather fond of speaking about "philosophy books."

The vacuity such a life produces can only partially be concealed behind a policy of what he calls "zhuirovat' zhizn'ju" ('enjoying life', from the French verb *jouir*). Enjoying life has a very specific meaning for Ivan Savich: running after girls. Nor is he particularly choosy. All *she* has to be is young and moderately pretty. After witnessing four flirtations, the reader can only conclude that the sole purpose they serve is to deaden the boredom of an unfulfilled existence. Boredom can become dangerous, for both the person stricken by it and his surroundings, and while in the case of the modest mental and emotional make-up of Ivan Savich this danger constitutes not great threat, its abstract presence still hovers ominously over the action.

As the sketch begins, we find the hero enveloped in boredom. In fact, he fritters away all his time and energy, oscillating between pleasure seeking and ennui. Boredom makes him irritable, and he takes out his frustrations on his dog and his servant, giving a solid completely unmotivated drubbing to the former and forbidding the latter first to snore, then to yawn, and finally to cough.

Following the practice of the "Natural School" (natural'naja shkola) in vogue at the time, Goncharov scatters his sketches with trivial details that point up the lowly, prosaic side of human behavior. As an example of how he handles this device, here is his description of Ivan Savich's boredom: "He was apparently quite bored. He didn't know what to do. To pass the time, he would bring his legs up under him and extend them out full length along the rug, he would yawn, stretch, or drop the ashes from his cigar into a cup of coffee and listen to them hiss. In other words, he was so bored he didn't know what to do." [1]

Avdej, Ivan Savich's servant, comes even closer than Elisej to Goncharov's classical portrayal of the servant Zakhar in *Oblomov*. The conversations between Podzhabrin and Avdej exhibit many of the qualities that made the Oblomov-Zakhar colloquies so famous.

---

1) VII, p. 7.

As soon as Ivan Savich moves to a new house, he starts up a flirtation with every eligible female tenant. And because his hanky-panky invariably brings him to the brink of an unpleasant showdown, he is invariably forced to move on. Both the beginning and the end of the four sketches finds him between apartments. We meet him — on the run from his last fiasco — taking new lodgings, and after following him through four adventures, we have him fleeing from the prospect of a forced marriage.

His four targets are very different. Anna Pavlovna, the first, is having an affair with a fat retired major by the hardly fitting and therefore funny name of Strekoza (the Russian word for 'dragonfly'), whose energetic jealousy keeps Ivan Savich on his toes. Anna Pavlovna's vacillations between "romanticism" in her speech and a keen business sense in her actions provide many amusing passages. Goncharov's ironic stance with respect to romantic clichés is more marked here than it was in "The Galloping Disease." At one point in the narrative for example the good Ivan Savich wants to leave his sofa in her appartment temporarily: " 'Here's what you do, angel. Keep one of my sofas at your place for a while. This green one,' Ivan Savich answered. 'I've got two and a couch besides.' 'What for?'. . . said Anna Pavlovna indecisively. 'I'd need a rug to put under it, and I don't have one . . Fortune doesn't smile on everyone' . . . (ne vsem rok sudil schast'e). 'Take one rug. I've got two.' 'Well, if you're that kind, then let me take the mirror too. It will help me to forget the blows of fate for some time.' " [1] The same thing happens with his clock: " 'Oh dear! I don't have a clock. How am I to know when you get here? The hours will seem like ages to me, and there are so few joys in life as it is.' 'Oh, don't forget darling,' said Ivan Savich, 'that life is short, as a philosopher said. Don't fret. Enjoy yourself. And take my table-clock, you know. It's dependable,' said Ivan Savich. 'Yes, but what shall I stand them on? I don't have such a nice little table. Not everyone is so fortunate as . . . ' 'Then take the table along with it. Avdej! Take it away!" [2]

Of course Ivan Savich himself cultivates quite a stock of stereotype phrases from the vocabulary of cheap romanticism. Every one of his prospects gets treated to an opening line of "Alone with you at last! Can it be true?

---

1) VII, p. 30.
2) *ibid.*, p. 31.

Or am I dreaming? " His "philosophical" position comes out in the maxim "Life is short, as a philosopher said," which he repeats with variations on every possible occasion. Goncharov is quite fond of using speech traits — and especially often repeated phrases — to mark his characters. The major's constant threat to Ivan Savich "I'll get even with you" (Ja s vami razdela-jus') is as funny and telling as Avdej's standard response to his questions "How should I know" (Ne mogu znat'). By varying the situation in which Avdej's answer occurs, Goncharov gets out a surprising number of nuances from it.

As his second "victim" Ivan Savich chooses the chambermaid of the Baroness Cejkh, occupant of the houses's most elegant appartment. To ensnare her he pretends to be his own servant. The good, simple girl falls for him immediately. They use to sit together and to kiss (he never seems to go any further). But after some time Podzhabrin feels his boredom again, whose appearance, by the way, made Strekoza's interference quite welcome to him in the former case.

It is interesting to note how many generalizations crop up here and there throughout the work. Generalizations were standard fare for the genre that authors of the "Natural School" called the physiological sketch. Here is an example of Goncharov's variety: "The maids are forever chewing or nibbling something. Their apron pockets always contain nuts, raisins or a half eaten rusk left over from the mistress's breakfast, or a biscuit, or wafer proof of the affections of one or another of the chefs." 1)

There is something most affecting about the case of the naive, uncomplicated chambermaid. She soon becomes an unsuspecting tool in Ivan Savich's attempt to meet her mistress, the baroness, and the discovery that her beloved was not the servant he claimed to be, that he has already wearied of her affections, touches a strain of genuine grief within her. Even down-to-earth Avdej, who in a moving scene suggests she try a bit of his master's liqueur (which he adores calling it bad stuff, /drjan'/ at the same time, and turning the normally masculine liker into likera, a feminine noun) to make her feel better, does not succeed in cheering her up. Podzhabrin, by the way, basically a good chap, tries to console her successfully with money.

---

1) VII, p. 42.

Baroness Cejkh is an arrant gold digger who swindles Ivan Savich out of large sums. Goncharov gives a very lively picture of a drinking party she throws for the *jeunesse dorée* of her acquaintance. True this description does not escape the tendency toward social criticism prevalent in so many stories of the period dealing with high society, but its brilliant humor goes a long way to file down its rough edges.

Ivan Savich's last exploit nearly ends badly for him. The upstairs tenant, a damsel, who is getting on in years, proves so extraordinarily virtuous as to be unapproachable. When after sparing no pains he finally wins an opportunity to break the ice, he finds himself almost immediately in the midst of wedding preparations. His moving is a real flight this time.

Goncharov obtains his comic effects in this final section by contrasting the girl's indignation at Ivan Savich's advances (which she fends off with the stereotype words "What are you doing to me? Whom do you take me for?") with her obvious hope that something permanent will come of them. He also draws an amusing portrait of the girl's godfather, an upright official who admiringly capitulates before the machinations of his not so upright colleagues.

Goncharov's friendship for Evgenija Majkova assumes a humorous semi-literary garb in the three part "letter" (Reproach, Explanation, Farewell) he wrote her on June 14, 1843 "after an eight-year acquaintance." [1] Mme. Majkova was about to take a trip abroad, and the letter was to be a farewell note. It is yet another example how the Goncharov of this period liked to combine romantic pathos with a highly personal, ironic treatment of his characters and their plights.

Floundering in his attempts to determine the sort of love he feels for the addressee, the author finally gives up altogether. His love cannot be neatly pigeonholed (it is neither erotic, filial, fraternal, nor merely a feeling of camaraderie), yet it is quite real.

He has trouble bringing himself to pronounce the fatal word Farewell. It is not something that can be written or said; it must be . . . borne. And by analyzing this image with an "If I may be allowed to express myself thus," he imbues the preceding solemnity with an ingenious sincerity.

---

1) Published in Cejtlin, pp.444-445.

This descent from the heights is even more precipitous when the intruder in the radiant temple is greeted at the "altar of love and friendship" with the words "Where do you think you're going?" (Kuda lezesh?) Goncharov often uses this "plunge technique" for comic effects. The author then compares himself to an old, dogeared book that contains nothing new, but is always comforting to pick up and on this elegiac note, which lends the letter a charm all its own, the elegant beautifully structured little work draws to a close.

Close contact with the Majkov family was of great importance to Goncharov because the other part of his life, his post in the Service, offered him scant satisfaction. For all his proficiency and conscientiousness he lacked the desire — to say nothing of the ambition — to build a career. Though now and again he would be given gifts for "excellence in service," it is clear that his extraordinary talents reduced his work to child's play and that he could therefore maintain above-average standards with a minimum of effort. This seems to be all he was interested in doing.

A Common Story

After giving up work on *Old Men*, he undertook a new project, *A Common Story*. "The novel was thought out in 1844 and written down in 1845," he says in retrospect. "By 1846 only a few chapters remained to be completed." [1]

Early in 1845 Goncharov read the first part aloud at the Majkovs. Work was evidently proceding apace. He gave this section to his friend Mikhail Jazykov, who had in turn agreed to hand it over to Vissarion Belinskij, — the most influential critic of the time, whom he knew personally, — and find out what he thought of it.

Several months went by. Goncharov refrained from inquiring after the manuscript's fate. What happened apparently is that Jazykov lost interest after thumbing through the first few pages, and laid the manuscript aside. [2] It was not until he casually mentioned it in a conversation with the new editor of the journal *The Contemporary* (Sovremennik), the later celebrated poet Nikolaj Nekrasov, that plans for publication got off the ground.

Nekrasov grew quickly excited about the work and passed it on to Belinskij. Belinskij, too, was much impressed, and in mid-April 1846 Goncharov spent several evenings at Belinskij's apartment reading the first part of the novel aloud for the critic and a circle of his friends. According to Panaevs's description of the readings "Belinskij followed Goncharov's reading with increasing sympathy and curiosity and from time to time would almost imperceptibly bounce up and down on his chair with glowing eyes at the passages that he especially enjoyed ... Belinskij was enraptured by the brilliant debut of this new talent." [3] Goncharov gives a similar account: "About three months after the reading, Belinskij showered me with ardent praise at every meeting and prophesied a good future for me." [4] In September 1846 Nekrasov acquired the novel for *The Contemporary* (Sovremennik). This journal, founded by Pushkin and after his death taken over by Petr Pletnev, had

1) N.I., p. 7.
2) Ivan Panaev, Literaturnye vospominanija, Moskva, 1950, p. 308.
3) *ibid.*
4) N.I., p. 7.

been going through a period of decline. Hoping that Goncharov's novel would liven up the journal a bit, Nekrasov planned to feature it in the first issue for 1847, but his co-editor Panaev was set on seeing his own work — a story of no particular literary merit, "The Relatives" — in print.

"I.A. Goncharov beams as he reads his proofs," wrote Panaev to Turgenev somewhat ironically. "He trembles with rapture. Yet at the same time he takes great pains to appear indifferent." [1]

Finally in issues three and four of *The Contemporary* (i.e. in early March and April 1847), the first and the second part of *A Common Story* made their appearance.

Critical reaction was quite positive. It came as no surprise that the principal exception was Faddej Bulgarin's *The Northern Bee* (Severnaja pchela). The objections in Bulgarin's review may be laid down to personal and political difference between him and the editors of *The Contemporary*. They may also have been born of jealousy or the desire to cut back the competing journal's sales.

Belinskij rated the novel very highly in his survey article "A Look at Russian Literature in 1847." [2] In a private letter to the writer and critic Vasilij Botkin, Belinskij wrote: "Goncharov's novel (povest') has caused a *furore* in Petersburg. It's an unprecedented success: Everyone thinks highly of it ... He has a really remarkable talent. His special quality, his personality, so to speak, seems to me to come from a complete break with the language of all three: seminary, literary jargon, and literary salon ... (seminarizm, literaturshchina, literatorstvo). Goncharov shows no sign of having labored over his style. You don't even feel you're reading. It's like listening to a story from a master storyteller. I'm certain you'll be greatly impressed by it. And the good it will do society! What a terrible blow to romanticism, daydreaming, sentimentality, and provincialism." [3] This sort of criticism is typical of the Belinskij of this period. By judging literature ·according to its social utility, he completely misses the work's true meaning.

---

1) Alekseev, p. 26.
2) V.G. Belinskij, Polnoe sobranie sochinenij, Moskva, 1953–59, v.X, pp.326–344.
3) *ibid.*, v.XII, p. 352.

There is little in the novel to tie it down to one point in contemporary social history. And where it does enter into the novel, it serves only as an illustration of the basic problems of human existence or, at most, as an incentive to try to come to grips with them. The "common story" of the title refers to the metamorphosis of youth's gullible gushings to the rational, experience-based scepticism of maturity and thence, in the face of imminent death, to uncertainty and the questioning of all values. Both poles of human experience, emotion and reason, can be justified, but neither is to be preferred over the other, and even their equilibrium is no solution to the problems life poses. Life and the purpose of life remain disappointing and enigmatic.

What, in the last analysis is life? Goncharov gives his answer many times over in his letters and his works: the struggle to take the edge off ever present existential boredom. In youth an irrepressible lust for life usually takes care of the problem; in maturity, useless, artificial activity, busy work. It is only in old age that we come to understand that emotion and reason serve the same end — that of filling out life enough to ward off boredom. And armed with this knowledge we live out our lives as best we can.

Women have a special role to play in the novel. Apparently Goncharov did not deem them capable of experiencing the boredom dilemma. Women *need* feeling; feeling is more important for them than reason. By finding a feeling they can reciprocate, they also find full gratification. Quite often this process is accompanied by a rather alarming dismissal of reason, but in the ideal cases a sensible equipoise can be established.

The first chapter of Part I immediately introduces the hero, twenty-year old Aleksandr Aduev. Son of well-to-do squires in a remote Russian province, he has led a sheltered, slothful existence. His widowed mother has loved and spoiled him as one loves and spoils one's only child.

His nurse has sung him lullabies of a life that would know no grief and bathe him in gold. The teachers in the provincial town prophesied a fine future for the intelligent boy. And home from school, he has tasted the first excitements of love, a pure and tender love, with the neighbor's charming daughter. It is a wonder that Aleksandr's character remains untainted by this undue adoration. Goncharov makes a persuasive remark in this connection.

"Home life had spoilt Aleksandr, but it had not corrupted his heart.
Nature had done so well by him, that the love of his mother and
the adoration of those surrounding him had only affected the better side of his character, developing in him emotional susceptibility,
and implanting in him an excessive trustfulness. Perhaps they were
the cause of the first stirrings of vanity in him; but vanity itself is
a mere mold, everything depends on the material we pour into it." [1]

Romantic idealism was apparently the reigning ideology at his University,
as it was in most Russian intellectual circles at the time. The action of the
novel begins in about 1830, when romanticism and idealism were the great
fashion in Russia. Like so many foreign intellectual trends in Russian culture, it was embraced with the most glowing fervor as a kind of life-consum-
ing creed. Aleksandr seems to know romantic literature very well; he is imbued with lofty, high-flown ideas about heroic life (vague as this notion
may be); the purifying power of true, passionate love; holy self-sacrificing friendship; the sublime vocation of art, and especially poetry; the eternal
values of artistic creativity descending from the heavens upon the elected
without any effort on their part; and the importance of enthusiasm, the
main force in life. For the romantic, life conceals a beautiful mysterious
secret. He feels it, he loves it, he is sure he belongs to the elected, those des-
tined for all sorts of heroic deeds. Full of such idealistic enthusiasm, Aleksandr feels he must leave the quiet, well-protected nest of his childhood:

"Of grief, tears and disasters he knew only by hearsay, as people know
of some disease which has never come their way, and only lurks remotely among less fortunate folk. And so the future presented itself
to him in rainbow colours. Something seemed to beckon him from
afar, though what it was he did not exactly know. Delightful visions
flitted by before he could make out what they were. Blended sounds
rang in his ears — the voice of glory, the voice of love. And all this
kept him in a state of delicious agitation." [2]

---

1) I, p. 11.
2) I, pp. 10-11.

No doubt he feels among the elected: he is capable of noble feelings, he will be capable of noble deeds. He is a great poet; his potential for love is inexhaustible.

But in the last analysis this hyper-romantic attitude is nothing more than egoism. Aleksandr is interested only in himself. His dreams touch solely upon his own person. He has no trace of love or pity for others, no genuine religion, and certainly not the slightest social concern. He has molded his romanticism to his own image, but in his genuine youthful enthusiasm, his honest delight and ardent faith in life, he does not and cannot notice this.

Full of great illusions, he leaves for Petersburg. In the capital he is sure he will find the proper field for the exhibition and application of his unusual gifts, and make an easy and conspicuous career.

The second chapter introduces the second hero Petr Ivanovich Aduev, Aleksandr's uncle. He is 37 years old when we first meet him, and has been living in Petersburg for 17 years. His nephew wants to "embrace" him on arrival, and expects help from him in launching his brilliant career.

Petr Ivanovich, we learn by degrees, came to Petersburg as a youth under much the same circumstances as Aleksandr. As a result of his adaptation to the realities of Petersburg life, however, he appears the direct opposite of the young and innocent boy. Petr Ivanovich is a highly placed officer in the government and the owner of a blossoming glass and china factory. Money, he has learned, is a most important factor in human life, and he knows how to go after it. Realizing early in his career that idealistic dreams would never lead anywhere, he simply gave them up, and apparently without any great struggle. (Herein lies a sharp contrast to the reactions of his nephew.)

By now his world view has clearly crystallized. Reason is superior to uncontrolled feeling, no matter how noble the feeling may be. Since indeals are always vague and unattainable, there is no point in yearning for them and ignoring the realities of life. We must cultivate an interest in everything life has to offer (including love, imagination and art), but insist that everything be controlled by reason. Reason teaches us the role that wealth and comfort play in enabling us to lead a life full of varied interests. One must accept life's teaching and analyze, weigh, and calculate all decisions. And

above all, one must work, work hard, to keep the intellect busy and procure the means for a comfortable life.

Of course everything one does has to be honest. Dishonesty would rob
us of peace of mind, trouble our conscience. And well-reasoned analysis
will show that this is not worthwhile.

On the other hand idealism in human relations will not stand analysis
either. Friends should be trusted and loved to a certain degree, but there
can be no question of self-sacrifice and no passionate love for a woman. If
it should come as a kind of malady (Petr Ivanovich envisages this possibility), it should be cured with reason, never indulged in.

You should not marry too early in life, but when you do marry, you
should choose a woman with whom you are not in love. She must be rich,
but since "one marries a woman with money, not for money," she should
also be younger than you. You should try to develop a fondness for her and
bind her to yourself by all reasonable means, educating her in an inconspicuous manner, subduing her will to your own, and thereby making her a
pleasant companion to your domestic life. Petr Ivanovich gives a very revealing portrait of himself in the letter he dictates to his nephew. [1]

Alexandr's enthusiastic idealism, which is actually merely a slightly veiled variant of "unreasonable" egoism, is opposed to the matter-of-fact realism of his uncle, which, although a brand of egoism, is eminently reasonable and free of all pretense. It is clear that these two approaches to life
must eventually clash, but it is just as clear that with time they will meet.
In the last analysis they are merely two different aspects of a single quality:
egoism.

The main ideological content of the novel lies in the account of how the
young idealist loses his illusions, and becomes a matter-of-fact realist under
the blows of life. The disappointments he suffers in his career, loves, friend-
ships and artistic ambitions are constantly anticipated and commented upon
by Petr Ivanovich.

His conversations with his nephew occupy a large part of the book. They
are brilliant dialectical performances on the part of the author — sometimes

---

1) I, pp. 49-51.

witty, sometimes serious stimulated by the deeds of the inexperienced idealist passing through the school of raw experience.

Aleksandr's disappointments begin on a small scale. The "love" he brings to his "dear relative" is curtly rejected. (He cannot even succeed in embracing him. Indeed, at first Petr Ivanovich thought of refusing to see him outright, but remembering his own youth and the financial support provided by Aleksandr's parents to help him get started on his own, he fears a troubled conscience and changes his mind.) — Petersburg, the great, resplendant city of his dreams, turns out to be a gray mass of unpleasant houses. The brilliant social circles in which he expected to shine are filled with indifferent, if not hostile, people. His provincial diplomas and the idealistic projects he composed at the university (where they caused quite a stir) count for nothing; his uncle wants to use them as lining for the wallpaper. Worst of all, his beautiful poems (quoted varbatim) evoke nothing more than his uncle's objective, but uncomplimentary comment that only hard work would reveal whether he had any talent. In his endeavors to make a career in the administration, his disappointment is just as complete: instead of the high position he had dreamed of that would enable him to carry out his projects, he can do no better than a post for which he must prove that he has a good handwriting and knows how to copy documents without forgetting the commas. His colleagues, so nice to him at first, are merely playing up to him, as he sees only too soon, because they want his money. They cause him to lose considerable sums in doubtful gambling, or borrow from him without the least intent of returning what they have taken. When his uncle promises to obtain a well-paid translation assignment for him, he is sure it will be something literary, a vehicle for his fine style. What he gets is an article about the use of manure from the Department of Agriculture. All these failures which follow one another in quick succession in Chapter Two and cover a period of about one month, do not really affect Aleksandr. They are external vexations, which leave the core of his ideas and beliefs untouched and do not really involve his basic personality or egoism.

Chapter Three begins with the words: "Over two years had passed." Aleksandr has changed to a certain degree.

"At last he gradually began to admit the thought that there are thorns as well as roses to be met with in life, and that the thorns

sometimes inflict pain, though not so severe as his uncle had fore-
told." [1]

Still he is far from coming round to the cold analysis of feelings his uncle
suggests, and

". . . would not as yet admit that all the mysteries and secrets of the
heart could be brought to the light of day."

Then comes the first real blow straight to the heart. Chapters Three to
Six, the rest of Part One, are devoted to the account of this personal tragedy, the first to genuinely affect Aleksandr. Indeed, it becomes a milestone
in his development, even if, looked at from the cold analytical viewpoint of
his uncle, it is not a tragedy at all, but rather a normal and predictable event.

Aleksandr falls in love for the first time. Eighteen-year-old Naden'ka Lju-
beckaja is a charming girl, full of life, joy, and passion. She lives with her
mother, a friendly and weak elderly lady, who understands the ways of
youth and does not interfere when her harmless attachment to Aleksandr
starts to develop. The romance proceeds in the manner Aleksandr feels it
should: shy and ardent looks, the first touch, the first kiss, sighs of ecstasy,
meetings in the dark — or even better — in a moonlit garden, recitations of
love poetry, oaths of eternal love and faithfulness, and so on and so forth.
He is happy, the girl is happy. Both are in love, and Aleksandr decides to
marry, neglecting in the meantime his office duties, his translations and his
literary studies.

The third chapter consists almost entirely of the rapturous outpourings
to which he subjects his uncle, and his uncle's icy warnings of impending
disaster. At the same time, Petr Ivanovich tells Aleksandr of his own intention to marry soon, but of course his idea of marriage differs radically
from that of Aleksandr's. He loves his future wife, but with a controlled
almost premeditated love.

Chapter Four contains a description of budding love in all its minute
peripeties. In Chapter Five misfortune strikes. Naden'ka's romantic raptures do not last. Much to her own surprise, when Count Platon Novinskij,
a handsome, strong, intelligent and spirited young man begins to court her,
she quickly bores of Aleksandr's rapturous and exigent love.

---

1) I, p. 64.

Naden'ka regrets her inconstancy, but cannot do anything about it. Aleksandr's behavior points up the real nature of his love. Jealousy makes him simply intolerable, and his wounded self-love is the main spring of his reactions. First he decides to humiliate her, only to grant her a magnanimous pardon once she has given ample proof of her willingness to repent. Then he thinks of taking a frightful revenge upon her. But at last, after her final word and several hours of genuinely deep despair (a very impressive achievement on the part of Goncharov), he curses her, resolves to despise her, and in the long run forgets her. The last (sixth) chapter of Part One, which takes place just after Aleksandr and Naden'ka break up, is again devoted in its entirety to conversation. Petr Ivanovich proves to his nephew that all the sad developments of his lofty romance were his own fault: his fatuous jealousy, his pose of the hurt and righteous lover, his reproaches, his importune perseverance, and his lack of energy to fight the count with his own weapons: detachment, elegance, and wit. Petr Ivanovich's speeches, his quips about duels, love, and marriage become more and more witty and more and more personal (on all other occasions he has preferred to talk in general aphorisms, scrupulously avoiding his personal life) related as they are over a bottle of good wine. To underline the depths of his despair, Aleksandr has declined to join him. Petr Ivanovich's description of the cunning system he has derived in order to dominate the household is interrupted by a remark from the corridor by his eavesdropping wife, Lizaveta Aleksandrovna, who has apparently already outfoxed the system and taken the necessary countermeasures. When the disconcerted Petr Ivanovich tries to finish expounding his reason-based theory of love, he is once again cut short — this time by Aleksandr's sobbing. Disconcerted for the second time and completely helpless, he appeals to his wife for assistance. She manages to console her new nephew, and as she does so by means of genuine compassion and understanding, Goncharov speaks only of the results. Thus, with the hero's first real experience of suffering and the introduction of a kind of heroine in Lizaveta Aleksandrovna, the first part comes to an end.

Goncharov has deliberately created a heroine with something of the unreal about her. Though he carefully discusses the backgrounds and characters of his two protagonists, about Lizaveta Aleksandrovna we learn only that she was twenty years old when she married the nearly forty-year old

Petr Ivanovich. Goncharov does not say a word about her former life, nor
the circles she comes from. Knowing Petr Invanovich's ideas about marriage,
we must assume that she is rich, but it would be difficult to assert anything
about her personality. As the plot develops she shows herself to be endowed with a wisdom of the heart, which sets her above the two men. She sees
their extreme onesidedness, but is spiritually attracted to the younger one
because he needs her and her warmth now and again, and because she feels
that he would be capable of understanding her own longings. Her husband's
coldness makes her feel superfluous, and his controlled love is not sufficient
to fulfill her desire for genuine, unrestrained feeling. She certainly began by
loving him, and would like him to rekindle that love, but his correct behavior stifles her emotions. His "knowledge" about feeling both prevents
him from feeling and causes her much suffering, and her all too serene, well-
protected life leaves her empty and sad. On the other hand her influence
upon Aleksandr is in many cases decisive, and Goncharov sees a kind of
heroism in her ability to conceal her own frustration and help others.

A year has passed since the fiasco of Aleksandr's first love. Chapter One
of Part Two begins at this point. It is devoted first to the analysis of Lizaveta Aleksandrovna's plight and then to the hero's next serious blow. Aleksandr feels he has reasons to believe himself deeply wounded and betrayed
by on old friend. (We must assume this friend is Pospelov, the youth who
came to bid Aleksandr an ardent farewell on the day of his departure from
the provinces and to whom Aleksandr wrote just after his arrival in Petersburg; however, Goncharov does not refer to Pospelov expressly.) When
Aleksandr meets him by chance on a Petersburg street, he takes his down-
hearted countenance as a sign that he is in trouble, and offers him all sorts
of assistance, including — horribile dictu — aid of a material nature. Just as
money is the high symbol of reasonable well-being for Petr Ivanovich, it is
the low symbol of cold calculation for Aleksandr. This encounter leads
Aleksandr to deliver a biting tirade against the unfeeling world about him,
containing some malicious concrete examples from among mutual acquaintances and concluding with the conviction that no one can understand him
and his superior, ardent soul. In a few cool, polished sentences Petr Ivanovich reduces his arguments ad absurdum, proving to him beyond dispute
that his ardent soul and the warm embrace he has prepared for mankind
have not prevented him from overlooking his own genuine, — if controlled —

friendship and — what is worse — the loving friendship of Lizaveta Aleksandrovna. He also reminds him that the love he bears his old mother, whom, as he inadvertently exclaims he adores and "for whom he would give his life," has not prevented him from failing to write her for four months. These concrete examples of actual love blinded by an over-exuberant idea of love, hit Aleksandr hard. He is too intelligent not to see that his uncle is right, and the hard clear light of his examples shatters much of his belief in his superiority as a "genuinely feeling man."

But there is another aspect of Aleksandr's superiority complex which has yet to be destroyed and Chapter Two deals with its destruction. Aleksandr had never really given up his ambition of becoming a poet and writer. He continued to compose verses, and at the peak of his romance with Naden'ka he even wrote a comedy and a hyper-romantic novel, but all his efforts were returned to him by the publishers. Encouraged by Lizaveta Aleksandrovna, who does not want to see all his ambitions shattered at once, and despite the warnings of Petr Ivanovich, who would rather have him continue his articles on agricultural problems, he spends six months composing a "real" novel, a "bitter" novel.

> "The scene of this novel was no longer laid in America, but in some Tambov village. The characters were ordinary people — gossips, liars, monsters of all sorts in frockcoats, traitresses in corsets and picture hats. It was all perfectly correct and appropriate." [1]

So as not to be accused of partiality, Petr Ivanovich sends it to an experienced publisher. The verdict is annihilating. The author has much in his favor, writes the editor in his report. He is intelligent, his language is correct, and he has a good personal style. Unfortunately he is completely without talent, and prone to let his feelings run away with him.

> "Tell your protégé that in the first place a writer only writes to the purpose when not carried away by self-absorption and prejudice. He must cast a calm, radiant glance at life and humanity, otherwise he will express nothing but his own ego, which nobody cares a rap about." [2]

1) I, p.174.
2) I, pp. 179-180.

This is basically what Petr Ivanovich meant when he told Aleksandr that feeling and understanding life is one thing, but reflecting it in one's works is something else again, something which requires talent. Again Aleksandr is intelligent enough to acknowledge his shortcomings. In the tragicomic scene in which he and his uncle burn all his literary productions he discards yet another illusion.

But the last and (as far as he is concerned) most solid piece of Aleksandr's romantic creed still remains untouched: his *own* capacity for infinite, true love, his *own* superior power and wealth of feeling. Even if certain doubts have begun to trouble him — after all, he did forget Naden'ka rather quickly, — he finds excuses for them. Clearly he needs a new lesson to teach him the truth.

Chapter Three recounts his love-affair with Julija Pavlovna Tafaeva, a young widow with every quality he had ever pictured in the woman of his dreams. She is goodlooking, intelligent, and loves and feels art, especially literature. She is sentimental and romantic, perhaps even a little more so than he himself, and she loves him with a genuine, constant love. What is more, she is rich, a pleasant though not decisive aspect for him. Their happiness is complete, and Goncharov takes care to make this clear. No exterior obstacles interfere. Even Petr Ivanovich is silent. Tafaeva gives herself to him, and he promises marriage. But as his happy year with her wears on, Aleksandr feels his infinite love gradually losing its original luster. At first his "angel's" presence merely ceases to excite him, but eventually she becomes insupportable, and true to his inexorably egotistical nature he pitilessly abandons his ever passionate, ever loving "ideal."

The defeat is complete now, and the consequence quite logical: absolute pessimism. Aleksandr no longer believes in anything. To mortify his spirit as others mortify their flesh (so he puts it), he indulges in utter misanthropy, reasoning that life is not worth the effort he had been putting into it. He neglects his work, abandons society (a short attempt at finding oblivion in debauchery ends badly: his health suffers), and falls into complete apathy. For the first time even Petr Ivanovich is frightened, but nothing he does succeeds in extracting him from it.

Aleksandr takes up with a retired old eccentric, a certain Kostjakov, whose only claim to originality lies in his limitations. All he talks about are

price changes and the sort of minor scandal he picks up from the daily press
or ferrets out of his neighbors' dirty wash. All he does is play checkers in
winter and go fishing in summer. Aleksandr shares the two last pursuits with
him and finds the old man's conversation a perfect means of keeping his
mind off old wounds.

Chapter Four describes this self-imposed retreat and relates another rather
unpleasant, but characteristic episode. Fishing one day, Aleksandr makes
the acquaintance of a lovely young girl named Liza, who lives in the country
with her father. She falls in love with the handsome Aleksandr, or rather
with his enchanted, indifferent, mysterious pose. Though no longer capable
of love, he is still too weak to resist. Finally the father notices the turn
things have taken, and one evening Aleksandr finds him instead of his daughter at a prearranged rendezvous. After a very humiliating scene, Aleksandr
is fairly pushed out the door. Not only has he fallen short of his ideal of
heroism, he has exhibited a lack of the most common decency. This discovery leads him to attempt suicide but he bungles the job so miserably
that he can only conclude he is also severely wanting in matters of courage.
Returning home is the only possibility left, and in Chapter Five Petr Ivanovich convinces him to take advantage of it.

The sixth and last chapter deals with Aleksandr's return to the country.
He lives an idle life, without passions or thought, enjoying nature and the
company of the very plain people around him, especially his loving mother.
Gradually, however, he tires of this state of half sleep, and after one and a
half years in the country, he suddenly awakes, stripped of all his former
ideals. He has grown older and cooler and become his real self. The essence
of his (rather mediocre) personality finally comes to the fore, and he feels
it is time to decide what to do with himself. Two paths of action lay open
before him. He can stay where he is, introduce improvements on his estate
(especially after the sudden death of his mother), and become a provincial
pater familias. Or he can return to the capital, follow in his uncle's footsteps and carve out for himself a brilliant career in the administration. He
decides in favor of the latter.

His letter to Lizaveta Aleksandrovna represents a spiritual portrait of
his new self: a simple man, an ordinary man, neither madman nor dreamer,
nor disillusioned nor provincial. He has gained a peace of mind, which, he
admits, may stem from egoism, and though he misses his former dreams,

he sees clearly that the time of meditation, of scrutinizing all his emotions has begun. He does not regret having suffered: suffering purges the soul, and an ignorance of suffering necessarily excludes a knowledge of the fullness of life:

> "It contains many important elements, the significance of which we perhaps shall not see in this world. I see in these emotions the hand of Providence, which, it seems, sets humanity the infinite task of progressing, achieving an aim imposed from above, while incessantly struggling with deceptive hopes and maddening obstacles. Yes, I see how necessary this struggle, these emotions are, how without them life would not be life, but stagnation, a dream . . . . When the struggle ends, lo! life, too, ends. When a man is busy, he loves, enjoys, suffers, feels, goes about his business, he lives." [1]

Aleksandr finds life beautiful when taken as it is, with its pleasures and all its bitterness. He wants to live it out with his fellow men, whom he accepts as they are, with the full understanding and modest conviction that he is the same as they are.

This wise and beautiful letter encourages high hopes, but the Epilogue — describing Aleksandr's situation after four years — shows that the same old story has run its course once again. The letter's beautiful wisdom has no lasting effect on its author. Aleksandr has become the same busy bureaucrat as his uncle — interested only in the administration, business affairs, promotions, and money. He is just about to embark on a loveless marriage with a young, rich girl, and he lives the ordinary life of a man striving for an external well-being unencumbered by ideals or illusions.

At the same time his uncle has begun to entertain doubts about the validity of the very theories he has inculcated so well into his nephew. Rheumatism plagues him; he is getting old. He takes little joy in his wealth and distinguished position. Still worse is the lot of his wife. Having longed in vain for love, for feeling, and yielding finally to resignation and utter indifference, her psychic frustration has begun to reflect upon her physical condition. Petr Ivanovich has decided to abandon his career to take her to Italy, where he hopes she will recover strength. But will she? . . .

1) I, pp. 293 — 294.

Very revealing is the new discription of Petr Ivanovich given in the Epilogue:

> "Petr Ivanovich was a kindly soul. He would have given anything,
> if not from love for his wife, then from a sense of justice, to set the
> evil right. But how was this to be done? " [1]

The pragmatic uncle has won a complete victory over his idealistic nephew, or so it seems. Even while proudly congratulating himself he realizes how wrong he was, how he wasted his life in idle pursuits, and what difficulties he will have in justifying it before himself in the face of imminent death.

We cannot be too surprised by this conclusion. The transformations which both Aleksandr and Petr Ivanovich undergo are very natural. In the last analysis, Goncharov is treating two aspects of basically the same personality: the mature uncle in his youth reacted exactly like his immature nephew; the immature nephew became exactly what his mature uncle had been for the large part of his life. We must assume that the nephew's end will approximate that of his uncle; he too will be overcome by grief and the realization that he has not really lived. But Goncharov makes us feel that the story he has told is a common story, one which happens with some variations to everybody. He confronts *idealistic* youth (characterized by love for all mankind, belief in the good, faith in itself) with the *real* mediocrity of human beings and human matters. Youth must adapt or perish in the unequal battle. This theme is certainly not new to literature but Goncharov presents it very poignantly.

No doubt one should point out that the idealism vs. positivism conflict was especially strong during the transitional period – 1830 to 1845 – in which Goncharov places the action of his novel. The mixture of sentimentalism and exaggerated romanticism in Russia as represented in the thirties by such writers and poets as Aleksandr Bestuzhev-Marlinskij, Nestor Kukol'nik, Vladimir Benediktov, (to mention only its most characteristic and most successful practitioners) gave way to a critical, almost pragmatic attitude, which was based in literature on the works of Gogol' (even if their true

---

1) I, p. 304.

meaning was misinterpreted) and developed first into the so-called natural school and then into the overly positivistic and socially oriented literary activities of the sixties. The natural school saw its main task in the study and evaluation of life's mediocrity. Though regretting the severe limitations this topic subjected it to, it maintained that mediocrity required minute scrutiny as the main factor at work in sucking up and destroying the ideals which make life worth living. Soon, however, their research became an aim in itself, and they developed a positivistic, utilitarian creed which militantly denied the validity of any ideal.

Aleksandr bears comparison with Pushkin's Lenskij, an idealistic poet, killed as a youth in a duel (by the title character of the famous novel in verse *Evgenij Onegin*). Pushkin stronly suggests that had he lived he might well have turned into a philistine mediocrity. But the Lenskijs disappeared in the thirties to give way to a more realistic generation, and we have every reason to assume that Goncharov himself developed from a young enthusiast, arriving in the capital with great expectations, into a modest officer in the administration trying diligently to build up an unambitious career.

This sort of development is not limited to Russia of course. While writing *A Common Story*, Goncharov seems to have been especially conscious of French literature. Balzac's *Le Père Goriot* (1834) and *Les illusions perdues* (1837-39) and George Sand's *Horace* (1842) have clear similarities to Goncharov's concept: a romantic, young man from the provinces arrives in the big city and is transformed by its "realistic" influence. André Mazon points expressly to a novel by Gustave Drouineau (an author mentioned in Goncharov's book [1]), *Ernest ou le travers du siècle* (1829), dealing with an over-confident young provincial who is forced to suffer the irony of his fiancèes skeptical father. Another well-known work, Frédéric Soulié's *Les mèmoires du diable* (1837-38), read and praised by Naden'ka's mother, tells the tales of the Baron de Luizzi, who loses illusions he harbored about himself after a conversation with a highly cynical devil.

Yet, as much as the transition from idealism to a realistic approach to life may be bound to the time when the novel was written and as much as it may reflect the Zeitgeist, the phenomenon as such remains eternal, and Goncharov makes us feel it in both its aspects: timebound and eternal.

---

1) I, p. 201.

The novel's structure is well balanced and well coordinated. Each of the two parts has six chapters, while the epilogue represents a final summary as drawn from the events. Sometimes one even has the impression that a logical formula is being worked out.

The main bulk of the novel consists of dialogues between nephew and uncle, in which the latter always correctly predicts the failure of the former's undertakings. Some motifs occur again and again, serving to make the symmetry clear. Money is an example of such a motif. From the beginning practical Petr Ivanovich warns Aleksandr not to try to borrow money from him. Money becomes a symbol for the practical attitude toward life, and as long as Aleksandr retains his claim as idealist par excellence, he does not bother Petr Ivanovich with pecuniary matters. In the epilogue, however, he asks for a considerable sum, symbolizing by this request the dissolution of his idealism. Petr Ivanovich is happy at this extraordinary event; the reader sees it as yet another sign that Aleksandr is going the road of his uncle.

Aleksandr is the novel's hero; it is his spiritual development that attracts the exclusive interest of the author. This development leads the hero mercilessly and painfully along the well-trodden path of the same old story. Because *his* development alone is under consideration, all other characters are enlarged upon only insofar as they have an immediate connection with him. His main adversary, Petr Ivanovich, earns the most thorough treatment. As a matter of fact, the novel is constructed on a double level. All events, feelings and ideas are first presented in the illusionary form in which Aleksandr sees them and then from the matter-of-fact viewpoint of Petr Ivanovich. As already mentioned, Lizaveta Aleksandrovna's development into the highly sympathetic human being she represents is completely omitted, a somewhat doubtful device (which Goncharov repeated in *Oblomov* with Ol'ga Il'jinskaja), considering her ideological importance to the plot. We never discover what happens to Naden'ka, Count Novinskij, Mrs. Tafaeva, or Liza, to say nothing of the lesser characters. Nor do we learn anything about their lives previous to their appearance in the novel. There is only one conspicuous exception: Tafaeva's education is dealt with at great length. But this was unavoidable, because the close relation of her "soul" and mentality to Aleksandr's had to be shown in order to explain his ardent love and make his subsequent cooling all the more striking. Goncharov may have derived this technique of abandoning characters as they become unnecessary from the preface of Atar-Gull by Eugène Sue, which André Mazon very persuasively quotes. [1]

Goncharov dwells upon the character of Petr Ivanovich's associate Surkov somewhat more than necessary. Here it seems his theoretical interest is in the type of the "lion", an empty salon dandy whose portrait Goncharov drew more circumstantially in the feuilleton "Pis'ma stolichnogo druga k provincial'nomu zhenixu." [2]

Rarely does Goncharov try to depict the functioning of a secondary character's feelings. He reserves this aspect of his art for the main characters, but even with them his analysis procedes more along logical than intuitive lines and is quite different from that of Tolstoj, for example. He is content to rely upon outward description as a mirror of inner character. Here is a comparison of the two protagonists in which the outward appearance reflects inner disposition:

> "What a difference there was between them — one a head higher than the other, well-built, stout, a man of powerful, healthy disposition, with assurance in his glance and manners. The thoughts and character of Petr Ivanovich were not to be guessed at from his glance, his movements, or his words — so skilfully was everything in him concealed by his manners and self-control. Every gesture and glance seemed to have been calculated in advance. His pale, imperturbable countenance showed that in this man the play of the passions was held in strict subservience by the mind, that his heart beat high or subsided according to the dictates of his mind.
> In Aleksandr, on the contrary, everything betrayed a weak and delicate constitution — the changing expressions flitting over his face, a kind of languor, slowness and uncertainty in his movements, the limpid glance which showed every sensation of his heart, every thought stirring in his mind. He was of medium height, but thin,

---

1) Mazon, pp. 313–314.
2) Cf. p. 75.

and his pallor, unlike that of Petr Ivanovich, was not natural to him, but the result of an incessant inner agitation. Unlike his uncle's, his hair did not show abundant growth on head and cheeks, but descended from his temples and to the back of his head in long, light locks which shimmered like silk." [1]

Goncharov once said that he felt at home only in describing what was personally known to him, close to him. This may be another reason why he provides such masterful detail in some cases, and is so brief and incomplete in others. Well aware of his sometimes uncanny gift of observation when dealing with people and environments he is well acquainted with, he deliberately sticks close to them. The excellent first and last chapters of the novel are fine examples. Both deal with life and people in Aleksandr's home, the provincial estate of Grachi. Goncharov gives beautiful descriptions of the nature he knew so well. The following excerpt is taken from the beginning of the last chapter:

"It was a glorious morning. The lake the reader knows so well, on the banks of which the village of Grachi is situated, rippled faintly beneath a light breeze. The dazzling brilliance of the sun's rays, reflected in iridescent sparks on the surface of the water, made the passer-by involuntarily screw up his eyes. The weeping birches dipped their branches in the lake, and here and there the bank was overgrown with sedge in the midst of which hid great yellow flowers, resting on broad, floating leaves. Every now and then a light cloud passed across the sun, which seemed to turn away from Grachi for a few moments, and then the lake, the copse and the village were instantly plunged in shadow. Only the distance was radiant with light. But the cloud passed on, and again the lake gleamed, and the cornfields seemed to be flooded with gold." [2]

This picture is followed by a glorious evocation of a thunderstorm (a frequent speciality among Russian writers). But his most outstanding feat is the account of how things *usually* looked around the house. This every-

---

1) I, p. 188.
2) I, p. 268.

day scene is clear proof of Goncharov's virtuosity. He rightly mentions
Teniers in this connection.

> "Sometimes he would go up to the window and look out on the yard
> and the village street. There the picture was different, a Teniers can-
> vas, full of busy domestic life. Barbos lay in front of his kennel, over-
> come by the heat, his nose on his front paws. Half a dozen hens
> greeted the morning, clucking in turns. Cocks fought. The herd was
> driven through the street to pasture. Sometimes a cow, falling be-
> hind, lowed dismally, standing in the middle of the road and look-
> ing all round. Men and women with rakes and scythes on their
> shoulders went to work. Every now and then the breeze carried
> a word or two up to the little bridge, and after it a load of hay
> crawled lazily past. Boys, with coarse, flaxen hair, wandered about
> the puddles, lifting the hem of their shirts. Regarding this scene
> Aleksandr began to grasp the poetry of the *grey sky, the broken
> fence, the wicket gates, the muddy pond, the folk-dance.* He chang-
> ed his elegant tight-fitting frock-coat for a loose, home-made dress-
> ing-gown. And in every manifestation of this peaceful life, in every
> impression, in the morning, in the evening, at meals and during rest-
> time, the vigilant eye of maternal love was present." [1]

From the literary point of view it seems to be an echo of Pushkin's Flemish school (cf. Onegin's Journey [XIX]: Flamandskoj shkoly pestryj sor!
[The Flemish School's variegated dross]), but one senses at the same time
how much a part it is of Goncharov himself.

His description of Petersburg is quite remarkable too. For the usual
blanket admiration, he substitutes an accumulation of curious gray details
of buildings and men, hardly counterbalancing them by a brief nod at Ad-
miralty Square, the Bronze Horseman (the famous monument in memory
of Peter the Great and subject of Pushkin's famous narrative in verse) and
the busy crowd, all of which stunned Aleksandr. Here again Goncharov
prefers the familiar everyday view to abstractions. He includes several such
miniatures of Petersburg and its suburbs. A very fine contrast is the im-

---

1) I, p. 290.

mediately preceding picture of the cosy provincial town where everybody knows everybody else.

". . . He remembered the district town, where the most casual meetings in the street were, in some way or other, interesting. Ivan Ivanovich goes to see Petr Petrovich, and the whole town knows why. Mar'ja Martynovna comes out of church, Afanasij Savich goes fishing. A policeman rides at breakneck speed from the Governor's house to the doctor's, and everyone knows that Her Excellency has deigned to bring forth an infant, although, according to the cronies and grannies, no one ought to have known anything about it. Everyone asks: is it a boy or a girl? The ladies get out their best caps. And there comes Matvej Matveich, stepping out of his house with his stout stick at six o'clock in the evening, and everyone knows that he is taking his evening constitutional, without which his digestion would not work, and that he will not fail to stop at the window of the old privy-councillor who, as is also well known, takes tea at that hour. A greeting and a few words are exchanged with every person you meet, and even if you do not greet a person, you know exactly who he is, where he is going, and what for, and in his glance you can read: and I know who you are and where you are going, and what for. If it *should* happen that strangers, who have never before met, come across one another in the street, the faces of both become living question-marks. They halt and look back once or twice, and when they get home they describe the dress and gait of the unknown individual, and many are the surmises as to who the stranger could be, where he came from, and what he had come for. But here in Petersburg, people look at one another, jostle one another in the road, as if they were all sworn foes." [1]

The same holds true of the characters. We get a fine portrait of Aleksandr's mother, Anna Pavlovna. Her self-sacrificing love for her son, her virtues as mistress of the house — a mixture of domineering serf owner and good heart, her narrow moral code combining Christianity with a well calculating mind (cf. her charming advice on how to treat beggars) [2],

1) I, p. 35.
2)' I, p. 13.

her basic altruism interlaced with idiosyncratic egotistical impasses — all
this combines into a living human being, whose simple soul does not leave
anything open to question.

   Simple souls generally succeed best in this novel. Anton Ivanovich, for
example, is a Russian variety of parasite, a man without occupation living
at the expense of landowners in the neighborhood by making himself indispensable to them with small services and concern about their concerns
in such a way that they do not even notice how he is fleecing them. But
is he really fleecing them, one may ask. They all like him and they all
derive some satisfaction from his activities. On his own low level he has
found his place. No one begrudges him his good-natured sponging expeditions, and Goncharov draws a sympathetic picture of him. Aleksandr's
new wisdom is exemplified by his attitude to Anton Ivanovich in the letter
to Lizaveta Aleksandrovna:

> "Here is an example of my meekness: a certain crank called Anton
> Ivanych visits me, stays with me, presumes to share my grief. To-
> morrow he will go to a wedding at some neighbours, and share
> their joy, and then to some other place, where he will perform
> the function of a kind of midwife. Neither grief nor joy prevents
> himfrom eating four times a day wherever he is. I see that it is all
> one to him — whether a man dies, is born, or weds, and I regard
> him without disgust, without irritation. I bear with him and do
> not drive him away. A good sign this, is it not, *ma tante?* What
> will you say on reading this self-praise of mine?" [1]

   The family serfs also belong to the simple soul category. Parallel to the
sad farewell scene between mother and son in the first chapter runs the
tragicomic farewell of the housekeeper Agrafena and her sweetheart Evsej,
who is to accompany Aleksandr to Petersburg as his man-servant. The way
in which she tries to conceal her grief under a mask of anger and he vacil-
lates between self-pity and jealousy of Proshka, his possible successor to
Agrafena's favors, is presented very comically. The feelings of both are very
genuine, but their limited intellectual capacities seem to reduce the emotions

---

1) I, p. 294.

involved to the level of low comedy. Evsej's further development as a character centers around his foolish delight in well brushed boots, which becomes a kind of fetish for him. Yet his return and the "silent, sheepish ecstasy" he exhibits, are once again both touching and humorous.

Goncharov's attitude toward servants is peculiar. Rather than resorting to Gogol's out and out scorn (in most of Gogol's works servants and peasants are presented as half idiots at best) he adopts an ironical touch aimed at their intellect, and excludes any possibility of "social compassion." Evsej talking about Petersburg in the last chapter sounds exactly like a character in a comic skit. Goncharov used this approach for the whole of his life (cf. his sketches "Old-Time Servants").

Kostjakov's simplicity has already been noted. Goncharov limits himself to a description of his clothes (a cap with a varnished peak and dressing-gown belted with a kerchief) and an enumeration of his matter-of-fact interests.

Goncharov often makes do with no more than a generalized type which he needs as a touchstone for the analysis of his hero's emotions. He does not even bother to introduce a family name for Liza and her father, at first referring to them as Oedipus and Antigone, later as the old man and his daughter, and only then mentioning that the girl's first name is Liza. Even so her portrait does not exceed generalization: a lock, an exquisite profile, a white neck, a slender figure, small feet — this is all.

Another way of supplying "description" is used for the still more episodic character of Sof'ja, Aleksandr's first — pre-Petersburg — "love". The eyes and expression of the plump, rosy girl plainly state:

> "I will love simply, without any nonsense, I will look after my husband like a nurse, obey him in all, and never try to be cleverer than he is. For who could be cleverer than a husband? It would be a sin! I will see to the housekeeping diligently, and keep the linen in repair. I will bear him half-a-dozen children, whom I will nurse and look after, dress and mend for, myself." [1]

---

1) I, p. 19.

But the presentation of small, characteristic details which become general, sometimes even symbolic, predominates. The best example of this " symbolism" is the motif of the "yellow flowers" blossoming in the pond of the remote provincial estate. They stand for sentimental love, for the kind of youthful abandon of which Petr Ivanovich completely disapproves, but which he is proven to have been guilty of in his youth and which Aleksandr embraces so wholeheartedly. Goncharov brings them up again and again, and by combining pure feeling with soft irony he makes the feeling shine out all the more radiantly. Although as a symbol they may seem almost simple-minded, the very fact of their reappearance adds much to the logical coherence of the plot.

The same holds for the introduction of minor characters. Kostjakov is mentioned and even briefly characterized in the good, naive Vasilij Zaezzhalov's hilarious letter to Petr Ivanovich. The characterization of him as a young man in the beginning of the book (I, 2) completely contradicts his appearance as an old man toward the end (II, 4), but the formal continuity is there. The same is true of Surkov, Petr Ivanovich's associate, who is separated from Mrs. Tafaeva as a result of Aleksandr's services. He begins his role in the second chapter of Part Two, but is briefly characterized (though not named) in the second chapter of Part One, more than 140 pages earlier.

Several other "signals" apart from the yellow flowers stress the logical correspondences among the novel's parts. Their appearance saves Goncharov the necessity of repeating himself on important psychological or ideological issues. The "yellow flowers" are mostly connected with the old maid Marija Gorbatova (Aleksandr's aunt), who is referred to as "tetka" − an expression with a distinctly unromantic ring. As soon as Aleksandr starts weaving plans which may become injurious to his wealth or career, Petr Ivanovich "pricks up his ears," or when Aleksandr quotes his pronouncements (as he does toward the end) which he does not want to be heard by his wife, he immediately makes a "ferocious face." After every one of Aleksandr's new misfortunes, his uncle poses with slight variations the same question he asked upon Aleksandr's arrival: "Now tell me, please. Why did you come here?" Aleksandr's great outbursts are usually dampened by Petr Ivanovich with the request to "shut your valve." But the most frequent and most humorous repetition is Petr Ivanovich's feigned propensity to forget the first name of Aleksandr's sweetheart Naden'ka. He brings her up no less than fifteen times, always referring to her as "your what's-her-name, . . . , isn't that right?", and substituting a different name each time. In addition, Petr Ivanovich insists on referring to Naden'ka as "the girl with the wart," though it is her mother who actually has it.

This brings us to the main characteristic of Goncharov's novel: its exuberant humor. A constant source of witticisms is the nature of the dialogues between uncle and nephew. Whatever Aleksandr says in romantic literary language is immediately translated into matter-of-fact, everyday expressions by his uncle. A great deal of the verbal charm is lost in translation. For "elevated subjects" Russian tends to use "archaic" bookish sounding Church Slavonic forms; for everyday topics it uses the more neutral-sounding Russian word stock. Aleksandr's speech mannerisms reflect a delight in high flown phrases characteristic of Russian romanticism. Emotion had to be expressed in elevated terms, using unusual words in a ponderous, rhetorical style. Pushkin claims to have "translated" Lenskij's tirade into clear speech (cf. "Evgenij Onegin," Chapter Six, Stanza XVII). To Aleksandr's complicated means of expression, to his preference for abstractions (frequently substantives with the verbal derivative suffixes — -enie, -anie or -tie), to his archaic forms (e.g. *vesi* for *sela* 'villages'), to his "grammatical pathos" (e.g. "I know deception" instead of "I have been deceived"), to his typically romantic vagueness ("somebody," "somewhere," "all" etc.) Petr Ivanovich opposes dry, official phraseology.

The "sincere, soulful effusions" which Aleksandr feels should form the basis of human communication are labeled "wild language" by Petr Ivanovich and ridiculed in a very off-handed, comic sort of way. After learning of his uncle's intention to marry, for example, Aleksandr marvels at his ability to continue "to discuss love with such infernal coldness." "Infernal coldness," replies Petr Ivanovich, "that's new! It's supposed to be hot in the nether regions." [1] When Petr Ivanovich decides to give a dinner, Aleksandr immediately interprets it as a farewell dinner before his wedding for "your true friends, those you sincerely love, with whom you would recall for the last time, raising the chalice of wine, your joyous youth, and, per-

---

1) I, p. 75.

haps, on parting would embrace them warmly." Petr Ivanovich's reply is
by this time predictable:

> "Well, in those five words of yours there is everything that does not
> or should not exist in real life. With what delight your aunt would
> have thrown her arms around you! Really, you say *true friends,*
> when there are simply friends; you say *chalice,* when people use
> to drink out of goblets or glasses, and you say embraces *on parting,*
> when there is no question of parting. Oh, Aleksandr!" [1]

When, after weighing it carefully in his hand, the uncle throws Sof'ja's gift,
a hair lock and ring, out the window (Aleksandr calls them a "tangible sign
of intangible relations"), he calmly describes his action as "the throwing out
of the window of intangible signs and all sorts of rubbishy trifles which
ought not to be kept in your room." [2]

When in the same scene it turns out that Petr Ivanovich has used Aleksandr's letter to Sof'ja for lighting his cigar, a philosophical conversation
ensues:

> "You're an extraordinary man, Uncle! Constancy does not exist
> for you, promises are not sacred. Life is so beautiful, so full of
> charm and sweet bliss. Like a smooth, enchanting lake —"
> "In which grow yellow flowers, of course," interrupted his uncle.
> "Like a lake," continued Aleksandr, "life is full of something
> mysterious and alluring, concealing so much —"
> "Slime, my friend." [3]

Aleksandr's vocabulary (wild jealousy, impulses, celestial bliss, colossal
passion, hot tears) undergoes a humerous debasement in Petr Ivanovich's
mouth.

Goncharov obviously derives pleasure from his highly successful comedy
scenes. One such scene occurs when Petr Ivanovich, having asked Aleksandr
to win Tafaeva away from Surkov, notices he has fallen in love with her,

---

1) I, pp. 83–84.
2) I, p. 46.
3) I, p. 52.

despite the fact that he had at first declined the mission, explaining that after Naden'ka's betrayal he had come to despise all women. In a dialogue with his nephew, Petr Ivanovich pretends that Aleksandr's success is due only to his desire "to do a favor for a relative," enumerates gratefully everything Aleksandr did "for him" during the courtship, and tells him innocently that he may stop seeing Tafaeva now, knowing full well that Aleksandr is head over heels in love.

A mixture of genuine drama and hilarious fun results from the scene in which Aleksandr arrives late at night to tell his uncle about his break with Naden'ka and Petr Ivanovich decides to have a late supper while hearing him out:

> "And you can eat supper?" exclaimed Aleksandr in astonishment.
> "I most certainly can. Can't you?"
> "I? Have supper? You too won't be able to swallow a bite your-self when you hear that this is a matter of life and death."
> "Life and death?" repeated his uncle. "Well, of course, that's extremely important, but let's just try — I think we'll manage to swallow a bite." [1]

The combination of Aleksandr's grief and his uncle's wandering interest (divided between the quality of the food and Aleksandr's misfortunes) is charming. Petr Ivanovich's transpositions of Aleksandr's bombastic, but genuinely felt speech (as e.g. the Pushkin — "O, human beings, unhappy race, fit theme for tears and laughter!") into "huma language" are especially felicitous here, and his irony at its best: "Stop talking nonsense, Aleksandr! As if there weren't any amount of girls like your — Mar'ja or Sof'ja, what's her name?" "Her name is Nadezhda." "Nadezhda? and which one is Sof'ja?" "Sof'ja ... is the one in the country," replied Aleksandr unwillingly." [2] It was not that long ago he had maintained that he would never, ever forget her!

Very frequently Goncharov achieves his humor by means of literary patterns or quotations. The letter of the old maid Mar'ja Gorbatova, Aleksandr's

---

1) I, p. 129.
2) I, p. 134.

aunt, to Petr Ivanovich, her former sentimental lover, is a charming parody
on the style of Nikolaj Karamzin, the most important representative of Russian sentimentalism:

> " . . . If I had known of his departure I would have sat day and night
> embroidering a cushion for you — a Negro with two dogs. You can-
> not imagine how often I have wept, glancing at the design. What can
> be more sacred than friendship and faithfulness? I now have only
> one thought, to which I devote my days, but there is no good wool
> here, and so I humbly request you, my dearest Brother, to send me
> the very best English wool to match the pattern enclosed in this let-
> ter, as soon as you can, bought at the best shop. But how I run on!
> What a terrible idea halts my pen! Perhaps you have quite forgotten
> us, after all, why should you remember a poor sufferer, who lives
> and weeps far from society. But no! I cannot believe you could be
> a monster like other men. No! My heart tells me that, amidst the
> luxury and pleasures of the metropolis, you still cherish your former
> feelings for all of us. This thought is balm for my suffering heart.
> Forgive me, I cannot go on, my hand shakes . . ." [1])

At the end of her letter she asks him to send her the novels of Zagoskin
and Marlinskij (the one, the author of several rather naive historical novels
à la Walter Scott, the other, a famous author of often hyperromantic tales
and novels) and the work "On Prejudices" by Mr. Puzino. (Polikarp Puzino
[1781-1866] published his *Vzgljad na sueverie i predrazsudki* [*On Superstition and Prejudice*] in 1834. Assuming that the action of Goncharov's
novel begins in 1830, we must charge him with a slight anachronism.)

An especially humorous feature is Goncharov's use of his own early
poems to poke fun at Aleksandr's poetic aspirations. He shows his uncle
a poem he has written and considers to be good. It is "Grief and Joy"
(Toska i radost') which Goncharov published in the Journal *Snowdrop*
(Podsnezhnik). Petr Ivanovich reads it aloud, interrupting his recitation
with critical remarks. Goncharov even goes so far as to modify the original
text for the worse in order to afford Petr Ivanovich's remarks greater justifi-

---

1) I, pp. 29-30.

cation. In the original we read that "the silence of sleeping nature seems frightening to us at such a moment," whereas in the novel it appears as "the silence of the distant skies is terrible and frightening at such a moment," which of course leads Petr Ivanovich to note that "terrible and frightening are the same thing." The beginning of the poem "Romans" is used later in the novel to provide Petr Ivanovich with a springboard for ironical observations.

Aleksandr is also fond of quoting his favorite poets. He uses lines from Pushkin as a rather doubtful illustration of his ecstatic feelings, from the fable writer Ivan Krylov to vilify the "world" and from Aleksandr Griboedov, whose bitter comedy "Woe from Wit" Goncharov greatly admired.

We do not know too much about Goncharov's first steps toward writing fiction, but perhaps Aleksandr's attempts ("He wrote a comedy, two stories [povesti], an essay and a book of travels") [1] reflect his own. One of the novels, which Aleksandr wrote according to his own "theory of aesthetics" invoking the "shade of Byron and referring to Goethe and Schiller," sounds again like a self-parody, even if one may assume Chateaubriand (whom Goncharov mentions as early as in "Nimfodora Ivanovna," completed by Goncharov at about the age when Aleksandr was making his debut) as Aleksandr's pattern and victim in this case. The plot is hyperromantic, it takes place in America, à la "René" or "Atala," and the parodistic overtones are clear. [2] The same parodistic attitude can be found in Aleksandr's novel from the provinces quoted above.

Aleksandr makes use of an unusual literary quotation to show how "two of the latest French novelists define true friendship and love." He claims to have agreed with them at first, but to have become disenchanted by experience. The two definitions of friendship and love are, as André Mazon persuasively argues, "pseudo-quotations," paraphrases of passages from Gustave Drouineau's "La manuscrit vert" and from Eugène Sue's "Atar-Gull." [3]

---

1) I, p. 102.
2) I, p. 103.
3) I, p. 160; Mazon, pp. 310–311.

Again Goncharov tampers with his original, stressing its exaggerations, so that they rightly arouse the indignation of Petr Ivanovich.

The list of authors presented in connection with Mrs. Tafaeva's "sentimental education" constitutes a kind of ironical survey of second and third rate literature. Aleksandr's cautioning Liza to avoid Byron in favor of Walter Scott and James Fenimore Cooper is another amusing literary sidelight.

A device which Goncharov put to good use in "The Happy Mistake" appears again in this novel. In the midst of a humorous scene, of comedy verging on slapstick he introduces psychological or ethical deliberations, sometimes in the form of aphorisms, sometimes as short essays. The tension between these incongruous elements generates a charm all its own and accounts for much of the special flavor of Goncharov's prose.

Frequent concise statements as: "It has long since been proven that a woman's heart cannot exist without love," or "It is, however, well known that no one ever wasted away from the sorrows and troubles of others. That's only human nature," or "The human heart, it seems, lives entirely from contradictions. If it were not for them, we might forget we even had one," alternate with short digressions on happy or unhappy love, its various aspects, its effect on unequal marriage, women, feeling, passion, jealousy, existential boredom ("how boring life is," cf. 264), "powerless desires," the essence of happiness, the role habits play in life, contrasts between generations, the nature of genius and talent in artistic creation, art as such, and music and literature. Some of them are very remarkable, reflecting no doubt Goncharov's own opinions, e.g. that statement that a writer can write to the purpose only when free of personal involvement and prejudice. And Petr Ivanovich is certainly speaking for Goncharov when he observes:

"Everyone experiences all those things," pursued Petr Ivanovich, turning to his nephew. "Who is there that is unmoved by the stillness, the darkness of night, or, let us say, by the rustling of leaves in a grove, by a garden, pools, the sea? If artists were the only ones who

felt all this, there would be nobody to appreciate them. But to reflect all these sensations in one's work is quite another matter. That
requires talent, and I don't think you have any. It can't be concealed — it shines from every line, from every stroke of the brush."[1]

Irony and humor are kept under control by this technique. Moreover, it
enables Goncharov to put his message across without a trace of didacticism.
A well-balanced distribution of accents creates the impression of a fluent
easiness in his narrative style.

Goncharov's prose does not display any striking stylistic devices. Metaphors, similes and personifications are frequent, but they are not intended
to dazzle. By *A Common Story* Goncharov had pretty much abandoned the
Gogolian ornamental style he had adhered to in his early stories. Similes
like the following one are quite rare and mostly serve to elaborate a recurring "symbol":

> "Steam, steam," said Aleksandr faintly, scarcely able to defend him-
> self. "You think and feel and speak exactly like an engine rolling
> over the rails — smoothly, evenly, calmly."
> "Well, and that's not so bad. Better than going off the tracks, bump-
> ing into a rut, as you have just done, and being unable to get up
> again. Steam, steam! Why steam, look you, is an honor to humanity!
> . . ." [2]

Goncharov prefers to derive his effects from an "astonishing correctness of
vision and rare aptitude for grasping a concrete impression." [3] This is clearly born out by such scenes as Naden'ka bent over the piano whispering the
word which signifies Aleksandr's first failure in love, early evening in the
village church, the boatride on the Neva, and the violin recital. Especially
impressive is the rendition of seemingly insignificant gestures or minute details as in this picture of Petr Ivanovich:

> That same night, at about twelve o'clock, when Petr Ivanych, a
> candlestick and a book in one hand, the other hand holding up

---

1) I, p. 172.
2) I, p. 144.
3) Mazon, p. 60.

the skirts of his dressing-gown, was going out of his study to his bedroom, his manservant told him that Aleksandr Fedorych wished to see him. [1]

Viewed as a whole, Goncharov's first novel is a fascinating work. It combines a well-balanced structure with an original treatment of its subject matter. What begins as a genuinely humorous story told in a genuinely humorous style leads inexorably, yet almost unbeknownst to the reader, to a hopeless catastrophe. Wittily rationalized ideologies place their proponents in an impossible impasse of tragic and irremediable pessimism.

---

[1] I, p. 127.

Goncharov wrote *A Common Story* when he was thirty-four, the age of young Aduev in the epilogue as he starts out on his career. But Goncharov did not follow the example of his hero; he did not run after wealth or fame. For he was certain of the futility of it all. What he was after, was a quiet life, a life without strain, a life with just enough restraining wisdom to keep boredom at bay.

Surely he felt a life of literary pursuits would further his ends. For Goncharov the creative impulse was the most satisfactory means of filling out life in the desired manner. What Aleksandr Aduev's emotional rantings and ravings failed to accomplish (he never became a writer), Goncharov set about in a state of prudent scepticism — with complete success.

After the completion of *A Common Story*, Goncharov apparently started in immediately on a new novel. At the same time he contributed various articles and reviews to periodicals but since all of them were written anonymously or under a pseudonym, it is quite difficult in some cases to determine his authorship.

An ironical review of a book compiled by D. I. Sokolov: "The Society Gentleman or A Guide to the Assimilation of the Rules of Social Intercourse" appeared in Volume Five of *The Contemporary* for 1847. In Volume Eight Goncharov published an anonymous obituary of his former pupil Valer'jan Majkov, who was drowned at the beginning of a promising career as a literary critic. In 1848 (Volume Twelve) he published a feuilleton called "Letters of a Friend from the Capital to a Bridegroom in the Provinces."[1] The signature is A. Chel'skij, but there can be little doubt about Goncharov's authorship.

These "Letters" (three in number) appeared in the fashion section. The signature refers of course to the fictive letter writer, not the author.

As can be surmised from the text, the author of the letters is a wealthy and quick-witted man of the world, who has given much thought to the art of *savoir vivre*. He has been asked by an old friend living in the provinces to procure a wide range of articles for him in the capital, starting with a complete wardrobe and ending with a coach. The reason for this request is his imminent marriage, and his desire to make a radical break with his bachelor existence.

---

1) "Pis'ma stolichnogo druga k provincial'nomu zhenikhu."

But the instructions Chel'skij receives as to the kinds of objects he should buy and the prices he should expect to pay greatly annoy him. He sees in them the proof of a certain *mauvais ton* to which the formerly elegant and refined young man has succumbed. His letters represent a sort of codex of the *comme il faut*. It is suffused, however, with a clearly ethical strain, a strain which removes the letters from the realm of "fashions" and "modern living" and places them in the much broader category of human relations.

This ethical bias forms the theme of the first letter, an exposition of four types: the fop, the salon lion, the well-bred man, and the upright man or better yet the man of high moral stature. The first two types run after cheap and purely external effects and are therefore shallow and scarcely worth mentioning. The third finds satisfaction in elegance and good taste as such, and although it has little to do with ethics (its representative is a master of politesse and of seductive *savoir vivre* not of moral rules), it does stand in close proximity to the final and highest type. This highest type is an ideal whose actual existence is open to doubt. "The man of high moral stature (porjadochnyj chelovek) is an intimate and harmonious combination of the external and internal moral art of living." [1] His elegant manners are no more than the naturally pleasing external form of his all-important inner strength; they are the "delicate and refined" reflection of his ethical qualities. He is the "perfect man," the whole man; he unites the external and the ethical sides of the great art of *savoir vivre*. [2]

Only the first two types need riches. The sterling qualities of the other two will shine through even the bleakest poverty: the well-bred man has his manners, the man of high moral stature both manners and ethical qualities. Like precious stones they may be mixed together with dust without losing their worth. Though the extent to which this banteringly presented theory of the harmonious man adheres to Schiller's "Briefe über die ästhetische Erziehung des Menschen" (Letters on the Aesthetic Upbringing of Man) is unclear, certain parallels on completely different levels cannot be denied.

The second letter deals with the ways of achieving external elegance. Point for point and in great detail (from linen on) Chel'skij demonstrates

---

1) Ogonek, VII, p. 73.
2) *ibid*., p. 74.

the importance of a "beautiful household" in all its ramifications as a factor in the formation of the inner man. If nothing else, he notes, then the mere presence of a woman requires special attention to beauty and harmony. His friend is obviously a bookworm, a scholar far removed from the world around him (he bears a distant resemblance to Kozlov in *The Precipice*), whose major interests are Greek, Latin, and the ancient world. At times Chel'skij teases him about these pursuits, but he also sings the praise of the ancients' love of beauty and bemoans the low place to which it has been relegated in modern classical scholarship. "How is it possible that you have failed to understand so colossal a hero of antiquity as Lucullus, you who can appreciate Plato, divine Homer, glorious Virgil?" [1] Goncharov's own knowledge of antiquity (his Winckelmann translations had evidently left their trace) find expression in the hymn-like parallels between the ancient and modern worlds.

Chel'skij runs two thousand silver rubles over the amount placed at his disposal by his friend. His excuse is that he is taking care of his internal and external needs, and he makes it clear to his friend that by making good the difference without offering any resistence he will be proving himself worthy of entrance to the category of men of high moral stature. The response he receives sorely disappoints him: his friend, clearly hurt and far from convinced, sends him the money without resistence, but also without a word of acknowledgement. Chel'skij's response is a third and very short letter in which he sadly affirms the temporary miscarriage of his attempt to create a perfect man (a condition to which he himself ardently aspires)[2], yet reaffirms his willingness to help.

Doubtless, this lively feuilleton expresses Goncharov's personal views and characterizes his personal aspirations. Like all his works it freely interweaves comical and serious elements. As for possible biographical parallels the provincial sholar may well be meant to represent Goncharov's brother Nikolaj, who led a life quite similar to the life Goncharov describes.

Work on "Oblomov" began as early as 1847. We do not know too much about its progress, nor about the plot as it originally presented itself to Goncharov's mind. It seems that in October 1848 Goncharov wrote "Ob-

1) Ogonek, VII, p. 80.
2) Cf. p. 302.

lomov's Dream", which — after several revisions — he published in *The
Contemporary* (1849, Volume Four) with the subtitle "Episode from an
Unfinished Novel." The success was encouraging, and Goncharov apparently
decided to procede at full speed, applying for a four-month leave of absence and traveling to Simbirsk to be able to work in peace. Before leaving,
he promised the unwritten novel to the journal *The Annals of the Fatherland* (Otechestvennye Zapiski), and received an advance from its editor,
Andrej Kraevskij.

In a humorous and well written letter to Nikolaj Majkov and his family
(July 13, 1849), Goncharov describes the far from comfortable journey.
Moscow, where he stayed a week, disappointed him: "The poetry of me-
mories and places has disappeared." [1] After short sojourns in Nizhnij
Novgorod and Kazan', he arrived in Simbirsk at the beginning of July 1849.

After fourteen years of absence, people and things had changed considerably. Goncharov speaks lovingly of his mother, who met him "plainly — without a great to-do, with an almost mute joy — and therefore very sensibly. A
wonderful, extraordinary woman." [2] He makes humorous remarks about
the changes in his brother and sisters. Tregubov had died shortly before his
arrival. He speaks of his nephews and the strange, unfamiliar name of "uncle" sounding in his ears. He feels himself loved and welcomes and appreciates it as much as he can. But ominous thoughts are never far from his
mind. "I've been here more than a week now, and I am still not bored.
Where have I ever stayed as much as a day without succumbing to boredom? Even if I do get bored this time, I'll try to conceal it." [3] Towards
the end of the letter, his fear becomes more concrete: "I'm still alright now,
but what will become of me when boredom — the scourge that follows me
everywhere — assumes its rights and overtakes me here: where will I hide?
Even now I feel it coming. Oh, God! Have mercy and save me." [4]

He speaks of the club, the provincial theater, and in another letter (to
Junija Dmitrievna Efremova, a niece of Mrs. Majkova and a close friend he
loved to tease good-naturedly) of the poetry of laziness, the only poetry

---

1) VIII, p. 243.
2) *ibid.*, p. 244.
3) *ibid.*
4) *ibid.*, p. 245.

to which he will remain faithful until death. He also makes vague allusions
to some amorous adventures, which lead us to believe that his relations to
the recipient of the letter were not completely innocent. But again he mentions "the whip of boredom." "Byron was right," he goes on, "when he
said that no self-respecting man should live beyond the age of 35. The only
people over 35 who live well are officials; after all, it isn't until then that
they've stolen enough to accumulate houses and carriages and the like.
'What more do you want? What more do you need?' they ask. 'What?
Tell us what.' How do I answer such a strange question? I refer my inquisi-
tors to Byron, Lermontov and their kind. That's where they must look for
an answer." [1]

The good life and this "poetry" account for the fact that he does not
accomplish anything on the novel. Shortly before returning to Petersburg
he writes a letter to Kraevskij telling him that he had better not count on
the novel he had promised and that he was therefore returning his advance.
In the same letter he mentions "another story" for which he had collected
some material. The story he is referring to later becomes *The Precipice;*
Goncharov writes about its conception in *An Uncommon Story* (1874).[2]

By the middle of October 1849 Goncharov was back in Petersburg,
where he spent the next three years in the civil service, rising in the ranks
and presumably working on *Oblomov* and *The Precipice,* though publishing hardly anything.

In connection with his mother's death in April 1851, he wrote a letter
to his sister, Aleksandra Kirmalova, praising the reasonable upbringing their
mother had provided them with and placing special emphasis on her justice.
"I am proud of and praise God for having had such a mother." [3] In the
same letter he gives his sister advice about bringing up her own children,
stressing the preferability of a university education over the rigors of the
Military Academy. [4] This is in keeping with his own very positive experience in the university and one of the many proofs of his interest in
problems of education.

---

1) Ogonek, VIII, p. 275.
2) N. I., p. 13.
3) Ogonek, VIII, p. 278.
4) Cf. *Vestnik Evropy,* 1907, II, pp. 586-588.

The Frigate "Pallada"

These uneventful years were suddenly interrupted by the most exciting event in Goncharov's life. The Russian government decided to undertake an expedition to Japan and America in the hope of opening commercial relations with Japan. Japan had remained nearly completely isolated and was closed to all foreigners despite the fact that several big powers, and notably the United States, had tried to effect a peaceful settlement with Japan. Admiral Count Evfimij Putjatin was entrusted with Russia's attempt to break Japan's resistance. To this end, he was given command over a small squadron, the main ship of which was the frigate *Pallada* (Pallas). Putjatin wanted a secretary who was skillful enough to describe the voyage. When the position was offered to Apollon Majkov, he suggested Goncharov, and to the astonishment of his friends, Goncharov accepted.

> "Everybody was surprised that someone as lazy and spoiled as I could make up my mind to go on such a long and dangerous voyage! No one who really knows me would be surprised at my resolve. My character is one of sudden changes; I never stay the same for more than two weeks in a row, and if on the outside I seem steady and true to my habits and propensities, it is only because the forms that frame my life are stationary." [1]

Things developed very quickly. The offer was made in the middle of August 1852. On August 22nd Goncharov met Admiral Putjatin, and apparently made a favorable impression. Putjatin applied for Goncharov to be transferred from the Department of Foreign Trade of the Ministry of Finances to the Ministry of the Navy, and permission was granted without delay. By September 9th all formalities had been basically taken care of and Goncharov had no choice but to go ahead with the venture.

It is difficult to determine whether he felt he was doing the right thing. His letters show him quite undecided. On the one hand, he hoped the journey would help him to escape the fits of melancholy and monotonous,

---

1) Alekseev, p. 36. Letter to E. Jazykova.

gray boredom of his life as an official in the administration. And of course he was curious about the world outside Russia, especially the more exotic regions; perhaps reminiscences of Tregubov's tales excited his interest. On the other hand, however, he was plagued by the fear of leaving a life he was accustomed to, the fear of the unknown and the dangers he would surely have to face. A voyage around the world on a sailing vessel implied perils of all sorts, and there were certainly times on board and in port when Goncharov deeply regretted his rash decision. His only consolation was that he might return before the voyage was out if things turned out too badly.

The start was none too promising. Three times Goncharov had to travel to the Kronstadt port where the ship was docked. But finally on October 7, 1852, a good ten days after he first reported in at Kronstadt, the "Pallada" set sail.

The frigate *Pallada* (length 173 feet, beam 43 feet 8 inches, draught 23 feet, 52 guns) was an old ship; it was not really fit for such a long voyage. The crew was a new one and had not been well trained. [1] And the expedition was beset by natural misfortunes from the very beginning. The Baltic Sea was unusually stormy that fall. The masts and sails were constantly in need of repair. The heavy pitching and rolling caused a series of leaks. Disease ran rampant: five sailors died in the first three weeks. Then the ship met with a major accident: it ran aground off Cape Dragör in dense fog and was so severely damaged that a complete overhaul became necessary. For two months the *Pallada* lay in dry dock in Portsmouth.

Reading Goncharov's letters from Portsmouth, one would scarcely guess that things had been going so badly (although his epistolary reports are much more "realistic" than the rosy text of his book *The Frigate Pallada*). His humorous touch varnishes many of the hardships. Apparently he did not want to complain and admit defeat. But in his sketch "Twenty Years Later" he states clearly how unbearable the voyage was and how at times he was driven to despair. Indeed for a short time he was resolved to turn back. He relates how he came to the decision of abandoning the expedition in a witty letter to the Majkovs (November 20, 1852). [2] At first he thought he would justify his sudden departure by claiming sea sickness,

---

1) The crew comprised 485 men, 31 of them officers.
2) Literaturnoe nasledstvo, pp. 359–361; Utevskij, pp. 61–63.

but when it turned out he was completely immune to it, he decided to
complain of nervousness and hypersensitivity to noise. Then it was discovered he slept so soundly that he had slept straight through the firing
of the ship's cannon, which was located right beside his cabin. At last he
confessed that he was not enjoying the voyage and had lost interest in
traveling. As soon as permission to return home was granted, however,
a reaction set in. Goncharov began to regret his decision, partly because
he felt that many of the officers were sorry to lose him, partly because
he was unwilling to make the long and strenuous trip from London to
Petersburg alone, but mainly because, one must assume, the reasons that
induced him to leave Petersburg still remained valid: curiosity and fear
of the boredom of routine. And perhaps he was spurred by the ambition
of becoming the "Homer" of the expedition.[1]

Insofar as his letters throw any light on the matter, it may be assumed
that Goncharov was on good relations with his travelling companions. Almost every time he mentions one or another of them, it is to approve of
them. His position occasionally required a measure of diplomacy: differences of opinion between Ivan Unkovskij, the Pallada's commandant,
and Putjatin arose quite frequently. Moreover, Putjatin ruled with an iron
hand, a policy which not everyone on board subscribed to. There is only
the slightest mention of these problems in Goncharov's letters, and the
book passes over them in complete silence. Even so promising an incident
as the time when a monkey who had been taken on board as a mascot gave
the napping admiral's hair a tug, was sentenced by the enraged plaintiff to
death in the briny deep, and finally, after a protracted chase through the
masts, was granted absolution — even this tempting incident went untouched. [2] On the other hand some of the officers, like Captain-Lieutenant
Pos'et, Lieutenant Baron Kridener, Midshipman Zelenyj, and Senior Navigation Officer Khalezov (who was nicknamed *ded*, 'the old man, grandpa') —
are quoted quite regularly. Semen Faddeev, the sailor assigned to serve
Goncharov during the voyage, proved to be a source of constant vexation —

---

1) There is no evidence for N.W. Wilson's assumption that Goncharov stayed under
   pressure from the Russian ambassador in London, exercised because of Putjatin's
   embarrassment at not being able to find a substitute secretary in England. Cf. The
   Voyage of the Frigate Pallada, edited and translated by N.W. Wilson, London 1965, p.19.
2) Cf. Utevskij, pp. 69–70.

and constant amusement. In the book Goncharov emphasizes his good points, thereby making him a new addition to the line of excellently chiseled servant types; in his letters, however, he has fewer positive things to say about him. At one point, he even felt it necessary to have the impudent Faddeev given a sound thrashing. [1]

The stay at Portsmouth was not very pleasant. During the repairs Goncharov was billeted on an old English boat with three officers to a room. Though the weather was bad, it did not take him long to learn Portsmouth by heart.

> "When it gets boring on board, I roam about the streets of Portsmouth. But after walking all through the city, I still have to turn back and take up once again with the people I must live with for three years. When I look at some of them, I get quite upset at the idea of having to come face to face with them every day. Others are more bearable, and there are some who are even quite nice — but very few. Anyway, I don't worry myself much about it, especially when I ask myself impartially: "What about me? Am I so wonderful?" Because once I've answered my question again as impartially as I am able — I always extend my hand without the slightest bile to all — the nice, the not so nice, and the bearable. Patience is a great virtue, or rather, the aggregate of virtues that determine a man's character, in other words — everything. Anyway, I always try as hard as possible to reconcile myself with all the present and future inconveniences of the voyage. I even mentally — in my imagination — smooth over the bumps, and sometimes succeed in cushioning the jolts. By using this artificial method, I have developed the valuable ability of keeping myself from getting bored." [2]

Goncharov spent eighteen days in London, and despite the weather — it rained nearly every day — he tried to see as much as possible. He was upset by the crowds assembled for the funeral of the Duke of Wellington

---

1) Literaturnoe Nasledstvo, p. 385: "Some days ago I ordered Faddeev thrashed. He fulfills his duty badly, you know why? I do not beat him, I do not yell, but I ask him for things and I pay him a salary. Incredible, but it is true."
2) *ibid.*

and delighted by the great quantity of pretty women. Like several other Russian writers (e.g. Nikolaj Karamzin, the sentimentalist), he never tires of extolling the beauty of English womanhood.

After repairs were finished, adverse winds kept the boat at Portsmouth until January 6, 1853. To Goncharov's great disgust, the sailors celebrated Christmas in drunken revelry.

No sooner had the *Pallada* set sail again than it was met by a fierce storm. Goncharov gives a witty description of the consequences and treatment of sea sickness, being among the very few not to be inflicted with it.

After the storm they covered the 1200 mile journey from England to Madeira in a little more than five days and nights, but only because of an extremely strong wind, which made travelling a torture. Again Goncharov speaks of despair and repents of having undertaken the venture at all. But in a letter from Madeira he sings a joyful hymn of praise, underlain as always by his soft, gentle humor: "I nearly wept when my lungs inhaled air of a purity they had never before enjoyed." [1] He describes an opulent dinner at the Russian consul's house which naturally features "Madeira wine of all grades and colors," masses of flowers and fruit, and the consul's beautiful wife (both Portuguese). The high point of his stay there was a five-hour excursion into Madeira in a palanquin; Goncharov refused to ride a horse. "It's impossible to describe all the places they carried me through, or exactly where I stopped or what I saw. I can only say that if I were never to see anything else again, I would have enough to reflect back upon for the rest of my life. And they kept telling me it was still winter and nature had not yet come alive, etc." [2]

The frigate remained in Funchal for twelve hours only. From January 18 to March 10 it made its way to Simonsbay in False Bay at the Cape of Good Hope, making one short stop at Praia on the Cape Verde Islands (January 25–27th).

Crossing the Tropic of Cancer, the Equator and the Tropic of Capricorn did not make much of an impression on Goncharov. He did enjoy a long

---

1) Utevskij, p. 67.
2) *ibid.*, p. 68.

calm, even though it put them behind schedule; "the resplendent summer over tranquil expanses of tropical waters" [1] delighted him. It was not even boring, he states in a letter to the Majkovs. [2]

It was one of Goncharov's secretarial duties to conduct a general diary of the voyage, and at the request of the admiral he also taught literature to the naval cadets. He tried to put everything he saw down on paper, but he was constantly beset by doubts as to whether he was the right person to compose such a chronicle. Work proceeded slowly because of his "unfortunate weakness for polishing and repolishing ... Someone else in my place would have done much better; all I like to do is draw and joke." [3]

About 300 miles before the Cape the wind picked up again, and Goncharov was glad to arrive at Capetown, where he stayed intermittently until April 12th. Admiral Putjatin arranged for a trip into the more accessible parts of Cape Colony. Goncharov was among the six officers and officials selected for this venture. From Capetown the party went as far as Worcester via Somerset West, Stellenbosch, Pearl, and Wellington. The Kaffir War was drawing to a close, and Goncharov felt obliged to read about its history, the better to write about it in his diary. This duty he considered rather boring, but on the whole the excursion was no doubt fascinating. Goncharov was impressed by the mountains and abysses, the hot springs, and the striking fauna and flora, so far removed from everything he had known in Russia. He discourses extensively on fish (to please Majkov, a passionate angler) and snakes (a hobby with his friend Ivan L'khovskij). The Kaffir War also provided him with a new experience; he passed crowds of returning Kaffirs, Hottentots, and other natives, and visited a prisoner camp and prison.

Goncharov singles out the natural beauty of Pearl and Stellenbosch for special praise, but in general South Africa is too barren and too hot for him, at least insofar as he can judge by his limited experience. Complaints of boredom run through almost all of his letters. Sometimes they seem to reach a point of near despair. In a letter to the Majkovs after a lively description of the excursion inland and a ride around Lion Mountain, he ex-

---

1) Literaturnoe nasledstvo, p. 313.
2) VIII, p. 251.
3) *ibid.*

claims "What boredom, what boredom. My God, the trials you visit upon us! To hell with them! To hell with Africa! We haven't even gotten to Asia yet, to say nothing of America. [1] I keep wondering what I'm doing here. America or no America, I'm no good to anyone. I have absolutely no desire to turn what I see to good stead. In fact, I've even stopped taking in new impressions. Someone else could have gotten so much more out of it all. I'm afraid I may not hold out. My strength seems to be failing me even though I'm gaining weight." [2] Goncharov makes a distinction between boredom *(skuka)* and spleen *(khandra)*. The latter seems to be synonymous with a certain general, purposeless yearning *(toska)*. *Khandra* and *toska* are the states he fears most, and they are constantly lurking just beneath the surface of his every thought and action.

The *Pallada* set sail from the Cape on April 12, 1853, but on the 14th she was so seriously damaged by a severe storm that Putjatin decided to ask for a substitute, sending Lieutenant I. Butakov as courier to Petersburg with a request for the newly launched frigate *Diana*. Butakov was to catch the mail steamer at Batavia in Java. The voyage to Batavia took a month; the weather was pleasant, and the *Pallada* sailed free. A calm prevented her from entering the Sunda Strait for three days. but Goncharov did not mind. He had become accustomed to the sea and was beginning to enjoy "this strange, unusual life more and more." [3] To his regret the frigate called at Anger instead of Batavia, and since it turned out that the mail steamer departed at unpredictable intervals, it was decided to take Butakov on to Singapore.

Despite the burning sun and the foul exhalations from the swamps in the virgin woods, Anger's tropical beauty enchanted Goncharov. "Once ashore, I was nearly happy. I was finally travelling the way I had dreamed of traveling — through woods and thicket, through unrestrained beauty. Until now — even in Africa — we had ridden from clearing to clearing along

---

1) The first schedule was to sail to Japan via Cape Horne. Because of the delay at Portsmouth plans were changed in favor of the Cape of Good Hope. But still there was the intention to sail from Japan to San Francisco and return via Cape Horne. This was frustrated by the Crimean War.
2) Literaturnoe nasledstvo, p. 376.
3) *ibid.*, p. 378.

smooth roads and spent the night in comfortable hotels. Here there was nothing of the sort. We hack our way into virgin forests — forests of coconut palms, fig trees, and many other species far beyond the scope of my severely limited knowledge of botany — which seem impossible to get through." [1]

In a letter to Evgenija and Nikolaj Majkov, he describes the luscious vegetation, praises the coconuts, and jokes about the natives' clothing and the fireflies, ending with a rare exclamation: "I still have far to go, perhaps I will return to Russia, but it will be a long time before I forget Java." [2]

The pleasures of Anger lasted only one day. On May 18th the frigate sailed for Singapore, arriving there on the 25th. "New, unusual, and striking" [3] exclaims Goncharov in a letter to his friend Mikhail Jazykov and his wife. The mixture of Asian peoples intrigues him, and he dwells extensively upon their characteristics. He admires the pulsating life, feels attracted to it, and misses no opportunity to take part in it. Even an accident enhances the feeling of life: "Something unfortunate has happened. A sailor had both his hands torn off while loading a gun. They're operating on him now, and I can hear him moaning. It's an unpleasant business, but what can be done about it? This tragic incident somehow seems to complement the lively morning scene and our new activities. I'd so much like to go on a buying spree, but where would I store it all? I keep what I can; it would be terrible if we had to change ships." [4]

This statement is quite characteristic of Goncharov's attitude to life. He always makes a conscious effort to keep his equanimity and prevents excessive emotions of any kind from gaining control over his psychological balance.

On June 1st the *Pallada* left Singapore, and on the 14th docked in Hong Kong. Putjatin went on to Canton to negotiate for sea-borne trade with China, but Goncharov, who was laboring under a severe fever, was unable to accompany him. His mood had sunk rather low, and his letters touch on the possibility of his returning to Russia. "You know, I'm the type of

1) Literaturnoe nasledstvo, p. 381.
2) *ibid.*, p. 382.
3) *ibid.*, p. 386.
4) *ibid.*, p. 383.

traveler who finds traveling a kind of torture." [1] Nonetheless he watches "with great curiosity" the clever and intelligent Chinese faces around him, observing "what they do, what and how they eat and drink." [2] When able to go for a walk, he indulges in a harmless hobby: buying trinkets of all kinds in great quantities even though he is perfectly aware that he will have to leave them behind or that they will either break or molder on the boat.

On June 26th the frigate left Hong Kong for the Bonin Sima Islands. On the night of July 8th, she was battered off Batan by a typhoon of unusual strength, only narrowly escaping disaster. "Fortunately," says Goncharov in a letter to the Jazykovs, "we were only skimmed by its tail, or it would have been all up with our old boat. It tore three sails to shreds and shook the main mast so severely that it nearly fell. God knows whether we would be able to escape if it had!" [3] The entire trip was fraught with misfortune. Instead of a week it took a whole month; the typhoon was followed by a calm, and the frigate did not put in to Port Lloyd, Peel Island until July 25th.

Goncharov fell ill. A rash and erysipilas on his leg caused him great pain. Official duties became a burden, and his only consolation were the letters he received from many friends when the corvette *Olivuca,* the transport *Prince Menshikov,* the schooner *Vostok,* and two couriers from Russia joined the frigate. The heat on the island was fierce, and when the damage done to the *Pallada* by the storm had been repaired, Goncharov was happy to leave it. The whole squadron set sail on August 4th for Nagasaki, and, meeting with no adverse conditions, arrived there on August 9th. Goncharov and the *Pallada* stayed on for three months (until November 11th).

Negotiations with the Japanese were very complicated and timeconsuming. Japan would not brook any change in its rigid social system and rightly feared that foreign influence would force it on them. Everything was done to prolong negotiations in the hope that the Russians would grow tired and leave. Putjatin had orders to be pliant and patient and to treat the Japanese

---

1) Literaturnoe nasledstvo, p. 383.
2) *ibid.*
3) *ibid.,* p. 394.

as equals, despite their manifest military weakness. His progress was therefore much slower than that of the less scrupulous Americans.

All this gives Goncharov a chance to scrutinize Japanese customs, reception ceremonials, the importance of social differences, the rigid gradation of ranks in a totalitarian state and the fear and spying it entails.

He is grateful for any kind of distraction, but the motif of boredom recurs repeatedly in his letters. At one point he thinks himself seriously ill. His liver and heart bother him constantly, he begins to lose hope of ever seeing Russia again, he complains of terrible winds that make life on the anchored boat impossible.

But all these troubles fade before the rumors reaching the *Pallada* of an imminent war. If war were to break out the situation of the squadron would be quite precarious; the English and French would not hesitate to attack it, and "our people say that they will not give themselves up alive, that if necessary, they will fight, you see, to the last drop of blood." [1]

Putjatin decided to obtain precise information about the political situation, and despite the fact that the Japanese finally promised high officials from Yedo (Tokyo) would soon arrive for negotiations, he left Nagasaki for Shanghai on November 11th. On November 15th *Pallada* anchored at the Saddle Islands near the entrance of the Yangtsekiang. Goncharov had had enough of life on board, and decided at the last moment to join the admiral and several officers for a trip to Shanghai. Putjatin was obviously much pleased with his secreterial services, and commended him several times in reports to his Ministry.

In Shanghai, described by Goncharov very vividly in a letter to the Jazykovs [2], Putjatin learned about the declaration of war between Russia and Turkey, and fearing that France and England might join immediately, he left Shanghai and the Saddle Islands on December 17th for Nagasaki, arriving there for the second time on December 22nd. The Yedo "groote Herren," as the Japanese called them, had arrived. A series of official receptions ensued, partly in Nagasaki, partly on board the frigate, but

---

1) Literaturnoe nasledstvo, p. 399.
2) *ibid.*, p. 400.

negotiations remained at a standstill. The Japanese protracted them so
adroitly that Putjatin finally lost his patience and decided to sail south-
ward to Manila, where he hoped to put the old boat through a drastic over-
hauling. He had not abandoned the project of a commercial treaty with the
Japanese however, and promised to return in the spring for further negotia-
tion. Staying in Nagasaki without any news of political developments would
have been quite dangerous, and so the *Pallada,* the corvette, and the transport left Nagasaki on January 24th 1854.

On January 30th the *Pallada* nearly went down. Near the entrance of
Naha harbor in Okinawa (Ryukyu Islands) a violent storm forced it to
anchor at open sea, no more than two miles from the perilous coral reefs
guarding the harbor's entrance. The gale was so strong that the anchors
began to drag; the ship came nearer and nearer to the reefs. Collision would
have meant instant destruction. Goncharov describes the situation very
eloquently in his sketches *Two Incidents of Life at Sea* and *After Twenty
Years.*

Okinawa delighted Goncharov. He saw in its landscape a resurrection
of the Golden Age as posited by Theocritus or described in the idylls of
Albrecht Haller. He writes to the Jazykovs [1] that he had suspected the
English traveler Basil Hall of overdoing his 1818 descriptions of the islands.
But he found his statements not only unexaggerated, but even incomplete.
The landscape — "enchanting dales, hills, murmuring brooks under the
vault of beautiful trees" and the people, for instance, "some long-bearded
old men who carried staffs and greeted the guests with deep bows and
fruit" — made one believe in the Russian fairy tale in which rivers of honey
and milk flow freely.

After leaving these "blessed isles" (February 9th), the frigate sailed on
to Manila, where it anchored on February 16th. Putjatin had intended to
have the frigate repaired there, but the Spanish authorities, afraid of a possible English or French attack on the Russian ship in case of war, made it
clear to the admiral that he was unwelcome. This was a great disappointment for Goncharov; he liked Manila, enjoyed the Spanish atmosphere,
and had looked forward to working there in peace for some time. He had

---

1) Literaturnoe nasledstvo, p. 402.

begun to write up the stretch of the voyage just behind them, made acquaintances, wandered happily around the bustling city, and reveled in the surrounding country. Even the heat was unable to disturb him. Then, after only eleven days, the *Pallada* had to move on.

Sailing became very tense. The constant fear of an attack from English and French ships necessitated a close watch of the horizon. The frigate was battle-ready, and in case of defeat would be blown up.

Putjatin decided to try to reach Siberian shores. The ship's poor condition made it impossible to even think of crossing the Pacific to San Francisco, as was originally intended. From Manila the frigate sailed to Batan to take on fresh provisions. A bad storm nearly broke the two main masts on March 8th. In Batan Goncharov experienced a strong attack of homesickness which was only exacerbated by the unavoidable decision to overhaul the boat. It turned out that the overhaul could best be done, with relatively little danger, by retracing their route south to Port Pio Quinto on little Camiguin Island (one of the Babuyans) where the *Pallada* stayed from March 12th to 21st. The repairs were successful, the masts firm again. But Goncharov remained homesick and unhappy. Though he still did not really regret his decision to undertake the voyage, privations and anxieties did sometimes overwhelm him.

The frigate now sailed straight north to Hamilton Island off the South Korean coast, the first major stop on its way to Russia. She arrived there without any incident on April 2nd. The transport sent by Putjatin to Shanghai for news of the war in Europe arrived on the same day, but provided them with little fresh information. (War had been declared on March 24, 1854). Putjatin decided to wait for them, but not on cold, unpleasant Hamilton Island, whose inhabitants proved quite hostile towards the sailors. He sailed for a third time to Nagasaki to remind the Japanese of his existence and insistance. The passage was smooth (April 7th to 8th), but of course there was no news from Yedo. Nor did Putjatin count on any. He sent a letter proposing a later meeting nearer the residence of the Mikado and the Shogun (the actual ruler of Japan), took on fresh supplies of food, and sailed on April 14th past the island of Tsushima to Engilman Bay (Korea), arriving there on the 20th.

As it was impossible to make normal headway until the ice off the Siberian coast had been broken up, Putjatin ordered a survey of the little known Korean coastline. But even pushing forward at an extremely slow speed was made prohibitive by bad weather. Naturally Goncharov was irked with life on the humid ship. The climate was cold, the shore bleak, uninviting, and peopled by hostile natives. In addition, supplies of fresh food began to grow scarce. The fact that a hitherto nameless little island was called Goncharov in his honor offered him little consolation.

The survey was completed on May 11th, and the frigate headed for the Tatar Strait (between Russia and Sakhalin). Reaching the Strait on May 17th, she fell in with the schooner *Vostok* which had been sent from Nagasaki to Shanghai for news and was hurrying on to Imperatorskaja Gavan' (now Sovetskaja Gavan') which Putjatin had selected as a meeting place for his squadron. The *Vostok* confirmed the declaration of war as fact.

A ciphered order from Petersburg ordered Putjatin to proceed to De Kastri (about 300 miles north of Imperatorskaja Gavan') to join the frigates *Diana* and *Aurora* and the corvette *Navarin*. Putjatin had to disregard this order. He sailed to Imperatorskaja Gavan', arrived there on May 20th, but could not enter the harbor because of heavy fog until the 22nd. Lack of provisions made life extremely difficult. Of the men on board of the two Russian ships that had wintered in the harbor, thirty-three had died of scurvy. The crew was kept busy with fortifying the harbor and building barracks.

On June 21st Nikolaj Murav'ev, the Governor-General of Eastern Siberia, arrived in Imperatorskaja Gavan' with orders that the *Pallada*, battered and bruised and no longer fit for normal voyages be towed into the Amur River, the ultimate plan being to return her to Kronstadt after the war. In accordance with this order, the *Pallada* sailed north on June 28th, called for one day at De Kastri, and proceeded with great difficulty (there was no wind) to the estuary of the Amur. After two and a half months of vain attempts at floating her down the Amur [1], however, the frigate had

---

1) There was a dangerous running aground again described in Two Incidents of Life at Sea.

to return to Imperatorskaja Gavan', and there she remained as a blockship until she was sunk in 1856 to prevent her from falling into the hands of the enemy.

On July 26th 1854 Putjatin transferred his flag to the frigate *Diana*, which was assigned to him to succeed *Pallada*. The transferral involved a major change in personnel, and Goncharov took advantage of the opportunity to ask for his release. Putjatin valued Goncharov and his services very highly, and did not at all like the idea of letting him go. But Goncharov was tired of traveling "I ought to return, if only because the voyage has exhausted me. For a long time now I've had the feeling that instead of traveling, *je fais un mauvais rêve*." [1] Nothing excited him any more, but then again there was nothing very exciting in the barren shores of Korea and Siberia. What is more, the prospect of cruising in rough waters under the constant threat of a French-English attack was less than attractive. He also doubted Putjatin would have much need for a secretary under such conditions. Putjatin, however, was sad to see Goncharov go. In a letter he wrote to the Secretary of the Navy, he has the following to say on Goncharov's account. "I cannot refrain from expressing once again my gratitude for your kind intercession in assigning Mr. Goncharov to this expedition. To the very end of his stay with me, he distinguished himself . . . in both his action and assiduity . . . His abilities and education render him highly useful to the service, and I can without hesitation recommend him to Your Excellency for the execution of important assignments of all kinds." [2]

On August 2nd Goncharov was transferred to the schooner *Vostok*. In Nikolaevsk, General-Governor Murav'ev and his retinue joined the party from the *Pallada*. The schooner arrived in Ajan on August 15th and around August 20th Goncharov began the long and difficult journey home across Siberia via Yakutsk and Irkutsk.

"In Ajan they told me that you can't take much with you, that all baggage is carried on packhorses, not in carriages, and that each horse carries from three to five poods. I gave all my books to one of our new settlements in the Tatar Strait and distributed my whole provision of Manila cigars

---

1) Literaturnoe nasledstvo, p. 409.
2) Alekseev, p. 46.

among the men on board. Then they told me that you go horseback for
the first 200 versts, for the next 600 you take a boat along the Maya River,
then you get back on your horse for the 180 after that, and then finally
for the last 200 versts to Yakutsk you can take a carriage. And as you
come up to Yakutsk, you cross the Lena, which at that point, you see, is
nine versts wide." [1]

Such are the terms in which Goncharov wrote the Majkovs of his journey
in a humorous letter from Yakutsk, where he arrived around September 12th.
The hardships of the overland route were so great that the sea voyage seemed
benign in retrospect. The worst part of it all was that Goncharov got frostbitten feet, which prevented him from continuing immediately to Irkutsk.
Even after partially recovering, he could not leave Yakutsk for more than
two months; he was forced to wait for the Lena to freeze over. Life in Yakutsk was not too unpleasant for him, thanks to the friendliness of the governor Konstantin Grigor'ev [2] and the bishop Innokentij, a learned man
whom Goncharov praised several times in his letters. But he longed for
home, and comical as his adventures may seem, they merely served as a
screen to cover his impatience. On November 26th he finally left Yakutsk
and, again after a strenuous journey, arrived in Irkutsk on December 25th
with a badly frostbitten face.

The three weeks he spent in this relatively big city were quite agreeable.
Governor-general Murav'ev and his French wife apparently liked Goncharov
very much and invited him daily for dinner. He admired Murav'ev's intelligence, energy, and efficiency. In his sketch "Through Eastern Siberia. (In
Yakutsk and Irkutsk)" written in 1890 and published in January 1891,
Goncharov also mentions that he visited some Decembrist families, a note
the censorship would not have let pass in the fifties.

On January 16, 1855 Goncharov left Irkutsk, and making short stops in
Kazan', his native Simbirsk, and Moscow, he reached Petersburg around
February 25th. He immediately reported to his department at the Finance
Ministry and resumed his post in the civil service. The most exciting part
of his external life had come to an end. Its literary result is one of the best
travel books in Russian literature, *The Frigate Pallada*.

---

1) Literaturnoe nasledstvo, p. 413.
2) Called Petr Igorev in "Through Eastern Siberia:"

Between 1855 and 1857 Goncharov published each of the book's chapters as separate articles in a number of different journals. [1] Moreover in February and March 1858 Vladimir Majkov's *Snowdrop* carried an account, aimed at younger readers, of two of his voyage adventures. It was called "Two Incidents of Life at Sea."

In the introduction, which he stylizes in the form of a talk for children, Goncharov makes the claim that life at sea is no more dangerous than any other kind of life, arguing that although life itself never changes it does offer an array of variations. He compares life to an opera motif which undergoes a number of modifications from one act to the next: "The theme, i.e. life, is one, but the variations change." [2]

The short diatribe against wetnurses that follows shows Goncharov to be far from sympathetic to the nursemaid brand of child raising. He particularly rails at their fairy tales, denouncing them for the unnecessary terror they strike into the hearts of the young. Real danger, Goncharov points out, is everywhere. Is it better to fall from a wagon drawn by frightened horses and die in the gutter with a shattered skull or to be rocked into death, or rather sleep, by a gentle wave with an emerald head and a mane of pearls — painlessly and without disfiguration? "Nothing in life should be taken on blind faith. Fate keeps an eye out for the moment when man stops looking around to see whether there isn't a stone about to fly out at him from somewhere, and as soon as he forgets himself she brings him back from oblivion . . ." [3] As examples he describes the Okinawa coral reefs and the treacherous sandbank at the mouth of the Amur.

Goncharov did not feel entirely at home in this special children's style. In a letter to Vladimir and Ekaterina Majkova he makes a good case for the position that a children's writer must accomplish the impossible: blot from his mind that he is writing for children, write unaware that he is writing for them. "Children don't like to be regarded as children. The idea that children's literature already exists and needs only to be selected from

---

1) Cf. Bibliografija, pp. 10–11.
2) VII, p.79.
3) VII, p.91.

among adult literature is entirely accurate!" [1] The *Frigate Pallada* is an excellent example of children's literature written unawares. [2]

"From Memoirs and Stories of a Sea Voyage," a sketch appeared in the 1874 miscellany *Pooling Resources* (Skladchina). [3] Here Goncharov describes the stranding at Cap Dragör and, once again, the perilous confrontation with the Okinawa coral reefs. The tone of this version is somewhat milder than that of the children's version. For the latter he wrote: "Nearby stood a gaping grave from beyond which life with all its beauty and splendor looked out at us." [4] For the former, "It gave me a certain pleasure to watch the breakers seething with foam and leaping across the rocks like wild white horses." [5] As before Goncharov muses upon the dangers that life encircles us with, dangers we fail to notice and therefore to take fright at. He concludes that danger and horror are by no means synonymous.

In addition to the above-mentioned adventures Goncharov gives a vivid eye-witness description of the earthquake in Simodo harbor that led to the destruction of the frigate *Diana*. He also paints a highly engaging portrait of the Archimandrite Avvakum, who accompanied the *Pallada* on its voyage and who is mentioned several times in the book with much the same affection as here.

The last time Goncharov returned to his travel reminiscences was in 1890, shortly before his death. "Through Eastern Siberia," the resultant sketch, was published in the following year in the journal *The Russian Review*. Its style is reminiscent of Nikolaj Leskov's verbose stories about high officials and church dignitaries; it has a somewhat obtrusive positive bias and is composed mainly of long conversations in anecdote-like episodes. The most fully developed characters are Konstantin Grigor'ev (the governer of Ya-

---

1) VII, p. 453.
2) The young Chekhov, who was later to come out with a statement about children's literature remarkably similar to Goncharov's, highly recommended Frigate Pallada to his younger brother Misha (Polnoe sobranie sochinenij i pisem, Moskva, 1948, v. XIII, pp. 29–30).
3) Cf. p. 256.
4) VII, p. 92.
5) III, p. 428.

kutsk, portrayed here under the name of Petr Igorev), Nikolaj Murav'ev, and the Bishop Innokentij.

The Frigate Pallada appeared in May 1858 in two volumes. At the time of the third edition, in 1879, Goncharov added a foreword plus a concluding chapter — the sketch from "Pooling Resources" with a new title: "Twenty Years Later." This chapter has since become an integral part of the book.

The work is divided into seventeen chapters, all of which are in the form of letters. Goncharov expressly notes in the above-mentioned foreword that the epistolary form is not a mere device, that he did in fact send the letters to friends, using a regurarly kept diary as an *aide-memoire*. This claim is only partially tenable. Substantial sections of the diary were clearly reworked into letter form well after the voyage. Only Chapter Three, which bears the subtitle "Letter to V.G. Benediktov," appears to have started out as an actual letter; it is a response to Benediktov's poem "To I.A. Goncharov Before His Voyage Around the World." The remaining "letters" are a mixture of passages from the diary and paraphrases of his correspondence with the Majkovs and the Jazykovs.

By using the letter form to structure his narrative, Goncharov provided it with an animated, easy-going, entirely natural narrator — the letter writer. In the guise of letter writer Goncharov was free to omit anything he pleased and forced to resist the temptation of playing the scholar. He therefore makes only the sparsest reference to secondary sources, stressing over and over that he wrote exclusively about what he saw with his own eyes, not what can be gleaned from "official accounts, tables, and almanacs." [1] "Remember our agreement," he says at another point, "the only things I write about are those that I see myself and experience from day to day." [2] Immediately following his extensive reflections on China he stresses that although sinologists and sinophiles may object to some of what he says, he has set forth everything as he observed it. [3]

---

1) II, p. 106.
2) III, p. 217.
3) III, p. 304.

Running through the entire work is a wise, good-natured understanding for all varieties of life. The "easy-going style" is of course the result of careful calculation; the polish and grace of the smoothly flowing narrative bears elegant testimony to Goncharov's artful attention to detail and his feeling for a clearly defined structure.

The first part of the first chapter is meant to sound as if it had been dredged out of the writer's memory. Writing from the Tatar Straits in June 1854, he retells his readers that because the early letters from England never reached Russia, he is forced to recap the early part of the voyage without their help. This ruse gives him the opportunity to evoke the uneasy feelings he had about the voyage before embarking on it. And removal in time from the feelings lends his presentation of them objectivity. He speaks of a deep-seated desire to visit exotic, far-away lands, a desire he has had since childhood and can now suddenly satisfy; the acute boredom (a continuous motif) that has driven him to reject his everyday routine; his uncertainty as to whether his mettle will hold up once the reality of the voyage begins approaching "like an ever more threatening storm cloud".[1] What is a sailing vessel? "A shaving, a basket, an epigram on human power." [2] And where is the strength necessary for putting down a profusion of new and intense impressions? "And when these wondrous guests will invade the soul, will they not put the host out of coutenance in the midst of the festivities?" [3]

After this outburst of despair comes an attempt at selfpersuasion: How many men had undertaken such voyages — when they were much more hazardous, when they explored unchartered regions — and lived to tell the tale. And nowadays everything is so civilized. "Australia has carriages and coaches, the Chinese have begun to wear Irish linen, everyone in East India speaks English; American savages straight from the woods set their sights on Paris and London and apply to universities, in Africa the negroes are beginning to be ashamed of the color of their faces and are gradually acquiring the habit of wearing white gloves. It would take a great outlay of money and labor to fall prey to the coils of a boa constrictor or the claws of a lion or tiger." [4]

---

1) II, p. 16.
2) II, p. 16.
3) II, p. 16.
4) II, p. 17.

But there is yet another problem — how to mold everything together into a gripping whole. From Aristotle through Lomonosov not a single writer has set down rules for travelogues. And so much of the poetry of travel has been lost. Will the readers not be disappointed? The only satisfactory answer to this question is the work itself. As it turns out there was really little poetry and no miracles. Everything — the sky, the sea, the tropics, the earth itself — is monotonous as soon as one comes to know it well . . . But at this point Goncharov breaks off, realizing that he has been letting hind sight do the talking for him. It is here that he begins his step-by-step account.

If one were to ask what the specific charm of this report is, the answer would probably have to be: Above all it is its basic idea, which runs through it: The sameness in diversity; life as such, the substance of existence is everywhere the same, only the surface, the appearances differ; it is the cleverly worded aphorisms that comment upon this idea; it is the sympathetic humor that, in Goncharov's treatment, so neatly counterbalances the serious passages; it is the fresh, unhackneyed similes that are always to contrast nature and objective reality with the human side of things; it is the masterful portraits of individuals and whole peoples; it is the witty and sensitive dialogues; and, last but not least, it is the nature of descriptions, whose abundant detail successfully tempers the author's frequent rapturous outbursts.

Against the backdrop of the ever looming threat of boredom Goncharov paints a picture of the universality of the human character's basic contrasts — happiness and sorrow, fervid activity and sloth, intelligence and stupidity. Yet he makes no more than occasional direct reference to it. Some of these references are quite abstract: "Intelligence is identical everywhere; despite differences in nation, dress, language, religion, and even world outlook all intelligent people — like all fools — have certain characteristic traits in common." [1] Or: "It has been said that carelessness is a characteristically Russian trait. Not at all! Carelessness is characteristically human." [2] Other references to universals of the human temperament generalize from a speci-

---

1) III, p. 178.
2) III, p. 249.

fic instance. After observing a woman mourning for a loved one at a funeral in Shanghai, Goncharov writes: "Of course we could not understand what she was saying, but the language of grief is everywhere one." [1] After observing the workings of a Shanghai tavern, he remarks that it is basically the same as its Russian counterpart, though on the surface it appears quite different. [2]

Nature too varies on the surface, while remaining true to form on a deeper level. African sparrows are much more beautiful than Russian sparrows, yet all their elegance notwithstanding they have identical habits. Africa has its swallows and crows, yet they do not correspond exactly to the homegrown, Russian varieties. "A dog began to bark, and even that was not entirely what we expected. There was something unfamiliar about it — almost as if the dog were barking in a foreign language." [3] There were strange insects crawling along the hotel walls, not the "homely bedbugs and cockroaches," [4] yet they probably served the same purpose. China has a tasty fruit that must be peeled, but when the peeling is done one eats the peels and throws away the pulp. [5]

Of course the frequent aphorisms also claim universal validity. In love, writes Goncharov, the nerves and blood are decisive, which is why lovers weep when parting; friendship, on the other hand, "weaves its nest in the head, the consciousness, rather in the nerves or blood." [6] The following statement is meant to be universal, yet it is at the same time typical of Goncharov's attitude toward storms of all kinds: "Storms, raging passions are not the norm of nature or of life. They are merely a transitional element. Disorder and evil are a creative process, the unskilled labor necessary for the production of well-being and happiness in nature's laboratory . . . " [7] It also sheds light on Goncharov's reactions to concrete storms. At first he says, "How hideous, or, if you will, how beautiful !" [8]

---

1) III, p. 135.
2) III, p. 113.
3) II, p. 138.
4) II, p. 187.
5) III, p. 133.
6) II, p. 41.
7) II, p. 130.
8) II, p. 82.

Later, however, the negative aspect takes precedence; the "classical" storm off the Cape of Good Hope that he was called up on deck to admire evokes in him the one-sided "How hideous! What disorder!" [1]

Structured around an aphorism chain that climaxes in a dramatic personification, the following passage well illustrates Goncharov's aphoristic penchant: "Vanity and coarse over-indulgence are the distinctive traits of a life of luxury. Hence the fact that such a life is of short duration. It is too feverous and ephemeral to be otherwise. It will not help a Croesus reach the Pillars of Hercules. It grows weak in satiety and finally falls, dragging down commerce as it goes. Luxury is always accompanied by its invisible enemy, poverty, who is forever on the lookout for the moment when the tawdry goddess shows signs of teetering on her pedestal: dressed in cynical rags, it gives the empress a quick push, seats itself on her throne, and gnaws away at the glorious remains." [2] Indicative for Goncharov's attitude towards art is the caustic aphorism about a beautiful Jesuit Church in Manila spoiled for him by the poor quality of its paintings: "Man can feel no charity or indulgence once his aesthetic sense has been outraged." [3]

As in his early works Goncharov directs his sense of humor against the clichés of romanticism. Talking of the ocean, which he has long been looking forward to seeing, he notes that poets have told him it was "boundless, gloomy, sullen infinite, unfathomable, and indomitable" while his geography teacher called it simply "Atlantic." [4] In contrast to the "sullen, gloomy, and potent" of Byron, Pushkin, Benediktov, and the like, Faddeev (his servant) adds "angry" and Goncharov "briny, boring, ugly, and monotonous." [5]

The description of the ship's pitching and rolling are truly classical in their inventive variations. One such account of the raging elements takes the reader inside the cabin, where objects seem to come alive: "The ship

---

1) II, p. 255.
2) II, p. 285.
3) III, p. 257.
4) II, p. 76.
5) II, p. 89.

was tossing terribly. Things that had been made fast to the wall and floor tore themselves loose and began flying back and forth, from wall to wall. Three massive armchairs in the captain's cabin decided to become independent, and off they went at breakneck speed. But by the time they reached the center of the cabin, the boat had lifted so steeply that all they could do was take a flying leap, first smashing to bits the coffee table in front of the sofa then falling apart themselves, and finally landing on the sofa with a crash. Some people ran in and began rummaging around in the debris, when all at once both debris and people flew back at full speed straight into my corner. I barely managed to lift my legs in time. The glasses, plates, cups, and bottles in the sideboards gave out a clatter and fairly leapt from their places." [1]

Goncharov likes it to use personifications to heighten the comic effect. He talks about "beautiful rocks in eloquent silence," of "sand lying quietly (smirno)," of "waves . . . trying to climb on board," [2] etc.

Everything touching on the Japanese is filled with irresistible humor. Goncharov's description of the intricate ceremony connected with receptions (for example, Japanese vs. European way of sitting), the receptions themselves, the Japanese penchant for obstacles and procrastination add up to a dazzling display of wit. Here is one example for many: At the first official reception with the governor of Nagasaki the guests were requested to put a pair of calico slippers over their shoes as they entered the house. They then moved into the reception hall: "We started walking through the rooms: on one side a window frame, reaching to the floor, was papered instead of glazed. On the other side there were movable screens, made either of paper and painted rather handsomely or of gilded or silvered paper, that made it hard to decide whether there was one huge chamber or several rooms. — Several rows of tightly packed together human figures, richly dressed and comically pompous, were squatting at the far end of the halls. Neither eye nor eyebrow stirred. There was no way of hearing or seeing whether the figures were breathing or blinking or whether they were alive for that matter? And what a multitude! Row upon row in that big room; then two massive old men with grey hair had been put in a narrow

---

1) II, p. 312.
2) II, pp. 33, 188, 255.

aisle like porcelain dolls, then again row after row. Both old and young were there, they all had pigtails — some thick, some thin — like rats' tails. What faces and what expressions! Not one figure was looking at us or was watching us with eager curiosity, and yet, you know, nothing like this had happened to them for forty years and almost none of them had ever seen anyone other than their own kind. Yet they all stared at the wall or the floor, seemingly engaged in a contest to see who could make the silliest face. They all did quite well at it, many of them, to be sure, unintentionally. —

The general appearance of the picture was original. The strange, fantastic spectacle could not have pleased me more. The silence was absolute. Only our own footsteps were to be heard. — 'Slippers, slippers!' I suddenly hear someone whisper. I look — I have boots on. But where are the slippers? 'You lost them three rooms ago', I am told. I go back and the slippers are indeed lying on the floor. The figures sitting in that room were just as still as they had been in our presence; not a glance did they cast at me. I overtook my companions, but I was not the only laggard; first one then another bends down and picks up the slippers. At last we entered a chamber brighter and larger than the others . . . . . At the same time as we entered the governor of Nagasaki, Osawa Bungono kami-sama appeared in it . . . . . We bowed to one another, When bowing I happened to look at my feet. The damned slippers had again come off; they were lying beside my boots. Leaning on the hand that Baron Kridener sympathetically stretched out to me I pulled them with difficulty on to my feet again. 'No good,' whispered the Baron and laughed with a laugh like a cough audible only to me and himself. Instead of an answer, I pointed to his feet: they were slipperless. 'No good' — I whispered in my turn." [1] Beside fully exploiting this sort of description — it runs through the entire work —, Goncharov can make a situation comic merely by placing the events in an effective order. Here is his first impression of Welch's Hotel in Capetown: "Lost in admiration of the mountains, we failed to notice that we had reached the wide porch of a two-storied building, Welch's Hotel. We were met at the entryway, on the lowest step, by a jet-black servant; then by a Malay servant, who was neither all black nor white either and who wore a red kerchief around his head; in

---

1) III, p. 51.

the entrance hall by yet another servant, a somewhat whiter Englishwoman; then, on the stairs, by a beautiful girls of twenty who was most definitely white; and finally by the proprietress, an old woman, the *nec plus ultra* in whiteness; she had gray hair." [1]

Goncharov excells in bringing out new sides of people by playing on their national characteristics. He especially enjoys poking fun at the English. Whenever Englishmen meet, he says, they first try "to tear each other's arm out of the socket" and then do they inform themselves of each other's state of health. [2] In contrast the son of a Dutch farmer "silently palpated the palms of all of us." [3]

At a banquet in the home of the American consul in Shanghai, Goncharov was invited to "have a drink" with the master of the house: "Having a drink of wine with someone means raising your glass and showing it to the person with whom you are drinking. He shows you his, and then you both nod at one another and drink." [4] The banquet was preceded by a courtesy visit; Goncharov was received in the study and had to sit on a high revolving chair: "I somehow managed to clamber up onto this anti-haemorrhoidal sitting device, and Mr. Cunningham followed suit. After looking one another over from our new heights, Mr. Cunningham asked me: 'How did you get here?' I was just about to answer when inadvertently I moved my leg: the circular seat with a screw executed an exquisitely smooth half-turn, and I found myself facing the wall. — 'On a shooner', I answered to the wall, thinking angrily at the same time, 'Whose contraption is this — English or American?' and rotated myself into my initial position with my legs. 'Shall you be stopping long?' — 'That depends upon circumstances', I answered, keeping my hand on the cushion of the chair, which again tried to move under me." [5]

Scenes like these follow one another in fast succession. Many, like the long, fascinating, and somewhat surprising digression about the Russian

---

1) II, p. 144.
2) II, p. 46.
3) II, p. 201.
4) III, p. 132.
5) III, p. 201.

squire [1] or a shower bath in Manila [2] are told with obvious relish. In conjunction with the humorous snatches scattered throughout (the remark for example, that neither women nor hens are allowed to attend cockfights [3]) they make the work a constant pleasure to read.

Goncharov's similes are unfailingly original and frequently comic as well. Although the hotel room outside Capetown is dark and sooty, it presents a friendly mien to the traveller like "an unshaven and unwashed man with a sullen, yet friendly look in his eye." [4] In contrast to a steamership, the sailing ship is like "an aging coquette who covers her face with rouge and powder, dons ten petticoats, and laces herself up in a corset all to make an effect on her lover; perhaps she even succeeds for a time; but just let the fresh forces of youth happen by, and all her efforts are reduced to naught." [5]

Children are a favorite subject for Goncharov's similes: The ever beaming sun of the tropics can grow irritating; "you remember those Petersburg nights in May when, toward midnight, the sky seems to want to grow dark and then suddenly lightens up again, like a frowning child who looks as if he will burst into tears at any moment and then lets out a laugh and runs back to his toys!" [6] A quiet breeze in Manila blows as softly "as a mother blowing on the face of a sleeping child to chase away a troublesome fly." [7] A Siberian river turns as cloudy "as the face of a lively, loving child clouding over with sadness." [8]

At the same time Goncharov also uses serious "philosophical" similes. "Sleep and tranquility envelop sea and sky like the ideal of a beautiful, comforting, tortureless death, the kind of death that would be attracting to a man overburdened by passions and adversities." [9]

Goncharov's talent for painting lifelike portraits develops to its fullest extent in his two last novels, but it is very much in evidence here too. Whether he is describing his servant Faddeev or a venerable old Japanese, the assurance with which he applies the telling detail is always the same:

---

1) II, pp. 67–72.
2) III, p. 248.   6) III, p. 220.
3) III, p. 262.   7) III, p. 237.
4) II, p. 185.   8) III, p. 351.
5) II, p. 30.   9) II, p. 128.

" 'Reporting for duty, Sir,' he said, standing at attention and facing me with his chest rather than his face. His face was always slightly to the side of the object he was looking at. His blond hair, pale eyes, pale face, and thin lips are more reminiscent of Finland than his native Kostroma. . . . I learnt him thoroughly in about three weeks, that is while we were on our way to England; he learnt me, I think in three days. Resourcefulness and cunning were not the least of his qualities, which were masked by the apparent awkwardness of a Kostromitan and the discipline to which he was subjected as a sailor." [1] Or: "We could not take our eyes off the old man; he had charmed us from the very first. There are little old men like that everywhere; every nation has their own variety. Ray-like wrinkles encircled his eyes and lips. His eyes, his voice, all his features shone with that intelligent, affable kindness old people have — the fruit of a long life and practical wisdom. To see this old man was to want him for a grandfather. Moreover, his manners showed him to be a man of good breeding. He began to speak, but his lips and tongue lost their strength and he spoke slowly. His speech was like a liquid being poured gently and evenly from one bottle to another." [2]

When Goncharov characterizes whole peoples (see his passage on the Indians nad Chinese [3]), he combines precision of detail with typical, general traits. — Also worthy of note is the fact that Goncharov never draws a portrait of any of his fellow travelers on board. He was apparently unwilling to run the risk of stepping on somebody's toe.

The expressive portraits get a special liveliness by the interspersed dialogues. Here is the talk he has with his old servant (Matvej from "Old-Time-Servants") just before setting off: " 'Master,' he said in agitated and imploring voice. 'For heaven's sake, don't go off to sea!' — 'Don't go off where?' — 'Where you're going, to the end of the world.' — 'How would you have me go?' — 'The sailors said you could go by land.' — 'But why not by sea?' — 'Heavens! The awful things people say about it. Why, they say that from that log hanging up there . . .' — 'From that yard,' I corrected. 'Well, what happened?' — 'During a storm the wind blew fifteen men over-

---

1) II, p. 24.
2) III, p. 154.
3) II, p. 270.

board. They had a hard time pulling them out, and one even drowned. For heaven's sake don't go.'" [1] Occasionally, he sets the stage for a veritable comedy routine. Here is the talk with a midshipman who offers him a snack shortly before departure time: "'You must excuse us. We have nothing hot,' he said, 'All the fires are out. We're taking on gunpowder.' — 'Gunpowder? Are we carrying much of it?' I inquired with great interest. "We've taken on about five hundred poud: and we'll be taking another three hundred poud.' — 'And where do you stow it?' — I asked with even greater interest. 'Oh, right here,' he said, pointing to the floor. 'Right underneath you.' The thought that there were five hundred poud of gun powder under my feet already and that at the moment the 'all hands' job' was concentrated on putting another three hundred poud stopped me from chewing for a little while. 'It's a good thing the fires have been put out,' I lauded their prudence." [2]

This sort of rapid give and take, punctuated by Goncharov's incidental remarks, is a recurrent feature. It injects an element of dynamic energy into the narrative.

Goncharov's nature descriptions are masterpieces of carefully calculated effect. Instead of taking pains to sidestep romantic exuberance, he makes effective use of it to provide contrast in the context. After describing the sailors taking an ocean bath, which is cut short by a shark attack, he turns to his letter's addressee, the Romantic poet Benediktov, with the words: "Take the first boat you can and come here to tell me how to call the gentle air, which bathes, pampers and caresses as only warm waves can; how to call the shining sky in its fantastic, ineffable raiments, the colors cradling the evening sun? The ocean in gold or gold in the ocean, a crimson flame, pure, clear, transparent, sempiternal, and unbroken fire with neither smoke nor the least blade of grass to bring back thoughts about earth. The tranquility of the sky and sea is not a dead, lethargic tranquility; it is what might be called a tranquility of sated passion, in which sky and sea, at rest in one another's arms after voluptuous torments, each feasts his eyes on his partner. The sun departs like a joyous lover who has left a long thoughtful imprint of happiness on the face of his beloved. — Entire worlds of magic

---

1) II, p. 27.
2) II, p. 25.

cities, buildings, towers, monsters, and beasts stretch over this boundless, flaming gold field; they are all made of clouds. Look how that giant fortress is slowly, noiselessly falling to pieces. First one, then another bastion tumbles down. A lofty tower sinks into oblivion, crushing its own foundation, only to take on a new form, the form of a mountain or of islands with forests and cupolas . . ." [1]

After an amusing report of supper at the Capetown hotel, Goncharov launches into a description of the southern night: "The night was warm, but so dark that you could not see your hand before your face, even though the stars were out. Everyone who came down the stairs into the street from the brightly lit entrance hall felt as if he were falling into a pit. The southern night is mysterious and sublime as a beautiful woman in a black mist: it is dark and mute, but beneath its transparent veil everything is throbbing and trembling with life. You can feel every breath of air building up your health; it is refreshing to your chest and nerves as a bath in fresh water. It was so warm it seemed as if the night had its own dark invisible sun to warm it. It was quiet, calm, and mysterious. Not a leaf was stirring. We walked down the pier and sat for a long time on some large rocks, looking out at the water. At about ten the moon came up, throwing its light over the whole bay. The ships rocked gently in the distance, and off to the right we could see the white outline of a sandbar and the dark jags of distant mountain peaks." [2]

And here is how he sees Okinawa: "Yes, this is an idyll cast amid the endless waters of the Pacific. Now, listen to a fairy tale! Each tree, each leaf has its niche. Nature has not tangled or intertwined them as she usually does. Everything seems as well proportioned, well outlined, and well placed as in a stage set or a Watteau painting. As you may have read, all the people, horses, and bulls here are dwarfs, while hens and roosters are giants; the trees are colossal, with silver threads of barely audible bubbling brooks running between them and the pleasant roar of theatrical cascades . . . I caught sight of natives from a distance already. There they stood, leaning on their long bamboo staffs. There were some in their midst — it would be wrong to call them "old men," what I would have to call them is "elders" —

---

1) II, p. 129. The Gogolesque style of this description is obvious.
2) II, p. 153.

who displayed great dignity and had thoughtful, serious faces. They were dressed in broad, simple, but very clean shifts with broad belts, and wore long gray beards and long hair combed upwards and gathered together in a tuft on top. When we got closer, they made us a low bow, bending their heads and allowing their arms to hang. Their children hid behind them in fear." The idyll ends with somewhat of a surprise: " 'What is this?' I kept saying, growing more and more astonished. 'If this goes on, I'll begin believing not only Theocritus, but Gessner and Madame Deshoulières and their Menalcases, Chloes, and Daphnes. The only thing missing is lambs with ribbons around their necks.' And wouldn't you know it, at just this moment our rams were let ashore for an airing, as if for no other reason than to complete the idyll." [1]

The storms give rise to magnificent and ever changing seascapes: "The wind bellowed. It stripped the caps off the waves and sowed them over the ocean as if forcing them through a sieve; it crowned the waves with clouds of liquid dust. Once again I held to may simile: yes, this is a pack of wild beasts tearing one another apart in their fury. It is like lions and tigers constantly pouncing and rearing, the better to get at one another's throats. They race upwards only to crash down again in one big pack, leaving nothing but a pillar of dust. Our vessel flies after them, into the abyss, but a new force pushes it back toward the surface and then even lays it on its side. All of a sudden the shallop begins cracking on its hoist. Two or three of us — and I seem to be one — are thrown from one corner to other, and a gigantic billow strikes the nets, leaps on board and floods the deck, reaching as high as the sailors knees. The horizon here is covered with a gray dust. There is almost no steady motion: the water is as bubbly as if it were aboil, and the waves have lost all contour." [2]

Though Goncharov's palette is especially rich in these descriptions, he is also more than competent in capturing the monotonous Siberian landscape: "There is nothing ghostly in these wild landscapes, though there is much that is sad. Dense deciduous forests flank the road; you ride along a narrow, stump-ridden path. Then the forest opens up to reveal a vast swamp strewn with rocks, which is probably impossible to cross in the rain. The

---

1) III, p. 191-192.
2) II, pp. 311-312.

stream beds have a natural covering of crushed stone, while larger stones, which seem to serve a decorative function, fall from wall-like cliffs that in some places have become overgrown with trees and in others are bare and savage. Nowhere is there any sign of life, nowhere a chance for human contact." [1]

The Frigate Pallada is hardly the children's book that the reading public and Goncharov himself thought it was. Its wealth of nuances, its judicious reserve, its humor, and its conscious avoidance of anything the least bit tinged with sensationalism required deliberate, intelligent reading. The precise, carefully constructed language deserves to be savored sentence by sentence. There is no doubt that the impeccable style of this calm and collected narrative served as a preparatory exercise for the style of the novels. [2]

The Love-Episode

The year 1855 meant more for Goncharov than starting anew after his return home; it was the year of what was perhaps the only serious love he ever experienced. In a letter to Anatolij Koni written many years later (July 11, 1888) he noted: "By the way, nonsense is the only word I have

---

1) III, p. 341.
2) There is unfortunately no complete English translation of The Frigate Pallada. In 1965 The Folio Society of London published a relatively short excerpt from the work, based on the already abridged 1949 Moscow edition edited by S.D. Muravejskij. The Folio Society's editor and translator, N.W. Wilson, states in his preface that "the old-fashioned interpolations and flowery passages show the influence of Sterne and his sentimental journeyings," adding laconically, "They have been cut out" (p. 14). Quite apart from the fact that Sterne has nothing whatsoever to do with Goncharov's style, the cuts in the English edition deprive the work of much of its special charm and give an utterly false impression of the original. This state of affairs is all the more deplorable in that apart for slips like 'water' for 'vodka' (p. 20) the translation is quite acceptable.

for those dramas that show women as heroines in men's lives. Women play
an enormous part of course, but the only time any joy, contentment or
pleasure is involved is when relations with them have a sense of comedy.
Then they add an *air-fixe* to life, a spirited, playful character. Living becomes easy. There's nothing to hold back our work, our daily pursuits. But
watch out when a man takes love *au sérieux* and starts to love 'cheerlessly
and harshly.' [1]

This is the sort of drama that robs us of our forces, plucks the flower of
our forces, so to speak, and distracts us from our work, duty, and calling.

What I have just said refers to myself: an admirer — as a result of my
extreme nervous sensibility and artistic nature — of all kinds of beauty,
especially feminine beauty, I have lived through several dramas and though
"pale, unshaven and half-starved." [2] I have emerged from them the victor
thanks to my powers of observance and sharp analysis and to my humor.
Even while convulsed in the spasms of passion, I could not help but notice
how silly and comic it all was. What I mean is that while suffering subject-
ively, I would look upon the entire course of the drama objectively and
— resolving it into its component parts and finding a combination of pride,
boredom, and impurity of the flesh — would regain my sobriety. It was all
just so much water of a ducks back. But what pains me is that sometimes
years have been wasted in this inane bondage, our finest years and days of
fresh, vibrant activity, creative work — i.e. of normal, human life." [3]

Very little is known of the "several dramas" he refers to having experienced. There are reports that in the beginning of the forties in Petersburg he was attracted by the two sisters of his brother's wife Elizaveta Kar-
lovna Goncharova, Adelaida and Emilia Rudol'f, in fact, Adelaida, the elder
sister, is said to have traits similar to those Goncharov gave Vera in *The
Precipice,* while Emilia, the younger sister, apparently resembled Marfen'ka. [4]

---

1) Quotation from Pushkin's "The Gypsies."
2) Inprecise quotation from Pushkin's poem "N.N." (1819).
3) Utevskij, p. 81.
4) Cf. Vosp. sovr. pp. 103–109. This parallel has no foundation whatsoever; Goncharov states clearly that Vera never existed, and that he never knew a Marfen'ka
   (cf. VIII, 400). But a passage in Oblomov (Part Two, Chapter Four, IV, p. 189)
   about the two sisters whom Oblomov used to visit may be an autobiographical
   reminiscence.

He was far from indifferent to Varvara Luk'janova, governess to the children of his sister Aleksandra Kirmalova. This romance during Goncharov's visit to Simbirsk in 1849 went so it seems very far. She later became with Goncharov's help headmistress of the Nikolaevskij Orphanage in Petersburg. Goncharov saw her probably rather frequently, but finally she married a Mr. Lebedev, who could not stand Goncharov. [1]

Not very clear are the relations of Goncharov to the niece of his friend Mikhail Jazykov Avdot'ja Kolzakova. It seems to have been a flirtation which started shortly before his departure in 1852, and which was resumed after his return, when she was married to a Mr. Rostovskij. After his death in 1859 the connection has continued, but it came to an abrupt and it seems unpleasant end in 1862. All the details of this story are unkown.[2]

Finally his flirtation with Junija Efremova, a niece of Mrs. Majkova whom he depicts in "The Galloping Disease" under the name of Zinaida, has overtones (especially noticeable in certain of his letters) pointing to deeper emotion.

Compared with his infatuation with Elizaveta Tolstaja, however, all these "loves" lose their luster. A friend of the Majkovs, she first met Goncharov in the early forties. His highly flattering prose entry in her poetry album, dated February 1843 and signed de Len', stresses that since prose is the language of reality and consequently of truth all his compliments partake of the truth.

Until his return from his voyage we hear no more about her, but from the period between August 1855 and February 1856 we have some thirty notes and letters to her from his pen chronicling his hopes, his love in the ascendant, and finally his disillusionment. The attempt of the forty-three year old writer to fall in "controlled" love with the attractive twenty-six year old lady ended in failure.

It is quite clear Miss Tolstaja never loved him. By the fall of 1856, only several months after Goncharov ceased corresponding with her, she had be-

---

1) Cf. Vosp. Sovr., p. 112, the apparently reliable reminiscences of Goncharov's grandnephew Mikhail Kirmalov.
2) Chemena, pp. 17–18.

come the bride of her cousin Aleksandr Musin-Pushkin. Ironically enough
it was Goncharov, who was asked to help and helped overcome the red
tape involved; marriage between relatives required special permission from
the church authorities. —

Goncharov initiated his correspondence with a series of notes concerning arrangements for parties or excursions; he offers to pick her up or get
her opera or theater tickets or run any one of a number of little errands
for her. Their invariably whimsical tone covers a serious strain, which
sometimes breaks through and gains the upper hand. Here is a typical
early note (dating from August 22nd 1855: "Would you care to go to the
Majkov's, and if so, will you allow me to accompany you? And if you
stay at home, will you allow me to bring you the Chinese albums, or would
you have sent them? And if in the end you do not care for any of these
prospects, would you perhaps have me simply go to bed? As a last resort
I am willing to consent even to this. Awaiting your orders will be yours
faithful to the very grave and including it, Ivan Goncharov." [1]

As the letters proceed, it becomes more and more evident that Goncharov was toying with the idea of marrying Miss Tolstaja, but that he was un-
sure of her feelings toward him. Furthermore, he was unable to close his
eyes to certain faults he found in her and was trying to rid her of them
through his influence.

To turn her away from the popular French adventure novelist Paul
Féval ("Do you really enjoy him?" he asks reproachfully [2]), he sends her
works he approves of (by Pisemskij and Turgenev, for example). He gives
her his travel notes, which had appeared in print, and "Pepin'erka," as he
calls it, an old manuscript of his (perhaps "Is Life on Earth Good or Bad?").
He also indulges in a bit of literary witticism, when she shows him a note-

---

1) The letters were first published by P. Sakulin in the journal The Voice of the Past
   (Golos minuvshego) 1913, vols. XI, pp. 215-235 and XII, pp. 220-252. In his introductory article (vol. XI, pp. 45-65) he tries to prove that Miss Tolstaja was the
   pattern for Ol'ga Il'inskaja in Oblomov, but his arguments lack persuasiveness.
   There is no similarity whatsoever between the two. Very persuasive on the other
   hand is the contention of O. Chemena that she was the pattern for Sof'ja Belovodova in The Precipice; cf. Chemena, pp. 29-31. The letter quoted above cf., vol.
   XI, 1913, p. 220.
2) *ibid.* , p. 227.

book, in which she has entered some jottings about feelings, esp. love and hope, *confidences* as he calls them. From his "constructive criticism" it is clear that he found little to his liking in her literary exercise, but he is careful not to hurt her. [1]

Although he calls his feeling for her one of friendship, he prefaces the word with leading points, thereby giving her to understand that "friendship" actually stands for something else. By refraining from an out-and-out avowal of his feelings and desires (his letters leave much unsaid), he guards himself against the humiliation of rejection. Her hints of "nets" and "bird catching" touch him to the quick, and in his last letter to her during her stay in Petersburg (where he saw her frequently) he tries to convince himself that it is only his own "unfortunate, suspicious character" that insists on detecting innuendos where there are none. [2]

Miss Tolstaja's departure (on October 18, 1855) only served to intensify Goncharov's feelings. Two days later he wrote her a letter that ends in a "whole scene" or "chapter from a novel," as he puts it. In the middle of the letter he suddenly launches into a fabrication which when complete consists of three installments (October 20th, October 25th, and November 5th). A friend of his, he claims, has fallen madly in love with Miss Tolstaja, and he, cool and reasonable as ever, wishes to calm him down with an objective discussion of the positive and negative aspects of his beloved. Therefore the title of this "chapter" is "Pro et contra."

Using the form of a heated dialogue Goncharov tries to analyze the character of the "most delicate and most cherished" lady and to interpret her actions. Those actions are by far not always satisfactory and so jealousy and criticism mix with endeavors to excuse her or at least to explain her behavior. [3] The "literary" form and the fictitious friend are of course meant to provide the distance their cautious creator wished to preserve.

The response was discouraging. After a note immediately following her departure (Goncharov's letter of October 25, 1855 bears witness to his delight at receiving it), her letters were scarce. She apparently had little sym-

---

1) The Voice of the Past (Golos minuvshego) 1913, vol. XI, p. 222.
2) *ibid.*, p. 227.
3) *ibid.*, p. 229.

pathy for his allegorical way of expressing himself. His November 3d letter
is typical in the way it tries to justify his approach: "I keep dreaming of an
outsider's eye peering into my letter. It might be the pretty eye of your
dear cousin, that wouldn't be so horrible. But what if it's a cousin in the
masculine? . . . Then you intend to die, don't you. How then can I write
you letters, to say nothing of sending you a portrait. Well, and if you die,
— excuse me —, if you ascend to heavens without a will. In whose hands
will it all land?" [1] And yet this letter ends with Goncharov's most outspoken confession of love: "And now good-bye — *for a while,* until the
next letter, my wonderful friend, my dear, clever, kind, fascinating friend
. . . Liza!!! suddenly escaped my lips. I glance around in horror, hoping
there is nobody in the vicinity, and respectfully add: Good-bye, Elizaveta
Vasil'evna, and may God grant you the happiness you deserve. I thank you
from the bottom of my heart for your friendship; it keeps an old man warm.

No one can say this time that my letter is silly, don't you think? But it is
silly, I began with a flourish and ended with a sigh. And it's all your fault.
You think that I am joking and that therefore I must be happy. Well I've
joked on occasions when there was horror and trepidation in my heart: at
sea, in a hurricane, faced with imminent death, I grew pale and I joked.
Joking is my element." [2]

Here Goncharov returns to one of his frequent themes. When he praises
joking, he is paying hommage to the bittersweet irony, he often used to
avoid cheap sentimentality.

"Pro et contra" provides another clear example of this sort of joking.
The imagined friend says " 'Yes, I've met an angel. He stopped me, looked
at me agreeable, flapped his wings. . . .' 'And sang out cockadoodledoo,'
I interrupted. 'Do you always joke like this in moments of triumph and of
mourning as well?' he asked indignantly. 'Yes, all the time, everywhere. A
joke never grows old or perfidious or tiresome. A joke provokes a smile in
times of torment. A joke . . . Well, what about your angel?' " [3]

His "angel" was on the point of leaving him forever.

---

1) The Voice of the Past (Golos minuvshego) 1913, vol. XI, p. 231–232 .
2) *ibid.,* p. 234.
3) *ibid.,* p. 228.

On November 14th he wrote a letter brimming over with reproaches: he
had as yet received no answer to his quasi-declaration of love. Sadly he reports the following dream: "I was waiting for you at the Majkovs. You were
a long time arriving (almost as long as it once took you to get to dinner
there: where were you that day? ... I don't know, but I can guess). My
impatience grew into an illness. Finally you arrived, but what had happened
to your beauty? You were disfigured, yet I was incredibly happy seeing you,
as it would have happened also not in a dream. But I — just think — I didn't
have a stitch of clothes on. I'd covered myself with some sort of sheet. That
supposedly means bad luck. So be it. Just as long as it's not for you." [1]

He mentions *en passant* the success of his articles on Japan (he had received a personal letter of commendation from Grand Duke Konstantin Nikolaevich), and Putjatin's intention to secure him a leave of absence, so as
to free him for work on the travel journal. This as well as his December 1st
reference to an offer (made by the Minister of Education Petr Valuev) for a
high post in the Department of Censorship, sound like nothing so much as
delicate attempts on Goncharov's part to bolster his social standing in the
eyes of his beloved.

For a long time there was no response, but from his letter of December
29th and its continuation on December 31st we can deduce that a very cool
letter did finally arrive. Goncharov's tone changes completely. He asks his
"faithless" friend whether she dare question his motto "que la plus sûre des
choses est la doute." [2] No longer does he harbor any doubts about where
he stands. Analyzing her letter with bitter irony ("You are as right as I am
wrong" [3]), he proves "logically" that by remaining silent she remained
true to her character and that by this "jabbering" he remained true to his.

His "friend" from "Pro et contra" no longer exists. "He has disappeared,
evaporated, crumbled into dust. I remain alone with my apathy — or spleen,
with a pain in my liver and without my 'gift of words.' So there's no one
left to frighten or alarm you with his ravings. As he vanished, he uttered

---

1) The Voice of the Past (Golos minuvshego) 1913, vol. XI, pp. 236–237.
2) *ibid.*, p. 235.
3) *ibid.*, p. 243.

your words with his last breath: 'Tout va pour le mieux.' It's a good thing she went away. It's a good thing she was so long in writing: tout, tout est pour le mieux." [1]

The final two letters of this period (dating from February 8 and February 20, 1856) resume the old friendly, humorous tone. Though a drop of bitterness does creep in now and then, it is clear that Goncharov has given up all hope.

Reading his intelligent and perspicacious analysis of Miss Tolstoj's character and examining his pointed no-nonsense advice to her on how to behave, how to overcome moral weaknesses and how to think more clearly (see his remarks concerning her use of proverbs, for example [2]), one can hardly blame her for her coolness. In all likelihood Goncharov would have been a demanding and strict husband, for a girl of an apparently not very serious nature.

———————— · ————————

After returning from his great journey, Goncharov remained only one year (the year of his love) at the Finance Ministry's Department of Foreign Trade. The hints at and doubts about some change in the letters to Miss Tolstaja took definite shape now.

In November 1855 Count Petr Valuev, an influential statesman whom Goncharov may have come to meet through the offices of Admiral Putjatin and whose relations with Goncharov grew quite close in the course of the years, had offered him the post of censor for the Petersburg Censorship Committee, a division of the Ministry of Culture.

Professor Aleksandr Nikitenko, a good acquaintance of Goncharov, who had been a censor himself and was very much interested in matters of censorship (see his excellently written and informative diary), did everything in his power to help put through the appointment. [3] Goncharov accepted, and on February 19, 1956 his transfer to the Ministry of Culture from the Ministry of Finances was made official.

————————————————

1) The Voice of the Past (Golos minuvshego) 1913, vol. XI., pp. 244–245.
2) *ibid.*, p. 231.
3) Nikitenko, I, p. 467.

The reactions of his friends to his new and quite delicate position were varied. Some criticized him on principle, claiming it was not right for a writer to double as a censor. Goncharov was not the only writer with this double role, by the way; the novelist Ivan Lazhechnikov worked in the same department. These rumblings notwithstanding, Goncharov was quite happy at the post, at least for quite a while.

One important advantage of his job was that he could stay at home and read. Of course the material was not of his own choosing, and the quantity was nothing short of staggering: besides numerous books, he was assigned to several of the "fat journals," and from February 1856 to December 1858 he officially read through 38 248 manuscript and 3 369 printed pages. [1] All the same, the work was both lively and responsible, and it gave him a great deal of satisfaction. Critic Pavel Annenkov, who always spoke of Goncharov somewhat maliciously wrote to Ivan Turgenev: "Goncharov and his little paunch fly from Norov (the new Minister of Culture, V.S.) to Shcherbatov (director of the Censorship Committee, V.S.); he is forever bustling about. He has subdued all his colleagues to his influence, conducts a sly policy with us writers, and has so blossomed in these pursuits, that his cheeks are even beginning to take on a bit of color." [2]

It is difficult to judge to what extent the critical implications about the "flying" and the "subduing" are true. In any case Goncharov was well received in important writer's circles. Critic and author Aleksandr Druzhinin gave Turgenev the following report: "Our circle has been convening more often than ever, almost every day. Its central personalities are Botkin, Tolstoj, Annenkov, to say nothing of Ermil (nickname of Aleksej Pisemskij, V.S.), Goncharov, Zhemchuzhnikov, and Aleksej Tolstoj." [3] Frequent get-togethers with the finest representatives of Russian literature and journalism provided Goncharov with ideal opportunities for mixing business with pleasure: the better to advance his professional interests — both public and private — he regaled himself with the choicest company.

Though basically a reasonable, liberal censor, Goncharov was also quite cautious. As soon as he came upon a borderline case, he would refer it to

---

1) Mazon, p. 198.
2) Alekseev, p. 68.
3) *ibid.*, p. 69.

his superiors, accompanying the work in question with a lucid explanation of why *he* would be in favor of seeing it published. Here, for example, is a report on a collection of N. A. Nekrasov's poetry: "I consider it my duty to point out that Nekrasov's book will continue to provoke the intense interest of poetry lovers, circulate in manuscripts, and be learned by heart as long as the ban on its free publication remains in effect. Numerous precedents in literature show this to be so." [1]

Only twice in four years did he make what authorities considered to be an error, letting works through that they would prefer to outlaw. But these slips did no harm to his position and in no way alarmed him.

There is no doubt that the criticism of the liberals (including Aleksandr Herzen) leveled at him was very unjust. It is only because of Goncharov's favorable and eloquent reports that such works as the "Novellas and Narratives" (Povesti i rasskazy) by Turgenev (1856), the novels *The Ice House, The Last Novik* and *Basurman* by Ivan Lazhechnikov, the seventh supplementary volume of Pushkin's *Collected Works* edited by Annenkov (1857), the novel *One Thousand Souls* by A. Pisemskij, a two volume edition of Aleksandr Ostrovskij, containing a previously forbidden play (1858) and the *Complete Works* of Lermontov (1859) were allowed for publication. This list is not complete: Goncharov's activity as censor was beneficial from all points of view. [2]

The year 1857 was marked by a great upsurge of his creative faculties. Though *Oblomov* still lay unfinished, his other works had begun to win him substantial recognition. His travel sketches, for example, scattered throughout various periodicals, enjoyed a remarkable success. *The Frigate Pallada,* their synthesis, was nearly ready. "Ivan Savvich Podzhabrin" had been reprinted in the anthology *For Light Reading* (Dlja legkogo chtenija) in June 1856. *A Common Story* received constant praise and was so popular that it required a second edition which appeared on December 31, 1857.

The hopes "Oblomov's Dream" had aroused found expression in persistent requests even demands for the whole novel. On November 11, 1856

---

1) Alekseev, p. 94.
2) Cf. Vosp. sovr., p. 17, the introduction by Anatolij Alekseev.

e. g. Turgenev wrote to Goncharov: "I refuse even to think of your having put down your golden pen. Let me say to you as Mirabeau said to Sieyès: 'Le silence de Mr Gontcharoff est une calamité publique!' I am convinced that despite your numerous censorship duties you will find it possible to do your work, and certain hints you gave just before I left lead me to believe that all hope is not lost. I will continue to harrow you with my cry of 'Give us Oblomov!' " [1]

Finally Goncharov made up his mind to make a concerted effort. He applied for a four-month leave of absence on the strength of the medical certificate issued — oddly enough — by a Dr. Oblomievskij. A tendency to gain weight had begun to bother him, and he decided to combine the cure at Marienbad with the strenuous travail of writing. He did not even admit to have *Oblomov* in mind — perhaps out of superstition.

Leaving Petersburg on June 7th he travelled via Warsaw and Dresden to his destination. In an amusing letter to his friend Ivan L'khovskij [2] from Warsaw he speaks again and again of the boredom he fears will overwhelm him and prevent him not only from getting any work done, but also from deriving any benefit from the waters. The closing is especially characteristic of his attitude to writing: "And you, my friend, do put up with my letters. Be a scapegoat just this once. Because writing is as necessary a process for me as the process of thought, and absorbing everything without letting anything go, is tantamount to moral asphyxiation. So if I write often and amply, please be patient and remember that it's neither a whim or an affectation (especially in today's letter), I write for the same reason as a bird sings or a cricket in the grass chirps." [3]

His fears of boredom proved completely unjustified this time: the Marienbad letters of 1857 teem with enthusiastic accounts of his progress with *Oblomov*. On August 2nd he wrote to the same L'khovskij: "Yes, my dear Horatio, there are more things on heaven and earth than our journalists have dreamed of. Picture this, if you can: I arrived on June 21st by the Russian calender and was so bored after the first three days that I wanted to leave. For three or four days I wrote letters — to you, to Jazykov, to my

1) Alekseev, p. 67.
2) For more information about L'khovskij cf. Literaturnyj arkhiv, 3, pp. 91-96.
3) VIII, p. 280.

family in Simbrisk. I didn't know what to do. And then somewhere around
the 25th or the 26th I opened up *Oblomov*, caught flame — and by July
31st I had written forty seven sheets in my own hand! *I finished the first
part, wrote all of part two, and have gotten quite a way into part three.*
I can't tell whether I've been improving or not. I only know that all I need
is three weeks of concentrated work to finish off *Oblomov*. The elbow
scene has long come and gone. The poem of delicate love is complete; it
took much time and will take up much space. Does it seem unnatural for
someone to finish in a month what he hadn't been able to finish in years?
My answer is that if it hadn't been for the years, nothing would have been
written in that month. What happened is, the novel — down to the most
insignificant scenes and details — had matured in me, and the only thing
left for me was to get it down on paper. I wrote as if I were taking dicta-
tion. And a lot in fact did come unconsciously; there was someone invisible
sitting beside me and telling me what to write." [1]

When he left Marienbad on August 4th, the novel was practically finished.
His letters show him fairly bubbling over with high spirits. After some days
in Frankfurt, he took a boat from Mainz down the Rhine to Cologne. "The
Rhine is inimitable in its own way. Its steep banks are dotted with vineyards
and one ruin more picturesque than the next," he wrote to L'khovskij. [2] In
Cologne he admired the cathedral and bought Eau de Cologne. And next
day he set off for Paris.

Throughout his stay in Paris he remained happy and active. "I've done
a good deal of driving and even more walking through Paris," he wrote to
Junija Efremova on August 25th. "I've seen everything a tourist is told to
see: Notre Dame, the Hôtel des Invalides, the Louvre and the Tuilleries, the
Champs Elysées, the Bois de Boulogne, the Bal Mabille, the Près Catelan.
But I get more pleasure out of taking my own "equipage" (Goncharov no
doubt means walking, V.S.) through the old sections of the city beyond the
Seine and walking into the markets and shops. During each outing I cover
seven versts (just under five miles, V.S.). Botkin, his sisters, and Fet are
living right below me. Korenev left for Dieppe yesterday. Menshikov and
Nikitenko and his wife are within a stone's throw." [3] For the Petersburg

1) VIII, pp. 290-291.
2) VIII, p. 295.
3) Alekseev, p. 77.

literary acquaintances whom he mentiones in his letter — along with Turgenev, who was in Paris at the time — he gave a reading of *Oblomov,* and
after receiving a very positive reaction, he began reworking and polishing
a passage here and there. Clearly he had never been happier.

He arrived at home on October 8, 1857 and immediately took up the
responsibilities of his old routine of reading and report writing. Official recognition for these services followed his arrival by only two days: on October 10th he was named a Court Councilor (nadvornyj sovetnik) in the Civil
Service. Another sort of recognition, the plaudits of his friends after readings of *Oblomov* excerpts (a careful selection of the friends was made according to Lev Tolstoj [1]), also gave him a great deal of satisfaction.

No doubt he was also flattered and encouraged by the offer he received
at the end of November to act as private tutor in Russian and Russian literature to the fourteen-year-old heir apparent, Nikolaj Aleksandrovich (who
died young — in 1865 — and never ascended the throne). At first Goncharov declined, pleading an already tight work schedule, advancing age, and
a lack of professional background. But under the pressure of Apollon Majkov (who had himself declined the honor and recommended Goncharov),
he soon gave in, and in January 1858 the lessons began. Despite Professor
Jakov Grot's the well known Slavist's slightly critical remarks about Goncharov's training in the theory of the Russian grammar [2], he seems to have
made quite a good teacher. Elena Shtakenshnejder, in her sagacious and
rather reliable diary comments that Goncharov was thrilled with his student and that the tsarevich took such pleasure in his Russian lessons that
he asked for three a week instead of the customary two. She also notes
that as a result of the tutoring position and his duties as a censor "our *new*
people . . . don't care for Goncharov, but that he cares little at being
frowned upon." [3]

Nonetheless the pressure of "liberal" opinion must have become a bit too
strong for his liking: in May 1858 he resigned his post as tutor and when the
offer was repeated in the fall of the same year he declined it again — this
time definitively. The fact that August Grimm, the heir apparent's head

1) Alekseev, p. 78.
2) Mazon, pp. 340–341.
3) Shtakenshnejder, pp. 209–211.

tutor was rude to Goncharov during the preliminary negotiations — he received him lying on a sofa — probably accounts in part for his decision. Moreover, he does not seem to have been happy with wages he was to receive. [1]

At Goncharov's request a copy of *The Frigate Pallada* [2] was presented to Alexander II. The Czar was greatly impressed with the book and sent Goncharov three hundred rubles and a diamond ring with a ruby.

---

1) Mazon, pp. 340-341.
2) It came out in May 1858.

Oblomov

After many reading sessions with friends and the consequent rewriting,
which lasted more than one year, *Oblomov* came out in the first four issues
of the *Annals of the Fatherland* (Otechestvennye Zapiski) in January to
April 1859 and was published as a book in the same year. A small fragment
from Part Three (Oblomov's first meeting with Agafja Matveevna) was
printed in *Atenej* (1858 No. 1, pp. 53–60).

The reworking consisted in many alterations. The style and the vocabulary were polished (more than 200 instances alone in "Oblomov's Dream"),
but also some new scenes were added and old ones changed.

The character of Ol'ga caused the greatest difficulties. O. Chemena is
right to a certain degree in maintaining that Ekaterina Majkova, the wife of
Vladimir Majkov, one of the painters sons became a prototype which Goncharov tried to portray.[1] Her ideas about the "progressive" attitude of
Ol'ga Shtol'c have no support in the text of the novel, still it seems very
probable that Goncharov wrote the eighth chapter of Part Four before he
went to Marienbad and thinking of Majkova. She certainly became "progressive" afterwards, [2] but in this chapter we see only a woman, who is
troubled metaphysically, without any social involvement whatsoever. [3]

The hypothesis that chapters nine to eleven of Part Four were also conceived and sketched before Marienbad, i.e. after Goncharov returned to and
carefully reread Part One written years before, seems to be true. Apparently
Goncharov wanted to be sure how to end before he filled in the main plot.
A proof is that Shtol'c's first name was Karl in the manuscript of the first
part *and* in the manuscript of the last chapters (same in the first printing
of the "Dream" in 1849), until Goncharov hit upon the scene where it
turns out that Oblomov's son was named after Shtol'c. Of course it was

---

1) Cf. Chemena, pp. 34–51.
2) Cf. p. 191.
3) It is characteristic that Chemena comes very near to a deeper interpretation of
   Shtol'c, calling him a mystic philosopher striving to raise Ol'ga's doubts to the
   level of Weltschmerz, but does not dare to draw all the obvious consequences.
   Cf. pp. 47–48.

impossible to name him Karl, and so Shtol'c became firmly Andrej and his father Ivan. Before that time Shtol'c changes his patronymic several times and even in the final text (Part One Chapter Three towards the end) he is once called Andrej Karlovich. This mistake was corrected only in the very last edition of Goncharov's works (1953).

It is interesting to note that in the early drafts, afterwards abandoned by Goncharov, there existed beside Shtol'c a very energetic Russian by the name of Pochaev, who exhibited many of Shtol'c's features. We have a chapter obviously belonging after Chapter Eleven of Part One of the final version, in which he makes his appearance. This chapter is similar to Chapter Three of Part Two of the printed text in its content, but it is Pochaev, who takes the role of Shtol'c. Shtol'c is briefly mentioned in the dialogue between Oblomov and Pochaev. At that time his part apparently was far from being firmly established. [1]

The main character of *Oblomov* and the philosophy he represents possessed Goncharov from the beginning of his career as a writer. We have the strange "fat man" in "Nimfodora Ivanovna", we have Tjazhelenko in "The Galloping Disease", we have some Oblomovian traits in "The Happy Mistake" and "Ivan Savvich Podzhabrin", and we have indications of Oblomovian possibilities for the hero of *A Common Story*. Although "Oblomov's Dream" published ten years before the complete version, deals exclusively with the hero as a small boy, it points clearly to the general line of the future work.

The chronological beginning of the novel is Part One, Chapter Nine, "Oblomov's Dream," an account of the hero's childhood which explains in retrospect the situation in which we find him in the first chapter.

"Where are we? To what blessed nook on earth has Oblomov's dream taken us? What a lovely country!" This is how the dream begins. It sets the tone for an idyll which deliberately uses classical references (Kolchis, the Gates of Hercules, the Olympic gods) to suggest the dream of a classical Golden Age, the peaceful, untroubled life, the ideal way of life as praised by Greeks from Hesiodus to Theocritus and by an uninterrupted tradition in European literature from the Romans to modern times. There

---

1) Cf. Mazon, p. 427.

is no doubt that Goncharov meant his Russian idyll to be taken somewhat ironically, but the irony involved is quite benign and should not be over-stressed.

All in all, the dream conveys the impression of a happy life, a happy life on a low intellectual and emotional level without any dynamic force behind it, a life of limitation and stagnation without any desire for "progress," a life of deliberate inactivity and laziness — but still a happy life. What is more, it was a happy life for everyone involved: little Il'ja's parents, small country landowners somewhere in a remote region of southeast Russia near the Volga, almost in Asia, reigning over their estate Oblomovka, their own beautiful, petty world; the host of poor relatives living with them, the many serf-servants, even the peasant-serfs — they all, rich and poor, enjoyed the somno-lent status quo and protected it carefully from any attempt at change. The days of this peaceful life were segmented by meals and their meticulous pre-paration, the years by religious feasts and family anniversaries, again care-fully prepared and always falling into indentical patterns. The servants and peasants both participate in this cycle and live out their own private exist-ence of leisurely work and harmless amusements like dancing, singing, and playing the balalaika.

Goncharov carefully avoids anything which might tend toward urgency on the one hand or gloominess on the other. Landscape and climate are as benign and unexciting as the people they form. There are no mountains, no rocks, no abysses, no roaring sea; only a small sparkling river winding its way through sandy banks, wide fields, soft slopes, and rich birch groves. The seasons come and go as prescribed by the calendar without blizzards, violent thunderstorms, or any other such unpleasant surprises. Even the usual simile for rain — rain like mournful tears — is avoided. "If there is rain, refreshing summer rain, it falls quickly and abundantly, splashing mer-rily with big drops like the warm tears of a man overcome by sudden joy." [1]

Death comes from old age or a chronic illness, but "for the last five years there had been no deaths at all among the several hundred villagers, not even natural deaths, let alone violent ones." [2]

---

1) IV, p. 105.
2) *ibid.*, p. 108.

Into this idyll little Il'ja is born. One day in the life of the seven-year-
old boy (the year is apparently 1819; Goncharov makes Oblomov his own
age) gives us the impression, in flashback, and generalized descriptions, of
a quiet and very happy childhood, surrounded by love and protected from
everything which might demand any physical or mental effort. No doubt,
Oblomovka is no training grounds for the struggle for existence outside its
bounds. It cannot provide a healthy all-round education. But its own blissful situation has much to recommend itself. Even the naive egotisms it
necessarily fosters can do no harm in the prevailing atmosphere of goodness. Goncharov quite deliberately excludes the intrusion of any character
with the power of disturbing the placid picture.

Il'ja himself compensates for the lack of real experience (all his childlike enterprises are thwarted by his solicitous parents) with a vivid imagination, and his fantasies find plenty of new material in the tales of the old
nurse (cf. the charming pages which survey Russian fairy tales), supersti-
tions (which, while temporarily disturbing the idyll, also add a certain spice
to its routine), and his own lively mind, so eager to play with the unknown.
The melancholy strain in the character of the mature Oblomov is a re-
mainder of these childish fantasies: "Even if the belief in phantoms disappeared, fear and vague anxiety remained in its place." [1]

The day of the seven-year-old merges as it uses to happen in dreams, into the reminiscences of a boy of 13 or 14. His studies as a boarder in the
home of Shtol'c, a German, "a strict and business-like man, like most Germans," [2] might have been profitable if his own village, Oblomovka, had
not been so near the Shtol'c residence. The constant interference of the
parents, fearing lest their son's brains be overburdened, prevents any real
scholastic progress. But Shtol'c's son Andrej, becomes his lifelong friend
and the second hero of Goncharov's novel. The mind of a young, intelligent
human being with a feeling heart and a balanced disposition was indelibly
stamped by the purposeless vegetative life he saw around him.

> " . . . Ilyusha's childish mind may have decided long ago that the
> way the grown-ups around him lived was the right way; and how
> could he have decided otherwise?

---

1) IV, p. 116.
2) *ibid.*, p. 125.

And how did the grown-ups live at Oblomovka? Did they ever
ask themselves why life had been given them? God only knows.
And how did they answer it? Probably they did not answer it at
all: it seemed very simple and obvious." [1]

Goncharov excells in evoking this unruffled life. He depicts it without
problems or demands, and one wonders whether its placidity might exceed
the level of physical saturation. It is life in a hermetic society, where everybody has his place in a definite hierarchy and everybody is happy, be it in
the most petty and primitive way. The "dream" ends at this point.

When Il'ja reached the age of 16 his parents reluctantly sent him to a
boarding school in Moscow. Financially well provided for, he fulfilled the
requirements satisfactorily enough, but without any real interest in the
subject matter. "His timid, apathetic character prevented him from giving
full scope to his laziness and caprices among strangers." [2] Only literature
succeeded in arousing him for a certain time. Here again his imagination
stood him in good stead, and youth came to him as it comes to everyone:

" . . . The happy age that fails no one and smiles upon all had
dawned for him too — the age when one's powers are at their
best and one is full of hope and longs to do good, to work, to
leave one's mark in the world, when the heart beats faster and
the pulses quicken — the age of enthusiastic speeches, of emotion
and happy tears. His heart and mind grew clearer; he shook off
his drowsiness and his soul demanded activity." [3]

Shtol'c, who went to the same school, studied with much more gusto. At
times his irrepressible ardor infected even Oblomov. Himself a great poetry
lover, he took advantage of Oblomov's love for verse to keep him under a
spell of meditation and learning for a time. He introduced aims other than
pure delight into their reading of poetry. He pointed out sterner goals for
his own and Oblomov's lives. They took solemn vows to ever pursue the
road of light and reason. The then slender, almost lively Oblomov even

---

1) IV, p. 125.
2) *ibid.*, p. 64.
3) *ibid.*, p. 65.

made attempts to influence others. Shtol'c remembers how in Moscow
" . . . in the garden there . . . you haven't forgotten the two sisters? You
haven't forgotten Rousseau, Schiller, Goethe, Byron, and how you used to
bring their works to the girls and take away from them Cottin, Genlis . . ."[1]
Oblomov wanted to travel around the world, see the originals of the great
paintings he admired, understand political economy and law, learn languages,
and even penetrate into the secrets of higher mathematics. But this period
of enthusiasm did not last. Life and knowledge did not blend thoroughly
enough; his natural apathy prevailed. By the time he had completed his
studies his head was like a library consisting of stray volumes from manifold branches of knowledge; he would not and perhaps could not apply
this knowledge to life.

A certain ambition, however, had not yet left him. Even though youthful enthusiasm had begun to taper off, he still contemplated entering into
an administrative career and assuming a responsible role in society. He sometimes imagined family happiness. At the age of 20, he arrived in Petersburg;
his parents had died, leaving him a decent income from the estate. At first
he chose to become a kind of dandy, living according to the rules of the
jeunesse dorèe, going to balls and parties, dressing after the latest fashion,
nurturing gourmet tastes and spending much money and time on his mistress, Minna. Very soon, however, he tired of this life. At about the same
time he discovered that making his way in the administration was both
strenuous and unrewarding. He gradually began to develop a personal philosophy in which

> "Life was divided, in his opinion, into two halves: one consisted of
> work and boredom — these words were for him synonymous — the
> other of rest and peaceful good humor." [2]

Government service, it seems, belonged very definitely to the unpleasant
half, and when after two years of work, he made the slight error of sending
an urgent document to Arkhangel'sk instead of Astrakhan', he used the incident as a pretext for retirement, thus avoiding a possible reprimand from

---

1) IV, p. 189.
2) *ibid.,* p. 58; compare to this the beginning of "Is Life on Earth Good or Bad?".

his superior. All this happened about ten years before the action of the novel begins. The intervening years were marked by a gradual extension and consolidation of his philosophy according to which he began to live. At first he suffered twinges of conscience which interrupted his steadfastness of purpose, but before long he came to live it fully, secure in the knowledge that it suited him perfectly. The peripeties of Oblomov's life as guided by this philosophy constitute the content of the novel.

> " . . . Having given up the service and society, he began to seek
> another meaning for his existence; he pondered what he could
> have been destined for, and at last discovered that he could find
> enough scope for activity in living his own life." [1]

With this statement Goncharov introduces the basic ideological problem of his work. Oblomov's discovery leads by degrees to utter paralysis of any activity. The same fantasy that played such an important part in his childhood gradually takes over. It helps Oblomov to create a life of his own within himself, and this inner life becomes a substitute for the dangerous life outside. Instead of dreaming of doing something, he ponders the state of affairs that will come about once this or that has been done. He draws up an excellent and quite costly plan of how to manage his estate. He knows very well that acquisition is far from being a sin, that it is the "duty of every citizen to keep up the general welfare by honest labor." [2] And yet he cannot bring himself even to visit the estate. The action involved would be too much for him.

He knows the delight of lofty thoughts. He is not a stranger to human sorrow. There are times when he weeps deep and bitter tears over the misfortunes of mankind. He suffers for humanity. He yearns for something indefinable. But none of this, nothing can induce him to action. He feels contempt for human vice, lies, and slander, for all the evil masquarading as good in the world. He wants to point it all out to men and show them their sores. But the best of intentions — which begin with Oblomov changing his position in bed two or three times in one minute, then sitting up with shining eyes, and perhaps stretching — invariably lead to naught.

---

1) IV, p. 66.
2) *ibid.,* p. 68.

Sometimes his dreams take a more egotistic bend. He imagines himself a great ruler and conqueror or a great artist or scholar. Everyone fears or admires him. He decides the fate of nations. He is crowned with laurels for all manner of feats. But he had dreams of anguish too, dreams in which he foresees some sort of danger, a storm threatening him, for example. Then he kneels down and prays to the heavens to avert it. But he soon forgets the storm, having expended his spiritual powers after days of deep emotion, he watches the sun sink "magnificently behind the four-storied house" [1] facing the window opposite his bed.

Nobody suspects the richness of this inner life except Shtol'c, who "could have testified to his abilities and to the volcanic work of his ardent mind and his tender heart." [2] But Shtol'c spends hardly any time in Petersburg. Whether Shtol'c would have been able to change Oblomov's development, even if he had been constantly in attendance, is more than doubtful. Oblomov realizes that his mind is gradually atrophying. He is well aware of his growing apathy. He does not *want* to do anything about it however, because inactivity becomes more and more a metaphysical issue for him, a kind of persuasion, a philosophical system, in which reason and will finally coincide. When the novel opens, he is already quite far along in this development, though he still has moments of uncertainty, and vacillation.

Oblomov is about 32 years old. He lives in a comfortable, if neglected apartment, and spends most of his time lying on a comfortable bed, dressed in a comfortable oriental dressing gown and long, soft, comfortable slippers. On the morning we first meet him (which, we have reason to believe, is Saturday, May 1st 1843) he is called upon to cope with two unpleasant pieces of news. First, a letter from his steward informs him that his badly mismanaged estate has ceased to yield enough money to enable him to continue living in the manner to which he has become accustomed, and second — and still worse — his landlord wants him to move, because he intends to remodel the apartment. Both events require just the sort of action Il'ja Il'ich despises taking, and yet he realizes that sooner or later he will have to do something. For a start he "discusses" the problem with his manservant Zakhar — a classical Goncharovian creation: clumsy, unclean, lazy,

---

1) IV, p. 70.
2) *ibid.*

impudent, limited, not overly honest, and given to gossip, he is at the same
time completely and passionately devoted to his master and his master's
whole family, and is basically a kind man. Goncharov compares him
ironically to the Calebs of old times, alluding to the faultless, faithful servant from Sir Walter Scott's "The Bride of Lamermoor." [1] Servants of
that age were "knights of the servant's hall, without fear or reproach," but
Zakhar belongs to *two* epochs "each of which had left its mark upon him.
From one of them he inherited a boundless devotion to the Oblomov
family, and from the other, the later one, sophistication and corrupted
morals." [2] Oblomov's conversations with his servant are sheer comedy
scenes, especially in the first part of the novel. Despite a kind of mutual
appreciation, their outward relations are rather hostile. Having always lived
together they grew tired of each other, and the result is a constant nagging
at one another. This failing gives rise at times to very funny situations, the
most famous of which occurs in Part One, Chapter Eight, when Zakhar
tells his master that "other people" move, so why shouldn't he. The notion
of "other people" spurs Oblomov on to a great tirade, in which he tries to
prove to Zakhar that he is not like "other people" using what Zakhar calls
"heartrending words" (zhalkie slova) as the mainstay of his argument. Though
Zakhar does not really understand these words (they are mainly bookish or
of Church-Slavonic extraction, e.g. *prostupok* 'transgression', *blagodetel'-
stvovat'*, 'to do good') their unusual, solemn, pathetic tone goes so much
on his nerves that he bursts into tears, and master and servant finally talk
without understanding each other.

Chapter Two demonstrates, a bit artificially, Oblomov's lack of interest
in the most common pursuits of life. Four visitors appear in quick succession: Volkov, a dandy interested in fashions and flirtations; Sud'binskij, a
careerist in the state service; Penkin, a journalist and adherent of modern
accusatory, socially oriented literature (he induces Oblomov to an inspired,
if brief, diatribe against it); Alekseev, the incarnation of human mediocrity,

---

1) Strangely enough the most recent and complete Soviet edition of Goncharov (cf.
   Bibliography) states in the commentary that Goncharov is referring here to the
   hero of William Godwin's (1756–1836) novel "Caleb Williams", in spite of the
   fact that it does not contain an impeccably honest servant. Moreover there is no
   evidence that Goncharov even knew it. Cf. IV, p. 517.
2) IV, p. 70.

interested in everything and nothing. To him Oblomov reads the letter from his steward, a very funny imitation of uneducated style, that contrasts sharply with the sad news it brings.

Chapters Three and Four are devoted to a fifth visitor, Mikhej Tarant'ev, an unpleasant character from the same province as Oblomov. Oblomov tolerates him because of his energetic ability to make plans and develop theories of how to get out of complicated situations. True, Tarant'ev does not indulge in much more action than Oblomov (and when he does act, it is certainly to further dishonest causes), but his insolent pushiness somehow attracts the soft Oblomov. Tarant'ev's role as a connecting character justifies his rather circumstantial introduction. (He is even supplied a short biography.)

Chapters Five and Six recount in retrospect the Petersburg life of the hero. Chapter Seven paints the portrait of Zakhar and describes his relations with Oblomov. Chapter Eight provides a logical follow-up: the hilarious row between master and man, which ends by exhausting the master and sending him back to sleep. Chapter Nine contains the famous dream, and Chapter Ten shows Zakhar in action during his master's sleep confirming in his almost simultaneous praise and abuse of Oblomov what Goncharov has already told us about his character. We also meet a number of other servants — his audience. Goncharov portrays them in the same ironically negative vein we know from *A Common Story*.

Chapter Eleven, which closes Part One, is very short. Zakhar has terrible trouble waking his master who ordered him to do so himself. The uproarius scene is interrupted by the laughter of Andrej Shtol'c, who — just back from a travel — has been observing the procedure unnoticed.

Thus, by the end of Part One (about 160 pages long) the primary hero has hardly gotten out of the bed and the secondary hero is just being introduced in person (his name has been mentioned again and again in the preceding chapters, and his unexpected arrival on the scene is quite effective).

The first chapter of Part Two is devoted to a description of this second hero's formative years: his childhood and early youth. Andrej Shtol'c's father, a German "bürger" with a thorough university education was an

agriculturist and technician by profession, and the steward of the estate of
a wealthy prince. He taught his son the practical side of life. Without infring-
ing upon his personality, he forced him to fulfill his orders to the letter, and
took care that he received a sound basis in both the sciences and the humanities. The down-to-earth, a little rough and prosaic education given Andrej by
his father was counterbalanced by the teachings of his Russian mother. She
imbued him with a love for poetry and music, attuned his heart to romantic
feeling, and toned down his boyish ways. She was assisted in her endeavors
by the influence of the atmosphere surrounding the princely palace with its
inhabitants. Though most of the year the prince and his family were away
in the city, the boy became acquainted with the aristocratic tradition by
wandering through the long galleries and admiring the prince's family portraits. And whenever the prince visited the estate, he would play with his
children and learn from them about life in the capital. Still very young, he
tried to adapt to their city manners.

Andrej was lively and intelligent, energetic and healthy, and the upbringing he received could not fail to develop a well-balanced personality. Discussing Shtol'c's character in Chapter Two, Goncharov stresses that nothing
about him was excessive, neither his appearance, nor his behavior, nor his
mental and moral reactions. He took care to reconcile the practical side of
life with the more ephemeral claims of the spirit. He was genuinely interested in a wide range of topics, he was capable of a wide range of feelings, but
he held everything under careful control:

"... It seemed as though he controlled his joys and sorrows like
the movements of his hands and the steps of his legs or as he treated the good and bad weather. He put an umbrella up while the rain
fell — that is, he suffered while the sorrow lasted, and even then
with vexation, with pride rather than a timid submissiveness; he
bore it patiently only because he blamed himself for his troubles
and did not lay them at other people's doors. He enjoyed pleasure
as one enjoys a flower plucked by the roadside — until it begins to
fade, and never drained the cup to those last dregs of bitterness
which lie at the bottom of every enjoyment."

"... Above all he feared imagination, this two-faced travelling
companion with a friendly face on one side and a hostile one on

the other, a friend the less you believe it and an enemy, the moment
you fall asleep trustfully to its sweet murmur. — He feared any dream
(mechta) and if he entered its province, he entered it the way one
enters a grotto with the inscription: ma solitude, mon hermitage, mon
repos, knowing the hour and the minute, one will leave it again." [1]

Though certainly not unemotional (the novel offers sufficient examples
for this), here too he is wary of any excess which might upset his equilibrium:

"He considered himself lucky even because of the fact that he knew
how to remain at a certain height, and while riding the hobby-horse
of emotion he never transgressed the thin line separating the world
of emotion from the world of lie and sentimentality, the world of
the true from the world of the ridiculous, and on the return ride
never blundered into the sandy desert of hard-heartedness, sophistry,
mistrust, pettiness and emasculation of the heart." [2]

"The sphere of the heart's functions" is still "terra incognita" to him at the
beginning of the novel, but we are sure that he will be able to handle it
when time comes. He is unwilling to give himself up to the first passion
that happens to come his way. He refuses to create idols for himself. He
behaves as if he were living his life a second time over, as if he already knew
what problems he would have to face and whether it was worth expending
the effort to deal with them. If after clear calculation he decided it was not,
he would not try to show off, but follow the dictates of reason. One
should point out however, that in spite of Shtol'c's strong dependence on
reason, Goncharov assures us again and again and shows us in his actions
and thoughts that he is far from being a dry, unfeeling machine. Neither
onesided, nor prosaic, he merely opposes illusion, fantastic speculations
and dreams, and self-assured idealism.

Shtol'c's professional activities are not clearly defined. After retirement
from government service, he seems to have gone into business and acquired
a respectable fortune. When we first meet him, he belongs to a trading

1) IV, p. 168.
2) *ibid.,* p. 169.

company. There is not the slightest hint of dishonesty or exploitation in
his dealings. Under the influence of the article "What is Oblomovism?"[1]
written by the contemporary critic Nikolaj Dobroljubov (who discussed the
novel exclusively as a kind of social pamphlet in keeping with the trend of
the time), the majority opinion in literary scholarship about Shtol'c runs
as follows: Instead of the 'positive hero' that Goncharov meant to create,
we get a lifeless invention. Instead of the appealing altruist he intended,
we find an unattractive egotist, a cold 'entrepreneur' ruled by reason, an
operator whose moral character is not beyond reproach. No less a person
than Anton Chekhov goes to great length in this direction, commenting
significantly enough that no one in *Oblomov*, – not even the hero – is
worth much, because none of the characters "are characteristic of their
time." He denies Oblomov's validity as a social type (though Goncharov
never maintained he was one; it was Dobroljubov who initiated this interpretation). "Stol'c," we read further, "inspires no confidence in me. The
author says he is a splendid fellow (velikolepnyj malyj), but I don't believe
him. He is a thoroughgoing rat (produvnaja bestija), who thinks very highly
of himself and is quite satisfied with himself. He is half invented and three
quarters stilted." The climax of the entire tirade comes when Chekhov
claims to be deleting Goncharov from the list of his demigods. (It should
be noted, however, that this humorously malicious letter to A. Suvorin
of May 1889 is signed Akakij Tarantulov!)[2]

Still and all, what Chekhov so light-heartedly formulated, is the essence
of what has been written about Stol'c from Dobroljubov's celebrated article all the way to the recent voluminous monograph on Goncharov by
A. Cejtlin. Cejtlin enumerates negative judgments on Stol'c [3] and fully
agrees with all of them. He reproaches Goncharov with his failure to give
a clear enough demonstration of Stol'c's predatory attitude to the peasants
(why should he, if it never existed?) He maintains that although Stol'c is
typical in his indifference to the "damned issues," supposedly characteristic
of all strata of the Russian bourgeoisie, and in his "intellectual satiety,"
Goncharov is still wrong in his moral evaluation of Stol'c, which in his
opinion is the prime reason for the failure of this character as such.

1) "Chto takoe oblomovshchina?", Sovremennik, V (1859) otd.II, pp. 59-98; reprinted
   many times.
2) A.P.Chekhov, Polnoe sobranie sochinenij i pisem, XIV (Moskva, 1949), p. 354.
3) Cejtlin, pp. 175 sq.

That Goncharov himself could much later (1879) characterize Stol'c as pallid and weak in his Critical Comments "Better Late Than Never," that he could think the conception of his character much too obvious [1] is only a further instance among many of the desire of Russian writers to justify themselves in the eyes of criticism. Such self-justification usually resulted in rather questionable attempts at accomodation, which frequently contradicted the writer's own text.

If we turn to the text of the novel, we find that Goncharov's Shtol'c (in contrast to the critics' version of Shtol'c) is in no way a definite social type (nor for that matter is Oblomov). What he does represent, in fact, is one positive solution to the problem of living in the midst of modern culture, a solution that would be desirable and practicable in any country. Reason and sentiment are perfectly balanced in him, and although he unites them with a strong will, it is not so strong as to upset the equilibrium of his total personality.

Stol'c is certainly interested in social questions, but he is aware that they constitute only a partial complex within a much deeper problem, and he knows that they do not yield to any ultimate solutions.

There is, to repeat it once more, nothing in the novel to indicate that Shtol'c was greedy or indulged in any unscrupulous practices while amassing his fortune. Shtol'c works hard and attains a comfortable situation in life, but he knows better than to *idealize* work. Work is life. It has no ethical value. And Shtol'c is far from preaching the "sanctity of labor." In view of life's realities he believes it necessary to identify work with life, and finds it only reasonable to expect the work thus discharged will lead to a certain well-being and enable him to take part in the cultural pursuits of his time. He does not think he can solve life's riddles; one lives because one has to live.

Chapter Three and Four of Part Two are mainly devoted to dialogues between Oblomov and Shtol'c clarifying their philosophical positions and approaches to the practical questions of life.

Oblomov is not yet completely sure about his final position, but he knows that his heart is at rest, and his mind sound asleep. He realizes he

---

[1] VIII, p. 80.

is too lazy even to live, and still he does not see any particular reason for changing this situation. When Shtol'c succeeds in dragging him out of his seclusion into society, he discovers that the gray base for all the gaudy activities around him is boredom; the same boredom of life which he overcomes with fanciful dreams and honest sleep, society strives to escape with vain and variegated occupations and interests, leading nowhere and giving no satisfaction. "All these society people are dead men, men fast asleep, they are worse than I am. [1] To his great tirade against the "empty world," its boredom and its sleep, Shtol'c has no real answer. Shtol'c calls Oblomov "philosopher" when he pleads for rest and peace, he calls him "poet" when Oblomov spins dreams of the ideal family life in the country, he insists on calling the passive life "non-life," and even coins the word "Oblomovism" to characterize Oblomov's weltanschauung. But he cannot give a satisfactory answer to Oblomov's triumphant question of whether "the purpose of all your running about, your passions, wars, trade, politics (is not) to secure rest, to attain this ideal of a lost paradise?" [2] Oblomovism, we must conclude, is the ideal, the lost paradise of peace, which mankind hopes to regain. Shtol'c argues that this is a kind of Oblomovian utopia, that one must live for life's sake and work for work's sake, but it is clear that he realizes he is not speaking to the ultimate metaphysical sense of Oblomov's question. He reminds Oblomov of his youthful activities and interests, but to Oblomov's description of how he began to decline from the moment he became aware of himself (a passionate speech, built on the repetition of the word *gasnut'* (to die out, become extinguished, decline'), Shtol'c has no reply. [3] He listened in gloomy silence, and at last proposed a trip abroad. This last section of Chapter Four prepares the further spiritual development of both protagonists.

Though not completely persuaded by Shtol'c, Oblomov still feels that he must make a choice. Like Hamlet, he asks, "to be or not to be." The result is a weak attempt at following his friend's advice: he prepares to travel abroad.

Suddenly, however, another possibility "for life" presents itself. Only touched upon in Chapter Four, it arises unexpectedly in full blossom at

1) IV, p. 179.
2) *ibid.,* p. 187.
3) *ibid.,* p. 190.

the beginning of Chapter Five: Oblomov thinks that he has fallen in love. Whereas there was little hope that traveling would alter Oblomov's mentality (Onegin's journey is an ominous precursor in Russian literature), [1] it is plausible that love may rehabilitate his life and modify his personality. Oblomov's love story occupies nearly all of Part Two and the whole of Part Three.

Here Goncharov repeats the strange mistake he made in *A Common Story*. He says not a word about the development of his heroine, Ol'ga Il'inskaja, previous to her appearance at the age of 20. We learn that she is intelligent, unpretentious, and straightforward, that she has broad interests and is an excellent singer. All these qualities are confirmed by her behavior, but considering the careful way in which the formation of Shtol'c's character was explained, Ol'ga's sudden appearance as a sort of *fait accompli* seems too abrupt. Shtol'c introduces Oblomov to Ol'ga. She — apparently a rich orphan — lives with her well-to-do aunt Mar'ja Mikhajlovna. Shtol'c and Ol'ga have been friends for years. He appreciates her sincerity, her genuine interest in all aspects of life, and her fresh, healthy charm. She admires his unpretentious superiority and values the attention he pays her when talking about serious things and the wit he exhibits in his humorous, ironically tinged remarks. Ol'ga is proud that Shtol'c has chosen to tell her about Oblomov and his peculiar attitude to life. She develops a desire to awaken him, to make him change, to breathe life into his passivity. Goncharov compares her ambition to Pygmalion's resolve to make Galathea live. Oblomov is immediately impressed by her. He notices that she knows a lot about him from Shtol'c, and is curious in an inobtrusive, friendly, even loving way. Oblomov's response to Ol'ga's voice is in keeping with his ebullient fantasies. Ol'ga sings beautifully; her rendering of "Casta diva" from Bellini's *Norma* becomes a kind of leitmotif. It is not surprising that they fall in love, even if, — considering the situation and the characters, — we cannot be sure their love will withstand all the trials ahead.

Ol'ga cannot help but want to dominate Oblomov. Above all she wants him to become active. She learns how to prevent him from sleeping in the afternoon; she is able to make him go to the theater or read a book — as long as she is there alongside him. But before the marriage, he must settle

---

1) Cf. A. Pushkin, Evgenij Onegin, Fragments from Onegin's Travel.

his affairs, get his estate organized, obtain various documents from official chanceries. Because he must take care of these things himself, they prove too much for him, and by degrees he falls back into his lazy apathy.

The culmination point of his happiness comes at the end of Part Two. After torturous doubts about whether he is worthy of Ol'ga, he accepts her reassurances; reason and her genuine feeling for him win out for a while. But there are also some indications of danger:

> " 'I am not afraid, any longer,' he said gaily, 'With you I do not fear the future!'
> 'I have read that phrase somewhere recently . . . in Sue, I think,' she suddenly said, mockingly, turning to him, 'only there it's a woman who says it to a man . . . '
> The color rushed to Oblomov's head." [1]

As soon as any action is required of Oblomov, he loses his composure. Goncharov gives a fine analysis of Oblomov's psychology when he describes how Oblomov reacts to the hypothesis that Ol'ga's friends may start gossiping about their relationship:

> "Although Oblomov's youth had been spent among companions who knew all about everything and believed in nothing, who had settled all vital problems long ago, and analysed everything with cold wisdom, he still believed in friendship, in love, in honor, and however many mistakes he made or might still make about people his heart suffered, but they did not undermine his conception of goodness and his faith in it. He secretly worshipped feminine purity, admitted its rights and power, and was ready to make sacrifices for its sake.
> But he had not enough character openly to recognize the principles of goodness and of respect for innocence. He enjoyed its fragrance in secret, but in words he sometimes joined the cynics who dread being suspected of chastity or of having respect for it, and added his frivolous remarks to their ribald conversation." [2]

---

1) IV, pp. 268-269.
2) *ibid.*, pp. 280-281.

But finally all obstacles seem to have been removed from their path; the last sentence of Part Two is: "He uttered a cry of joy and sank on the grass at her feet." [1]

The contrast in mood at the beginning of Part Three (Tarant'ev's visit) is very well done. Tarant'ev "instantly brought him down, as it were from heaven into the mire." He spent the summer in the country in order to be near Ol'ga. Problems with a new apartment — rented before he considered marriage, but not yet payed for — take on alarming proportions. And once when Oblomov goes there to get rid of it, he sees his familiar furniture stored there and meets the landlady Agaf'ja Matveevna Pshenicyna (her household reminds him vaguely of Oblomovka), it becomes clear that he will once again follow the law of his own nature. He moves in "temporarily," and begins to invent excuses to get out of seeing Ol'ga. When he pretends to be ill, for example, she believes him and to his horror comes to see him. He does nothing about his estate, leaving the management to the friend of his landlady's brother, whom he does not know and who turns out to be a rascal. He decides to postpone the marriage until everything is settled, and is proud of his new "resolution." But it is just this which makes Ol'ga finally admit to herself the hopelessness of the venture she has undertaken.

In the sad parting scene (Part Three, Chapter Eleven), Ol'ga asks Oblomov whether he feels he has the strength for life with her and her demands on life. When he finds he cannot answer in the affirmative, Ol'ga pours out an avowal of what she had expected from him:

"I have only lately understood that I loved in you what I wanted
to find in you, what Stol'c had pointed out to me, what we had
both invented. I loved the Oblomov that was to be! You are gentle,
you are honorable, Il'ya; you are tender ... like a dove; you hide
your head under your wing — and want nothing more; you are ready
to spend all your life cooing under the roof ... but I am not like
that: this isn't enough for me, I want something else, and what that
something else is — I don't know! Can you teach me, can you tell
me what it is I miss, can you give it me, so that I ... And as for
tenderness ... anyone can give it! ... " [2]

1) IV, p. 296.
2) *ibid.*, p. 381–382.

Oblomov reacts to this "cruel" but honest speech by weeping and by berating "Oblomovism." Yet he makes no move to seek out a remedy, nor even seems desirous of finding one. Nonetheless, he is deeply affected by the rupture and contracts a violent fever as a consequence. The first snow of the year, which Oblomov sees through the window before losing consciousness marks his definitive break with the world and symbolizes the cutoff point in his development along Shtol'c-like lines. It provides an effective contrast to the resplendent summer of his strong but hopeless love.

Part Four is the account of Oblomovka reincarnated. In its way it is the most fascinating and most metaphysically significant part of the novel. It covers the seven years in which Oblomov gradually kills the desire for life in himself, learns to live with the monotony of absolute inactivity and develops his ability for contemplation.

As he approaches a state which completely satisfies his spiritual requirements, however, he begins feeling the physical effects of his sedentary existence. The process of physical decay is quickened by Agaf'ja Matveevna, his amiable landlady, who falls in love with her refined and grateful tenant. Agaf'ja Matveevna is a widow and has two children Oblomov dotes upon. She is simple and very limited intellectually, and her lovethirsty heart is clearly in need of one to care for. Her virtuoso cooking and excellent management of her little household prepossess Oblomov in her favor. What is more, her soft white body (for which her active elbows become a frequently repeated metonymy) and kind face come to excite him sexually, and she becomes first his mistress and then his wife.

Shtol'c's visit in the second chapter (approximately one year after Oblomov's break with Ol'ga) makes it amply clear that this time he will not be able to induce Oblomov to undertake any changes in the *status quo*.

A bit of suspense is injected into the narrative when Tarant'ev and Agaf'ja Matveevna's brother blackmail Oblomov (as a seducer) into signing obligations which bring him near to financial ruin. The good woman does not even sense she has been used in these machinations. Even Oblomov, typically enough, hardly realizes what he has perpetrated by his signature. Agaf'ja's attempts at concealing their resulting poverty (Chapter Five) are quite touching; she pawns her belongings to feed Oblomov the expensive food he is accustomed to eating. But none of these episodes have any influence upon the development of Oblomov's life and philosophy.

Shtol'c arrives as a *deus ex machina*, unravels the nasty plot, and uses his influence in higher circles to explode its supposedly air-tight legality. Once this "attempt" on Oblomov's new mode of life (at the same time a "false" peripety in the plot), has been properly dealt with, he is free to take definitive possession of his newly created Oblomovka. Oblomov has given up his reluctant struggle for life and has found peace and happiness. In Chapter Nine Goncharov paints the idyllic picture of a warrior resting after a defensive but victorious battle. Oblomov "decided at last that there was nothing further for him to aim at, nothing further to seek, that he had *attained his ideal of life*" [1] even if he has had to renounce the poetry with which his imagination used to adorn it. He easily represses any occasional regrets that arise and recognizes once and for all that "his life had not merely *happened* to be so simple and uneventful, but had been created and designed to be such, in order to demonstrate *the possibility of the ideally restful aspect of human existence.*

It was other people's lot, he thought, to express its tempestuous aspects, to set in motion the creative and destructive forces; everyone had his own appointed task!" [2]

It is clear that Goncharov approves of the philosophy evolved by his "Oblomovian Plato", [3] stating categorically that there are no reasons for him to repent, work toward another goal, or alter any aspect of the life he has carved out for himself. He even goes so far as to compare Oblomov to the ancient Christian hermits, who, turning away from life, dug their own graves. (Of course, there is not the slightest Christian bias in this statement.)

Even the stroke he suffers as a result of his all too peaceful existence does not have much effect on his "preparation of a wide and simple coffin." On his last visit, Shtol'c learns (along with the reader) that Oblomov has married Agaf'ja Matveevna and had a son by her. Then we read that he dies peacefully, in his sleep. Death comes to Oblomov without pain, without

---

1) IV, p. 486 (Italics mine, V.S.).
2) *ibid.*, p. 487.
3) *ibid.*

suffering "like a clock that stops because it hasn't been wound up." [1] A
description of his quiet grave and of Agaf'ja Matveevna's deep and lasting
grief (one of the most touching pages in Russian fiction) ends his story.

The last part contains two long chapters (Four and Eight) completely devoted to Shtol'c and Ol'ga. In Chapter Four Goncharov gives a psychological explanation for the quick development of the genuine love which grows
up between them after they unexpectedly meet in Paris. In Ol'ga it is surprise that her first love can be so easily superseded (only because she does
not realize that it was in fact Shtol'c whom she had always loved), and
the feeling of guilt towards Shtol'c, to whom she does not dare to confess
the sad experience she just had.

Shtol'c had always thought of Ol'ga as an intelligent, charming, natural,
but inexperienced girl. When he meets her after her disappointment, he
senses that she has grown into a woman who can be his equal and satisfy
both his intellect and his emotions. Once more Goncharov stresses that
Shtol'c is not solely a rational being, that he is capable of passion, and that
he is looking for passion in Ol'ga too; he wants to be certain that her feeling for him as a person is not limited to an admiration of his intellectual
capacities. "He was not a dreamer," says Goncharov. "He wanted gusts
of passion no more than Oblomov, though for different reasons. And yet
he did wish that before flowing quietly into its even stream, feeling should
surge up hotly at the source, and one should be able to draw from it and
drink one's fill and so to know for the rest of one's life where this spring
of happiness flowes from." [2]

In Shtol'c this longing for passion develops into love; moreover his
"continual ardent and intelligent devotion" [3] brings Ol'ga to understand
her real feelings, which culminate in her dreams of a magnificent happiness
on "the wide arena of many-sided life with all its depth, with its charms
and sorrows — happiness with Shtol'c." [4] The very commentators who
condemn Shtol'c, see in Ol'ga the ideal woman (Chekhov, in the letter
mentioned above, is perhaps the only exception), and they never tire of

1) IV, p. 499.
2) *ibid.*, p. 417.
3) *ibid.*, p. 418.
4) *ibid.*, p. 422.

propagating this dogma. It is odd that this ideal woman is so completely under the influence of a character who, if one is to believe the critics, stands so far beneath her level.

Her open confession of her love for Oblomov makes no impression upon Shtol'c; he gives a clear analysis of her feelings at the time she thought she loved him and discards her former flame as a "mistake." No doubt he is right in his evaluation.

In Chapter Eight we find the definitive philosophical message of the novel. In the form of a conversation between Ol'ga and Shtol'c, Goncharov gives clear utterance to his own ultimate insights. Strangely enough, Oblomov commentators have failed to interpret this discussion in the way Goncharov beyond all question intended it to be understood.

Without the slightest basis in the text it has been declared (first by Dobroljubov and repeatedly since) that Ol'ga, dissatisfied with her limited family happiness and recognizing Shtol'c's "true" character, begins to yearn for a broader field of activity and that this activity is social work — in other words "going among the people." As I have already indicated, there is no textual basis for this interpretation. Ol'ga is concerned with the question of happiness as such, not family happiness. She and Shtol'c live a full, many-sided life; they are perfectly happy with one another, with their children, their interests, their work, their comforts, and their wealth. "Man is odd!" says Goncharov after describing their happiness. "The fuller her happiness was, the more thoughtful and even ... apprehensive she became." [1)]

And what follows is a description of the phenomenon which, as Walther Rehm has demonstrated in his above mentioned study, provides the axis for Goncharov's work: the existential boredom which seizes man just as he reaches a state of absolute satisfaction, the Nothingness the modern intellectual faces, the man to whom all material goods are available, but who is incapable of finding an answer to the ultimate questions and is terrified by the obvious senselessness of life: " 'What is it?', she thought with terror. 'Is it necessary, is it possible to wish for something else? Where am I to go? Nowhere! The road does not lead any farther ... Doesn't it? Have I, then, completed the circle of life? Is this all ... all?'

---

1) IV, p. 468.

her heart asked, and left something unsaid ... and Ol'ga looked round anxiously lest someone should overhear this whisper of the heart ... Her eyes questioned the sky, the sea, the forest ... there was no answer anywhere: there was distance, depth and darkness. — Nature said the same things over and over again; she saw in it the continuous but monotonous flow of life without beginning, without end." [1]

What her heart has left unsaid is one possible road to salvation: belief in God. But Goncharov deliberately leaves this out as a possibility for modern man. It is quite striking, although never pointed out, that in his first two novels neither religion nor the church play the slightest role. His personal attitude to faith is irrelevant here, but he himself knew well why he so thoroughly banished it from his work. Vera's desperate prayers in *The Precipice* play only a subordinate role within the pilosophical conception of the novel, but in *Oblomov* even this touch is missing.

What has seized Ol'ga is the 'sickness unto death' (to use Kierkegaard's expression), the 'strange affliction" *(strannyj nedug)* [2], as Goncharov says, using, significantly enough, the same expression Pushkin uses to describe the affliction of his Onegin in an analogous situation (cf. *Evgenij Onegin,* I, 38); Onegin's symptoms coincide, not without cause, with those of Ol'ga.

When she turns to Shtol'c for help, he immediately diagnoses her problem as 'skuka' — boredom (the word, which appears throughout Goncharov's writings and letters in striking profusion). She is obliged to admit that it is some sort of hypochondria — 'kakaja-to khandra,' [3] again an expression used by Pushkin in a similar context.

And after her description of this emotional state — ("What is then all this happiness ... and all life ... — ... — all these joys, grief ... nature ... — ... all this is drawing me still somewhere else; I grow discontented with everything ... " [4] — Shtol'c answers hesitantly: " 'It may be an excess of imagination: you are much too alive ... or perhaps you have matured to the point of ... ' he finished in an undertone, speaking almost to himself." Upon

---

1) IV, p. 469.
2) *ibid.*, p. 470.
3) *ibid.*, p. 472.
4) *ibid.*, p. 472.

Ol'ga's insistence he makes his idea more explicit: " . . . it may be that you
have reached maturity, the time when life stops growing . . . when there
are no riddles left and the whole of life is wide-open . . . ." [1] "The search-
ings of a mind, which is alive and irritated, at times try to break through
beyond the workaday limits, find of course no answers, and there appears
sadness . . . a temporary dissatisfaction with life. It's the sadness of the
soul questioning life about its mysteries . . . . " [2] Such questions may
drive those unprepared for them to the brink of madness, continues Shtol'c,
and to Ol'ga's dismayed remark: "Happiness is brimming over, I so want to
live . . . and all of a sudden there is an admixture of some bitterness . . . ,"
he replies: "Ah, that is what one has to pay for Prometheus's fire! It is not
enough to endure, but you have to love this sadness and to respect your
doubts and questions: they are the overflow, the luxury of life, and appear
for the most part on the summits of happiness, when no coarse desires are
left; they do not spring up in ordinary life: people in need and sorrow cannot be bothered with them; the crowd goes on and knows nothing about
this mist of doubts, this yearning to understand . . . . " [3] To Ol'ga's plain-
tive question about what can be done to counteract this yearning, this indifference to everything, Shtol'c offers an answer which is consistent, clear,
and entirely in keeping with *his* life: " 'Nothing, − . . . − Arm yourself with
fortitude and follow your path patiently and perseveringly. You and I are
not Titans − . . . −, we will not, like the Manfreds and Fausts, go to struggle
defiantly with rebellious questions, we shall not take up their challenge, but
humbly bowing our heads will live through the difficult time and then again
life and happiness will smile upon us and' . . . 'But what if they never will
leave us alone and the sadness goes on upsetting us more and more?' she
asked. 'Well, what of it? We will accept it as a new elemental force in
life . . . But no, that does not happen, it cannot be so with us! It is not
your sadness, it is the general affliction of mankind. One drop of it has fallen
upon you . . . . ' " [4]

   It is clear: Ol'ga and Shtol'c will find in their love for each other the
strength to overcome the time of *"nedug"* and yet even before they are rid

---

1) IV, p. 473.
2) *ibid.*, p. 474.
3) *ibid.*
4) *ibid.*, pp. 474–475.

of it, both of them look on life with open eyes. They accept it with its joys
and sorrows and live for the sake of living. They harbor no illusions (least
of all "social" illusions) and need no faith for consolation; even in a conversation that does touch on the ultimate issues they never mention the
name of God. This however does not prevent compassion, the main Christian
virtue, from taking root in Shtol'c and certainly in Ol'ga. Shtol'c's compassion is most obvious in his kindly treatment of Oblomov (his helpfulness
is sabotaged until the very end only by the absolute and philosophically
well-founded inertness of the object of his solicitations). But there are other
instances where Goncharov makes it clear that Shtol'c is not a mere "man
of reason." Agaf'ja Matveevna, simple loving soul that she is, instinctively
recognizes his human worth; she wants to thank him, "to lay before him
at last all that was pent up in her heart and lived there always: *he would
have understood,* but she did not know how to say it; she merely would
rush to Ol'ga, press her lips to her hands and burst into such a flood of
scalding tears that Ol'ga could not help weeping with her too, and Andrej
deeply moved would make haste to leave the room." [1] So many relevant
details of Shtol'c's character have gone unnoticed, obscured by dogmatic
views of him.

Striking parallels with Schopenhauer's philosophy strongly suggest themselves in the analysis of the metaphysical concept of the novel, and although
we have no basis for assuming that Goncharov was acquainted with Schopenhauer's work, the possibility is not excluded. Goncharov knew the literature
and philosophy of his time much better than it is generally supposed. As a
result of the gradual publication of his letters, which due to his own veto
have long remained unknown, many facts of his so far largely obscure
spiritual biography have been coming to light.

The question of whether Stol'c is successful as a fictional character, whether he is 'alive' and 'convincing' can only be answered if one first establishes
his spiritual concerns on the basis of the text. A judgment of his actions and
reactions must be postponed until after the philosophical conception of his
personality has been defined. The answers to questions about whether
fictional characters are 'lifelike' usually tend to be rather subjective, and a
line can be drawn beyond which objective judgments seems almost impossible. Shtol'c offers a good example.

1) IV, p. 503 (Italics mine, V.S.).

In his debates with Oblomov, Stol'c does not always express his deepest convictions, and psychologically he is quite right to hold back. Basically Shtol'c and Oblomov see life the same way: their view is hopelessly pessimistic. Both of them *know*, for both of them 'life has stopped growing,' for both 'there are no riddles left,' both live only for the sake of living, without illusions, without ideals, without faith, simply because one has to live. And because both have the means to arrange their lives as they see fit, neither has to participate in the struggle for life of the masses which Shtol'c speaks of to Ol'ga.

Yet while Oblomov considers passivity to be the proper mode of existence and seeks "happiness" in peace and the absence of will, Shtol'c sees the possibility of his "happiness" in activity, movement and strength of will. Hence his attempts to arouse Oblomov from his inertia and win him over to his own way. Oblomovism irritates him all the more because he senses in it another valid possibility. This is why Oblomov finds it easy to refute Shtol'c's arguments. Shtol'c is unable to answer the question "What is it all for?" — the crucial question —, for he knows as well as Oblomov that no answer exists.

Goncharov spares no effort to give equal weight to the values of the spokesmen for each possibility of living for the sake of living. Therefore Oblomov and Shtol'c are both ethically beyond reproach, both endowed with strong intellect, and both capable of true feeling. How else could their lasting friendship and mutual respect be explained? The only difference between them is that Oblomov sees the possibility of avoiding insoluble problems in reducing the will, whereas Shtol'c opts for its augmentation. Both depend only on themselves; neither expects any help from the beyond.

The last chapter, a kind of epilogue, introduces a new character: a writer (literator) who is described as being "stout, and having an apathetic face and thoughtful, almost sleepy eyes." [1] In this description it is not difficult to recognize Goncharov's self-portrait. To him Shtol'c relates the story surrounding the concept of Oblomovism — the novel we have just read — without trying to define the term. But by now we know what it means. It is the label for a philosophy of life, an attitude deliberately renouncing all activity,

---

1) IV, p. 503.

denying the value of life as such, and turning away from all manifestations of it. Oblomovism can claim a certain kinship with Buddhism. Above all they share a respect for nothingness, and surely Oblomov's final state of inertia constitutes his own special brand of Nirvanah. In any case there is certainly no way of justifying it from the Christian point of view. Christianity cannot approve of this kind of quietism because it rules out the possibility of man being made in God's image. Furthermore, for the mortification of the flesh it substitutes a mortification of life through indulgence in the elementary pleasures of the flesh. Oblomov buys his late happiness with his life. At first he loses life figuratively in the form of strife and endeavor, triumph and defeat; then in the form of premature death. But it cannot be denied that the *modus vivendi* he has worked out for himself brings him happiness, even bliss, and Goncharov rewards him for it with an easy and "happy" death. In this respect the novel, and with it the whole of Goncharov's *oeuvre,* becomes so metaphysically powerful that any social conclusions are quite subordinate.

As in *A Common Story* we have two protagonists who though seemingly poles apart, are basically the same and a woman who represents the eternally feminine, intuiting more about life than the two heroes can "learn" or "deduce." That *she* is satisfied with Shtol'c's pessimistic and resigned view of life, that he can console *her* and even kindle her love with his sad acceptance of life as it is, makes it clear where Goncharov's own beliefs lie.[1]

Lizaveta Aleksandrovna in *A Common Story* feels that both Aleksandr and Petr Ivanovich were onesided, that they lacked a metaphysical basis for their attitudes and did not really "know" what they professed. Their fundamental instability dooms her to a slow death in utter frustration. Ol'ga feels intuitively that both her men do "know." And while approving of Shtol'c's way — the activist way — of coping with "knowledge," she also feels the basic identity between Shtol'c's attitude and that of Oblomov. This explains her sincere love for Oblomov and her unshaken sympathy and interest in him. The exalted position Goncharov alots to his heroines may to a certain extent account for the absence of any biographical details prior to their appearance in the novel. Perhaps Goncharov wished to surround them with an aura of mystery so as to better justify their higher intuitive wisdom.

---

1) Cf. IV, p. 475.

Despite the triad in both novels, they have each one clear protagonist. In *Oblomov*, of course, everything revolves around the title character; in *A Common Story*, it is always Aleksandr who stands at the center of the action. It would be impossible to imagine Shtol'c or Petr Ivanovich as the main hero; both serve principally as antitheses to their respective protagonists. In each of the two novels, therefore, Goncharov presents us with a monograph about a man whose character he considers typical of a certain attitude toward life.

Oblomov follows a symmetrical structural pattern. The first and fourth parts are divided into eleven chapters, the second and third parts into twelve. Goncharov was apparently anxious to create a form which would prevent any overflow. The division between Parts Two and Three is somewhat artificial, however, because there is no break in psychology or time as after Parts One and Three.

The symmetrical structure was necessary because *Oblomov* has no plot in the usual sense, especially compared to other novels being written at the same time. Although the story of a life from cradle to grave, a kind of *Bildungsroman*, it deals with a life which was extremely poor in external events. *Oblomov* is an anti-adventure novel. Everything that goes into making a novel "interesting" — dangerous situations, extraordinary experiences, suspense, dynamism of plot — all this has been deliberately avoided.

The idea of undertaking such a novel was certainly a bold one, and Goncharov's unquestionable success shows that he found the right form for what he had to say. *Oblomov* is best characterized by the tone of disconsolate merriment running through it. The tension between its basically hopeless philosophy and playful surface details forms one of the main springs of its very special dynamism. Just before the "Dream" at the end of Part One, Chapter Eight we find an example of this tension when the doctor predicts an early death for the over-sedentary Oblomov. By juxtaposing Oblomov's two reactions, fear plus the inward decision not to follow the doctor's suggestions, Goncharov introduces humor into a life-and-death situation (which is made even more immediate by the news of a dying neighbor). This visit is followed by the famous above-mentioned dialogue with Zakhar concerning "other people." Both Oblomov and Zakhar are genuinely involved in the argument, Oblomov's speeches breathe genuine pathos, yet it cannot help but strike the reader as ridiculous. The outlandish vocabulary and comical repartees enhanced by funny similes (e.g. description of Zakhar's weeping in terms of "a tone impossible for any instrument, except perhaps some Chinese gong or Indian tam-tam" or "two dozen beetles (that) had flown into the room and started buzzing")[1] overlay the real feelings behind the quarrel with a veneer of humorous antics.

Oblomov's meditations just before falling asleep to dream his famous dream play a very important role in his spiritual development. They represent a last flaring up of his doubts as to whether abandoning willpower in favor of inactivity will provide him with the right way of life. Comparing himself to "other people," he wonders whether his quietistic leanings have a place in "human destiny" and whether he has not buried his treasure under a "heavy load of rubbish and dirt." [2] This "secret confession to himself" in "one of the lucid conscious moments of Oblomov's life" (it comes from within, it is not induced by Shtol'c or Ol'ga) is an attack by the natural force of life against its negation. The conclusion he reaches — that his intellect and his will are already paralyzed beyond resuscitation — leads him to what might be called a positive evaluation of negation. His inner struggles are reflected in sighs, groans, and a restless tossing and turning in bed. At the end of the most serious passage in Part One Zakhar, who has noticed the noise, comes out with the amusing "That's how he carries on after *kvass* (Èk ego tam s kvasu-to razduvaet)." [3] Here once more Goncharov has accentuated Oblomov's genuinely tragic mood with a snatch of superficial humor. That Goncharov considered the combination a characteristic feature of life and its reflection in art may perhaps be inferred from the program Shtol'c puts together for Ol'ga's recital. "She sang many songs and arias at Shtol'c's request; some expressed sorrow, with a vague presentiment of happiness, others joy, though there was a hidden spring of sadness in the sounds." [4]

This tension between serious problems and the comic is constantly played upon in several symbolic details that come up again and again: Throughout

---

1) IV, p. 97.
2) *ibid.*, p. 101.
3) *ibid.*
4) *ibid.*, p. 203.

the novel Oblomov's dressing gown ("lacking the slightest hint of Europe")
and his slippers, for example, serve as symbols of his conscious rejection of
active life, but as objects in and of themselves they hardly command much
respect. When Oblomov reinforces his "now or never" decision to follow
Shtol'c with Hamlet's "To be or not to be," Goncharov continues "Oblomov got up from the chair, but failed to find his slippers at once with his
feet and sat down again." [1] Oblomov's habit of putting on his slippers
without looking down for them is one of his amusing idiosyncrasies. But
the fact that his failure to find them prevents him from getting out of bed
is certainly symbolic of his future development.

Seemingly over-minute descriptions of a scene, object, or character also
take on a kind of symbolic meaning. The "microscopic" details engulf the
very life they are meant to depict; they diminish and in the end devour it.
The same device is common in Gogol', who shares with Goncharov a concern with the pettiness of so many people's lives. The crucial difference
between them is that Gogol' regards the myriad of petty cares plaguing man
as machinations of the devil, whereas Goncharov sees the possibility of at-
taching a positive value to them.

A good example of the minute descriptions which continue throughout
the novel may be found on the very first pages: "Dusty cobwebs hung in
festoons round the pictures on the walls; mirrors, instead of reflecting objects, might have served as tablets for writing memoranda in the dust; there
were stains on the carpets; a towel had been left on the sofa. Almost every
morning a dirty plate, with a salt-cellar and a bone from the previous night's
supper, was to be seen on the crumb-covered table." [2] The "inventory" of
Pshenicyna's house provides an equally good example from the final pages:

> "The kitchen, the pantries, the sideboard were full of crockery, of
> big and small, round and oval dishes, sauce-boats, cups, piles of
> plates, cast iron, brass, and earthenware pots. Agaf'ja Matveevna's
> silver, redeemed long ago and never pawned since, was kept in the
> cupboards, together with Oblomov's. There were rows of tiny and
> of huge round teapots and china cups, plain and gilded, and painted,

1) IV, p. 193.
2) *ibid.*, p. 9.

with mottoes, flaming hearts, and Chinamen. There were huge glass
jars of coffee, cinnamon, vanilla, crystal tea-caddies, cruets of oil
and vinegar. Whole shelves were taken up with packets, bottles,
and boxes of household remedies, herbs, lotions, plasters, decoc-
tions, camphor, fumigating powders; there was also soap, material
for cleaning lace, taking out stains, and so on, and so on — all that
every good housewife in a country house keeps by her." [1]

Goncharov also uses details to characterize people. Often he supplies them
with comic overtones (e.g. Zakhar's side-whiskers, thick enough to make
three beards and nest two or three birds, the "talking nose" of his wife
Aksin'ja, or the big paper parcel, the thick stick, and galoshes of Agaf'ja
Matveevna's brother). On the other hand, the carefully detailed portraits
of Ol'ga's aunt Mar'ja Mikhajlovna and the Baron von Langwagen are perfect examples of aristocratic *comme il faut,* refined manners and absolute
self-possession. The rumor of a former love affair between the two adds a
human touch to the otherwise strictly external portraits. Sometimes a detailed external portrait is introduced when the character is hardly even
secondary, but purely episodic. Such is the case of the doctor who appears
only once and for a very short time.

Innokentij Annenskij is surely correct in assuming that Goncharov lived
mainly in the sphere of "optical impressions." [2] Description is his forte,
and just as description predominates narration, so concreteness predominates abstraction, color sound, and typicality of character typicality of
speech. Goncharov's so-called artistic objectivism, the *sine ira et studio* he
was so proud of, is in fact nothing more than a sharply delineated predo-
minance in his writing of descriptive over musical elements.

Valid as this characterization of Goncharov's style may be, we must not
lose sight of the above-mentioned symbolic function fulfilled by super-
abundant detail. Just because the concrete predominates the abstract in
Goncharov, we must not neglect his important abstract philosophical message. Yet this is precisely what Goncharov scholarship has done.

To the abundance of detail one must add an abundance of similes as
among the novel's most important formal devices. Many similes are used

1) IV, pp. 482–483.
2) Cf. his article "Goncharov i ego Oblomov", Russkaja shkola, 1892, IV, pp. 71–95.

to make feelings or abstractions concrete. Thoughts, cares, and problems
are like birds, clouds, and stones; life is compared to a river, to a green
hilly field; intellect and will have sails; difficulties in life are a dense forest
with overgrown paths; fear and passion are like ice and fire. Such similes
may seem like literary formulae, colorless and unoriginal, but Goncharov
nearly always sprightens them up with a detail or two, thereby giving them
a new life and harmonizing them with the details used in concrete descriptions. Problems, for example, wake up one after the other and fly around
in anxious disorder like birds awakened by a sudden ray of the sun in a
slumbering ruin; the path of life becomes more and more overgrown; in the
transparent water of life Ol'ga sees every pebble, every undulation – and
then the pure depths. Goncharov never overdoes the concrete pictures in
his very frequent abstract similes, and achieves thereby a distinctly original
effect. Ol'ga compares her power over Oblomov to the role of a leading
star whose light will be shed over a stagnant lake and mirrored in it. After
describing the changes reflected in Ol'ga's face as she comes closer and
closer to understanding Oblomov's hints, Goncharov continues: "This is
how the sun, coming out from behind a cloud, gradually lights one bush,
then another, then the roof of a house, and suddenly floods the whole landscape with light." [1] Quite remarkable is the frequency with which he uses
animals – mostly domestic – for comparisons and surprising "concretiza-
tions." Germans crudely keep insisting on their old *Bürger* rights much as
a cow inevitably fails to hide its horns on time. For the most part, however,
animal similes serve to give a better idea of a character's appearance or behavior: Zakhar loves Oblomovka like a cat loves its attic, a horse its stable,
a dog its kennel. Agaf'ja Matveevna is compared by her brother both to a
cow and a horse. Goncharov apparently liked the simile because when Oblomov kisses her neck, he has her stand like a horse having its collar put on,
and he describes her love for Oblomov as a sweet yoke. Her brother, on the
other hand, sniffs the air in the market like a setter, and brings home the
best capon under his cloak. In these cases Goncharov gives us more than a
simile; he adorns it with a "homely detail" to make it "special." The guilt
ridden Oblomov follows Ol'ga quietly, "like a dog somebody has stamped
at and which walks with its tail between its legs." [2] Here, as in many

---

1) IV, p. 239.
2) *ibid.*, p. 272,...."Kak sobaka, na kotoruju topnuli" ...

similar cases, the colloquial folksy Russian is difficult to translate. Anis'ja's talking is likened to the sound of chopping splinters (in Russian: treshchala, kak budto luchinu shchepala). Not only the "homely" detail, but also the sound effect gets lost in translation. Some translators have omitted such spots completely.

The tendency toward the inconspicuous, the small, the cozy, explains the nearly complete absence of metaphors and the very restrained use of all figures of speech other than the simile. Goncharov's language is smooth and pure. What to do with "whiches" and "thats" in too close succession, a problem faced by Oblomov when writing his landlord, also seems to have concerned Goncharov. His style has much of Pushkin's purity and admittedly many of his idiosyncrasies, though there are cases where Gogol''s influence is more than clear. It becomes especially noticeable in passages dealing with detailed portrait painting of the characters and daydreams. In the last instance he uses Gogol''s pathos and sometimes even his rhythmicized prose.

The false fervor of the archaisms Oblomov uses (they drive Zakhar to tears) can only be construed as an ironical criticism of this kind of language (cf. also "Old-Time Servants"), and Zakhar's infrequent linguistic blunders (mozhedom for maiordomus) do little to delineate his character. The only conspicuous attempt to characterize a character by his speech patterns occurs in Agaf'ja Matveevna's references to her brother. She speaks of him in the third person plural *(oni)* a feature of petty bourgeois or servant speech indicating respect. Goncharov imitates this type of language in *his* narration partly for its comical effect and partly to show a modicum of ironical disrespect to the person in question (cf. "Her brother had gone in for Government contracts, but lost his money, and succeeded, by means of various stratagems and entreaties, in obtaining his old job of secretary 'in the office where they registered peasants'; once more he walked to his office and brought home half roubles, twenty- and twenty-five copeck pieces, to put them away in a secret box." [1]

---

1) IV, p. 499. "Bratec zanimalis' podrjadami, no razorilis' i postupili koe-kak, raznymi khitrostjami i poklonami, na prezhnee mesto sekretarja v kanceljarii, 'gde zapisy-vajut muzhikov,' i opjat' khodjat peshkom v dolzhnost' i prinosjat chetvertaki, poltinniki i dvugrivennye, napolnjaja imi daleko sprjatannyj sunduchok."

A remarkable feature of Goncharov's style (and one that connects him with the eighteenth century) is his use of extended aphorisms, most of which deal with human nature and human qualities in general. Ol'ga's behavior puzzles Oblomov, though he dismisses the idea almost as soon as it occurs to him, he does for a moment suspect her of guile. This is reason enough for Goncharov to insert a pithy characterization of cunning:

> "Cunning is like small coin with which one cannot buy much. Just as small coin can keep one going for an hour or two, so cunning may serve to conceal something, to deceive someone, to put a wrong construction on things, but does not enable one to see a far horizon, to connect the issues in the case of any big event. Cunning is short-sighted: it sees well only what is close at hand and is often caught in the trap it has set for others . . . . And cunning was like a mouse running round things and hiding." [1]

It is interesting that in such instances Goncharov also likes to introduce similes of the "homely" type as small coin or mice. Several aphorisms deal with the nature of love, happiness, and boredom. Here e.g. his aphorism on love, developed into a little disquisition: "Although love is said to be a capricious, unaccountable feeling that suddenly appears like an illness, it too, like everything else, has causes and laws of its own. And if these laws have been but little studied so far, this happened because a man stricken with love has no time to spare for watching with the eye of a scientist how an impression steals into his soul and casts a dreamlike spell over his senses, how first his eyes get blind, how and at which moment his pulse and then his heart begin to beat faster, how as if of yesterday suddenly a devotion unto the grave arises and a longing for self-sacrifice, how his own *ego* gradually disappears and passes into *him* or *her,* how his intellect grows either extraordinary dull or extremely subtle, how his will is surrendered to that of another, how his head bends, his knees tremble, how tears come, then fever . . . " [2]

It happens that such aphoristic disquisitions are put into the mind of a character. Oblomov for instance thinks about will: "One desired a thing

---

1) IV, p. 270.
2) *ibid.,* p. 392.

yesterday, today one got what has been passionately, desparately longed for, and the day after tomorrow one will be blushing for having desired it and then cursing life because the desire has been fulfilled — this is what comes of going along boldly and independently through life, of following one's own *will*. One must fumble one's way, shut one's eyes to many things, and not dream of happiness, not dare to repine at its slipping away — that is what life is!" [1]

The frequency of such philosophical digressions proves once more that Goncharov's *œuvre* has to be considered not only as an example of slow and detailed — so called realistic narrative —, but also as a philosophical and ethical system. This system is not being presented as outspokenly as by Dostoevskij or Tolstoj, but it is there and it is complete and consistent. That this consistency leads to a final question mark does not change the fact that all aspects of possible views on life are being artistically shown and pointedly discussed. The unusual, striking and artistically persuasive Oblomovian solution explains the deep impression this type left on world literature which can easily be compared to those of Don Quixote or Hamlet.

---

1) IV, p. 255.

First Retirement

Though working as a censor had advantages, it had become increasingly more trouble than it was worth. Perhaps Goncharov feared that the impetus, which had whisked him to the end of *Oblomov* would flag. He wished to take full advantage of his literary prowess while writing was still relatively effortless. At the end of May 1859 he obtained a long leave of absence (four months) and returned to Marienbad in the hope that a new wave of inspiration would help him complete or at least make some headway in his latest project, the novel *The Precipice*.

This hope remained unfulfilled. In fact, his disappointment at not being able to get down to work led to periods of deep depression. Here is how he described his mood in a desparate letter to Junija Efremova dated July 1st 1859: "Ask my oldest friends if I haven't lost all my spirit, if I can still look at anything or anybody with the vitality, sparkle, or whimsy I used to, if I smile or joke a lot? Ask and you'll say, 'Of course not.' You see, as a result of my age, my experience, as a result of ... I can't even list all the reasons, I've been overcome with a general apathy. That's the way I am; that's the way I'm constituted. I was alive, alert, feverish in my likes and dislikes, full of imagination, and then I cooled, ran down, lost my drive, put on weight, and felt nothing but boredom and indifference. This indifference doesn't apply specifically to you or anybody else; it's a general, all-pervading indifference ...

Try to find out where I went, with whom I was on friendly or affectionate terms and you'll see there was no one. I had literary friends, you say. Yes, I did. But that couldn't be helped. It was almost a service. Common interests bound us together. And even then we met mostly for dinner and would fly off in all directions afterwards. There were but few real feelings and very few attachments.

Time, illness, work, and various disappointments have done much to alter my character ... I no longer laugh, I have to force myself to make a joke ... instead of living, I doze through life, I'm bored, there's nothing else left. What sort of friendship or animation do you expect to find in a semicorpse?

You wish me health. Thank you. I don't know whether I'll reach the goal, whether I'll be cured. But when you wish that I find inspiration, you wish in vain. The wish will not come true. I have had no inspiration. I have not been in a mood for writing. But I stubbornly made up my mind to have a go at it and began. The results correspond to what I told you when I left: no one can outline and write a novel in six weeks; it's arrogant and ridiculous to think so. Maybe two or three years ago it would have been possible to lay a foundation or put the finishing touches on something outlined long ago and already in progress. Taking a good look at what I planned to write, I have come to the conclusion that it will take a good three years of solid work, under the condition of freedom, health and vibrant, unflagging strength. And I am glad, because now I no longer feel the onus of having to write: I've stopped work and breathed a sigh of freedom: where would I ever find three years of free time and vibrant strength? There's clearly no point in dreaming. And anyway I've been doing myself a lot of harm working so hard. I've been sitting so long I turned pale and tired myself out completely, and all because I set myself the silly, petty, bureaucratic task of writing at least one part — as if it were some sort of report. As a result I began to feel worse than before and renounced it, renounced it once and for all." [1]

On July 12th 1859 Goncharov left Marienbad for Bad Schwalbach, where he rejoined Vladimir and Ekaterina Majkov (all three had left Petersburg together). From Bad Schwalbach they made their way via Wiesbaden, Cologne, Brussels, and Paris (where they made a short stop) to Boulogne-sur-Mer. Goncharov hoped the baths there would counteract the consequences of his tendency to obesity: high blood pressure and rheumatic pains. But on September 20th he returned to Petersburg unsatisfied and unwell.

The desire to devote himself exclusively to his writing was not the only reason his censorship duties lay heavy on his hands. As the guidelines he worked by grew tighter, he had more trouble maintaining his own reasonably liberal outlook on the one hand, and satisfying both the government and his literary friends on the other.

Attacks from the left also became more vociferous. In the December issue of his journal *The Bell* (Kolokol) Herzen had assailed him in his frequently mean manner. His short notice "Unusual Story of the Censor Gon-

---

1) Utevskij, pp. 124–125.

Cha-Ro from She-Pan-Hu" combines critical remarks about Goncharov's travel sketches (for what he refers to as their flabby, drawn-out narrative style!) with the reproach that Goncharov had prepared himself for his censorship duties according to the Chino-Japanese school of mutilation in the "country that has uttered not a word since it dried up after the flood."[1] Among other unpleasant jeers and insinuations is a particularly venomous epigram by the minor poet Nikolaj Shcherbina, who clearly went out of his way to annoy Goncharov. What we know of Goncharov's reaction to Herzen and the others appears in a June 1859 letter from Marienbad to Andrej Kraevskij: "I know that no matter what I wrote, my position and duties would preclude all mercy," [2] he writes resignedly.

Elena Shtakenshnejder makes several references to the liberal's hate for Goncharov. [3] They saw in him a renegade from liberalism, and though he could easily have proven that he had never espoused the new and radically oriented views of writers like Saltykov-Shchedrin and was therefore in no way a renegade, it must have been painful for him to pass judgment on his colleagues. In a certain sense his position on the board of censorship made him a "superior," someone they had to watch themselves with. Finally this situation became unbearable.

Even though his work met with the full approval of his superiors (Evgraf Kovalevskij, the Minister of Culture at the time, wished to promote him to the post of the Special Chairman (osobyj predsedatel') of the Petersburg Board of Censors, but was refused authorization from above — another factor, perhaps, leading to Goncharov's decision to resign), Goncharov submitted his resignation papers on January 18, 1860. The reason he gave for his move was that the "chronic rheumatism in the temples and throughout the entire face" [4] necessitated an extended trip abroad.

The report of his immediate superior, Ivan Deljanov, to the Minister is unusually favorable and quite perceptive in its analysis of Goncharov's services: "The loss of Mr. Goncharov, one of its most enlightened and most beneficial members will certainly be deeply felt by the Saint Petersburg

---

1) Utevskij, pp. 102–103.
2) *ibid.*, pp. 103–104.
3) Shtakenshnejder, pp. 219–220.
4) Alekseev, p. 103.

Board of Censors. He possessed the rare skill of being able to establish
harmony between the demands of the Government and the present demands of society, thereby furthering literature — an invaluable virtue in
a censor — as well as freeing the Ministry of Education from the quarrels
and other annoyances the censorship so often meets with." [1] On February 1, 1860 Goncharov was released from his censorship duties.

The Quarrel with Turgenev

In the following month a clash that had been ripening for some time
reached its climax: the friendship between Goncharov and Turgenev suffered a setback from which it never really recovered. Goncharov was in the
habit of talking over with friends the ideas he had for his novels. He often
went into great detail and would read them extended excerpts aloud. He
was particularly open with such experienced and talented friends as Turgenev, who learned of both *Oblomov* and *The Artist* (Khudozhnik conceived
as already mentioned at the same time as *Oblomov* and later called *The Precipice) in statu nascendi*. When Turgenev's *Nest of Gentlefolk* appeared in
January 1859 and *On the Eve* in February 1860, Goncharov thought he
detected certain parallels between his friend's finished products and his own
oral descriptions of plans for a large number of details and episodic scenes
as well as certain characters and plot lines. As a result he felt he could not
write his novel in the form in which he had originally conceived it. Goncharov was all the more irritated because while ungrudgingly willing to recognize
Turgenev as a master of the short story, he refused to allow him any talent
whatsoever as a novelist. Now he had to witness that it was exactly in this
genre that Tugenev began to write and that his success was immense.

A long (166 page) chronicle of the vicissitudes of the Goncharov-Turge-
nev friendship-to-enmity relationship has come down to us in a little-known

---

1) Alekseev, p. 104.

manuscript by Goncharov himself entitled *An Uncommon Story (True Events)*. He composed it in December 1875 and January 1876 and supplemented it with several more sheets in July 1878.

The following note appears on the first page: "After my death those parts of this manuscript which are indispensable may be excerpted for publication, but *only in the case of extreme need* as indicated in a Note (at the end of the manuscript on sheet fifty), i.e. only if the opinion, the rumors and the lie that I here refute, should find their way into print. In case the need should not arise, I request that these sheets be set on fire (crossed out: January, 1876, I. Goncharov) or preserved in the Imperial Public Library as material for a future historian of Russian literature, July 1878, I. Goncharov." [1]

In May 1883 he entrusted the manuscript to his faithful friend Sof'ja Nikitenko. The Russian Public Library in Petrograd acquired them in 1920 (it is not clear from whom) and in 1924 published them in its own series in two thousand copies.

There can be no doubt that Goncharov wrote his *Uncommon Story* in a disturbed, almost pathological state. The evidence for his accusations is extremely feeble, but his representation of biographical background, leading to the accusations is — as far as we can judge at present — quite sound.

Goncharov reports having first made Turgenev's acquaintance at the critic Belinskij's in 1847. The meeting must have taken place during the early part of the year because in early February Turgenev went abroad, not returning until June 1850. Goncharov's first impression of Turgenev was unfavorable. He describes him as a cheap poseur, a dandy, who, although he "cut a fine figure," had ugly features and an unpleasant squeaky voice.

So a genuine personal relationship between the two writers could have developed only during the short period between Turgenev's return from abroad and Goncharov's departure for his journey on the frigate "Pallada" in October 1852.

---

1) N. I., pp. 176–177.

It was at this time already that Goncharov disclosed to Turgenev, whom he describes as "a very astute critic" [1] the overall plan and also many details of his *Oblomov.*

After Goncharov's return in February 1855, their friendship seems to have taken up where it left off. This is the period that saw most of the conversations between the two novelists about Goncharov's literary projects. Their private discussions were supplemented by readings from both novels in progress. Goncharov writes with obvious pleasure about the literary circle he found in Petersburg. Beside Turgenev the critics Annenkov and Vasilij Botkin, Nekrasov and Panaev (editors of the periodical *The Contemporary*) were its members. Goncharov recalls dimly having seen there also Lev Tolstoj and his distant relative the poet Aleksej K. Tolstoj. "We talked a lot, argued about literature, had noisy, merry dinners — in short, we enjoyed ourselves immensely." [2]

According to his *Uncommon Story* Goncharov began to notice as early as 1855 that Turgenev seemed extraordinarily attentive to whatever he said and that he took special interest in all his ideas and opinions. Flattered by Turgenev's attention, he unveiled to him the complete outline for *The Precipice,* all its episodes with all their particulars, all details, "everything, absolutely everything." [3] Turgenev's reaction to the scene between Vera and her great aunt, claims Goncharov, was: "Why, this is worthy of a Goethe novel." [4] Goncharov's remarks in this connection about the original plan for *The Precipice* are quite interesting. [5]

When Turgenev returned to Petersburg from his estate Spasskoe in the fall of 1858, he brought *A Nest of Gentlefolk* with him. He soon arranged a dinner after which the novel was read aloud (by Annenkov, because Turgenev was suffering from bronchitis). Goncharov, as he tells it, was not invited. Nor did he attend the dinner. He did make an appearance just after it though, — much to Turgenev's surprise and confusion, if we are to believe Goncharov. "And what did I hear? That which in the

---

1) N. I., p. 12.
2) *ibid.,* p. 14.
3) *ibid.,* p. 15.
4) *ibid.*
5) Cf. p. 270.

course of three years I had been telling Turgenev: namely, a compact, but quite complete outline of *The Precipice* (or *The Artist*, as the novel was referred to in the drafts)." [1]

The examples Goncharov adduces to prove his point are quite unconvincing. Clearly his temper had taken the upper hand. He told Turgenev point blank that what he had just heard was nothing but a recasting of his novel, whereupon Turgenev, — according to Goncharov — turned chalk white and offered to throw his work into the fire. " 'No, don't bother,' I said to him, 'I gave this to you. I can still make something else. I've got plenty!' That was how it ended. I left." [2]

From that evening on, Goncharov tells us, relations between him and Turgenev were strained. And in fact, whenever they happened to meet, Goncharov would hint at "loans." Turgenev would defend himself as best he could, but did admit there were certain similarities. He even cut an entire scene (a conversation between the heroine Liza and old Marfa Timofeevna) that Goncharov considered an imitation of the changed, but still later famous scene between Vera and her great aunt. It is not clear, however, whether he decided to omit it because Goncharov's arguments convinced him or merely because they were getting on his nerves. Turgenev gave Goncharov a letter, in which he listed everything Goncharov had told him. The purpose of this letter was to give Goncharov a firm hold over Turgenev. Although it has apparently been lost, it did exist; Goncharov refers to it in a letter to Turgenev dated March 27, 1860.

A convincing account of the background behind the quarrel is given in B.M. Èngel'gardt's fine book, [3] which makes Goncharov's difficult position after the sea voyage amply clear. On the one hand Goncharov needed to return to the Service to earn his keep (a problem that was solved by his stimulating, though somewhat grinding duties as a censor), and on the other he dreamed of pursuing a completely different career, a creative career, one for which he felt a natural penchant. Enter Turgenev, who not only devoted all his time and energies to writing, but had begun to

---

1) N.I., p. 20.
2) *ibid.*, p. 22.
3) Cf. Bibliographical Remarks, No. 4.

encroach upon a genre that Goncharov had singled out as his own. And if that were not enough, Turgenev's works fairly flowed from his pen, while Goncharov's as he stressed over and over were preceded by a long and agonized struggle. During that period Turgenev published one novella after another as well as three full novels, all Goncharov had to show for himself was his travel notes, which did not enjoy the success they deserved and *Oblomov,* which earned its reputation only gradually.

The great immediate — and lasting — success accorded to *A Nest of Gentlefolk,* paralleling as it did *Oblomov*'s more hesitant recognition, once again let loose Goncharov's wrath. In fact, he had not yet gotten over his annoyance at hearing the novel read at Turgenev's house.

On March 28, 1859, just after Turgenev left Petersburg for his estate, Goncharov wrote him a biting letter accusing him of plagiarism, ambition and an overassessment of his talent and skill. He praises the *Notes of a Sportsman,* but critisizes *A Nest of Gentlefolk,* and expresses reservations about Turgenev's conception of the heroine in the plan for his new novel, the future *On the Eve.* He also informs him that he has made significant changes in the novel he once outlined for him (probably in the winter of 1855-1856), obviously giving Turgenev to understand that he was working on something Turgenev knew nothing about. Just before concluding he makes reference to the passage Turgenev excluded from *A Nest of Gentlefolk* ("to avoid a certain similarity") and finally ends with the touching confession that he is praying for a day or two of inspiration and was waiting anxiously for it to arrive. [1]

Turgenev's reply, dated April 7, 1859, was perhaps a bit too conciliatory; he takes note of Goncharov's accusation of plagiarism without trying to refute it and concedes that Goncharov's criticism of his work is fully justified. But at the same time he asks what Goncharov wants him to do? To repeat the *Notes of a Sportsman ad infinitum?* And if his novels are nothing more than an aggregation of sketches, what should he do about it? People who "need the novel in the epic sense of the word," he adds, do not need him. He concludes with a general observation on the

---

1) Cf. VIII, pp. 305-311.

transitory quality of human existence and the resulting futility of all such quarrels. [1]

For a time Goncharov's mind was at rest. After Turgenev returned to Petersburg at the end of April, they saw one another now and then, and Goncharov attended Turgenev's farewell dinner when the latter went abroad again. In a letter to Annenkov he describes how "we feted Turgenev, that amiable, universal deceiver and everybody's darling. By now he's most likely forgotten all his Petersburg friends . . . . and is charming his friends over there, whom he surely convinced as soon as they saw him that he'd never given a thought to anyone else. Such is the power of his mild but magic winsome character." [2]

Engel'gardt is right in citing these "good-natured grumblings" [3] as evidence of Goncharov's feelings about Turgenev in times of psychic equilibrium.

The equilibrium did not last long. In February 1860 Goncharov read an excerpt from *The Precipice*, "Sof'ja Nikolaevna Belovodova," at a fundraising program for the Literary Foundation. Applause was moderate, in spite of Goncharov's good way of reading [4]; the resounding success of Turgenev's "Hamlet and Don Quichote," presented the previous month before the same audience, was still fresh in everyone's mind. When Goncharov published the excerpt in the February issue of *The Contemporary*, Turgenev's *On the Eve* came out at the same time in *The Russian Messenger* (Russkij Vestnik), and Goncharov's sketch went almost unnoticed.

Turgenev had talked over his plans for the novel with Goncharov, and once again Goncharov thought h e saw a continuation of the line that had set him against *A Nest of Gentlefolk*, the Vera theme. Although Turgenev again made some changes, Goncharov came to the conclusion that Turgenev fully intended to make use of all his situations and ideas, he accused him of slyly adopting them all *before* his own novel could be completed. In this way, he claimed, whatever he – Goncharov –

---

1) VIII, p. 537.
2) *ibid.*, p. 322.
3) Engel'gardt, p. 23.
4) Cf. Vosp. Sovr., pp. 75–77; reminiscences of Longin Panteleev.

might produce would then seem to be an imitation of Turgenev, not the other way around.

Turgenev's supposed intrigue made Goncharov furious. On March 3, 1860, after reading "about the first forty pages" of *On the Eve,* he wrote Turgenev a letter full of veiled, but unmistakeable attacks. The "first forty pages" deal among others with the painter and sculptor Shubin, whom Goncharov immediately identified with his Rajskij. Towards the end of the letter he notes that he has finally come to know and appreciate Turgenev as a writer and as a man. "There is one noble trait I admire in you as a human being: the affable, indulgent, undivided attention with which you listen to the works of others and with which you, by the way, listened to and extolled my insignificant excerpt, an excerpt still from the same novel whose plot I told you long ago, when it was still in outline." In a postscript he asks Turgenev to send him back his handkerchief: "Excuse me for reminding you. You're so absentminded and forgetful." [1]

Even after Goncharov began talking quite openly about how Turgenev had illegally appropriated material from his novels, Turgenev refused to react. Then one day Goncharov met the critic Stepan Dudyshkin on the street, and when Dudyshkin happened to mention he was on his way to Turgenev's house for dinner, Goncharov remarked: "You'll be eating off my money," hinting at Turgenev's *On the Eve* honorarium. "Shall I tell him so?" asked Dudyshkin. "Go right ahead," replied Goncharov. – And the "message" was really relayed. [2]

It resulted in a letter from Turgenev to Goncharov labeling all his charges as defamatory, demanding the matter to be placed before an impartial jury, and, in case Goncharov refused to comply — threatening him with a duel.

The "court of honor" met in Goncharov's apartment on March 26, 1860. Its jury consisted of Druzhinin, Dudyshkin, Annenkov and Nikitenko. Nikitenko has left behind an apparently very objective account of the proceedings in his diary:

---

1) VIII, p. 327.
2) N. I. p. 28.

"Today at one in the afternoon the celebrated explanation took place. Turgenev was visibly agitated, but set forth the course of the affair very plainly, simply and without the least show of indignation though not without chagrin. Goncharov's response was somewhat hazy and not satisfactory. The passages he cited from *On the Eve* and his own outline, did little to substantiate his claims. Victory, therefore, clearly favored Turgenev and it became obvious that Goncharov had been carried away, as he himself put it, by his alarmist character and had exaggerated the situation. Then Turgenev announced that all friendly relations between him and Mr. Goncharov were from that-time forth at an end, and took his leave. The essential bone of contention, which we all were afraid of, consisted in the words Goncharov had transmitted through Dudyshkin. But when Goncharov himself declared that they were nonsensical, uttered without any ulterior motive, and not at all meant as they might be construed, that they were supposed to be a joke which, by his own admission, was quite coarse and indelicate, and Dudyshkin affirmed that he had not been authorized by Goncharov to transmit them to Turgenev, we solemnly pronounced the word out of existence, thereby removing the main *casus belli*. All in all I must confess that my friend Ivan Aleksandrovich played a not very envious role in this affair. He showed himself to be an irritable, extremely unreliable and churlish person, while Turgenev, — especially during this explanation, which could only have been painful for him —, behaved with great dignity, tact, elegance and with that special grace characteristic of honorable members of well-educated society." [1]

Another account is to be found in Annenkov's " 'My Six-Years Correspondence with Turgenev. Literary Reminiscences." [2] Here Turgenev's final words appear as follows: "My business with you is now ended, Ivan Aleksandrovich, but allow me to add one last word. From this moment our friendly relations are ended. What has occured between us has given me a clear indication of the dangerous consequences that can follow from a friendly exchange of ideas, from simple, trusting bonds. I remain an admirer of your talent and I will most likely have occasion to delight in it

---

1) Nikitenko, II, pp. 114–116.
2) Shest' let perepiski s Turgenevym. Literaturnye vospominanija. St. Petersburg, 1909, p. 521; cf. Utevskij, p. 133.

along with many others, but from this day onward, there can be no thought of our former heartfelt benevolence or complete frankness.' — And nodding good-by to all, he left the room, thereby bringing our meeting to a close."

Goncharov's own version largely agrees with Nikitenko's in the externals, but is of course strongly prejudiced against Turgenev. Juridically he was unable to prove anything of course, and so Turgenev, who was obviously extremely uneasy at first, left triumphantly. [1]

In the course of the discussion it came to light that Goncharov had never read the whole of *On the Eve*. He promised to do so, and here is his reaction: "Afterwards I glanced through *On the Eve*: Lo and behold! There were indeed few similarities! But I did not recognize it in the printed version. It wasn't at all the story he told me! The motif has remained the same, but a number of details have disappeared. The entire milieu is new, the hero some Bulgarian or other. It's the same story and yet it isn't. While he told it to me, he must have been, you might say, testing to see if I recognized it as a sequel to Vera and Volokhov. And when he saw I had figured him out, he changed it around before it got into print. He's always been a genius at that sort of thing. He's kept it up too, making all his borrowings from me according to this system (as we will see later) distorting the milieu, that is, the place of action and the characters' professions (but retaining the character I gave them), names, nationality etc." [2]

For several years Turgenev and Goncharov did not see one another nor even greeted one another when they chanced to meet.

The Goncharov–Turgenev affair did not go unnoticed. In 1860 the journal *The Spark* (Iskra) published an amusing poem by Dmitrij D. Minaev entitled "A Parnassian Verdict." Goncharov, stylized as a droopy, lazy mortal with lackluster eyes and immobile like Oblomov, appears before the gods as plaintiff to demand punishment for a colleague, who stole the plot and outline of his novel. Even though the examples he adduces in his favor sound absurd ("his characters, walk, drink, chatter,

1) Cf. N. I., pp. 29–31.
2) N. I., p. 31.

sleep, and love the way mine do") the decision of Apollo and the gods is
not unequivocal. The thief of creative property is sentenced to playing the
walk-on role of one of the merchants in Gogol's *Inspector General*. And
Goncharov is sent on a trip around the world to allow him to write a better work than the one he had originally planned. Turgenev did actually play
the "appointed" role — at a charity performance on April 14, 1860. Rumor
has it, though it has never been proven, that Goncharov took part in the
same performance in a similar role. Strangely enough Goncharov was not
at all irritated by the poem. In a letter to Sof'ja Nikitenko from Marienbad
dated June 26, 1860 he shows himself very amused by it and finds everything said about him very close to truth, especially the "lackluster eyes."
"Our affair is funny, it reached the public and laughter should be general." [1]
But one of the following letters shows already how deeply the sting had
entered: "No, Sof'ja Aleksandrovna, he did not take just a *little grain* from
me; he took the best spots, the pearls and played them on his lyre; if he
had taken the plot, this would not have been as bad, but he took the details,
sparks of poetry, e.g. the shoots of new life on the ruins of the old one, the
history of the ancestors, the location of the garden, traits of my old lady —
one cannot help but be incensed. And in addition to this he staged a
comedy, a show, a duel, knowing very well that nothing could be proved,
he called witnesses. All this troubles my soul, brings in a deep hypochondria, and adds coldness towards life and towards men — and one does not
want to see, to know, to hear them, one does not want to be involved in
anything; a moral paralysis interferes with living and action." [2]

No doubt Goncharov exaggerated Turgenev's "guilt," but it is hard
to maintain that so far Turgenev was completely innocent. Consciously
or unconsciously he used some of Goncharov's narratives. This feeling
apparently tinged the halfhearted verdict of "Apollo" and the cautious
resolution of the "Court of Honor" as reported by Annenkov: "Whereas
the works of Turgenev and Goncharov came into being on the same Russian soil, they had to have for this reason some similar situations, had to
coincide accidentally in some ideas and expressions, which justifies and
excuses both sides." [3]

---

1) Utevskij, p. 135.
2) VIII, p. 344.
3) Utevskij, p. 133.

Certainly in the following years Goncharov's suspicions developed into a persecution mania, but the *beginning* of his illness does not lack all foundation.

————— · —————

As a retired Civil Service Officer Goncharov received quite a decent pension and was therefore able, to take a trip abroad — to recover from the excitements of the previous months. In the beginning of May 1860 he took the boat bound for Stettin at Kronstadt with the Nikitenko family and went to Marienbad via Berlin and Dresden, where he stopped for two weeks. He obviously chose Marienbad in the persistent hope of repeating the creative upsurge that had brought *Oblomov* to completion three years before.

At first it seemed as if this dream were coming true. He wrote to Sof'ja Nikitenko, who was obviously still encouraging his work (or in Goncharov's words, who had pricked his conscience with more than one sharp needle), that he felt young, alive, even chipper and that his spirits would be turned to profit on the novel.

But these high spirits proved quite ephemeral. His next letters — addressed in part to Sof'ja and in part to her father — overflow with complaints of boredom, poor health, weakness, abulia, and general depression. He had failed to get the novel off the ground: both the hero and his entourage did not take a clear shape in his mind. [1]

After a month of fruitless effort he gave up and moved on to Boulogne-sur-Mer. Once there, he began seeking company in order to avoid setting to work. He spent a lot of time with Jakov Grot and with his friends Aleksandr Nikitenko and his wife, who arrived afterwards induced by his urgent recommendations of Boulogne.

Though he writes to their daughter Sof'ja (who had stayed on in Dresden) that creative work requires plenty of time for contemplation he also adds: "I will not conceal to you the despair that sometimes overcomes

—————————————

[1] Goncharov's letters to Sof'ja Nikitenko of 1860 were printed in "Literaturnyj Arkhiv" 4, 1953, pp. 110–162 and are among the most valuable documents characteristic for Goncharov's state of mind. Cf. about her *ibid.*, pp. 108–109.

me when I think that I may never come up with a hero and that I've taken
a task upon myself which is too much for me. It makes me want to drop
everything and let the world pass me by ... " [1]

In another gloomy letter he writes: "I ought to be planning my trip
home. Home! It makes my heart sink to think I've got to go back home,
where there's no one waiting for me, no one whom I need, and certainly
no one who needs me. But just the same I've got to. Why? Because of
hateful money. Without money there's no life, no nature, no happiness,
no poetry! All that comes of life without money is poverty and vice or
the sort of lofty inhuman virtue that makes a shiver run up and down
your spine. People endowed with this virtue live on nothing, go off to
the desert, stop eating and drinking, sleep on rocks etc. etc. and lead a
life that has completely gone out of fashion nowadays." [2]

On August 23, 1860 Goncharov left Boulogne for Dresden, where he
spent some time in the pleasant company of Nikitenko's two daughters
and his ten-year-old son developing a delightful relationship with the latter. Goncharov's love for children is a permanent feature of his character.
Soon the Nikitenko's joined them, and Goncharov read a chapter from
The Precipice he had just completed on the spot. In his diary Nikitenko
notes that Goncharov enjoyed the role of "master of ceremonies" and
guide around unknown cities. He also writes of his passion for acquiring
"useless" souvenirs (a passion which we know from his great journey). [3]

Goncharov returned to Petersburg via Warsaw in the end of September; extremely amusing letters to Nikitenko and to Ivan L'khovskij [4] narrate about his unpleasant adventures during the travel.

He continued to work on *The Precipice,* but progress was painfully
slow, with the result that he received no creative satisfaction from it.
On December 12, 1860 he was elected a correspondent member of the
Academy of Sciences, a great and no doubt flattering honor, even if Turgenev was elected on the same ballot. Turgenev's name comes up now
and then in Goncharov's letters of the period, and always accompanied
by some malicious comment or other.

1) VIII, p. 346.
2) Utevskij, pp. 143–144.
3) Nikitenko, II. p. 150.
4) Literaturnyj Arckhiv, 3, 1951, pp. 162–164.

A certain amount of diversion during this period was provided by his
nephew Viktor Kirmalov, who lived and worked in Petersburg. Kirmalov
was the son of his sister Aleksandra, whose husband had been murdered
by his serfs in July 1850. Oddly enough, we have no record of Goncharov's reaction to this event.

Goncharov followed Viktor's development during his career as a student with great interest, and when he fell in love with a poor girl completely lacking in connections and influential relatives, whom his own
meager income could barely support, Uncle Ivan, — backed by his sister,
who had refused the couple her blessing —, did all he could to dissuade
him from the marriage. He gives a humorous report of the affair in a
letter to his younger sister Anna Muzalevskaja: "Can you imagine, Madame, the thunderbolts I have hurled down on that crazed head of his for
the past two years, with what lightening flashes of experience and eloquence I girded him, what a case against wretched poverty I built up. At
first he was secretive and wouldn't say anything, but then he told me in
no uncertain terms that I should not spend my energies in vain, that such
is his fate, that he, she and even I would all die if the marriage did not
take place, that he felt his health failing etc. etc., that he would work,
that he would live with the utmost frugality, but that he would wed.
Finally I gave up and told him to do whatever he liked . . . ." [1]

All the same his nephew's firm resolve impressed him. In fact, it caused him to reverse his opinion and, convinced that Viktor's love was
genuine, to intercede for him with his mother (in which he was successful).

But freedom from all responsibilities does not seem to have agreed with
Goncharov. In a letter to Aleksandra he writes: "Everything, everywhere
bores me, and I don't know what to do with myself." [2]

One day Viktor gave his uncle a small mongrel he had bought from
street urchins. Mimishka, for such was the dog's name, became a source
of constant joy for Goncharov, and the two were soon inseparable — even
when Goncharov went out for visits. While maintaining an ironic stance

---

1) Vestnik Evropy, 1908, XII, p. 424.
2) ibid., p. 422.

vis-à-vis his affection for the animal, he nonetheless bought him a golden velvet collar. When Viktor wrote him in 1863 about his concern over his wife's illness, Goncharov answered that he could understand the problem very well. "Why, the day Mimishka falls seriously ill, I don't believe the newspaper will come out, and were she to die I would sell everything and move abroad." [1] Mimishka did not die until 1872. A day after this event Goncharov wrote a tragicomic letter to his publisher Mikhail Stasjulevich. It begins with the words "Yesterday, the seventeenth of February, at a quarter past seven in the evening, my wonderful, dearly beloved and loving friend, Mikha Trezorovna, passed away after short but severe suffering." [2] It ends, however, with the explanation that for this reason his proof-reading will take much more time (he was reading proof on "A Million Torments" at this time) and that he would need a second set of proof sheets. He was clearly out to tease the ever impatient Stasjulevich.

Another trip abroad from the end of May until mid-September 1861, taking him again to Dresden, Marienbad (where he spent one month), Switzerland, Boulogne, Paris and Berlin, was artistically as unproductive as the preceding one.

After his return he confessed to Anna: "When I ask myself why I went on the trip and why I returned, I find I have no answer. I have neither official nor literary duties any more. I just sit around and do nothing" (darom nebo kopchu)." [3]

Goncharov's unflaggingly high opinion of the works of Aleksandr Ostrovskij finds expression in a short report dealing with Ostrovskij's best known work, *The Thunderstorm,* — the only output of this year we know of. The purpose of the report was to recommend the play for a literary prize funded by Count Uvarov. It praises the play's structure, its dynamic dramatism, and its characters, as well as Ostrovskij's gift for accurate perception and for turning that perception into art.

---

1) Vestnik Evropy, 1908, XII, p. 432.
2) Stasjulevich, IV, p. 114. Goncharov uses here an invented form of the dog's name, which sounds half solemn, half funny, implying that the father of the deceased Mimishka was some Trezor — a frequent dog's name in Russia.
3) Vestnik Evropy, 1908, XII, p. 423.

Even at this early date Goncharov pays great attention to the theme of how a woman "falls" (both heroines "fall," he points out, yet their reactions show them to be different types of women), a theme he explored extensively in *The Precipice*. He singles out the "rich widow" Kabanova as the incarnation of blind tradition-transmitted despotism, of the concept of duty deprived of all humanity, and lavishes special praise on the dialogue, whose language he pronounces as true reality as the characters that speak it. He also brings up his pet theory of art as reality filtered through the artistic consciousness and talent of the artist.

Even supervising the new edition of *A Common Story, Oblomov,* and *The Frigate Pallada* afforded him little gratification; he detested reading proofs. "Don't scold me for not coming to see you," he wrote Panaev. "I'm constantly fussing with the proofs. At the moment I'm reading *Pallada*. What punishment!" [1)]

So it was that in mid-May 1862 he paid the visit to his brother and sisters he had put off the year before. He stayed until about July 12th.

He spent an enjoyable time with his relatives in Simbirsk, but there too his work barely inched along. His sister Anna, who was married to a popular and apparently excellent doctor, was proud of her famous brother and did everything in her power to make Goncharov's stay pleasant. She gave him the best room in the house and exclusive rights over the garden, so he could work undisturbed in the bower. His strict order forbidding her to force new acquaintances on him or even allow guests in to see him were a disappointment to her, but fortunately the sting of his anchoritic ways was diminished by the fact that during the summer there were but few landowners in town. The following letter to A. Nikitenko gives an idea of Goncharov's ups and downs during his Simbirsk visit: "I have been blossoming here on the banks of the Volga for more than a month now, most revered friend Aleksandr Vasil'evich. I am living with my relatives, who have gathered around me in a tight family circle in a little house crammed full as a hive with various and sundry inhabitants. I am comfortable, at ease, content and tranquilly — bored. This tranquil boredom and the soul's sound sleep, are sometimes

---

1) Alekseev, p. 119.

awakened by the wild, frantic wails, moaning, and grinding of teeth that
comes to me from the ruins of the fires. How horrible, what scandalous
practices! I'd like to find out exactly what went on, the truth, who did
it, what and how? But that's impossible here: the newspapers are full
of hints that they leave hanging up in the air and the rumors have reached such wild proportions that you can't believe anything.

Here, just as everywhere else, I am doing nothing: this, it seems, is
my main calling. With difficulty I have guessed it. And I do nothing as
much owing to this very calling as because of circumstances. The little
house in which I live is so small that a word spoken in one corner is
heard in the other. And now it is necessary for me to renew certain
maritime customs like falling asleep sometimes, for example, if not to
the noise of a storm then to the thunder of the William Tell Overture
being played by my nieces. Or else my nephews, of which I have many,
will come running, will make a lot of noise, will shout, and I will end
up being noisy myself, or I will go out with them to the Volga or into
the fields. Once and for all now I have decided that my ability to write
is irretrievably gone and that for me the time of heavy service labor has
come, if only with your or someone else's help I could find an opportunity to join up somehow. But if they won't have me anywhere, if no
one of those important friends, who are so affectionate with me as long
as I don't ask them for anything, supports me, then it will be necessary
to condemn myself to extinction, oh — perhaps even a prolonged one
in some crack in the wall somewhere —, . . . and then farewell Marienbad, Dresden, Boulogne: independent destitution will be my lot.

'Write!' some say hypocritically, as do others who cannot distinguish
bureaucratic writing from literary writing. 'Write!' they reiterate, when
it is impossible to write, when one is on the edge of storms and fires,
from which art timidly hides itself, when it is necessary to write in dirty
manner or else not write at all. 'Write!' they repeat when everything
has become loathsome: when tears fill your soul, when you feel you
have outlived your years of writing just as you have outlived the years
of passions and have withered away. It is impossible to write and I
won't even begin, or perhaps only if it will be necessary to write a
report or a memo. It is amusing to listen when they fancy that laziness

can detain one from creative work. No, not laziness, but a million other psychological, physiological or simply logical reasons." [1]

Goncharov, we see it again in this letter, had a gift of getting along with children and seems to have loved them very much. The fires he refers to are the famous St. Petersburg fires (set, apparently, by nihilist groups) that raged throughout the city during the last two weeks of May 1862.

Goncharov's somewhat exaggerated anxiety over the "destitution" facing him brought forth an immediate reaction from Nikitenko. Nikitenko had just resigned as editor-in-chief of the Ministry of the Interior's official newspaper *The Post of the North* (Severnaja pochta) (which had begun to come out in January of the same year), as a result of a series of disagreements with Petr Valuev, then the Minister of the Interior, and had recommended Goncharov as his successor. A telegram to Simbirsk describing this unexpected opportunity brought Goncharov back to the capital in a flash.

At his interview with the Minister Goncharov made the best of impressions. "Goncharov came to see me yesterday," wrote Valuev to his Deputy Minister A. Trojnickij. "I must confess that I liked him again a great deal. He is a highly cultured man (v nem est' èstetika). One can talk with him often, and that 'often' is essential for relations with an editor-in-chief. He wants to be editor-in-chief. His name will attract more than one subscriber and give proof that the journal is on its way up rather than down. Apparently he bears a grudge against certain writers. That too may prove useful." [2]

---

1) Utevskij, pp. 150–151.
2) Alekseev, p. 123.

Editor-in-Chief

And so by late September 1862 Goncharov was back in the Civil Service — this time with the Ministry of the Interior. From October 1862 until June 1863 he edited the *Post of the North,* yet he could scarcely find the work satisfying. *The Post of the North* was conceived as a paper, which had to expound and explicate the views of the government with respect to internal affairs. In addition to this it contained excerpts from the Russian press as a whole (but only those that coincided with the government's point of view) and official directives and circulars of various sorts.

In the following passage from a letter to his nephew's wife Dar'ja Kirmalova he describes his situation at this juncture: "What can I say? I'd say that I'm bored and that it's time to give up the ghost, but I have not a second to think about such things. Work takes up all my energies. Which has its good side: it keeps me from noticing time and life passing by. My indifference to everything makes me so diligent that the day before yesterday the Minister told how surprised he was to find me so hardworking. Taking me for Oblomov, he had expected anything but work from me. Yet I had told him long before not to expect anything but hard work, and so far I have kept my word. I never go anywhere and apart from *The Post of the North,* — in which there is nothing to read as you see, — I never read anything. It's not necessary to read it, it's not a paper that's meant to be read; its purpose is to publicize official news and statistics." [1] And to his nephew a few months later he writes in the same vein: "I am very busy, but on the other hand I am not bored." [2]

Work on *The Post of the North* proved more than strenuous, however, it also involved a fair share of danger, as evidenced by the following passage from Nikitenko's diary: "In point of fact, the lot of the editor-in-chief of an official newspaper is not far removed from that of a forced laborer. He is responsible for every letter, every comma that is put in or omitted. Until an issue appears he is uneasy. And once it does appear, he is even

---

1) Utevskij, p. 155.
2) Vestnik Evropy, 1908, XII, p. 432.

more uneasy. In the first instance he worries about whether some error
has been made, in the second, the error has already been made, and
there's no way of setting it right." [1]

This type of work was bound to sour on Goncharov in the long run,
and the continual political ferment, — student unrest and the Polish Uprising especially, — made news coverage and the choice of what to print
more and more difficult. According to a report he made to the Minister,
Goncharov favored "greater freedom to speak openly about out internal,
social and domestic affairs," [2] a standpoint finding less and less sympathy
in the eyes of Valuev. And so Goncharov resigned his post, — while remaining on good terms with the Minister, — and took on a new one,
equally as responsible, but less dangerous.

Censorship on a Higher Level

In March 1862 the Board of Censors was transferred from the juris-
diction of the Ministry of Culture to that of the Ministry of the Interior,
a move most probably made to remove the Ministry of Culture from an
ambiguous position; on the one hand it aimed at promoting intellectual
activities and on the other, in the form of police (because such was the
power the Board of Censors doubtless disposed of), at controlling them.
In July 1863 Goncharov was named a member of this newly created
"Ministry of the Interior Board for Publication Affairs," as it was called.
At the same time he was promoted to Actual Councillor of State, a rank
corresponding in military service to that of a general.

Part of his duty consisted in keeping track of a number of periodicals,
including the well-known and highly restless journal *The Contemporary*
(Sovremennik), edited by Nekrasov, and Ivan Aksakov's Slavophile newspaper *The Day* (Den').

In September 1865 after only two and a half years of operations the
Ministry of the Interior Board for Publication Affairs was disbanded to

1) Nikitenko, II, p. 89.
2) Alekseev, p. 125.

form a Central Government Board for Publication Affairs. One of the consequences of this development was the abolition of precensorship for all periodicals; newspapers and journals were no longer prohibited to appear, but were still subject to review after publication. If they failed to comply with the Board's instructions, they could, after two warnings, be either temporarily or permanently banned without even a detailed statement on the part of the Ministry. This move put the press under the autocratic supervision of the Ministry of the Interior and the members of the Central Government Board in a difficult position. Under pressure on the one hand to satisfy the minister, they also had to take care not to raise the ire of liberal public opinion.

As far as may be observed, Goncharov acquitted himself admirably of his new responsibilities, though of course the impossibility of being absolutely just absolutely all the time led him to tack now and then in his basic principles, those of an enlightened conservative or conservative with liberal tendencies. His attitude toward the status of Poland jibed unmistakably with the official government position. In many other issues, however, he took a stand based on pure common sense, a practice that got him into trouble with both sides.

Goncharov showed a clear tendency to go easy on less important writings so as to avoid creating a tempest in a teapot. Such cases were in the majority, of course. But when he felt something was at stake, he could make his objections amply clear. In the case of "The New Type," an article by Dmitrij Pisarev, an influential radical of the left with marked materialistic views, he made no bones about saying what he thought: "an amazing example of the utter misuse of talent and intelligence." [1] And it was with Goncharov's full approval that *The Russian Word* (Russkoe Slovo) — the journal, which printed the article — and the radical *Contemporary* were closed down in 1866.

Yet Goncharov considered sometimes even Pisarev unworthy of suppression. Here is his opinion of the third volume of Pisarev's essays: "Sophisms, paradoxes, and vainglorious pretension are the distinctive, self-evident traits of Pisarev's works in general and this book in particular.

---

1) Alekseev, p. 151.

And so I would guess that it will destroy none of the reigning principles of aesthetic criticism even in the eyes of the younger generation and can be left untouched." [1]

What with the enormous number of newspapers, journals, and books that fell to Goncharov's prudent perusal, it is understandable that he was loath to go to battle too often. But some of his friends felt he was carrying his pacifist penchant a bit too far. This is the point Nikitenko is driving at in the following insightful excerpt from his diary: *"The Contemporary* carried an article, by (M.A.) Antonovich, I think, entitled 'Food and its Significance' that openly propagated materialism, arguing that first and foremost man needs to eat. It goes on to speak of work and how compensation is incommensurate with work done and draws finally communistic and socialistic conclusions. If the article were only a popularization or the statement of the rudiments of a science, I wouldn't say a word against it no matter how delicate the issues it brought up. But it is nothing more and nothing less than a proclamation aimed at people with few brains and less knowledge to the effect that man lives and thinks and does absolutely everything by his belly alone and that the principles and aspirations of the belly must guide us in recasting the social order. The first censor to look over the article was I.A. Goncharov, who, as a result of his habit of straddling the fence, (playing up to a certain literary party for fear of being berated by them in their journals, while holding onto a job that supplies him with four thousand rubles a year), wrote a wishy-washy review of the article, but one that leaned toward the literary party. He also used a ruse which, though not particularly clever or shrewd, was clearly conceived with the clever intent of avoiding pronouncing the final sentence: he requested the Board to assign another of its members to read the article. It was I the Board charged with this responsibility. Since I refuse to recognize all literary parties and have no fear of them and since I would never play up to governmental authorities were they to require of me something absurd or out of keeping with the true interest of knowledge, thought, and general enlightenment, I vowed to act in this instance as I always try to act: with as much reason and conviction as I am able. A careful reading of the article convinced me it was just another example

---

1) Alekseev, p. 157.

of *The Contemporary* and *The Russian Word*'s usual tripe, the sort of
article that relies on immaturity and ignorance — especially among the
younger generation — for its effect and earns its popularity in their eyes
by preaching eccentric, communistic ideas. What are these gentlemen
after? Money and popularity. They neither wish nor need to work
seriously to earn them. Foreign literatures and books have everything they
could ask for. Every imaginable delight of radical or progressive hue is
there for the taking and will be novel here in Russia. Make believe it's
your own, and in no time you're a famous thinker or publicist. Besides,
the pen glides quite lightly across the paper here. It is very plainly wrong
to indulge in print any intellectual corruption or egotism which chases
after money and fame without the least concern for the consequences.
But unfortunately, this is the sad and irrefutable state of affairs. All this
went into my review. I showed that the government had no right to remain indifferent to such developments in the press liable to shake moral
sentiment, especially in Russia, where knowledge and public opinion are
still so weak they are unable to stand up against false and harmful doc-
trines and use their influence to neutralize them. The Board not only
agreed with my conclusion; it ordered my review to be circulated *as a
guideline* at the Petersburg und Moscow censorship committees.

Ivan Aleksandrovich (Goncharov) was amusing: he argued with me in
an attempt to prove — and quite a ridiculous attempt it was too — that
the time had come to acquaint our public with pernicious ideas, forgetting that society was well enough acquainted with pernicious ideas already,
that there was no point in adding new evils to old by means of the press,
which Russians believe like the Gospel, and that acquainting people with
all sorts of abominations before giving them the weapons to oppose them
was tantamount to depriving them of those weapons for life and thereby
promoting evil. Later Ivan Aleksandrovich agreed with me and even
enthusiastically supported approval of my review as a guideline. As a
result, he is now in a position to announce to the literary circle in question that he had stood staunchly behind the article, but that Nikitenko
had so lambasted it that his defense had done no good — that's the main
thing — but of course he never protested the Board's decision either. A perfect case of eating one's cake and having it too." [1]

---

1) Nikitenko II, pp. 416–418.

As has already been pointed out, Nikitenko's attitude toward Goncharov was a bit ambiguous. Their friendship, or rather amical relations,
lasted many years; they travelled together, and Nikitenko's daughters,
Sof'ja in particular, were sincere admirers of their father's celebrity friend.
Yet while Goncharov's letters to Nikitenko give evidence of genuine affection, Nikitenko's diary includes passages that criticize Goncharov quite
severely.

Goncharov remained on the Board of Censors until the end of 1867.
His four and a half years there were far from easy: work as a censor kept
him from work as an author. For the last three years he spent each summer abroad, haunting his old favorites — Marienbad (in hopes of a new
round of inspiration à la Oblomov), Paris, Boulogne-sur-Mer — but he remained as blocked as ever. His block was partly due to a strong reaction
to overwork. He complains of eye trouble — the result of reading constantly — a malady that later developed into a dangerous disease. But
mostly it derived from the self-imposed pressure of having to put something down on paper. Failure to meet his stringent standards paralysed
him to such an extent that he spent much of his time inventing excuses:
in his letters to Sof'ja Nikitenko for example, he laments (sometimes in
a very amusing way) over all sorts of noise preventing him from concentrating.

Another — and closely related — thorn in Goncharov's side was Turgenev's prodigious productivity. Yet his personal relations with the man had
improved. In 1864, four years after their quarrel, they met at Druzhinin's
funeral. Turgenev took the first step by asking Annenkov to tell Goncharov at the cemetary that he wished to shake his hand and find out how
he would react to the proposition. " 'I would shake his,' 'I answered,' "
writes Goncharov in his *Uncommon Story*, "and so we came together
again as if nothing had happened. And again we met, talked, and dined
together. I forgot everything. We never said a word about the novel. I
only told him in a few words that I was still writing — in the summer,
at the waters." [1]

As a result of the truce their correspondence picked up again (Turgenev's letter from Paris of March 1864 shows true affection for Goncharov),

---

1) N. I., p. 32.

and they would get together abroad several times. But Goncharov never ceased to look upon Turgenev's successes with a jaundiced eye.

Finding it difficult to work in peace, Goncharov constantly travelled from place to place. Marienbad and Boulogne-sur-Mer are the fixed points on his axes. In 1866 he stumbled on the theater of the Austro-Prussian War, an episode which he describes in a very funny way, but certainly the atmosphere was far from suited to his work.

In Baden-Baden during his 1867 vacation he spent some time (as he had done in 1866 by the way) not only with Turgenev, but at this occassion with Dostoevskij too. Dostoevskij, who was at the height of his gambling frenzy at this time, had varying success at securing loans from Goncharov. Goncharov gambled too, but was always careful and dispassionate. Dostoevskij's reports to the opposite were probably provoked by a desire to show that even as sedate a person as Goncharov could lose hold of himself. [1] At any rate, there appears to be no basis for Dostoevskij's claim that Goncharov lost "considerable sums."

The year 1866 marks a turning point in the development of Goncharov's friendship with the family of the younger Majkovs, Vladimir and Ekaterina. In 1852 Vladimir, a journalist and editor of periodicals for children, married a sixteen-year-old girl from the Ukraine. Ektaterina Kalita. The marriage was a very happy one at first, and the couple had three children. Goncharov felt completely at home with the family. He was attracted by the lively and passionate character of the young woman as well as her husband's sedateness. The latter's disposition had earned him the nickname "the old man" while he was still a boy, and his wife was consequently called "the old woman" from the time they were married. Goncharov enjoyed using these nicknames when writing or referring to them in letters.

Ekaterina Majkova had a talent for literature, and according to Chemena [2] it was her health that prevented her from becoming an independent writer. Though often confined to her bed, she nonetheless took an active part in editing her husband's children's journals, and it was for their *Snowdrop* (named after the earlier handwritten *Snowdrop* of

---

1) Cf. Utevskij, pp. 176 sq.
2) Chemena, p. 22.

the older Majkovs) that Goncharov reworked a portion of his *Frigate Pallada*, providing it with a foreword entitled "Dialogue with the Reader." [1]

Then the Majkovs' marriage began to deteriorate. Ekaterina fell in love with Fedor Ljubimov, a student nine years younger than herself whom the family had taken into their house in the winter of 1866. Ljubimov was an adherent of the then rampant nihilist movement. Ekaterina had previously showed "progressive" leanings, and the conservative attitude of the entire Majkov family clashed with her liberal outlook, which she nurtured by reading and even associating with such spokesmen of revolutionary materialism as Chernyshevskij, Dobroljubov, Pisarev, and Shelgunov.

In August 1866 she left her husband and children to follow Ljubimov. A year later she had a son by him, whom she immediately abandoned. When Ljubimov was forced to end his career as a medical student because of low grades, he and Majkova lived for a while in one of the "progressive" communes. He eventually took to drink and became so unpleasant that Majkova finally left him. After a period of peregrination she settled in Sochi, having completely revised the social and political aspirations of her youth. Vladimir suffered deeply from the break, and Goncharov followed his friend's sufferings with great concern.

A full account of this drama can be found in Chemena's book. She sees in Majkova the prototype of Goncharov's two main heroines: Ol'ga in *Oblomov* and Vera in *The Precipice*. She also speaks of Goncharov and Majkova's "joint literary work" on *The Precipice*. Even if her statements seem somewhat exaggerated (Majkova did hardly more than copy portions of *The Precipice*), there can be no doubt that many of them are valid and that Goncharov listened to Majkova's opinions and borrowed some of her features for both the interior and exterior portraits of his heroines. [2]

Majkova's formerly cordial relations with Goncharov began to take a turn for the worse in the early sixties, when Majkova's leftist leanings came to the fore. In 1863 she went abroad, and Goncharov wrote her

1) Cf. p. 95.
2) Cf. p. 127.

more than ten letters while she was in Nice. His goal was to reconcile her with her husband, for even several years before the definitive rupture she had begun to feel alienated from him. Evidence for this interpretation stems from his May 16, 1866 letter to her;[1] the correspondence itself was later destroyed by fire.

When in 1866 the tension in the Majkov family reached its climax, Majkova wrote to Goncharov from the Ukraine asking him for advice and apparently indicating her intentions of breaking up the family. Goncharov's immediate reply contains what might be looked upon as his anti-nihilistic confession. His long leter was printed for the first time in its enitrety by Chemena. [2] It constitutes a highly important testimony of Goncharov's political views.

First Goncharov expresses his surprise at the fact that Majkova — whom he had considered mature, completely developed intellectually, and equipped with a "sharp and subtle mind" [3] — could be carried away by new social and political currents, that doubts could have arisen in her. In a charmingly ironical vein he goes on to argue that the new ideas are not new at all (except perhaps to certain Russians) and that anyone who is well educated and intellectually alive ought to have been informed of them long ago. He ridicules what he feels are the inconsistencies of materialism and socialism. He rejects the idea that Majkova's idols can provide the world with a simple and honest organization of life, because he sees them as children playing with undigested theories. He compares the attitude of the young progressives to the irresponsible speeches and actions of the windbag Khlestakov from Gogol''s *Inspector General*. Moreover, he places special emphasis on love, praising it with genuine self-involvement as "an elementary force of life elaborated by delicate natures with a highly developed sense of humanity into a new religion, a cult that becomes the focal point of life itself. Some people, the sort of people we call 'cold,' do not comprehend this, they have simply either failed to develop their capacities or are organically deficient." [4]

---

1) Chemena, p. 146.
2) *ibid.*, pp. 140–149.
3) *ibid.*, p. 141.
4) *ibid.*, p. 147.

As for Majkova herself, Goncharov cautiously hints that a personal infatuation may have influenced her new ideology. He suggests that the quiet
happiness of her love for her husband has spoiled her and that she now longs
to leave the captivity in which it has held her. He also affixes an interesting personal confession to this statement: "I have become hardened in
laziness and selfishness, and I consciously do not wish to work and be
useful — even if I were able to." [1] Except for his sometimes bothersome
nephews, he continues, he has no "close ties": "I have left behind no
children, nor has any life's companion hung herself around my neck. And
had there been anything of this sort, I dare say I would not have been
frightened by my obligations and would have stood up to life with greater
stamina. Yet I think I would have been terrified by the responsibility of
bringing up children, and overly timid when it came to directing them
and molding their future. *Constant contact with them* would have both
consoled and horrified me: to guess the right roads for them and to give
them the proper preparation, that is the goal I would certainly have set
for myself; but at the same time I would have given out under the
burden. No, it is a good thing that I have no relatives closer than
nephews." [2]

This passage is one of the very few in which Goncharov speaks openly
about the family life for which he so obviously yearned. But the letter
had no effect. Majkova did not return to her family. A short exchange
of letters between the two took place during the winter and spring of
1869 in connection with her reactions (negative, of course) to *The Precipice*. It is quite characteristic of Majkova that although she preserved
Goncharov's letters she carefully crossed out a passage that was highly
uncomplimentary to her. Thanks to Chemena's efforts, [3] however, we
know that when making a serious attempt to convince her to return to
her children Goncharov accused her of neglecting the aspect of her personality "that deals with the notion of the heart." [4] After this letter all
correspondence between them ceased once and for all. [5]

1) Chemena, p. 148.   2) *ibid.*, pp. 148–149.
3) *ibid.*, pp. 150–152.   4) *ibid.*, p. 152.
5) Some generalizations of Chemena's book were attacked by S. Kajdash (Novyj mir,
   1966, Nr. 11, pp. 262–267) in the article "Razmashistost' i nebrezhnost'." Her
   overstatements were refuted by F. Prijma (Russkaja literatura, 1967, Nr. 2, pp.
   212–216): "Pod flagom 'nauchnosti' i 'nravstvennosti' ".

.The only literary output of 1866 we know of is a short note in the newspaper *The Voice* (Golos) — November 23, 1866 —. Goncharov praises the writer, poet and historian Nikolaj Karamzin, whose hundredth birthday anniversary was about to be celebrated, as the second after Lomonosov to bring knowledge, high thoughts, and noble, moral, humane principles to the great mass of society. He called for commemoration ceremonies for Karamzin similar to these held to honor Lomonosov a year ago.

We have an interesting portrait of Goncharov at this occasion (1865). Here is how Jakov Polonskij, a famous poet and neglected prose writer describes him at the official festivities marking the hundredth year of Mikhail Lomonosov's death in his novel *Unawares* (Nechajanno): "At that moment an elderly man of short stature with a clean shaven chin and a small bald spot appeared at the rostrum; he was in a dress coat and white tie, of course, and without removing his white gloves, he began to unfold a sheet of paper. Then, after a brief remark he began to read, 'Who is that?' asked Lelja. 'Don't know ma'am,' answered Pul'kin. 'That's Goncharov,' said Umekov. 'The one who wrote Oblomov?' 'That very one.' Lelja looked through the lorgnette. A deathly silence spread throughout the hall. Goncharov began to read verses by Rozengejm." [1]

Before The Precipice

Starting January 1, 1868, there was nothing to hold Goncharov back from completing his *Precipice:* he was no longer employed and received an adequate pension, which together with the royalties from his other works allowed him to get along quite comfortably. There was nothing to hold him back — except his inability to get down to serious work.

At this juncture an unexpected impetus entered Goncharov's life in the person of Mikhail Stasjulevich, a noted historian and new editor of one of the most widely read journals of the time, *The Messenger of Europe*. Look-

---

1) Ja.P.Polonskij, Polnoe sobranie sochinenij, St. Petersburg, 1886. vl. VI, p. 233.

ing for something that would put more life into the *Messenger* he hit upon
the idea of serializing a new novel by the well-known author of *Oblomov,*
and energetically set to spurring on his sluggish charge. His efforts in this
direction were greatly furthered by the lively intercession of the poet
Count Aleksej Konstantinovich Tolstoj and his wife. Goncharov had
known Tolstoj for some time, but with this new development they became much closer. By the end of the sixties he was a frequent guest at
the Tolstoj home. And because this was the period when Tolstoj was
working hardest on his trilogy of historical plays (which Goncharov
esteemed greatly and whose trial readings he attended), perhaps the
obvious pleasure Tolstoj derived from his work did in fact spur Goncharov on.

In late March and early April 1868 Goncharov gave readings of the
completed sections of *The Precipice* both in his own apartment and at
the Tolstojs. During the same period Stasjulevich was carrying on negotiations with him concerning publication. They apparently did not go
smoothly, because on the one hand Goncharov was chary of making
final commitments for a work that was still incomplete and on the other
anxious not to let it go at a too low price (Nekrasov was very interested
and would gladly have acquired the work for his *Annals of the Fatherland).* In the end Goncharov did promise the novel to Stasjulevich, who
with great skill and perseverance finally saw it through to completion.

Goncharov wrote about this to Sof'ja Nikitenko (whom he called the
Agaf'ja Matveevna of his works): "Stasjulevich knows how to stimulate
imagination by energetically conducted, intelligent, sober, mindful criticism and he acts in a very subtle way upon one's self-respect. Just think,
in my conversations with him my nerves and imagination started working again, and all of a sudden, clear as day, the end of the novel appeared before me, so that it seemed that I could just sit down and write
it." [1)]

Once again he thought back on the great upsurge of eleven years before and set off for the waters, choosing this time Bad Kissingen. That
a real enthusiasm for the project was not lacking is evident from this letter to Stasjulevich: "I am all bubbling inside like champagne in a bottle,

---

1) Alekseev, p. 170.

Everything is ripening, taking shape. The farther I go the easier it gets.
I can hardly hold myself back when I am alone, I sob like a child and
with a tortured hand I hurry to make notes, somehow, in disorder." [1]
In his mind he sees the end of the novel already clearly before him,
although not in the shape it took in the printed version: "In my mind
the novel is completely finished . . . the vista has all opened up before
me down to Rajskij's grave and its iron cross overgrown with thorns." [2]

The three weeks in Bad Kissingen did not find him in continual high
spirits — periods of great stamina and desire to work alternated with
periods of despair — both well mirrored in his letters to Stasjulevich. Yet
he never wavered from his decision to complete the novel so far.

Suspicions that Turgenev was jealously following his every move blazed
up again, and Goncharov began speculating about whether several of the
Russians at the spa were not in fact Turgenev's emissaries sent to spy on
him. He also expressed the fear that Berthold Auerbach's novel *Das Landhaus am Rhein* (The Country House on the Rhine) might have much in
common with his own country house on the Volga, by which of course
he means that he suspected Turgenev of having informed Auerbach about
his plans.

In the beginning of July Goncharov went to Bad Schwalbach, where
he met Stasjulevich on vacation, and then via Wiesbaden and Paris again
to Boulogne-sur-Mer. But he never stopped working on the novel as his
letters to Stasjulevich and to Sof'ja Nikitenko show. The letters to Stasjulevich are sometimes despairing enough to warrant credence in a full-
blown persecution complex, and all the comments he makes about himself and his character are tainted by the pressure under which he was
working and by his extremely bleak mood. Even his usual sense of humor disappears, although now and again it breaks through as e.g. in
describing an unsuccessful attempt at buying a revolver to shoot himself with: "Besides my nature and the weather I have to contend with
circumstances. There is nowhere I can go to escape misfortune. I have no
sanctuary, i.e. no close friends. All the people, who have offered to be-
friend me are such that I keep as far from them as possible. For fear of

---

1) Alekseev, p. 170.
2) *ibid.,* p. 171.

the consequences I myself have never offered friendship to anyone, and if there were cases when I made overtures, they always ended with my getting my fingers burned. People who are not my close friends have counterfeited and still counterfeit such a "liking" for me, and in such large numbers that it makes me want to go buy a revolver at Devins (he's close by) and blow my brains out. It's expensive, though, the bastard. I've priced it. A small one sells for sixty francs, and it's got such springs that when he showed me how to use it and put one into my hands, I didn't know where to begin. Why do they have five or six barrels when one of them could go through anything — even my stomach? He showed me a single-barreled model too, but this time I thought the better of it and decided in favor of life. So I set off, hapless creature that I am, in search of something close to life. After walking along for a while, I stopped in front of a window of drugstore items, next to which stood one lone book. My curiosity aroused I went inside and asked about the book. They gave it to me, and I read the title: Water Closet, 1,000 sheets of soft paper, 4 1/2 francs. I, who never buy books, bought this one. There it is now on the fireplace. — It wasn't until I bought it that I noticed the absurdity of it all. There I was, ready to buy a pistol to put an end to myself, and what did I buy in fact? A thousand sheets — in other words about three more years of life are guaranteed! — Tomorrow or the day after, I'll set it all right, I'll buy the pistol and put it next that book, and everyday I'll ask myself 'To be or not to be?' And in addition I'll get a skull somewhere, yes, I will." [1]

But opposed to spots like this are outburst of genuine grief, as e.g. "I'm bored and I feel vile. Excuse me and wish me — I don't even know what, really I don't! I don't want anything, or rather I want to close myself up in my room so that nobody can get in and nobody can pull me out." [2]

By the time he returned to St. Petersburg in August 1868, the novel was finished, but his depression had reached an all time low. Rereading the novel before settling down to prepare for its publication, he was so dissatisfied that he made up his mind to abandon it. Again it was Stasju-

1) Utevskij, p. 195.
2) Stasjulevich, IV, p. 48.

levich and the Tolstojs who exerted the pressure that finally brought him round.

Stasjulevich "forced" Goncharov into a gentleman agreement, offering him three thousand rubles for the novel (a considerable sum for the time) and on November 1, 1868 *The European Messenger* carried an announcement to the effect that the novel would be forthcoming. Work on setting the first part of the novel in type began immediately. Goncharov, torn between the desire to see his work in print and the fear of seeing his work in print, sank into an even deeper despair. Witty Aleksej Tolstoj caught the tragicomic aspect of the situation in this letter to Stasjulevich: "Let me express my admiration for your patience with our pregnant — but still affable — old maid. I am impatiently looking forward to the delivery," [1] and: "My heartiest congratulations to you for having deflowered our dear Aleksandra Ivanovna. Only your energy and stick-to-itiveness could have done it. Keep it up, and the kingdom of heaven is yours. Vivat Mikhail Matveevich!" [2]

After the announcement of the novel had appeared, Tolstoj wrote to Stasjulevich: "It was with the greatest of pleasure that I noted in the November issue of *The European Messenger* that you have burned our dear Ivan Aleksandrovich's ships behind him and that he, like Cortès, will have to conquer or die. I hope his victory is beyond doubt. The bridge spanning the Hellespont has been destroyed, and Xerxes will be forced to remain forever in the Hellas of your journal, though I don't doubt he'll be trying to jump across." [3]

On January 1, 1869 the first part of *The Precipice* appeard in *The European Messenger*. The next four parts followed on the first of each of the next four month.

---

1) Utevskij, p. 200.
2) *ibid.*
3) *ibid.*, p. 201.

The Precipice

Artistically and philosophically, *The Precipice* is doubtlessly Goncharov's most relevant work. Its artistry is obvious, but its ideological content does not lend itself to easy interpretation. The wealth of artistic and metaphysical insights it offers is so subtly presented that one cannot be too surprised at how long it has taken literary critics to discover them. Not until the past two decades has a new evaluation begun to take root — both inside and outside Russia. The average reader, by the way, has reacted quite differently from the critics. When it appeared in 1869, the novel was denounced and reviled by nearly every critic who reviewed it; yet it has become one of the classics of Russian literature. The reading public instinctively recognized the qualities in *The Precipice* that make it a genuine work of art and prevail against the timebound nearsightedness to which critics are prone.

As has been stressed several times in the preceding chapters, boredom played an important part in Goncharov's life and view of life. His letters abound with references to and descriptions of this phenomenon. *The Frigate Pallada* is an account of how he tried to escape it by travel. In his two previous novels it provides a distant but menacing backdrop for the spiritual development of the heroes. In *The Precipice* Goncharov brings it to the fore. He makes it the predominant philosophical issue, the mainspring for the actions of the hero Boris Rajskij, and raises it to the status of a crucial problem in both life and art.

The first scholar to recognize the pivotal position of Goncharov's concept of boredom and to interpret his last novel in its light was Walther Rehm. [1] Referring to Søren Kierkegaard's *The Concept of Dread* (1844), Rehm describes boredom as the most characteristic feature of nineteenth century culture. Boredom in this sense is basic, metaphysical, existential. It is boredom without any concrete *raison d'etre,* boredom as the ontological result of the loss of faith in God in the eighteenth century, when the enthronement of reason destroyed other, and perhaps more important qualities in man.

---

1) Cf. Bibliographical Remarks, No. 10.

Having lost all connection with the beyond, Man loses interest in the here and now. Life becomes meaningless. Ethical values lose their content when deprived of all affinity to an absolute value. God, the Good, and all sense of being become neutral, if not negative elements. The soul, the region of feeling and will, becomes void of any genuine, worthwhile beliefs or endeavors; dominated by analytical reason it stands before a dangerous abyss of nothingness. As the ability for emotion decreases, so does the ability for life. Faithless Man first turns in toward himself, but rational analysis of his personality decomposes his soul; all his feelings and desires, when subjected to the uncommitted light of reason appear senseless. Because, however, reason is powerless to solve the problem of what all the feelings are ultimately for, it soon gives way to existential boredom.

What can one do in a meaningless world? All activity may be reduced to an attempt to kill boredom, to escape it sting. As mentioned above, a certain material well-being is a condition for the development of this affliction. People who must strive for subsistence have no time to ponder over and yield themselves up to spiritual emptiness. But on higher levels of cultured society, this "sickness' becomes dangerous. Dissatisfied with his own inner life, Man begins to play with the lives of his fellowmen. He looks on life as a sort of theater in which he, a bored spectator, tries to excite his emotions by manipulating the "play" around him. His motivations are far from philanthropic; they stem from his own boredom, and have therefore basically egotistical roots. Of course the character of the play he stages depends upon his own character. It may be cruel, it may be benevolent. In any case, however, he is sure to use his fellow creatures as instruments for the satisfaction of the selfish desire to overcome his purposeless boredom.

Often this attitude goes hand in hand with a cult of one's own personality as reflected in one's outward appearance, i.e. a kind of aesthetic egoism. Russian literature provides striking examples of this combination of dandified exterior and cool, ironical *Weltanschauung* in Pushkin's Evgenij Onegin and Lermontov's Pechorin (the title character in *A Hero of Our Time*). To a certain extent Griboedov's Chackij (the protagonist of his brilliant comedy *Woe from Wit*) fits these specifications, and Chackij's personality very much interested Goncharov.[1] Gogol' too

1) Cf. p. 253 sq.

planned to introduce this sort of character in the persons of Tentetnikov
and Platonov (cf. the drafts to the second part of *Dead Souls*), and its
development in many variations and degrees is attested in Turgenev's
fiction and certain of Tolstoj's characters (e.g. Prince Andrej in *War and
Peace*), and culminates, in its most dangerous reincarnation, in Dostoevskij's atheists, Stavrogin of *The Devils* and Ivan Karamazov.

Behind all these tragic lives stands the dilemma of Man without God.
In place of God there is emptiness, boredom, nothingness. No matter how
Man tries to combat them, he is doomed to failure. Analytic reason is not
the most valuable faculty in Man, and if given too much power, it is
capable of destroying feeling and will, the main attributes of the sub-
conscious and — perhaps — the most important components of the human
personality.

Goncharov seems to have been keenly aware of these implications.
Convinced that existential boredom was one of the main forces behind
the life and culture of his time, he decided to underline its significance
as a metaphysical and ethical problem in artistic form. Metaphysical boredom thus became the main issue of a tense, highly original and ingeniously
constructed novel which can easily stand comparison with the best achieve-
ments of Russian nineteenth century prose. [1] Understandably enough, Goncharov tackles a variation of the problem especially akin to him; that of
the artist whose existential boredom relegates him to the ranks of a dilet-
tante.

In *The Precipice,* as in his former works, the hero is constantly at the
center of both concrete and ideological events. Everything that happens
emanates from him, and all characters stand in close relation to him.

Boris Pavlovich Rajskij is a well-to-do member of the provincial nobility
in his early thirties. Having lost his parents as a small boy, he was raised
on their estate by his great aunt, the sister of his maternal grandmother.
After boarding school, he tried his hand at the university, then left first
for the military and finally the administrative service, but as he failed to

---

[1] Incredible as it may seem there exists only one abridged and incorrect translation
of "The Precipice" into English published in 1915! [London, Hodder and Stoughton;
New York, A.A. Knopf, 319 p.]

achieve distinction in either studies or the service, he decided to retire
and devote himself entirely to his main interest in life: art. To that end,
he enrolled in the Academy of Creative Arts in Petersburg.

For Rajskij, however, art is far from an aim in itself. He uses art as a
way of overcoming the boredom that has plagued him since early childhood. In Rajskij, Goncharov wishes to portray a man suffering from the
illness of modern times. Deprived of faith and all connection with the
beyond, alienated from his own existence, yet at the same time spiritually refined, highly intelligent, and quite talented, he is searching for something, anything that will make his life worthwhile. All he can come up
with is creative work and passion. Surely none but a man with highly
developed intellectual and emotional capacities would succumb to a
disease whose main symptoms are culturally based.

Opening the novel with a portrait of Rajskij, Goncharov immediately
establishes his psychological concern by a skillful use of outwardly ominous
detail:

> "Boris Pavlovich had a lively, extremely mobile face. At first glance
> he did not look his age. His high, white forehead gleamed with
> health. His eyes were quick to change expression; one minute
> they would be burning with thought, emotion or joy, the next
> they would sink into a dreamy brown study — and even then
> they seemed young, almost boyish. Sometimes, however, they
> looked out at the world with a maturity, fatigue, and boredom
> clearly revealing their master's age. In fact, three barely distinguish-
> able wrinkles, those indelible signs of time and experience, had
> formed around his eyes. Smooth, black hair fell down over his
> ears and the back of his neck, but a few white hairs had begun
> to silver his temples. Around the eyes and mouth, his cheeks, like
> his forehead, retained their youthful color, but at the temples
> and around the chin they had grown darker, yellowish.
> It was easy to see from his face that he had reached the point
> in life when maturity had won its battle with youth, when a man
> has entered the second stage of his existence, when every new ex-
> perience, emotion, or malady leaves its trace. Only his mouth,
> in its smile and the hardly perceptible play of its thin lips, pre-

served a young, fresh, at times almost childlike expression.

 Rajskij, wearing a gray housecoat, was sitting with his
legs up on the couch." [1]

 We find him in conversation with Ivan Ivanovich Ajanov, a highly placed administrator in his forties, and member of the Russian *haut monde*.
He is a "reasonable" man, lacking in the subtle emotions necessary for
probing matephysical depths. (Even Macbeth's witches would come to
grief, says Goncharov, if they should try to tempt him away from the
established course of his ever so well-organized life.) He is restrained,
apathetic, and narrow. "Cynical egotism' [2] governs his opportunistic
approach to life and precludes him from experiencing the emotions which
Rajskij feels so keenly. In this confrontation Goncharov exploits one of
his favorite devices, sharp contrasts, to introduce the reader to the main
ideas of his book.

 It is indicative that in the short first chapter (only nine pages long) the
words "boring," "boredom," and "to be bored" appear no less than
thirteen times. Learning that Ajanov is never bored, Rajskij exclaims,
"If only the world were without boredom! Can any fiercer scourge
exist?" [3] Fortunately, however, he has found a remedy in beauty. And
since Rajskij describes beauty as that which excites passion and adoration, it is not surprising that he takes Don Juan as a sort of symbolic
character. He sees him in Byron, in Goethe, in all artists, and places his
search for beauty on the same plane as Don Quixote's ethical passion. He
even maintains that the search for beauty is more deeply rooted in Man.
Ajanov sees Rajskij as Don Juan and Don Quixote rolled into one, but
in doing so, of course, he is thinking in terms of the connotations Don
Juan and Don Quixote usually evoke: the skirt-chaser and short-sighted
bumbling idiot.

 Rajskij knows that his ideal of beauty is almost impossible to realize.
In the real world it simply cannot exist, and "what the fantasy creates,

---

1) V, p. 7.
2) *ibid.*, p. 42.
3) *ibid.*, p. 11.

analysis destroys like a house of cards." [1] The only beauty that is not doomed to annihilation is beauty that is adored in works of art.

Passion kills boredom. But when its object is a living being, it is transient and, once slaked, it dies away. Only a work of art can be an eternal stimulus. It follows, then, that in contemplating art and — still more — creating art one finds the greatest possible relief from boredom. Rajskij's ecstatic pronouncements sound shrill and irrational against the ironically cool background of Ajanov's quiet, matter-of-fact replies. "Passions interfere with life," he says, and suggests "work as a remedy for emptiness." [2]

This suggestion shows how little Ajanov understands Rajskij's position. Rajskij despises work; he sees it as a device which Man has contrived to help him escape boredom on the lowest level. Work may allay a working man's boredom, but it can in no way deal with the burden of a man who conceives of life as a metaphysical entity.

A further ironical touch lies in the incident which provides the springboard for this philosophical conversation. Rajskij has been attracted by a distant relative, Sof'ja Belovodova, whose placidly enigmatic beauty inspires in him a passion to know what lies hidden behind the mask. Straightforward Ajanov cannot understand Rajskij's metaphysical yearnings. By suggesting several times that Rajskij simply marry his cousin and have done with it all, he merely exasperates him still more.

Rajskij's "preoccupation" with Sof'ja is typical. It consists of turning her into an instrument for the satisfaction of his curiosity, a remedy against the emptiness of his own existence. He does it instinctively, not really knowing why. Sof'ja, as it turns out, is not a very rewarding object for investigation, but Rajskij's attempts to penetrate her innermost feelings serve as a kind of prelude to the great task that stands before him: solving the riddle surrounding the real heroine of the novel: Vera.

Sof'ja inspires him, as Vera will later, to paint a portrait and write a novel, to transform passion and beautiful reality into art. It is characteristic of Rajskij that he chooses *two* branches of art. On the one hand it

---

1) V, p. 13.
2) *ibid.*, p. 14.

points to his gifted nature (and as a matter of fact, he is quite a talented musician as well), but on the other it reveals that art is not his real vocation. If it were, he would be able to overcome boredom through concentrated work in one art. Passionate creative work would carry him away, and reason would not have a chance to interfere. As it is, however, his nervous, highly sensitive organism suffers from an overdose of reason. He longs for creative work, he longs for passion, but he is unable to give up his whole personality to them.

But for a while Sof'ja's beauty carries him away. It excites him, it excites his fantasy, and boredom vanishes — for a while. His new attitude becomes clear in the following conversation with Ajanov (Chapter Five).

> "'. . . I've been toying with the idea of painting her portrait. It would take a month, and then I will study her . . . "
>
> 'Be careful now you don't fall in love,' remarked Ajanov. 'You cannot marry her, as you say, but play passions with her you cannot either. In time you'll only get burned . . . '
>
> 'Dont't you think I realize that?' Rajskij interrupted. 'I know what I'm doing. Day and night all I dream of is getting burned. And if I were to be burned by an incurable passion, I would marry her . . . But no. Passions are either cured or, if incurable, they don't lead to marriage. There's no quiet harbor for me. It's either burning or sleep and boredom! . . . You know, Ajanov, for a long time now I've been seriously thinking of writing a novel . . . '" [1]

Rajskij expects a tragic flame to take hold of him and hopes to check his boredom by immortalizing his new-found passion in a novel. Farther on in his conversation with Ajanov, he sings the praises of the novel as a literary genre.

> "'The novel welcomes everything. It's not like a drama or comedy. It's an ocean without shores — or an ocean whose shores are never visible. It's so spacious. Everything has its place.' . . . 'All of life — life as a whole and in its parts — is fair game for the novel.' . . .

---

1) V, pp. 40–41.

'Merging one's life into the life of another, putting down on paper all one's observations, thoughts, experiences, portraits, scenes, sensations, emotions — une mer à boire!' " [1]

These remarks prepare the development of Goncharov's own novel. Rajskij *does* mix his life together with those of others. He *does* try to write a novel about it. He even succeeds for a time in numbing his boredom. But he never succeeds in finishing the novel. Art can never become an instrument for foreign aims. The novel is written in the end not by Rajskij, but by Goncharov, the real artist, the moving force that conceived the basis for the work and developed it into art.

In the first part Rajskij sets out to find the woman behind Sof'ja's beautiful mask and impeccable manners. Sof'ja is a twenty-five-year-old widow who lives with her two very rich and very aristocratic aunts. Proud of the old Pakhotin family name, they run their household in the stiff, cold tradition of the high nobility. Sof'ja's rigid but energetic mother raised her according to the firm, narrow rules of her society's code of behavior. Her death just before Sof'ja's marriage frees Sof'ja's long suffering father from the bonds of his strict wife. Goncharov gives a charming portrait of this old bonvivant, who, after squandering his fortune in a violent reaction to the fettered existence he had been forced to lead, finds himself reduced to the financial mercy of his sisters. He is the only "living" inhabitant of the house. His rooms contrast blatantly with the rest of the mansion, whose heavy old furniture and abundant vases resemble sarcophagi and sepulchral urns (Chapter Two).

Sof'ja's upbringing has effectively protected her against all strong emotions, let alone passions; it stifled nearly all feminine instincts in her. Indeed, her life consists of a series of sacrifices to the society in which she moves, all sorts of social conventions, and pride. "She is a beautiful statue, automatically doing everything that inexorable duty to her circle and upbringing required of her." [2] This is how Goncharov describes her personality. One should add, however, that she is not stupid; her witty ironical repartees to Rajskij's tirades give evidence of a keen intelligence. Further-

---

1) V, pp. 41–43.
2) VIII, p. 209.

more, she is artistically gifted, a more than competent musician. Trapped
in the limbo of her passion-free world, she refuses to come to grips with
Rajskij's attempts to liberate her. "I have no intention of trading my
ignorance for your dangerous knowledge," [1] she tells him.

Part of the reason she refuses (as does Vera later on in the novel) is
that she senses his interest is not altogether altruistic. She realizes that it
does not stem from heart-felt persuasions, that it is deeply egotistical. In
"stirring up her peace" all he really wants is to find something to keep
himself busy. Maxims like "The world is moving forward toward happiness, success, and perfection" [2] basically contradict his own beliefs. He
never succeeds in formulating what he wants Sof'ja to do once she has
abandoned the constraints of her former existence, the "cemetery," "the
dusty recollections," for which the ancestral portrait gallery becomes a
symbol. He shows her life in the streets, (by removing the heavy curtain
from her window), he makes social propaganda (in sketches with just the
proper infusion of shock value), he speaks for the serfs, at whose expense
the Pakhotins (and the Rajskijs) live, he preaches self-abandoning love (in
which he does not believe). That he himself knows precious little of life
outside the drawing room, that he ignored his own serfs' plight, and that
he cannot quite erase the egocentric tinge that characterizes all his passions — all this Goncharov makes amply clear.

When in Chapter Fourteen Sof'ja tells him of her former interest for
the poor teacher El'nin, he encourages her to let herself go. When in
Chapter Eighteen she pretends to be in love with Count Milari, he rants
and raves with anger and jealousy and in an excellent (especially from
the point of view of dialogue) tragicomic scene, it becomes clear that
Rajskij has put himself in the position of the hero. In his attempts to
find out "what is hidden under the ice," he has taken on the role of the
jealous lover and is out solely for himself.

For sufferers of Rajskij's disease, altruism is in fact nothing more than
egoism. It therefore goes without saying he succeeds neither in painting
Sof'ja's portrait nor in reshaping her life. He takes refuge from life in
fantasy. At the end of part one he abandons his mind to such vagaries as

---

1) V, p. 107.
2) *ibid.*, p. 29.

how to breathe life into a statue (from the beginning he thought of himself as Sof'ja's Pygmalion) and how to stylize Sof'ja's imagined romance
in novel form.

In art his failure is still more conspicuous. His first attempt at a portrait of Sof'ja catches all her unruffled, resplendant beauty, the harmony
of her features, and the innocent, tranquil look in her eyes. But Rajskij is
not content. He wants to create the Sof'ja he sees in his dreams, Sof'ja
as she will look after her "awakening." He changes the portrait according-
ly, and all similarity disappears. His teacher Kirilov, a devoted ascetic in
art, criticizes the work sharply. He feels the discrepancy between face and
expression, points up all Rajskij's deficiencies in technique and makes the
work quite amateurish. Kirilov is correct in accusing Rajskij of substituting an abstract, cerebral kind of passion *(strastnost')* for the real thing
(strast') and playing around with both art and life. [1] Rajskij's analytic
mind stifles his creative abilities. Creation requires the whole man. It requires the dedication and practice we find in Kirilov and in the cellist,
the second illustration of this thesis. Kirilov makes a religion of art, and
though he may go too far in his asceticism, he nonetheless comes closer
to the truth than Rajskij. It seems that Goncharov's model for the impressive portrait of Kirilov was the painter Aleksandr Ivanov.

Further proof of Rajskij's insufficiency as a human being may be found
in the sad story of Natasha, a sketch that Rajskij himself has composed
about an episode in his own life. Inserting Rajskij's version of the affair
is a clever device on Goncharov's part: in his very own words Rajskij demonstrates his inability to respond to true love. Love, like everything else,
begins to bore him after a time.

The Natasha in question was a poor, young, innocent girl, who lived
with her sick mother with the doubtful "help" of an elderly "friend."
Rajskij destroyed the friend's hold on her and saved mother and daughter
from shame and poverty. They fall in love and think earnestly of marriage.
When Natasha's mother dies of consumption, the deep emotions she experiences intensify her own case of the same illness. "The altar waited,
but love lured them ahead." [2] Natasha is on the way to recovery. She

1) cf. V, p. 135.
2) *ibid.,* p. 118.

loves Rajskij with a genuine, deep and serene love. But he tires of her: he wants passion. His fantasies plague him with a different kind of love: "that heat of strong, fiery, jealous love" [1]: which she cannot give. From the moment he attempts to analyze their love, his own begins to wane. Neglected, she suffers, but he — full of himself — notices nothing. His repentance and regrets come only with her death.

Chapter Fifteen, which deals with this sad event, reads like a study in morbid romantic writing, a sort of imitation of the early Dostoevskij. Meant as an example of Rajskij's talent as a writer and his notion of how life should be depicted in art, it is likewise an illustration of his character as seen from the side. At one point Goncharov reminds us of this: Rajskij writes about himself anonymously and in the third person except in one passage where "Rajskij" stands instead of the usual "he." [2] This is presumably a deliberate slip to demonstrate the reflection of life in art.

The first part of the novel is a kind of prologue to the actual plot. The "didactic" conversations with Sof'ja (which take up three chapters: Four, Fourteen, and Eighteen), the descriptions of the Pakhotin household (Chapters Two and Three), the dialogues with Ajanov (Chapters One and Five), and the painting of Sof'ja's portrait (Chapter Seventeen) take place in the novel's "present" and show Rajskij as he is. Goncharov intersperses his accounts of the present with flashbacks to explain how Rajskij became what he is. Chapter Six which is devoted to his spiritual upbringing, both summarizes and supports what has already been said about his inability for motivated work, his lively imagination, and his manifold gifts. Chapters Seven to Eleven give a long and detailed retrospective account of the vacations Rajskij spent at his estate (which was being managed at the time by his great-aunt). Several protagonists of the novel along with some secondary characters are introduced as they were about fifteen years before the action of the novel begins. The precipice, scene of the novel's most tragic events, is introduced here too. Chapters Twelve and Thirteen are again retrospective; they treat Rajskij's unsuccessful stints at the university, in the civil service, and at the academy. Chapter Sixteen contains letters from grandma (as his great-aunt is called) and

---

1) V, p. 118.
2) Cf. V, p. 117.

Leontij Kozlov, Rajskij's schoolfriend. Kozlov writes about the second hero
of the novel Mark Volokhov, and he and grandma urge Rajskij to come
to his estate Malinovka (literally "Raspberry Village"). Their letters make
Rajskij decide to leave St. Petersburg and proceed to the scene of what
will be the main plot.

Rajskij undertakes the trip in the hope of gathering material for a novel
he intends to write. He enters in the program his "conversations with
Sof'ja, the episode with Natasha and many other things that must enter
the laboratory of his fantasy" [1] to perhaps become "a prologue to the
novel." "The novel itself," he muses, "lies in the future, or it may never
materialize at all! What sort of novel will I find there in the provinces,
in the country! An idyll maybe, with hens and roosters, but not a novel
of living people with fire, spirit, passion!" [2]

As it turns out, he finds just that. And even though he becomes person-
nally involved in the passions around him, they are not enough to arouse
him from his indifference and boredom. He basically remains the amateurish artist observing everything from without, the cold analyst unable to
let himself go. He cannot forget himself, nor can he help studying other
people's lives and his own reactions to them.

The second part, which covers several weeks of Rajskij's sojourn in Malinovka, reintroduces many of the characters presented in retrospect or
shown in Part One in life and action. Grandma has remained the "feudal
serf owner" she had been. She does not for a moment question a landowner's right to own serfs, and is perhaps too proud of her geneology
and social standing. She is bossy and exigent, demanding great respect
for her age and experience. At the same time she is a real human being.
All her negative qualities are superficial; as soon as events become really
serious, and depth of feeling or judgment is involved, she forgets her
theories of right and wrong and reacts in a way which attests to the
beauty, — and at the end of the novel even the greatness — of her
character.

---

1) V, p. 155.
2) *ibid.*, p. 156.

Grandma — her name is Tat'jana Berezhkova — is described as having "black vivacious eyes and such a friendly and gracious smile, that when she gets angry and when a thunderstorm begins to flash in her eyes, you see behind the thunderstorm the clear sky again." [1] When Rajskij says he considers her a beauty, he refers both to her real inner self and her outward appearance. And certainly her passionate affair with Tit Nikonovich Vatutin, which though only hinted at in the beginning, grows into a crucial issue, implies a strong, uncompromising character together with unusual beauty. Rajskij, in his thirst for solving the "riddles" of the people around him, is constantly trying to find out what kind of woman Grandma really is. His gradual penetration into the depth of her personality and the secret of her love is an important plot line running throughout the novel.

Vatutin is one of Goncharov's charming, short character sketches. He is a gentleman by nature, a cavalier, noble in mind, refined in behavior and elegant without cheap dandyism in his dress. His "eternal" devotion to Grandma shows the constancy, decency, and depth of his personality. The slightly ironical touches which Goncharov indulges in when reintroducing him as an elderly man (e.g. his concern with what is healthful and his exquisite way of talking) do not detract from the impression of solidity he creates; there is no doubt he acts as a true nobleman in any given situation. He is opposed to the behavior of the new generation, represented by Mark Volokhov, in much the same way as Pavel Kirsanov opposes Bazarov's conduct in Turgenev's *Fathers and Sons*.

Marfen'ka and Vera, grandnieces of Grandma and distant cousins of Rajskij, were introduced in Part One when they were about five and six years old. Even then their very different personalities had begun to crystallize, and it turns out that Rajskij's guesses as to what they would become are quite right.

Marfen'ka was an uncomplicated child. Under Grandma's strict but loving guidance she grew up content and completely unaware that anything might be different from what it is. She grows into a charming, friendly girl with no ambitions other than those of becoming a good housewife and mother.

Vera, on the other hand, was self-willed from the start. She was always

---

[1] V, p. 64.

one for personal freedom and lived in proud inner seclusion. As she matures, she grows more and more dissatisfied with her spiritual surroundings. She cries out for change and a broader view of life, and when the possibility for novelty and knowledge beyond the moral prescriptions of Grandma and provincial society presents itself in the shape of the "nihilist" Mark Volokhov, her curiosity and desire to live life at its fullest slowly turn to love. Rajskij came a little too late. Before Mark introduced her to his world, he would have been able to "attack" Vera in much the same way he had attacked Sof'ja. And of course it is very probable that he would have become bored with the task had she responded. Entering as he does after Mark has had his say, however, he makes no headway whatsoever, and this resistence together with the secrecy of Vera's love drive him to a strange, but very genuine passion for her. It is the course of this passion that constitutes the chief plot line of the novel.

The first nine chapters of Part Two cover Rajskij's first day in the country. We observe his first meeting with Marfen'ka, as she is feeding the poultry (a charming scene, much appreciated by contemporary readers), his unwillingness to listen to Grandma's "accounts" of her estate management, his attempt to "awaken" Marfen'ka (with an amusing discussion of modern literature and music), his visit to Leontij Kozlov and his wife Ulen'ka, his reintroduction to Vatutin and to Mrs. Krickaja. The latter provides a sort of comic contrast and relief during the tragedy that is to develop. Vera is not at home, paying a visit of several days to a friend.

Leontij Kozlov and his wife represent two forms of passion in love. Their story is given in retrospect in Chapters Five and Six. He is a born scholar, completely dedicated to his field: Greek and Roman literature and culture. Absentminded, really alive only in the antique world of his books, he fails to see, what is going on around him. He especially neglects his wife, whom he adores and who he is sure adores him too. But Ulen'ka is the incarnation of a female libertine. The only reason she married Kozlov was that she had gotten herself into trouble and could not afford the consequences. To support her, Kozlov has found the secure, if lowly position he now holds as a provincial schoolteacher. She is faithless to her unsuspecting husband, running after every male who crosses her path.

Leontij, a devoted friend of Rajskij's and genuinely good soul, lives
a happy life in his narrow world. Rajskij cannot forbear trying to "reform" him too, but all his talk about "limited horizons," and the new
world of progress reflects nothing more than the confusion he feels
whenever confronted with a happy, intelligent person: How can a man
live like this and not be bored? In this case he receives a clear answer:
Leontij is a true scholar, and his conscious life is with his books. Progress for him would be a "second antiquity."

" . . . How can you help but believe in progress? We have lost our
way. We have failed to live up to our great models. We have squandered
many of the secrets of their existence. It is now our duty to pull ourselves back up onto that lost road and . . . try to gain back the strength,
the perfection of thought, scholarship, law, morals, and of your "social
economy" . . . a wholeness of virtue and maybe even of vice! Baseness,
pettiness, and trumpery will all lose their luster. Man will stand straight
again, firm on iron feet. That's what I call progress!" [1]

Rajskij has to give up. Leontij states decisively that he never suffers
from boredom. His only vulnerable point, as Rajskij recognizes, is his
wife. Leontij himself has no idea how much she means to him. His whole
life is built upon his quiet passion for her and her "Roman profile."
Once again passion appears to be the only alternative for boredom:

"It was clear that in addition to the books that nourished his mind he
nurtured a heart. He himself had no idea what it was that bound him so
tightly to life and his books. He never suspected that if he should lose
the books, his life would not be lost along with them. But if he were deprived of his 'Roman head,' his entire life would undergo paralysis." [2]

As the charm of the novelty of his new surroundings dies away, Rajskij begins to feel the approach of boredom. He has come to Malinovka to
turn provincial life into a novel but finds life in the country basically as
monotonous as it was in the capital. The only writing he does consists of
descriptions of people with bizarre or ugly features, and he does it very
well. Or rather Goncharov does it very well, in reporting what Rajskij

---

1) V, pp. 213–214.
2) *ibid.*, p. 217.

wrote. In these passages the identification of hero and author progresses at a fast pace.

A variegated round of colorful episodes fill Chapters Ten through Thirteen. Especially powerful is the story of the sexually uninhibited servant maid Marina and her rightly jealous husband Savelij, another variation on the theme of passion. In what amounts to a genuine folk drama, Savelij, an upright, sullen, and elderly peasant falls in love with a dissolute young woman, in whom Rajskij sees a "selfless priestess of the cult of the 'mother of delights,' " [1] Pushkin's description of Aphrodite in his *Egyptian Nights*. To keep her faithful he constantly spies on her, beating her black and blue at the least suspicion (most of which are justified).

No less impressive is the portrait of Polina Krickaja, the elderly woman who plays at being a "mother of delights," who wants every man at her feet, but shrinks back at every serious attempt on her virtue. Rajskij's remark after her second visit goes a long way toward characterizing her personality: "She isn't even any good for a novel — too much of a caricature! No one will believe in her." [2]

Rajskij spends his days painting and writing, and they soon begin to creep along tediously. What is he to do with all his sketches and episodes, he wonders. A real novel might console him; transforming life into the allencompassing genre of the novel might be worth while.

"He decided to write it in episodes sketching here a figure that caught his fancy, there a scene that attracted him or struck him as interesting, inserting himself wherever his senses, impressions, feelings, and passions — above all passions — might lead him.

'Oh God! Grant me passion!' he would sometimes pray, tormented by boredom. Boredom was about to get the best of him at Malinovka and he began to think of going off and seeking out 'life' elsewhere. He wanted to either gulp it down by indulging passion to the hilt or else refuse to compromise his ideals, in which case he would suffer from all sorts of indignities and torture himself with a lifeless indifference to everything around him." [3]

1) V, p. 246.
2) *ibid.*, p. 251.
3) *ibid.*, p. 252.

But once again reason, analytic reason, intervenes. It hinders him from giving himself wholly to his work and even provokes him to undertake some "experiments" of rahter doubtful validity: he is all ready to seduce the naive Marfen'ka when something from within her restrains him and prevents him from becoming "a terrible rascal," [1] as he puts it himself. By the end of Chapter Thirteen Rajskij reaches the peak of his boredom.

At this point Goncharov cleverly introduces the second hero and Rajskij's main antagonist, the nihilist Mark Volokhov. Mark is living under police surveillance in provincial exile. He was first mentioned during Part One in a rather strange connection. In a letter to Rajskij, Kozlov complained about Mark's tearing pages from valuable books that do not belong to him and using them to light a cigar or clean his ears and nails. This and many other unpleasant features establish Mark as a highly negative character. When he appears, however, his straightforward, energetic, and intelligent behavior makes it difficult to believe that he did such things. Indeed, it takes some time for Goncharov to smooth over the several inconsistencies in his characterization of Mark.

On the one hand, Goncharov hated the "new men", liberals, positivists, socialists, and finally the communists. He followed their formation as an interest group in the early fifties and their heyday in the sixties with a great deal of distaste. On the other hand, he recognized them as a potent force, even if basically an evil one. The tension between his disapproval of their principles and his attempt to do them justice with an objective appraisal resulted in a character who is not completely persuasive. Only towards the end, when his love affair with Vera takes a dangerous turn, does Mark become a human being apart from his "principles." Goncharov himself explains Mark's ambiguity by the fact that he conceived him differently from the way in which he finally drew him. The evolution is understandable if we take into account the length of the period over which Goncharov worked on the novel. [2]

Mark was at first a secondary character whose main role was to put Vera's personality into relief. A strong man with liberal ideas who could not abide the narrowness of government or society in Petersburg, he was

1) V, p. 266.
2) Cf. p. 234 sq.

finally sent to the provinces as an exile. There he continued to express
his independent views, but in a much less radical and more credible form
than in the final version. This rational, intelligent and skeptic liberal meta-
morphosed gradually into a rather cheap protester against the status quo,
reviling the guidelines and traditions of the "old morality" without bother-
ing to seek out viable replacements. This metamorphosis can be explained
by the fact that at the end of the forties the liberal trend showed few excesses; it was a truly idealistic movement of firm philosophical founda-
tions which advocated a number of changes in the Russian social order
that were completely acceptable to Goncharov. But when the inroads
made by cheap materialism and utilitarianism led it to a blanket rejection of all idealism (especially in literature), and its young and limited
followers began to exhibit more bravado than reason, Goncharov became
first disillusioned and then repulsed. He says he met dozens of Volok-
hovs during his visit to Simbirsk in 1862. [1])

Mark's nihilism, as reflected in the novel, is actually little more than
an expression of his physical ebullience plus the distorted view he has of
his "clear judgment" concerning conditions in Russia. He feels hampered
by conventions and tries to show his superiority by being rude to his
teachers, answering back his officers in military service, irritating the
police, trying to get away without paying in restaurants, intentionally
destroying books, borrowing money without any intention of returning
it, stealing apples, etc. At the same time he is capable of holding rigorous
discourses on the philosophical basis of materialism (complete with quotes
from Proudhon: La propriété, c'est le vol) and explicating a wide range
of arguments against idealism and religion. The contradiction between obvious erudition and intelligence, and rather childish actions might be interpreted theoretically as an expression of his basic boredom and indifference,
but in fact they do not really blend into a whole personality.

When Rajskij and Volokhov meet by chance one evening at Kozlov's,
Mark emphasizes his nihilistic tendencies by being as impolite as possible.
Goncharov gives an exact portrait.

"Mark was about twenty-seven. He was solidly built — he seemed
to be made of metal — and well-proportioned. Though clearly not

_____

1) Cf. Cejtlin, p. 243.

blonde, he had a pale complexion, and his palish brown hair, tossed
back over his ears and neck like a thick mane, left bare a large,
prominent forehead. His beard and moustache were scanty and
lighter than the hair on his head.
His open, almost insolent face was always slightly thrust forward.
His features were not quite regular, a bit oversized, though his face
was more lean than full. The smile that would flash across it from
time to time suggested annoyance or derision, never pleasure.
His arms were long, his fingers large, regular, and strong. His gray
eyes had either a daring, challenging expression to them or, as was
more often the case, were cold and aloof.
He had compressed himself into a nondescript mass and was sitting
motionless: his arms and legs were so still they seemed to have
ceased functioning, and his eyes looked out at everything calmly
or coolly." [1]

From the beginning Rajskij senses a kinship between himself and Mark:

". . . What is he like anyway? The same victim of discord I am?
Always struggling with equally objectionable alternatives. On the
one hand your fantasy tempts you by raising everything to the
ideal: people, nature, all of life, every sort of phenomenon; on the
other there's cold analysis to destroy it all without giving you a
chance to bury yourself in oblivion or go on living. The result is
constant dissatisfaction, indifference. Is that what he's like, or is
he different?" [2]

It turns out that Mark is not different. Mark, like Rajskij, cannot live
without analyzing everything that comes his way. Dominated by reason,
his materialistic nihilism promotes inefficiency and indolence by encouraging him to waste his time in barren criticism of society, and silly
practical jokes. Again, like Rajskij, he is highly gifted but unproductive,
and frustration makes him cynical, sometimes wicked, in spite of his
basically good heart. He believes in reason, truth, and freedom. He wants
to act, to propagate the "new ideas," to enforce them — if necessary —

1) V, p. 269.
2) *ibid.*, p. 272.

by terror, but like Rajskij, he is paralyzed by the nagging idea that in the last
analysis nothing has any meaning. He succumbs to boredom, and his forced
exile in the provinces enhances the malady. Boredom, we must conclude,
bears a deep relation to nihilism (the attitude of materialistic rationalism);
both are perched on the edge of a dangerous nothingness. Mark calls Rajskij a failure, but is he not a failure himself? He hints at a great idea he is
called upon to express and execute. When Rajskij queries what the idea
consists of, however, he answers by expressing a desire for sleep. Rajskij
rightly calls him a Russian Karl Moor, the unsuccessful rebel from Schiller's *The Robbers*, — and loses much of his interest in him. [1]

  Rajskij's boredom has returned in full force. What is more, it has taken
a more dangerous form than ever before.

> " 'What a dreary existence it is.' " he pondered, "looking on at this
> and that, digesting what occurs, becoming passionately involved
> for a moment, and then cooling off, growing bored, and forcibly
> or artificially renewing in yourself the periodic will to live like a
> daily appetite! The secret to the art of living is nothing more than
> the secret of how to make those periods last, or rather, not the
> secret — the gift, the instinctive, unconscious gift. Once we learn
> to live as if with our eyes and ears closed, we will live happily
> ever after. And certainly those are right who don't have a sting
> in the brain, who are short-sighted or have a bad sense of smell,
> who walk as in a fog without losing their illusions! And how can
> we retain the colors of things, how not to look at them with naive
> eyes and see that grass isn't green, the sky isn't blue, that Mark
> is a shallow liberal rather than an exciting hero, that Marfen'ka
> is a sugar doll, and Vera . . . . '
> 'What is Vera?' he wondered yawning." . . . . "His former thought
> 'to describe boredom' came to his mind. Life certainly is many-
> sided and diversified, and if — he thought — this boredom, wide
> and bare like the steppe, is contained in life itself, just as immeasur-
> able sands, bareness and poverty of deserts are contained in nature,
> then boredom too can and must be the subject of thought, analysis,

---

1) Cf. V, p. 287.

of the pen or brush as one of the aspects of life: well, I'll go
ahead and I'll insert into my novel a wide and misty page of
boredom: this coldness, revulsion and malice which have in-
truded upon me will become colors and tints . . . the picture
will be true to life . . .' " [1]

At this, the lowest point in Rajskij's depression — can there be any
deeper despair than that involved in hopelessly describing boredom to
rid oneself of boredom — at a point when the metaphysical relevancy
of boredom becomes so painfully clear, Goncharov introduces the heroine
Vera. He has delayed her entrance until Chapter Sixteen of Part Two:
and the moment is well chosen. Aching for strong emotion, passion,
material for his novel, in short — any remedy for boredom, Rajskij is
wide open. With Vera's appearance he has a new object for study and
new opportunities for letting his fantasy roam.

It is important to note that Goncharov never tells expressly what Vera
is actually like. All we know about her comes from Rajskij's lavish praise
of her beauty and ruminations over the key to her personality. The reason
he is so involved, so passionate is of course that Vera who is in love with
Mark, consistently resists his approaches. If, as mentioned earlier, Rajskij
had preceded Mark, Vera might have shown an interest in him, his art,
and his erudition. But any concern on Vera's part would quickly have
caused Rajskij to lose interest. It is her indifference and the mystery surrounding her that stimulate his curiosity, and lead him to over-rate her.
Once removed from Rajskij's raptures, Vera becomes nothing more than
a selfwilled and independent, but normally intelligent and good-looking
girl. Indeed, Goncharov does not really describe her in any detail. She is
apparently quite unromantic and has little sense for poetry or music. She
tends to be cool and matter-of-fact, and is dominated more by reason
than feeling. True, her love for Mark is genuine, but at the same time she
always seems to have it well under control.

Without Rajskij and his fantasies, Goncharov's heroine loses a great deal
of her attraction; it is he who puts her on a pedestal, not the author. The
last chapters of Part Two give an excellent picture of Rajskij's naive pos-
sessiveness, and his avid intellectual approach to life, contrasting them to

1) V, p. 292.

Vera's cold resistance and well justified anger at his egotistical attempt at usurping her personal freedom. Rajskij gets himself into quite an unpleasant situation. Ignorant of Vera's relation to Mark, he does not suspect that Vera is keeping Mark au courant of all his moves. Mark therefore has the advantage of amazing Rajskij with his gift of divination, teasing him in his rude, ugly manner, and enjoying a cheap victory over an honest and defenseless rival. As a result of Vera's resistance Rajskij's passion develops into a kind of disease. Partly it is his wounded ego that makes him persist, but it is also true that he has talked himself into much of his torments.

The third part of the novel is devoted to a description of these torments. Rajskij cannot stop following Vera, yet more and more indications — like the letter "on blue paper" and her elusive and teasing replies to his fiery questions — lead him to believe that Vera loves someone else. The reader is not told who the lucky young man is until the last chapter of Part Three (though he has most probably surmised as much quite a bit earlier); Rajskij must wait for the last chapter of Part Four (though at one point (Part Four, Chapter Nine) he comes dangerously near to the truth). This secrecy, of course, supplies Parts Three and Four — the novel's climax — with the necessary tension.

Vera and Mark's relations are depicted in an unusual manner. We see them together only three times in the course of the entire novel, and each time their conversation, far from being prettily romantic, consists of a struggle between persuasions, first against a background of mutual attraction, then against the background of love.

The first meeting takes place about nine months before Rajskij's arrival. Vera catches Mark stealing apples and Proudhon's "La propriété, c'est le vol" comes up. Proudhon notwithstanding, Vera considers stealing "ill-mannered," but Mark impresses her by his straightforward behavior and his appeal to "light, new science, new life." Thus begin their clandestine relations, which constantly overshadow the action of the novel, but are developed in only two more scenes.

In Chapter One of Part Four, immediately following the retrospective account of the first meeting, we are introduced to the main problem of their relationship. Mark, in accordance with his materialistic, positivistic, nihilistic precepts, wants to consummate their love without forming any bonds or resorting to such obsolete institutions as marriage. He feels that Vera should follow him unconditionally, enjoy love as long as it lasts, and then — see what happens. There is no doubt that Mark's love is genuine. Reason, however, retains the upper hand, and even in the face of Vera's stubborn opposition he refrains from making promises that he might not be able to keep and that contradict his ideal of free love as in nature. His dilemma bears a distinct similarity to Bazarov's plight in Turgenev's *Fathers and Sons.*

Vera's love for Mark is very genuine too, but she cannot help seeing that his negation of traditional values is not counterbalanced by any firm, constructive knowledge or belief. He has discarded all "conventional lies," yet offers no truths of his own in exchange. Vera's clear realization of this lacuna in his ideology makes her reluctant to follow him unconditionally. She wants a union for life, bound by wedding and marriage in the old tradition; he rejects matrimony outright, equating it contemptuously with "grandma's morals."

Their quarreling leads nowhere. He walks off, proud of his ideological consistency in submitting to the "laws of life," and she turns to what she truly believes is a higher value: religious faith, an eternal truth as great as her love.

Their last meeting (the third witnessed by the reader Part Four, Chapter Twelve) does not add anything to their arguments. Both are too strong and too sure of their inner persuasions to be able to yield, but they do love each other and cannot find the strength to part forever. "They realized that each was right from his own point of view, yet they senselessly hoped, he — that she would come over to his side, and she — that he would give in. They understood at the same time that this hope was absurd, that neither of them could suddenly change his nature at will; adopt new convictions, a different view of life as easily as putting on a new hat; share his partner's faith; or separate himself from it." [1] This senseless hope leads to catastrophe (and the pivotal point in the novel). Just as they are about to part their love flares up and Vera "falls." She

---

1) VI, p. 269.

gives herself to Mark, certain she has won him over and that her sacrifice
will reform him. He takes her, seeing in her surrender the acceptance of
his theories. Both are wrong; both misunderstand the passionate parting
gesture.

Goncharov omits all reference to a rude awakening, but Vera's tortures
and the premonition of tragedy that mounts throughout the last part,
leave little doubt as to the outcome of their romance. Chapter Six of
Part Five contains a minute analysis of Vera and Mark's psychologies, a
lucid retrospective account of the development of a relationship that ended "not in the victory of one or the other, but in mutual defeat and
parting forever." [1]

The two parts which feature Vera and Mark's meetings also see the
culmination of Rajskij's passion. In a highly dramatic scene he flings a
bouquet of orange blossoms, the symbol of innocence, into Vera's open
window after he learns she has given herself to Mark.

To the two main plot lines of Parts Three and Four (the relations between Vera and Mark and Rajskij's sufferings and passion) Goncharov
joins several secondary lines, some of them essential to the development
of the novel, others of an episodic character (though always closely connected to the main theme). Most significant is the introduction of a positive character, who fits much the same mold as Shtol'c and is meant to
contrast sharply with Mark Volokhov. His name is Ivan Ivanovich Tushin,
and he becomes more and more important as the novel moves on. He is
in love with Vera, proposes to her, and by a misunderstanding on her
part becomes one of the few to know of her "fall." Still, we have every
reason to assume that he will become Vera's husband.

In Tushin, Goncharov wished to embody his idea of what an average
man in the best sense of the word should be. In Tushin as in Shtol'c he
stresses the importance of a certain equilibrium, a "harmony of intellect,
heart, and will." [2] Such people are not conspicuous; they seldom make
a name for themselves. The glamour of sharp, subtle minds and ready
words often eclipse them, but the Tushins of this world are the real — though
invisible leaders of the life of the whole circle into which fate places them.

---

1) VI, p. 318.
2) *ibid.*, p. 392.

Tushin lives with his sister on an estate called "Dymok" (Little Smoke), which he has organized in a rational and extremely effective manner. The main source of the estate's income comes from its forests, and because forestery happens to be Tushin's hobby, the entire operation is ideally run.

He knows more than trees and the money they bring however: now and again he goes on the sort of spree that completely upsets the tranquility of the sleepy town, leaving nothing unshaken. He is also a serious student of agronomy and economics, and enjoys a good French novel. [1] Honesty is inherent in his character. So is an unfailing sense for right and wrong. He always knows how to react in the most difficult and delicate of human situations; he is always ready with a kind word and an understanding heart. He knows his worth, but bears no trace of egotism or selfaggrandizement. His love for Vera is strong and chivalrous in the true meaning of this word.

It is extremely difficult to draw positive characters that remain true to life. Goncharov appreciated the difficulty of the task he had set himself, and apparently tried to counteract the danger of Tushin's becoming a lifeless paragon of virtue by playing down his role in the plot, stressing his *average* qualities and denying him "virtuous" speeches. In his discussion of Tushin's character and in the scenes that show him get the better of several precarious situations, Goncharov makes it clear that this is his idea of a good man.

Literary critics who reproach Tushin with woodeness and lifelessness are hardly justified. Goncharov never goes too far, he does not make Tushin perfect. The scene in which Tushin breaks his whip with the silver handle for example shows him to possess a passionate temper; it is only a very strong will that can hold him back.

For Goncharov's "liberal" contemporaries and the majority of Soviet critics, Tushin is the epitomy of an asocial capitalist. Yet there is nothing in Goncharov's text to support such a claim as long as one does not assume *a priori* that being an employer is a sin in itself. In Chapter Eighteen of Part Five, in which Goncharov describes the huge enterprise, the

---

1) VI., pp. 104–105.

owner is the hardest worker and is revered by all his employees and serfs for his just management.

Another important plot line is the evolution of the relationship between Kozlov and his wife. What Goncharov hinted at as possible at the end of Chapter Eight of Part Two, becomes real in Chapter Six of Part Four. Kozlov lived happy and secure in the delusion that the wife he adores reciprocates his feelings. But the reader knows Ulen'ka's true character. Not satisfied with Mark, she seduces Rajskij too, the very evening he comes to "fulfill a friend's duty" (in other words, to accuse Ulen'ka of loose morals). His "fall" in Chapter Twelve of Part Three provides excellent comic relief. Among her numerous anonymous friends in town, she prefers Monsieur Charles, the French schoolteacher, and only Leontij Kozlov is surprised when she finally elopes with him. Kozlov's despair, his vague hopes of seeing her again (he would pardon her immediately), are among the novel's most touching pages. They also provide a case study of the passion Rajskij so longs for. Passion glows quietly in Kozlov, but it is so intense that if extinguished it would surely entail the extinction of his very life. Time has begun to heal his wounds by the end of the novel, but the process is a very slow one and never fully effective.

The healthy relations between Marfen'ka and Vikent'ev show Goncharov looking on the brighter side of love and marriage. Vikent'ev is a young official, whose widowed mother owns an estate in the neighborhood. His shy wooing and Marfen'ka's shy reactions maintain a delicate balance between playing a game and real emotion. Theirs is a story of an uncomplicated love in uncomplicated characters, of many tears, but little suffering. By introducing a touch of irony here and there Goncharov avoids sentimentality, even if he does deliberately use the nightingale as a recurring symbol for the pure and naive feelings of both "children." The official proposal, presented by Vikent'ev's mother and accepted by Grandma turns into another of the comedy scenes Goncharov scatters throughout the novel with such virtuosity; both the women are happy about the match, but family pride makes each of them anxious not to seem too eager. Grandma, vacillating between tradition and common sense, receives an especially sensitive treatment.

Another dramatic comedy scene (Chapter Two, Part Three) relates how wicked old Nil Andreevich Tychkov, the self-appointed keeper of the

town's moral code (being himself a rascal), is thrown out of Grandma's
house after some insinuating remarks about poor Mrs. Krickaja's age and
constant flirtations. Goncharov is very skillful at generating tension. Once
again he centers the climax around Grandma, who to Vera's and Rajskij's
great delight abandons all conventions at just the right moment and grows
into a "figure full of majesty." [1]

Grandma's traditional side comes through in her plan to influence Vera,
whom she rightly suspects of concealing a love affair from her, by an
"allegory": reading aloud a moral novel in the evenings. As in *A Common
Story* Goncharov takes advantage of the situation to compose a charming
parody, retelling the "moral" and highly didactic plot of a standard old
novel, dealing with the sufferings of a young couple, who prevented from
wedlock by cruel parents, receive severe sentences from fate for their dis-
obedience. The effect on Vera is completely lost, of course.

The dream divination scene is also a literary parody, spoofing the role
of dreams in novels, which was very much in vogue in Russian literature
at the time. It begins with harmless Marfen'ka's complicated and frightening mythologically based dream (which bears no relation whatsoever to
her happy future) and ends with Grandma's simple dream of a small
piece of wood on snow (which fails to give the slightest hint of the cruel
experience she will soon face). Vera's bridge ending abruptly in the sea is
too much of a premonition to be taken seriously (following Mark's teaching she explains it away materialistically as a fever), and Rajskij's flying
is too much of a character reflection. Moreover Vikent'ev's humorous
travesties are a clear indication of Goncharov's irony.

The Sof'ja Belovodova story is brought to a somewhat unpersuasive
end in a letter from Ajanov. By writing a completely harmless note to
Count Milari, she comits a "faux pas" that results in the departure of her
whole family "to a spa that even the old people could not remember." [2]
Sof'ja feels guilty and wants to expiate her "sin." All this is hardly in
keeping with the development Sof'ja seemed to be undergoing in the first
part of the novel. It was apparently added, when Goncharov decided
against reintroducing and reforming her as he had planned originally. [3]

1) VI, p. 26.
2) *ibid.*, p. 222.
3) Literaturnyj arkhiv, 3, pp.85–90, and N. I., p. 98.

After nearly every episodic event or appearance of a colorful episodic character (e.g. the drunkard Akim Openkin who speaks an impressive Church-Slavonic, or the old servant Ulita who takes care of the cellar and looks like a goblin), Goncharov remarks that Rajskij resolved to describe it or use it in his novel. In this way he never lets us lose sight of the double orientation: the fact that the hero and the author are starting from the same raw material creates a kind of deliberate ambiguity.

The fifth part of the novel begins just after a culmination point of tension: Rajskij discovers Vera's relationship with Mark and takes his "revenge" with the orange flower bouquet. The already strong suspense is heightened by Grandma's sufferings and confession, [1] but because the confession saves Vera, tension subsides and life returns to normal. There are no catastrophes, no deaths; but each ot the protagonists has undergone an ordeal and grown wiser and sadder.

Tushin first comes to the fore as an important character in Chapter Five, when Vera thinking he knows about her and Mark tells him about her "fall." Flaring up and then calming down under her influence, he gives proof of a dauntless, honest character and a genuine love for Vera. It seems only natural after this that she chose him to make it clear to Mark how hopeless his endeavors to see her have become. Their confrontation (Chapter Sixteen) is designed to show the complete bankruptcy of Mark's principles when faced with a strong representative of Grandma's morals. Inspired by his love for Vera, Tushin behaves inpeccably, while Mark intuitively aware of the legitimacy of Tushin's position is constantly on the verge of losing his temper and resorting to cheap insults.

It is reason that prevented Mark from giving up himself to his passion for Vera, a passion that might have turned into love. Reason kept insisting that constancy in love does not exist, that a cooling-off period inevitably follows the greatest love. By listening to reason, he loses his great opportunity in life to let constant love prove itself.

Reason did not prevent him from taking advantage of Vera, however, and he is forced to admit to himself that all his "logic" and "honesty,"

---

1) Part Five, Chapter Ten.

all his discussions with Vera about ideology were nothing more than sheer egotism. By blindly following his logical, honest, and natural principles, he nearly destroyed the life of his loving victim and certainly destroyed his own.

At the end of Chapter Seventeen, the last time we hear about Mark, we learn that "he is off to spend some time with an old aunt in the province of Novgorod and that he is then planning to reapply to the Cadet Corps and obtain a transfer to the Caucasus." [1]

The parallel between Mark and Pechorin, the protagonist of Lermontov's *A Hero of Our Time* seems to be deliberate. Both men are cold egoists, who lose all contact with the real life of faith, feeling and will and become victims of nihilism; both are strong, but one-sided; both despise and destroy their fellow creatures. The symptoms Lermontov captured so well have by Goncharov's time developed quite logically a full-fledged nihilistic movement. In Mark Goncharov characterizes and denounces that movement.

Chapters Seven to Ten are devoted to a description of Grandma's violent reaction to Vera's disaster, a reaction the more violent in that she considers Vera's fate to be God's punishment for her own sin. This conviction explains her "wanderings" and despair, so often criticized by literary historians, but psychologically quite well founded. Tat'jana Markovna sees that her forgiveness does not really console Vera; Vera is under the impression that she is moved only through pity. To prove her genuine involvement and save her beloved "child," the old woman resolves to sacrifice her pride. In a highly dramatic scene (Chapter Ten) she confesses her sin of forty-five years past. The knowledge that highly venerated old Grandma was able to survive gives Vera the force to overcome her shame and begin a new life. In Chapter Twenty-One the circumstances of Grandma's fall are told in the form of a rumor by Mrs. Krickaja to Rajskij, but neither he nor the reader can doubt their truthfulness.

The hero of Grandma's romance was of course Tit Nikonovich Vatutin. They fell in love, while Grandma was being wooed by a count, and he succeeded in surprising them at a *rendez-vous*. He gave a slap in the face

---

1) VI, p. 388.

to Vatutin, and the chevalier nearly killed him with a knife. Tat'jana Markovna separated the rivals. Because a duel would have made things public, the two men gave their word of honor: the count to keep silent, and Tit Nikonovich — not to marry the beloved woman. This romantic story delighted Rajskij of course, and added greatly to his admiration for Grandma.

With Vera's depression on the wane, Marfen'ka happily married, an important key to Grandma's life and character revealed, Rajskij has little choice, but to leave the estate. Now that his curiosity has been satisfied, he must once more face up to his dangerous *ennui*.

But on the eve of his departure he suddenly realizes he has all the material he needs for a novel and decides that his notes on boredom, passion, himself, and all the characters — principal and episodic — must be reworked on the spot, immediately: "I shall try, I will begin here, on the spot of the action," [1] he says to himself. By turning all the dramas and comedies he has witnessed into fiction and poetry, he will be able to see the pure essence of creation, — his heroine Vera in all her statuesque beauty —, without any admixture of realistic trifles. But exactly herein lies his failure. In his search for pure art, Rajskij loses sight of reality and his novel bogs down at the very start. An amateurish artist and at the same time a character in the novel, deceiving himself about his faculties; the real author, Goncharov, as if standing behind him, telling the story for him and being amused at his difficulties and somewhere at his own too, — this is the situation at the end.

Here is how Goncharov gently ironizes his hero's creative method: "Wasting no time, he picked up a blank sheet of paper and wrote:

VERA

A novel . . .

in large letters across the top. 'In how many parts?' he wondered and stopped writing. 'One volume — that's no novel, that's just a novella,' he thought. 'Two or three: Three — it might even take three years! No, two is enough!' And so he wrote: 'A Novel in Two Parts'." [2]

---

1) VI, p. 418.
2) *ibid.* (The first sentence of the quote is missing in this edition, apparently by an oversight).

And so it continues. Rajskij has no trouble in finding a motto: he chooses the forty-fourth poem in the cycle "Die Heimkehr" (TheReturn Home) from Heinrich Heine's *Buch der Lieder* (Book of Songs). (Aleksej Tolstoj translated it excellently expressly for Goncharov). It would hardly be possible to find a better description of Rajskij's plight: "a comedian, a comedian of life, who really only acted with death (death of the soul) in his own breast, the role of a dying swordsman." [1] "Ich hab' mit dem Tod in der eigenen Brust / Den sterbenden Fechter gespielet." (With death in my own breast, I have played the role of the dying swordsman).

Rajskij must admit with a sigh that playing passion is quite dangerous too. A look in the mirror shows him older and grayer. Next, he writes a dedication to womanhood, claiming the right to present them with a high feminine ideal (as a result of his honest and passionate sufferings), and requesting them to live up to this ideal. "After the dedication he wrote Part One Chapter I in large letters," [3] and then he falls to thinking about possible difficulties the publication of the novel might meet with (e.g. censorship). Finally he must admit to himself that he does not see the psychological problems of the novel too clearly, but he still writes "Once . . . " and then falls asleep.

Boredom has taken over again. No doubt the usual question — What's the use? — will arise again and prevent the novel from being written. We can be all the more sure of the fate of the novel when Rajskij suddenly gets the idea that writing might not be his true vocation after all, that the fact that he imagined Sof'ja and Vera as statues and dreamt of a statue in his sleep might be "hints, commands." [4]

So Rajskij decides to become a sculptor (the more so because he sneezes at the moment of the decision, which he interprets as a nod of approval from fate). And should sculpting (the only art he did not try so far by the way) fail him, then, he writes "I will go down for good in the waves of my mirages and perpetual (neiskhodnyj) boredom." [5] He

---

1) Rehm, p. 72.
2) VI, p. 418.
3) *ibid.*, p. 421.
4) *ibid.*, p. 423.
5) *ibid.*, p. 424.

will yield to the belief that he is fated never to be successful, never to achieve
anything. "But for the time being why not live and hope! To Rome! To Rome!
Where art is not a luxury or an amusement, but work, pleasure, life itself!"[1]

Every word here of course is to be taken ironically. All Rajskij is doing is
killing time to prevent boredom from creeping in. He will play out the comedy of his life, hoping and working without lasting gratification or a sense of
achievement, living exclusively for the moment. He will enjoy Italy, its "nature, art, history" and return to Russia and live on reminiscences. When Goncharov introduces "mother Russia" into the last sentence of the novel, he
does not wish to imply that Russia offers a solution to Rajskij's problem; he
merely sets her forth as a final resting place after a wasted life.

———— · ————

Whereas it is relatively easy to reconstruct the development of *Oblomov*
from the time Goncharov first conceived it until it actually appeared in print,
The Precipice presents a significantly more complex picture. Although Goncharov worked on both novels simultaneously, *Oblomov* progressed quite
smoothly — all things considered — while *The Precipice* kept running up
against difficulties.[2]

The impetus for the novel seems to have come from the rumor Goncharov
heard during his trip to Simbirsk in 1849 about the relationship between his
mother and Tregubov, a rather hazy story of an old love that for reasons unknown to anyone had not ended in matrimony. The parallel to the relationship between the grandmother and Vatutin is so obvious as to make the scene
with which Part V, Chapter 21 closes almost superfluous: Learning of the rumor about his grandmother, Rajskij looks at her with new eyes as she notices
immediately. Goncharov, who usually makes a point of denying the use of
prototypes for the characters in his novels, makes several references to the
parallel in this instance. [3]

Toying with the theme of a long past love affair that led to a woman's
"fall," Goncharov happened on the idea of reworking the story in modern
dress. The result was the figure Vera, who at this point had little in common with the Vera of the final version, being a high spirited young girl
who flaunts as many conventions as she can. The reciprocal confession
scene between grandmother and granddaughter still seems to have been

1) VI, p. 424.
2) My own account largely follows the quite convincing account of O. Chemena, op.cit.
3) VIII, p. 400, e.g.

conceived very early. At any rate Goncharov spoke to Turgenev about it. [1] The scene does figure in the final version, but its basic ingredient, the confessions, is obviously truncated.

Among the elements independent of this kernel probably the first to take shape was the figure of the hero: an artist struggling with the problem of representing reality in art. This problem was one with which Goncharov himself was constantly struggling, and there can be no doubt that Rajskij's thoughts on the process of creation to a great extent reflect his own standpoint.

Even at this early date (1849) Goncharov had apparently put down on paper many of the positions Rajskij takes in the first and second parts of the novel *vis-à-vis* art in general and the novel as a literary genre in particular. There is no way of determining what Rajskij the man as opposed to Rajskij the thinker was like at this time, though his passion for Vera seems to have been quite different, quite a bit more genuine.

In *Better Late Than Never* Goncharov talks about the order in which the individual figures came to him. "The first to appear life size was Grandmother, then Vera and Rajskij, and later Marfen'ka, Kozlov and his wife (who come from memories of university friends), and the domestics . . . " [2] As Chemena rightly notes, this order proves a fairly accurate means of ascertaining the sketchwork Goncharov completed between 1849 and 1852: Rajskij's biography (Part I, Chapters 6, 12, and 13), his first visit to Malinovka (I, 7-11, i.e. the chapters that appeared under the title of "Grandmother" in the first issue of *The Annals of the Fatherland* for 1861), Rajskij's arrival for his second decisive visit (II, 1-2), the four chapters devoted to Kozlov and his wife (II, 5-8), and the description of the domestics and of the comic figure Polina (II, 12). Two more sections seem to date back to this early period: first, the portrait of Openkin (II, 19) and second, the highly effective scene of the reception of Grandmother's which ends with the Tychkov scandal — because the guests at the reception talk of the political events of 1848-1851 as if they were going on at the time.

---

1) Cf. p. 171.
2) VIII, p. 79.

Not until 1855, after his long journey, did Goncharov take up *The Precipice* again. It is most likely at this time that the first chapter of the novel was written. The name of Ajanov — Rajskij's collocutor — points to Siberian reminiscences.

In the winter of 1856 Goncharov outlined the novel as it then stood for Turgenev. By this time Sof'ja Belovodova and Natasha had come into being. The prototype for the former may well have been Elizaveta Tolstaja. Ol'ga Chemena is probably correct in postulating that Rajskij's attempts to awaken the "beautiful statue" resemble Goncharov's attempts to win over Tolstaja. [1] Rajskij's bitter thoughts after his farewell to Sof'ja [2] ("Thus died the lover in him and awoke the selfless artist") apply to Goncharov as well. [3] The chapters dealing with Sof'ja (I, 2–5, 17, 18) were therefore written or at least drafted during the years 1855–1856.

In 1858 the first sixteen chapters of the novel were copied out by Goncharov's nephew Viktor Kirmalov. Goncharov appended chapters 17 and 18 in his own hand, though when he did so remains unclear. He also inserted Kozlov's statements about Mark into chapter 16.

At this time Goncharov was still uncertain as to what to call the novel and vacillated back and forth between *The Artist, Rajskij, Rajskij the Artist,* and *Vera.* It was not until the summer of 1868 that he settled once and for all on *The Precipice.* In any case he completely ceased work on the novel in 1857, so as to devote himself fully to *Oblomov.*

As soon as *Oblomov* appeared, in 1859, he went back to sifting *Precipice* fragments. After several months work he gave chapters 14 and 15 of Part II, in which Mark Volokhov makes his first appearance, to Ekaterina Majkova for copying. Goncharov seemed intent on endowing his heroine Vera with many of Ekaterina Majkova's traits. But neither Vera nor Mark had yet acquired a definite character, and the remains of Goncharov's lack of certainty can be discerned in the final text of the work. Chapter 17 of Part II ends with Vasilisa announcing that Mark has come to visit Rajskij, and Rajskij hurries off to meet him. Yet their meeting

1) Chemena, p. 30.
2) Part I, Chapter 18.
3) V, p. 155.

is never discussed (to say nothing of the fact that it would be unthinkable for an outcast like Mark to show himself at Grandmother's house by the light of day), and in Part II, Chapter 20 we learn that after their nocturnal meeting Mark and Rajskij had never seen one another again.

At this point there seems to have been another hiatus, due this time to Goncharov's feud with Turgenev. In the outline for *On the Eve* as Turgenev recounted it to Goncharov (probably in March 1859) the heroine follows her lover, a young man possessed with progressive ideas, to stand by his side in his work. Goncharov had originally intended the same fate for his Vera (who was to follow Mark to Siberia). Though there is little similarity with Turgenev's plot in the version that finally saw print, the similarity does seem to have been greater in Goncharov's original draft. And so Goncharov stopped moving forward (apparently at Part III, Chapter 4) and began recasting sections of the work he had formerly considered complete. He was also annoyed at Turgenev for having included a pair of sisters in his cast of characters since his *Precipice* outline had indicated that he would be using a pair of sisters. As a result of a complaint he made to Turgenev on this account, Turgenev changed the sister of Elena Stakhova (Goncharov's heroine was also Elena in his earliest drafts) from Zoja Stakhova to Zoja Mueller. In addition to this mistrust of Turgenev, which paralysed all his effort to continue work on *The Precipice* and nearly caused him to give up writing altogether, he was held back, beginning in 1862, by his extraordinarily time-consuming activities first at the *Northern Post* and then with the Board of Censors. This hiatus lasted until 1865.

In the summer of 1865 Goncharov went back to work on the novel, concentrating on Part III. The tenth chapter, in which Tushin, the "positive character," makes his appearance, is dated "Boulogne, July 30, 1865." Chapters 5–8 (Rajskij's jealousy of the author of "the letter on blue paper") also belong to this period. Work continued throughout the next summer, by which time it had become clear that Vera was not to be on Mark's side and would therefore not follow him. It was during this summer that the crisis in the Majkov family reached its climax. Ekaterina broke with "the bonds of convention" by leaving her husband to live

with her lover. This is what Vera was *not* to do. [1] The clearer it became
that Majkova would leave home, the firmer was Goncharov's resolve to
alter Vera's character and behavior.

The task he set out for himself was far from easy. Substantial portions
of the novel had been completed, and the plot line — as far as the Vera-
Mark relationship was concerned — was geared to climax in the Siberian
trip. Now, after five years of letting the manuscript lie and three more
years of forging uncertainly ahead, Goncharov felt it necessary to change
the ending while at the same time ensuring that both parts form an
organic whole without anachronisms or self contradictions. This extraordinarily difficult task required an extraordinary intellectual effort, and
Goncharov's despair of himself and the world at large during this period
is clearly related to the mammoth proportions of the project.

Goncharov began to add new material to the novel in Bad Kissingen in
July 1868, and by working steadily throughout his stay there, he left with
Part IV complete and Part V well under way. The figure of Vera had now
changed considerably. Now Goncharov very skillfully stresses her physical
passion for Mark. He had hinted earlier that they were bound by more
than abstract discussions, but by playing up the sensual element in their
relationship Goncharov could show that Vera's attraction to Mark was
merely physical not ideological or psychological. He also introduces an
element of religious fervor into Vera's character, which, though he makes
no mention of it earlier, is completely consonant with the picture of the
passionate truth seeker he has drawn of her. It is rather surprising that
this religious fervor first comes to light in Chapter 15 of Part III, but it
is nonetheless far from inconsistent. The sudden outburst of Vera's dormant religious feelings can easily be accounted for psychologically by the
gradual awareness that her love is foundring and by the profound grief
that accompanies this awareness. Her new religious outlook together with
the imminent breakup of her relationship make it possible for Vera to
develop a certain sympathy for Mark; they help her realize how lonely,
forelorn, empty, and dissatisfied he basically is despite all his swagger.

---

1) Ol'ga Chemena is no doubt correct in maintaining that Ekaterina Majkova influenced the figure of Vera. It must be stressed, however, that in this case the
   influence was negative, moving Goncharov to make Vera's actions diametrically
   opposed to Majkova's.

This realization only strengthens her love for him; it adds christian love for one's fellowman to the erotic love she had already felt.

Mark's development has already been discussed. From a complex positive characterization of the honest, idealist do-gooder he becomes a noaccount phrasemonger and nihilist who gives vent to his disillusionment with the world — the result of a wounded ego — in silly pranks and empty slogans. Because the original conception does at times come through, however, he has a certain ambiguity about him. Goncharov never succeeded in making a consistent character of the new Mark.

There is no way of knowing to what extent Majkova's lover Fedor Ljubimov or Goncharov's nephews Vladimir Kirmalov or Aleksandr Goncharov served as a model for Mark. What is clear, however, is that Goncharov blackened the positive figure of the enlightened liberal with many of the traits of the worst variety of shallow-minded nihilism to give vent to his anger over the events of the sixties. Given the ambiguity of Mark's character, it would be difficult to accept Vera's love for him on any other but an erotic level. And it would be difficult to accept her victory over herself at the end of the work, after her fall, if it were not for the common sense approach deeply rooted in the patriarchal and profoundly religious tradition in which she grew up.

Goncharov overhauled the entire novel and composed its conclusion while under constant pressure from Stasjulevich, who played deaf to his continuous pleas for more time. On the one hand Stasjulevich was looking out for the good of his journal, which had made great gains since it had begun serializing Goncharov's novel. On the other hand, however, he must also have realized that any kindheartedness on his part could well lead to unpredictably drawn out delays, and he was therefore relentless. The novel suffered from this pressure, some rough passages and some passages of dubious merit were either left untouched of inserted at the last minute. Yet there is reason to believe that if Stasjulevich had not stood his ground the novel might never have been completed.

After "The Precipice"

From the very first there was a great discrepancy between the reactions of the fraternity of critics and the Russian reading public: while the critics panned the work, the public ate it up.

It is easy to account for the critic's position. By interpreting the figure of Mark Volokhov, unacceptable to leading radicals and liberals, as representative of the younger generation, they turned the novel into a pamphlet against that generation, willfully overlooking the fact that Volokhov represented only one aspect of the work. The result was an anti-Goncharov campaign that gained in intensity with the appearance of each new part of the novel and culminated in a caterwaul of coarse, often mean invectives.

One of the leading critics of the time, Nikolaj Shelgunov, had this to say about *The Precipice:* "A novel, which fails to inspire a progressive way of thoughts or progressive conclusions in his readers could only have been written by a backward and dumb author. – In *The Precipice* Mr. Goncharov has buried himself. May he rest in peace! If the author is unable to see that the motive power behind contemporary writers is realism, not idealism, then we can not teach him. One more fresh grave for a writer who died for progress! But at least we know that if Mr. Goncharov publishes another novel fifteen years hence, it will be read by our grandmothers – and this only for the memories it brings back and for these piquant love scenes that older people find so charming. Russian literature has never had such a mighty talent for sensuous vignettes ... – Wo consider Mr. Goncharov's novel to be poorly conceived, harmful, and immoral, and it goes without saying that we would never put it into the hands of girls and boys still in learning stage." [1]

Most of the reviews were mere variations on this theme, which were far from agreeable to Goncharov. But he was absolutely sure of his right, so that there is not even an indication of any vacillation in his basic attitude. Still certain attacks like the nonsensical articles by Mikhail Saltykov-Shchedrin "Street Philosophy" [2] and Aleksandr Skabichevskij "An Old Truth" [3] could not but hurt.

1) Utevskij, p. 213.
2) The Annals of the Fatherland (Otechesvennye Zapiski), 1869, VI.
3) *ibid.,* 1869, X. Both articles were reprinted several times in the collected works of the respective critic.

For the time being Goncharov tried to escape this bombardment, by
going abroad; in mid-May 1869 he went via Berlin to Bad Kissingen,
then to Paris and Boulogne-sur-Mer.

But the strains of the previous year had left their mark. In a letter to
Sof'ja Nikitenko from Bad Kissingen he speaks of a "galvanic force" that
enabled him to complete *The Precipice* and see it in print. After serving its
purpose, that force turned into severe depression. Baiting by the critics
provided the coup de grace. At this time Goncharov's ever-present mistrust of Turgenev had developed into a full-scale persecution complex.
For now he thought himself surrounded by spies, who not only wanted
to draw on his literary plans, but who tried to enter his private life and
make him suspect from the political point of view. Some of his letters to
Sof'ja Nikitenko sound like the outcry of a desperate man: "I am not ill,
that is, I have not gone mad. Everyone knows that. Is it honorable, is it
just to mutilate a man's life by letting loose a band of assorted scound-
rals on him: dissolute women, cunning and brainless spies robbing him
of his every step, thought, word! — Anyone who tells me that I'm dreaming or delirious, or that *my nerves are upset* is a hypocrite and a liar. I
see it all. I can feel what's going on." [1]

When Goncharov returned to St. Petersburg in September the polemics
against *The Precipice* were still raging. He was especially piqued by a review from the pen of Evgenij Utin, Stasjulevich's brother-in-law, in the
November issue of Stasjulevich's *Messenger,* the very journal that had
published the novel at the beginning of the year. By bowing to the
younger generation Stasjulevich apparently wished to save his journal
from being labelled hopelessly conservative. But Goncharov, and not without justification, thought of himself as having been betrayed, and for
some years thereafter his relationship with Stasjulevich lacked much of
its original warmth.

In his article "Literary Controversies of Our Time" Utin, like his predecessors concentrated on Voloknov and the younger generation. Aleksej Tolstoj's amusing reaction to this review in a letter to Stasjulevich,
has the ring of truth to it: "Your last issue had an article by your brother-

---

1) Utevskij, p. 223.

in-law Mr. Utin on controversies in our literature. With all due respect for
Mr. Utin's mind, I cannot fail to observe — my candor prevents me — that
he is doing the younger generation an odd sort of service by acknowledg-
ing the figure of Mark as its representative in the novel. Tell me, why in
heaven's name doesn't the middle generation see itself in Rajskij? Why
don't the older people identify with the councillor who was turned out
by Grandma? Why does the *younger generation* yell fire every time a
scoundrel or other appears on the scene. *Salva venia et exceptis excipien-
dis,* it's like watching who grabs his hat when someone yells, 'The crook's
hat is on fire!' Take me, for example, I'm fifty-two. But, God is my witness, it would never occur to me to take offense if I came across a fifty-
year-old blackguard in a novel. There's something *nicht richtig* going
on." [1]

Wherever possible, Tolstoj sought to mollify him and set things right
between him and Stasjulevich. When Goncharov complained to Tolstoj
about Turgenev and his "organized ring," he received only "abuses" in
response. Writing to Stasjulevich, Tolstoj had this to say about their mutual
acquaintance: "Goncharov's malady seems incurable. What can be done
with him? People have been driven to despair by the thought of having
a glass nose;" [2] and: "Poor, poor Goncharov! He must constantly be
wrapped up in cotton, and when, as inevitably happens, he crawls out,
it is only to say, 'It's your fault I'm so cold!' What can you do with
him!" [3]

Turgenev's opinion of *The Precipice* as reflected in his letters was clearly
negative, but he never made any public pronouncements against the work.

Now Goncharov had to decide whether he wanted to bring out the
novel in book form, and after long and painful deliberations he decided
to do so, the critics notwithstanding. No doubt an important factor in
this decision was the friendly attitude of the reading public with whom
the novel proved very popular.

Stasjulevich discusses the phenomenon in a letter to Aleksej Tolstoj:
"Ivan Aleksandrovich's novel has given rise to the most incongruous

1) A. K. Tolstoj, Sobranie sochinenij, IV, Moskva 1964, p. 320.
2) *ibid.,* p. 321.
3) *ibid.,* p. 332.

rumors, but people are reading it, a large number of people are reading it. — In any case, only *The Precipice* can account for the journal's phenomenal success. For the whole of the last year I had 3,700 subscribers, and this year on April 15th (1869) I scaled a journal's pillars of Hercules, that is, 5,000. By the first of May I had 5,700." [1] And in *An Uncommon Story* Goncharov noted with great satisfaction: "*The Precipice* made a great impression even though it was dissected section by section. Stasjulevich told me that no sooner does the first of the month roll around than from early morning our suscriber's messenger boys crowd our offices like a *bakery* (his words), in order to get the issue of *The Messenger of Europe*. My novel came out between January and May inclusive, one part to an issue. As Stasjulevich told me with gratitude, the number of subscribers rose suddenly from 3,500 to 6,000." [2]

When *The Precipice* appeared as a book in February 1870, Goncharov was subjected to a new round of vociferously negative reviews from the "liberal" side. But there were some objective articles too and the book sold very well.

Just before the book was released Goncharov had to face the problem whether to write a forword answering the critics and justifying his position. He actually wrote a "Forword to the Novel *The Precipice*," which he wanted to include in the 1870 edition, but apparently because Stasjulevich and Nikitenko persuaded him not to enter into any discussion with his critics at the time, it was not included — after some hesitations on Goncharov's part. The manuscript was published for the first time in 1938. [3] Goncharov's second attempt to answer the novel's critics is his "Intentions, Problems, and Ideas of the Novel *The Precipice*" (Namerenija, zadachi i idei romana *Obryv*), which was presumably written about 1875 and was first published posthumously in 1895. [4] The third explanation came as a long article "Better Late Than Never (Critical Notes)" (Luchshe pozdno chem nikogda [Kriticheskie zametki]), which was written and published in 1879. [5] In this article Goncharov analyzes all three of his

---

1) Utevskij, p. 216.
2) *ibid.*, p. 217
3) Cf. VIII, p. 513.
4) Russkij Vestnik, Nr. 1.
5) Russkaja Rech', Nr. 6.

novels and sets forth his views on art and literature in general and the
novel in particular.

   This attempt of self interpretation suffers from the common flaw of
similar attempts by Russian writers: all analysis focusses on Russian
problems, Russian society and Russian life. The emphasis on this sort
of analysis must be blamed on the narrow "social" criticism of the time.
It lowers of course the ideological level of the works in question and
one has no other choice than to separate the discussion of the works
as they are written, from the necessarily biased opinions of their authors
about them. The following is a brief combined survey of the three articles
mentioned above. Goncharov obviously constantly returned to the unpublished sketches, when working on "Better Late Than Never," so they
can easily be incorporated in its discussion.

   From the beginning in his "Forword" Goncharov concentrated on defending himself against the charge that he had insulted the "new generation" in the character of Mark Volokhov. This remained the main issue
in the following two articles. Again and again he stresses that Volokhov
is meant to represent only a small unpleasant, negative minority of the
"new men" in Russia. He is not typical for the new generation as such,
but for its excesses and distortions, not its true countenance. He is one
of those semi-educated people who has dissolved the bonds of family,
school, work, and all socially productive activity; one of those restless
minds that are on occasion very much alive and spirited but lack the
preparation which learning and experience give, minds that aspire to
prominence and distinction but lack the right and means to do so, because these are usually gained by talent, knowledge, and hard work. He
is an impostor of "the new life," of the supposed "new force," an apostle
with no disciples preaching his sermon to the nooks and crannies of the
peacefully flowing life of our backwaters. [1]

   True Mark claims to be fighting for truth, reason and freedom, but
then again Goncharov asks ironically, who does not? He has no place
among reasonable, well educated young people; he is the type who pro-

---

1) VIII, p. 143.

tests against everything without the least idea of what to put in its place. Dazzled by the façade of the new Zeitgeist, he fails to grasp the meaning behind new concepts. He is ambitious and yet lazy; he will never be able to cope with the task he wants to take upon himself or serve the ideas he tries to propagate. The only positive thing that can be said about Volokhov is that he is genuine in his beliefs. He is an amateurish dreamer, but an honest one — from his point of view at least — hence the influence, though fleeting, he is able to exercise on Vera and various other unprepared Russian people, mainly schoolboys. With full justification Goncharov asks why the "negatively objective" attitude he takes towards nearly all his characters remained unchallenged except in the case of Volokhov, why in the case of Volokhov he lost the right to criticize?

Real representatives of the new generation Goncharov sees in Tushin and his like. Tushin is the "unconscious new man," a man formed by life itself whom Russia needs. Of a healthy natural bent, he is simple, honest, straightforward: he both understands and loves the task life has set him. Sincerity, belief in simplicity, an understanding of the charm of truth and the willingness to live by it (i.e. cultivating one's feelings and cherishing them as much, if not more than reason), such is Tushin's character as Goncharov would have us to see him.

The main goals of *The Precipice*, as Goncharov formulates them, were to describe "the play of passions," investigate the problem of the "fallen woman" and "analyze" in the figure of Rajskij, "the nature of the artist and follow up its manifestations in art and life." [1] Goncharov writes that the "process of different manifestations of passion, i.e. of love" [2] never failed to amaze him. He was perpetually struck by the immense influence it exercised over "fate — and men and the actions of men." "While at work on Vera's genuinely ardent passion, the novel forced me to set in motion and exhaust almost all the forms which the passions may take. Frist there is Rajskij's passion for Vera, one sort of passion, the sort particular to his character. Then Tushin's passion for her, a profound, level-headed, human passion, consciously based on a conviction of Vera's moral perfection. After that there is the teacher Kozlov's unconscious, al-

---

1) VIII, p. 216.
2) *ibid.*, p. 208.

most blind passion for his unfaithful wife. And finally the wild, animal-like, yet persistent and intense passion of Savelij the peasant for his wife Marina, that serf-girl Messalina." [1]

But Vera's love is of course the most interesting. Her passion, as Goncharov sees it, is an outcome of her thirst for a "new truth." Here again Goncharov reduces universal feeling to a specific situation in Russia. Having experienced the wrongs of patriarchal life of outmoded traditions and having recognized them as such, she sets about acquainting herself with new ideas. In Mark she hopes to find a new truth; she felt in him great strength, courage and fire. This made her fall in love with him.

As it turns out, however, she did not really know, where to seek her "truth." What is more Grandma had not prepared her for her personal ordeal; she was too self-willed, too proud. It is no surprise then that Vera's disillusionment is complete. "Not Vera fell," says Goncharov, "not a person, — the Russian maiden, the Russian woman fell as a victim in the struggle of the old life with the new one . . . " [2]

When critics chidingly asked how an intelligent and beautiful girl like Vera could fall in love with such a rude, dirty fellow, Goncharov refuses to answer: "People know, why they love, but no person in love will be able to decide why he or she is in love. The heart has afterwards to pay a bitter toll fo its imagination, as it happened to Vera." [3] At the same time Goncharov points to many cases during the sixties, in which "charming beauties" follow such "heroes" as Mark to their garrets or cellars, abandoning their parents or even their children. No doubt he had also Ekaterina Majkova in mind, when he wrote this. [4]

Concerning his treatment of Vera's fall, Goncharov stressed that the fact of the so-called fall is not decisive. His main concern in this respect was to raise the question whether the fall of a woman can be determined by the fact as such, the "certain fact," by which people got accustomed to determine it, or rather by the nature of the woman herself. Morally pure characters like Grandma or Vera are both guilty of the "fact," but

---

1) VIII, p. 209.
2) *ibid.*, p. 96.
3) *ibid.*, p. 219.
4) *ibid.*, p. 95.

have they fallen? Goncharov considered the society attitude towards fallen women "a crying injustice," and his novel is meant to prove it.[1]

The third goal, that of analyzing the nature of the artist, is much more central for Goncharov in this novel. Rajskij is of course a very concrete Russian artist, but in this case Goncharov does not limit himself to Rajskij's individual problems. He uses Rajskij as a springboard to highly significant pronouncements about the essence of creation.

Art was a luxury in Russia at the time, an amusement for the rich and a very poor source of income for professional artists. A member of the landed aristocracy, Rajskij is meant to exemplify a class of serious dilettantes. As living practitioners of this advanced variety of dilettantism, Goncharov cites Count Viel'gorskij in music, Tjutchev and Count V. Odoevskij in literature. "In all kinds of art the talents of such Rajskijs were not the content and aim of life, but just a means to spend the time pleasantly." [2]

Rajskij, Goncharov continues, is talented, but having grown up during a period characterized in Russian history by Oblomovian sleep, he lacks the arduous "prepschool," necessary to develop his talent. Too much of him still lies dormant. This is why he is unable to concentrate on art or the new ideals, "the approach of which one could sense in the air." [3]

When Goncharov speaks of "Oblomovian sleep," he is refering to his untenable conception obviously adapted post factum, that *A Common Story*, *Oblomov* and *The Precipice* have "the closest organic connection," and are in essence one huge edifice, one mirror, in which three eras "old life, sleep and awakening" are reflected in miniature. [4] Clearly these three eras seem rather contrived. What does "old life" mean? Why did it fall asleep? It certainly could not have escaped Goncharov's attention that socio-ideological movements like Russia's from the forties to the sixties had occured everywhere in the course of history. Evidently these reinterpretations resulted from an attempt on his part to comply with

---

1) Cf. VIII, p. 216.
2) *ibid.*, p. 85.
3) *ibid.*
4) *ibid.*, p. 162.

the demand of contemporary criticism that the writer respond to the
"accursed questions" (prokljatye voprosy) of Russia's present day.

Rajskij is a born artist; he has imagination and a "subtle nervous
organization." "But his lack of an artistic education coupled with the
idle life of nearly all of society fifty years ago and his secure existence
made neither an artist nor a writer of him, and his surplus of creative
imagination overflowed into his life, turning it into a paradise at one
moment and a hell at the next." [1]

Rajskij is by nature an "individual without individuality" (bezlichnoe
lico) reflecting the fleeting events and sensations of life and coloring
them with the hue of this or that moment. He is essentially honest, good,
and noble and though his heart and reason may rise to magnanimity and
self-sacrifice, decision concerning his vital interests seldom touch his heart
or reason. At every step nerves and fancies destroy the best of intentions.
His love for Vera is pure and simple fantasy; it exists only in his imagination. Without the least bit of evidence he conjures up an inward beauty
to match her charming countenance. He stubbornly sees what he wants
to see, and refuses to admit that Vera might differ from what he would
have her be. When he learns that she belongs to someone else, he loses
his passion in one evening, and from a nervous, sensitive lover, he becomes "her good friend and brother." [2]

As interesting and as much to the point Goncharov's explanations are
in some respects, they do no even tackle the main issue *The Precipice*
sets forth: the problem of boredom. The reason for this is quite clear:
Goncharov did not want to raise his interpretation to the metaphysical
level. He wanted to answer his critics, and they attacked him on socio-
logical, political, and nationalistic issues. Going beyond this limit would
have led nowhere, as there was little hope that any of the critics would
be willing or capable of discussing transcendental truths. It is difficult
to determine to what extent Goncharov conceptualized the problem as
an abstract metaphysical dilemma, but there is no doubt that – on an
intuitive level at least – he was keenly aware of it.

---

1) VIII, p. 214.
2) *ibid.*, pp. 214–215.

The Twenty Last Uneventful Years

Goncharov was forced to limit his 1870 trip abroad to Marienbad and Dresden; the Franco-Prussian war had dashed his hopes of visiting Boulogne-sur-Mer and take the healthy sea baths. By mid-July he was back in Petersburg. The following letter to Sof'ja Nikitenko reflects his low spirits: "Many people, as I notice, do not understand my sad situation – and it seems – they do not like it, that I live this way and not that way. But really it cannot be otherwise, after all what happened . . . Where should I take health, strength, the desire to live from! – Some people have been asking me whether I'm working on something new? Heavens! That's all I need! For several years running, everything has seemed to conspire to hinder me from being an author, and now people ask why I've stopped writing. A fortress is made of stone (in wartime one naturally turns to military figures of speech), but once it's been battered with bombs and artillery fire, it's left in ruins. What then is left of man! I must pull myself together. The main thing is to emerge from the darkness I've been living in and forget everything. And it wouldn't hurt to find another climate if I want to take up the pen again. The last time I felt even the glimmer of a desire to start something new was last year in Boulogne, by the sea. The weather was magnificent, there was nothing to disturb me, and the outline for a new novel almost began tracing itself in my head. The faces, types, scenes even the general contours and an epilogue to *The Precipice* began coming to me the way they always do. But as soon as I returned to our autumn the weight on my shoulders returned. It was even intensified by all sorts of intimations, threats, etc. I have lost heart once and for all and don't even think of myself as an author anymore. Now I'm sick, I'm a worn out invalid with the *idèe fixe* that there is no way for me to live my life but under lock and key. And that *idèe fixe* comes very close to truth." [1]

Concerning the war, Goncharov tended to favor the Prussians, but was willing to forgive Napoleon because of his desperate situation.

From the above reference to an epilogue for *The Precipice* we can only

---

1) VIII, pp. 430–431.

conclude that Goncharov was planning some sort of continuation to the work, which never materialized, however.

As a result of his self-inflicted literary idleness long letters become more and more a compulsion. Daily events, politics, literature and of course personal moods and sufferings — all these he handles with consummate wit and wisdom in his usual impeccable style. Goncharov was well aware of the compulsive nature of his letter writing and feared he might be trying the patience of his correspondents. Here is the touching conclusion to a long "literary" letter to Countess Sof'ja Tolstaja dating from November 1870: "You at least will not berate me, good, kind Sof'ja Andreevna, for my long, unseemly, Koz'ma-Prutkovian [1])letters! You realize, you understand what all this letter jabber means: it's my nature. *And chase nature out of the door, it will fly back through the window.* When I'm not writing books, I write letters! You will take this letter as you see fit. You will read it or let it be. But you will not use my jabber against me. You will not *raise a hue and cry over it — and me at the same time.* You will not betray my old-man's childlike trust in you; you will simply throw it away, because it's impossible to read (I realize that), it can only be written — and even that during a sleepless night!" [2)]

In 1871 Goncharov went back to Bad Kissingen and then on to Ostend for the healthful sea air and water. On his way back to Petersburg he stopped for a while in Berlin.

In December he saw Griboedov's famous comedy *Woe from Wit* at the Aleksandrinskij Theater, and the following March his article on the play, "A Million Torments," was published in *The Messenger of Europe.* This latest appearance in print was again accompanied by numerous obstacles and doubts, and the title, according to Goncharov himself, is ambiguous: It refers first to Chackij, the play's hero, but also to the article's publisher — Stasjulevich — and the author.

---

1) A reference to the "author" of satirical and parodical verse and prose invented by the Countess's husband Aleksej and the Zhemchuzhnikov brothers.
2) VIII, p. 440.

"A Million Torments"

The essay opens with the statement that Griboedov's comedy has exhibited an astounding vitality: While such great figures as Pushkin's Onegin and Lermontov's Pechorin — to say nothing of their inferiors — "petrify with time like tombstone statues," [1] Griboedov's work has lived its own irrepressible life for half a century and will go on living indefinitely. It is the purpose of the essay to supply the grounds for this statement.

Goncharov points out that professional critics have never known quite what to make of the work. They seem to agree that it is a model of its kind, but they cannot put into words what makes it so. The reading public has also esteemed it highly, paying it the extreme compliment of turning many of its lines into everyday sayings, thereby breaking up the continuity, the plot line, into millions of small coins.

Goncharov intentionally omits two aspects of the work from his discussion: the exquisite portrait the play affords of the period and individuals typical of the period, and its sparkling language. Both have been sufficiently dwelt upon by the critics. He adds though that there can be no doubt that in these respects many other literatures have yet to bring forth a Griboedov and gives a short but penetrating and astoundingly modern evaluation of Griboedov's language, his complete fusion of verse and colloquial dialogue, which he designates as conversational verse.

It is a third aspect of the work, however, that Goncharov proposes to concentrate on: the comedy as action, as "stage motion." [2] This aspect has been overshadowed by the other two, says Goncharov; yet it is the plot structure in this "subtle, clever, highly refined, and passionate" [3] work, or rather the plot structure in combination with the first two elements that makes it a comedy of life *par excellence*.

With great empathy and fine wit Goncharov proceeds to characterize the hero, Chackij. He then sketches in the plot so as to strengthen his thesis of its psychologically and objectively finespun movement.

1) VIII., p. 8
2) *ibid.*, p. 10.
3) *ibid.*, p. 13.

In Onegin and Pechorin Goncharov sees the sickly offspring of a dying
age; in Chackij the harbinger of a new age. The numerous parallels he
draws, the apt juxtapositions he makes are extremely skillfully formulated. For Goncharov it is mainly Chackij's feeling of partaking activ-
ely in life, together with its corollary, his ability to fall in love, that set
him apart from the other two heroes. Goncharov very adeptly retells the
plot, stepping it up gradually to the allimportant scene in which Chackij
declares his love to Sof'ja. "So masterful a scene in such masterful verse
can scarcely be found in any other dramatic work." [1]

Next Goncharov very convincingly demonstrates how as a result of
his passion Chackij gradually loses control over his reason. In the end he
traps himself by the untenable exaggerations of his social and political
views and his reproaches to Sof'ja. Sof'ja in Goncharov's interpretation
is far from the silly little miss critics have so often taken her for. She is
a woman who is genuinely in love and though she makes her position
abundantly clear, Chackij, blinded by his passion, refuses to understand
her. Her main drawback is her conventional upbringing; it dims her
positive qualities considerably. Yet it cannot annihilate them, and perhaps she sees light after the sad discovery she makes at the comedy's
end.

Another of Goncharov's original and convincing insights is that
Chackij serves as a catalyst, that his grand appearance in the final scene
prevents any further concealment of what has been going on and forces
each of the main characters to take honest stock of himself. Chackij —
intelligent, honest, and hot-tempered — has caused a split in the ranks,
and even though his own aspirations have gone awry, he has injected
some life into a dessicated, convention-ridden society. He brings away a
million torments with him, but the seed he has sown has not been in
vain.

According to Goncharov's interpretation men like Chackij generally
come to the fore when one age is about to give way to another. He
pioneers new concepts and new customs, in short, a life that opposes
stagnation, the stagnation of the outdated. And he suffers the fate of all

---

1) VIII, p. 19.

pioneers: he is "broken by the quantity of the old forces, but not until
he has dealt them their death blow with the quality of fresh, new forces."[1]
It is Goncharov's conviction that Chackij will live on as long as artists deal
with warring ideas and the succession of the generations, that he is the
typical representative of a specific situation, and that all Griboedov's followers will be able to do is compose variations on the master's theme,
much as the followers of Cervantes and Shakespeare have done with Don
Quixote and Hamlet. "The candid, fiery speeches of these future Chackijs
will always echo Griboedov's words and motifs, or if not his words, then
the feeling and accent of his own Chackij's petulant soliloquies. When
battling with the old world, our robust heroes will never stray from this
music." [2]

Goncharov names Belinskij and Gercen as his choices for Chackij's most
important successors in real life. He rejects in no uncertain terms the widely accepted critical view of Chackij as an abstract, an idea, a walking, talking moral. He finds Chackij's character so rich and manysided, so full of
life that its depths cannot be adequately probed within the boundaries of
a play. As far as Goncharov is concerned, Griboedov's creation is as perfect as is humanly possible.

The essay concludes with some remarks about the apparently disappointing performance of the play staged in honor   of the actor Ippolit
Monakhov, which Goncharov saw. — Griboedov criticism can claim few
examples of such acuity of thought. At the time it appeared Goncharov's
essay was extremely original, both in methodology and its conclusions.

Work on this article helped Goncharov over the hurdles of his psychological crises. Nikitenko says in his diary that Goncharov "seems to be
beginning to come out of his retinence and excessive melancholy that
for several months kept him in absolute seclusion." [3]

---

1) VIII, p. 32.
2) *ibid.*, p. 33.
3) Nikitenko, III, p. 227.

In 1872 he travelled abroad for the last time, following the usual Marienbad, Paris, Boulogne-sur-Mer route. He returned home in August relatively happy and quite refreshed.

Goncharov's life gradually fell into a routine that remained uninterrupted by major events. He read a great deal (French novels as his main fare), wrote letters, and took extended walks, which he considered extremely valuable. His health was not very steady, and because frequent colds confined him to his rooms, he would compose plaints — often quite witty — on having to refuse invitations or visitors. He also refused to be active on literary committees or work on editorial boards for charitable publications, and consciously reduced the scope of his own literary efforts.

In fall 1873 he taught, as it seems, Russian literature to the children of Grand Duke Konstantin Nikolaevich, apparently a short and uneventful episode. [1]

When asked to contribute to a collection of stories and articles entitled *Pooling Resources* (Skladchina) in support of the starving population of Samara province, however, he agreed to participate. At first he worked on a sketch called "A Trip along the Volga"(December 1873 and January 1874), but he abandoned it in favor of "From Memoirs and Stories of a Sea Voyage," renamed later "After Twenty Years," [2] which was published in the collection in 1874. He always had a particular fancy for everything connected with the popular *Frigate Pallada,* the only of his books to escape attack from almost all sides. "It's the one book," he wrote, "that like a rose without thorns has left me with a pleasant aftertaste, or rather, the one pleasant event in my career that has left me no bitter aftertaste." [3] Though he was long undecided as to whether to put out an edition of collected works, he saw the *Frigate Pallada* appear in four editions during his lifetime and greatly enjoyed polishing it up. [4]

'The Trip along the Volga" was meant to be a reminiscence of Goncharov's trip to Simbirsk (1862). It's main apparently fictitious character

---

1) Alekseev, p. 205.
2) Cf. p. 96.
3) Alekseev, p. 232.
4) Ogonek, VIII, p. 465.

is Ivan Khot'kov, a very gifted and very likable painter, whose career as an artist is in danger because his restless nature makes concentration all but impossible. Because Goncharov enjoys providing his readers with the motivation behind what he writes, he tells us that Khot'kov has painted his portrait and given it to him as a surprise and that he in turn had promised to paint the artist's portrait in words. Khot'kov reminds the author of his "debt" in the first section of the sketch, and the description of how the debt was contracted and the report on the trip along the Volga constitute the debt's liquidation.

Both the appearance and the temperament of the artist are evident from the first page. And the trip along the Volga has nothing to do with the Volga. It serves rather as an excuse to describe Khot'kov's behavior and his relationship with the wide variety of his fellow-passengers and thereby gives rise to a gallery of miniatures surrounding as it were, the main portrait. The most impressive of these miniatures is that of the completely destitute, senile ninety-year-old woman returning to her native province for the first time in decades, who expects to be taken in by relatives; the good and expansive Khot'kov takes up a collection for her on board.

A very lively description of harbor traffic and a short bit of landscape painting are all but lost among the human portraits and the sparkling conversations. Almost the entire sketch consists of dialogues even in episodic situations that could easily have been narrated. There is real reason to regret that Goncharov never tried his hand at writing for the stage; he would most likely have made a brilliant playwright.

The "Trip" was never completed. Goncharov would undoubtedly have put a lot more work into it before allowing it to be published, and there is no way of knowing how it would have ended. The fragment was printed for the first time in the periodical "The Star" (Zvezda), 1940, Nr.2.

As Dostoevskij was also working on the "Pooling Resources," Goncharov once again found himself in contact with him. In his "Small Pictures" Dostoevskij had sketched a village priest with nihilist tendencies, whom he believed to be a type that had remained unnoticed. Goncharov remarked to him — at first apparently during a conversation and later in writing — that a type did not become a type until it had been repeated so often that it could no longer remain unnoticed. Destoevskij had concentrated too many "liberal characteristics" in one personage and had thereby incurred Goncharov's displeasure: this sort of writing ran directly counter to Goncharov's. The tone of his letters is polite and cautious; he clearly has no desire to offend, and leaves the final decision to Dostoevskij. [1]

After vascillating for many years, Goncharov finally made up his mind to allow his portrait to be painted for the gallery of the rich art patron Pavel Tret'jakov. The result of his sittings with the well-known painter Ivan Kramskoj was the excellent portrait which Goncharov characterized himself in a letter to Tret'jakov as follows: "Thanks to Ivan Nikolaevich's talent, the portrait surpasses all expectation. Several of my art loving acquaintances admit they have rarely seen such mastery in a portrait, to say nothing of its remarkable likeness." [2] It is characteristic of Goncharov's lack of self confidence in the period following the publication of *The Precipice* that he originally assumed Tret'jakov's suggestion to be a joke. [3]

Goncharov had always been interested in painting. Names of painters appear throughout his letters and works. In 1874 he wrote an article entitled "Christ in the Desert: A Painting by Mr. Kramskoj," but it failed to see print, again seemingly because of Goncharov's lack of self confidence and almost pathological modesty. Laying it aside the better to "look it over in peace," he never picked it up again. It was first published in the journal *Beginnings* (Nachala) in 1921 and proved to be extremely perceptive.

---

1) VIII, p. 456 sq.
2) Ogenek, VIII, p. 439.
3) *ibid.*, p. 412.

The essay is of importance for its clarification of two aspects of Goncharov's thought: his attitude toward religious art and consequently his attitude toward religion.

Certain critics had asserted that modern artists who deal with biblical themes are nonbelievers because they rely too much on realism and too little on the traditionally sanctified attributes of their chosen material. Without trying to meddle in matters of belief or nonbelief (which lie entirely outside the realm of art), Goncharov points out that the recent attempts to portray scenes from the Scriptures rightfully aim at leaving behind the restrictive rules of the historical school and introducing a modicum of realism into religious motifs — an undertaking that has very little to do with faith or the lack of it.

Artistic truth, he asserts, is art's only objective, and neither formal nor truly religious piety can be disturbed by it. Paintings as such cannot even express world views, to say nothing of being able to alter them. The very art of painting is bound by time: it can represent only the fleeting state of a person, emotion, passion, or event. Within such a limited perspective there is no way of painting "tendentiousness" into the picture, and it is therefore impossible to paint Christ as God incarnate (though this is what the critics demand).

Belief in Christ's divinity must come to us through faith, Goncharov continues, and though faith flows in abundance from His life and teachings, it has little connection with His objective form. When critics demand to see "something special" shining through Christ's person, they are demanding the impossible. Apart from the fact that the divine is inaccessible to man, it was clearly absent in Christ's real person. For had it been present, people would have recognized it and fallen down at His feet, and there would have been no battle, no great deeds, no suffering, no mystery of salvation. Should the artist succeed through his own genuine emotion in appealing to the spectator's faith, we can only rejoice, but the goal of art has been reached if he has succeeded in expressing an artistic truth without distorting historical truth.

Goncharov feels that all attempts made by art to overstep human boundaries and move into the territory of the superhuman and miraculous are doomed to failure, that all attempts to determine the *essence* of the divine by means of the form of its attributes will fail. He argues that the artist's concrete perception is bound to break down, and that even supernatural *events* do not lend themselves to pictorial reproduction. He clinches the argument by calling to mind the attempts to capture on canvas Christ's ascension.

In line with this position the enthusiastic praise Goncharov lavishes on Raphael's Sistine Madonna is aimed entirely at the portrayal of the Blessed Virgin. Here, says Goncharov, the artist has succeeded in representing supreme humanity in motherhood and giving us a glimpse of divinity. But when he tries to show God in the figure of the child, he fails. He gives him a mature face — almost an old man's face — to make him seem wise and divine, but all he has done in fact is to affix an unusual, unlikely head to the body of a child. Yet Raphael proves many times over in other works that he excells at depicting the classical beauty of youth.

Far be it from Goncharov to suggest that any artist can produce a successful religious work of art or that faith or the lack of it has no effect whatsoever on the execution of religious art. "No, Christian faith has an enormous and unique influence," [1] and Goncharov continues with a long hymn to Christendom, which more than any religion has succeeded in "establishing new and everlasting ideals toward which mankind is presently striving and ever more shall strive." [2] "Do whatever they may, no ravishers, no sceptics, no philosophers will ever annihilate religion in man nor the ideals toward which it strives. And there is nothing purer or loftier than the Christian religion." [3]

Goncharov's manifestly genuine and profound religious feelings find what might be called passionate expression in this statement. Taking everything he says on the matter into account, we can establish his position to be the following: It is not absolutely necessary for an artist working with religious themes to be religious himself; he can capture supreme artistic truth even without religious conviction. And although the presence of religious conviction can add to the likenesses he paints the highest degree

---

1) VIII, p. 192.
2) *ibid.*
3) *ibid.*

of humanity, the divine remains impossible to represent graphically no matter how he tries.

After this introduction, which comprises over three quarters of the essay, Goncharov turns to the painting that provided the impulse for the remarks. Ivan Kramskoj's "Christ in the Desert." He gives it a sympathetic description, perhaps one of the most beautiful painting descriptions in all Russian literature. His exposition follows the theses of the introduction; he praises the artist for having depicted the highest degree of humanity and thereby allowing sparks of the divine to make themselves felt.

An artist does not paint his subject alone, states Goncharov in his conclusion; he also paints the tonality with which his imagination tints the subject. Carrying this point farther, Goncharov delivers a carefully developed attack on "realism." Realism constantly claims that it can depict reality, yet where if not in depicting reality does realism founder? Realism "aims at attaining some absolute, almost mathematical truth. No such truth exists in art. Art does not show an object as it is; it shows it as reflected in the imagination. The imagination then provides it with the image, colors, and tonality established by historical studies and illuminated by imagination. The artist does not work from the object itself because the object no longer exists; he works from the object's reflection." [1]

Goncharov is in fact expounding the same thesis for the visual arts as he did for literature, namely that instead of being a representation of reality, art is a reflection of reality, it is reality as the artist perceives it.

The following note was appended to the manuscript: "I must look this over when I find time. There seems to be enough material for a full-length essay." [2] One can only agree. Despite occasional haziness in the train of thought, a fault easily remedied, the essay is rich in candid, very personal and profound insights.

In an unsigned article carried by the newspaper *The Voice* (Golos) on May 9th Goncharov speaks about the acquisition of Vasilij Vereshchagin's paintings by Tretjakov. He expresses the hope that a "national Russian museum of painting" might be the result of this deal. [3]

---

1) VIII, p. 195.
2) *ibid.*, p. 517.
3) Alekseev, pp. 213–214.

The "Notes Made for a Critical Article on Ostrovskij" also most likely date to the year 1874. They were originally conceived as a discussion of Ostrovskij's latest play *Late Love*. But Goncharov stopped work on them before the intended article was finished. They first appeared in a collection of essays entitled *In Memory of A.N. Ostrovskij* which was published in 1923.

"Notes" they are called in the title, and notes they are. They have no clear coherence and are plainly far from completion. And yet they contain a number of stimulating comments. Instead of discussing the play he had proposed to discuss, Goncharov expostulates on Ostrovskij in broad terms.

Goncharov, as mentioned above,[1] always had great esteem for Ostrovskij, too great, perhaps. He was attracted by his cool objectivity, his sense of humor, and his ever fertile imagination. No doubt the friendly relationship between the two men also played a part in Goncharov's admiration for the playwright's work. When Ostrovskij's late plays began receiving cool reception from the press and public, Goncharov felt it his duty to come to his defense.

In Goncharov's opinion the unfavorable criticism reflected a general trend: the cool reception Russian society had begun giving all *belles lettres*. By turning to social and political activities and fostering scientific progress, large groups of the population had lost sight of art and no longer viewed life through art's prism. Goncharov seems to see this development in a positive light, though he expresses his approval somewhat equivocally: if everyone were to cease viewing life through art's prism, society would be condemned to "eternal youth." He also feels that under the pressure of the country's new attitudes art must abandon some of its hallowed traditions and turn to a *terra incognita* of new ideas.

Goncharov divides Russian society confronted with Ostrovskij into three classes: the artistocracy, which cannot comprehend him because he is foreign to their milieu (in this connection he goes into a rather detailed characterization of the *beau monde* and its tradition-bound sense of taste); the middle class, which is very close to Ostrovskij because its borders

---

1) Cf. p. 119.

converge with the borders of the circles Ostrovskij puts on stage; and the lower classes — from the merchant class on down — which find Ostrovskij uninteresting because "we can see it all at home." Clearly Ostrovskij can never have the broad influence Pushkin, Lermontov, Gogol', and even Griboedov had; the milieu he has staked out for himself is too limited. His lack in popular acclaim, predicts Goncharov, will be made up for by longevity. He has chronicled the life of the Muscovite State from its beginnings (in *The Snowmaiden*) to the first railroad station, as it went on in the masses of the people, and has so completely exhausted it that nothing more can possibly be added to it.

The Iliad of the Russian people, its heroic period, lasted until the reign of Peter the Great. An Odyssey never existed because there was no Penelope — a sarcastic allusion to the position of the Russian woman. Even in the heroic period, Goncharov seems to imply, there was little actual heroic activity. As a result, when Russian authors write about early Russian history, they write about two periods only: the reign of Ivan the Terrible and the Time of Troubles (the time of the False Dimitrij, Shujskij and Boris Godunov); these two periods give them raw material that looks more like life, not like a bear hunt or an insane asylum. Goncharov attributes Ostrovskij with having uncovered and portrayed a Russian Odyssey where nobody had ever expected to find one: among the simple people.

The rest of the "Notes" consists of fragmentary remarks on Russian history and Ostrovskij. The connection between the two, however, is not always discernable. They are the bricks of a building whose outline is not yet distinct.

————·————

"Hamlet Returns to the Russian Stage" is an essay Goncharov began in 1875 and again never completed. The occasion that prompted him to write about the play was the appearance of Aleksandr Nil'skij, an important actor and an acquaintance of Goncharov, in the title role. Goncharov later gave the manuscript of the essay along with other sketches to Sof'ja Nikitenko, instructing her to do what she saw fit with them. A capsule characterization of Hamlet taken from the essay appeared in the 1900 edition of the Grand Duke Konstantin's translation of the play. The fragment did not appear in its entirety until the Ogonek edition of 1952.

Goncharov begins by expressing his joy at the appearance of a classic on the stage. Even though he greatly admired Aleksandr Ostrovskij, he was clearly aware that Ostrovskij's narrow thematic range tended to make for overly specialized actors. And at the time Ostrovskij reigned supreme over the Russian stage. Actors were growing less and less skillful; they had trouble with the historical plays of their own Ostrovskij to say nothing of "the brilliant dramatic chronicles" of Aleksej Tolstoj or Shakespeare. In Goncharov's estimation Nil'skij was an exception, and while his skill was amply recognized by his audiences he was vilified by the press. A short excursus berating the press for its attacks precedes the main body of the essay.

Goncharov sees Hamlet as an atypical role that no actor can ever hope to master. Lear and Othello are playable because their characters are clearcut — almost to a fault. To play Hamlet an actor must be a Hamlet, as Shakespeare created him. Otherwise all he can hope for is to bring out one or another aspect of the part. "Delicate dispositions, hearts with disastrously strong feelings, implacable logic, and oversensitive nerves, all these elements contain to a greater or lesser degree the ingredients of Hamlet's passionate, tender, profound, and petulant nature." [1]

How is the actor to find the means to express all this in one evening? There are many men who have a number of Hamlet's qualities and are able to portray them. Goncharov expressly uses the word "qualities"; he does not speak of traits. The fact that Hamlet cannot be recognized by one trait or another proves that he is not a type. Goncharov would seem to be referring here to his minor controversy with Dostoevskij concerning the concept of types. [2]

If Hamlet's condition were normal, hypothesizes Goncharov, his qualities would not be perceptible; they do not exist under tranquil circumstances. Hamlet is no hero; he is a good, noble man, a gentleman, and would remain so if fate hadn't provoked him. When confronted with the world of evil, his positive qualities force him to stop at nothing. A

1) VIII, p. 203.
2) Cf. p. 258.

less honest or less rigorous temperament would either choose "not to be" or simply to allow evil to run its course. But the law of fate demands retaliation and assigns Hamlet the role of revenger. The drama of his situation consists in the fact that he is a man in the full sense of the word. Had he been more machine-like, he would have had an easy time of wreaking bloody vengeance and therefore of calming his conscience. But Hamlet eschews the way of sacrifice and bloodshed to go his own way, knowing full well that his organism, his person will be unable to stand the blows it will receive. These doubts lead him to despair, yet he moves steadily forward, incapable of flinching, incapable of striking with frigid apathy. He is aware that by fulfilling what has been ordained he too will be forced to succumb. He can be made to desist only if he is overcome on his way by death or by a miracle convincing him that all evil is a mere fiction. Whenever he seems disposed to doubt, the frightful reality of the deed he has to revenge convinces him again of the reality of evil and consequently of the necessity of battle, victory and his own eventual defeat.

At this point Goncharov returns to the concept of the type and stresses once again that types develop in everyday life from the repetition of identical traits in many individuals. He is less convincing when he tries to show why he considers Lear and Othello and even Macbeth to be "typical." Since the end of the fragment reiterates previously expounded material, we may assume that Goncharov was growing tired of developing and synthesizing his theory. But his analysis of Hamlet is doubtlessly original, even if it does contain parallels to Goethe's interpretation. Perhaps the article was also intended as a belated reaction to Turgenev's famous "Hamlet and Don Quixote" (1860).

———————— · ————————

Since the sixties Goncharov had been zealously collaborating on two Petersburg newspapers: The St. Petersburg News (Sanktpeterburgskie vedomosti) and The Voice (Golos). He contributed short book reviews, articles about personalities of the literary world, be it because of an anniversary or a death, but he was most at home with feuilletons, scenes from city life.

Practically all feuilletons went unsigned, and at this stage in the development of Goncharov scholarship it is all but impossible to determine which among them belong to Goncharov.

In a letter to his publisher A. Kraevskij he expressly requests that
all his articles be printed "without any signatures or initials." [1] In another letter he characterizes his journalistic endeavors as follows: ". . .
what variety: cabbies, dogs, music . . . finally Shakespeare! The reason
for all this variety is that nothing human is foreign to me." [2]

If a very few of Goncharov's feuilletons are in fact identifiable, it is
only because for some reason they remained unprinted. Referring to
"Christmas Time" (Rozhdestvenskaja elka) in another letter to Kraevskij,
he writes: "Don't scold me, Andrej Aleksandrovich, for failing to send
you the preholiday lines I spoke to you about. The trouble is I can't
keep my words down. Before I know it, I've lost control! Well, that's
just what happened this time. Instead of that short article, those few
short lines, I practically gave birth to a *feuilleton-monstre* half a sheet
long. Besides it has turned out to have a bantering sort of tone; it has
turned out a lollypop not at all suitable for the serious *Voice*. — I tried
and tried, but finally put it away unfinished. To finish it would have
taken another evening or two." [3]

The letter allows us to place the composition of "Christmas Time" in
December 1875. The first page of the manuscript contains the following
note in Goncharov's hand: "Abandoned feuilleton. Written for a newspaper because of Christmas." It was first published in the seventh volume
of the 1952 Ogonek edition and then once more the following year in
Literary Archives. [4] The latter, a critical edition, is much to be preferred.

Clearly the feuilleton is a lollypop if the term lollypop (limonadnyj) is
meant to include a somewhat bold sort of fun. Goncharov shows us both
sides of the coin; he captures the joy and excitement of those on the receiving end (children, in particular) and the trials of those who are expected
to do the giving (mainly no doubt the *patres familias*).

"Christmas Time" means the entire Christmas season. New Year is included, and this leads into an excursus about New Year's visits, basically
completely meaningless but traditionally "necessary" and exhausting every-

---

1) Literaturnyj arkhiv, IV, p. 106.
2) *ibid.*
3) *ibid.*
4) Literaturnyj arkhiv, IV, 1953

body concerned. People suffering both physically and financially under the festivities, would, no matter how they berate them, out of one side of their mouth, protest their suppression out of the other.

The sketch is very lively and contains many typically Goncharovian features, features characteristic of Goncharov as a man. For one thing, it shows off his touching love for children: "There are no stupid or nasty — that is, bad children. There are children who are ailing, but they are pitiable, not bad! All children are beautiful, as beautiful as childhood itself, the age of unconditional beauty!" [1]

Goncharov finds children most beautiful at the ages of five, six, and seven. Soon after, he feels, the child's awakening consciousness begins to attract corruption. In an amusing discourse, however, he defends the generally rejected theory that a child's innocence may in some cases be made to last until he is sixteen.

But the feuilleton ends in a minor key. After examining Christmas festivities among the people, Goncharov concludes they all pretty much boil down to drunken reveling. He himself was quite averse to alcohol. In his "Servants" he bemoans the fact that he, who looks askance at drunkards from all classes of society, is so often surrounded by them and calls the urge to drink "an intermittent, sometimes dangerous, insanity that can spark an unexpected catastrophe." [2] All three novels contain excurses on the bad effects of alcohol. Goncharov sees the situation in the lower classes as particularly acute and concludes that if serfs drank out of woe then their freeman descendents drink for joy. After an imaginary half-dialogue half-inner monologue by representatives of the people, the following lapidary assertion closes the feuilleton: "Having a few too many is a must for the holidays!"

It would be well worth the effort to identify Goncharov's feuilletons. They will surely be found to contain a wealth of humor and of melancholy.

---

1) Literaturnyj arkhiv, IV, pp. 100–101.
2) VII, p. 357.

Between 1875 and 1878 Goncharov remained in Petersburg, spending most of his time in the apartment he would occupy until his death. His life proceeded tranquilly and his correspondence and articles — some published, others left in rough drafts — give evidence of much intellectual activity. He worked steadily on *An Uncommon Story* and the long apology "Better Late Than Never." Both these apologetic works reflect with varying doses of venom Goncharov's reaction to Turgenev and the persistent attacks on his last novel. The latter article has been discussed in connection with the criticism directed against *The Precipice*;[1] the former apology and pamphlet does not stop at the "court of honor" and the following reconciliation at the funeral of Druzhinin described above. [2]

Turgenev was anxious to effect a reconciliation, continues Goncharov, because firstly he hoped that once the argument had been settled, the bone of contention — the plagiarism — would be forgotten, and secondly because he needed to reestablish contact so as to keep closer watch over him and prevent him from completing *The Precipice*. According to Goncharov, Turgenev had already expropriated many of his ideas for *Fathers and Sons* and *Smoke* from *The Precipice* sketches. True, Goncharov does acknowledge the priority of the figure of Bazarov in *Fathers and Sons;* he admits that Turgenev solved the riddle of the nihilist type at a time when it was still in the process of taking shape, and that he himself did not have to come to grips with his nihilist, Volokhov, until the movement was in full bloom. But he denies the least bit of literary merit to *Smoke,* denouncing it as a collection of cleverly disguised borrowings. [3]

Almost in passing Goncharov notes that Turgenev's *Spring Freshets* (1872) is a paraphrase of his first novel *A Common Story*. He claims that Turgenev undertook the project for two reasons: first, to demonstrate how much better he could handle the same thematic material, and second, to prove that the material was his own in case *A Common Story* ever appeared in French translation. After all, he argued, why would a Frenchman pay any attention to the fact that Goncharov's novel had been written twenty-five years before?

---

1) Cf. p. 244 sq.
2) Cf. pp. 168 sq., 190.
3) N. I., p. 46.

At the same time Goncharov contended that as soon as his works were translated the reputation of the jealous Turgenev would be utterly destroyed in France. He saw Turgenev as hellbent on depriving him of all his originality and even accused him of having passed around the ideas he had culled from *The Precipice* to other writers. What Goncharov is implying here is that his material is so rich that even Turgenev, whose prolific pen regurgitated plot after Goncharov plot in the short stories (Turgenev's "An Unhappy Woman" comes from the Natasha episode, e.g., he claims), could not dispose of them all on his own.

And yet, if we are to believe Goncharov, Turgenev was not satisfied with the themes, motifs, and ideas he had received directly from the master; he had therefore formed a spy ring to keep an eye on him and had gone so far as to direct its members to break into his hotel room and copy his papers. There was no doubt in Goncharov's mind but that all his private correspondence bearing the least reference to literary plans or anything remotely related found its way into Turgenev's hands. Even Stasjulevich did not escape his suspicion as an accessory.

As the most important recipients of this material Goncharov suspected Berthold Auerbach and Gustave Flaubert. A translation of Auerbach's *Das Landhaus am Rhein,* with a preface by Turgenev, appeared at the same time as *The Precipice* in *The Messenger of Europe,* and Goncharov — very innocently, he tells us — recommended Sof'ja Nikitenko to do the translation. It was not until too late that he learned that the novel was nothing more than *The Precipice* transposed to "German soil and German customs." [1] It is difficult to see what similarities between Auerbach's long and rather tedious novel and his own work Goncharov had in mind; except for some generalities there are none.

And Flaubert? Goncharov read *Madame Bovary* as a retelling of his own Ulen'ka-Kozlov story: "The novel's plot, its overall plan, its protagonists, incidents, and psychology all parallel the episode of Kozlov and his wife." [2] The fact that Flaubert's novel was first published in 1857 only substantiated his suspicion: had he not recounted his *Precipice* outline to Turgenev in 1855?

---

1) N. I., p. 70.
2) *ibid.,* p. 81.

In *L'éducation sentimentale* Goncharov tries to point up many correspondences by citing page numbers. His theory here is that Turgenev would give Flaubert an oral translation of each *Precipice* chapter as it came out in the *Messenger of Europe* and that Flaubert would set to work immediately after these translation sessions. It is certainly superfluous to say that all examples Goncharov gives do not stand up to close inspection. They are partly commonplaces and partly details that in context have completely independent validity. [1] And naturally the fact that an article in the January–February 1870 issue of the *Messenger of Europe* by an unindentified A. S-n and entitled "French Society in Gustave Flaubert's New Novel (On the Occasion of the Publication of *L'éducation sentimentale*, 2 vols., Paris, 1870)" which drew a harmless comparison between Flaubert's hero Frédéric and Rajskij added considerable fuel to his fire. [2]

Emile Zola, who Goncharov thought was also being used by Turgenev to discredit him, spoke in lavish praise of Flaubert in his "Letters from Paris" (which began appearing in September 1875 in the *Messenger of Europe)*, making specific mention of Flaubert's slow, laborious method of writing. On the one hand, Goncharov took Zola's praise of Flaubert as a reflection of Zola's wish to belittle him, Goncharov; on the other, he saw in Zola's description of Flaubert's writing habits a true reflection of his own. Recalling that he had often complained in his letters about how difficult it was for him to write, Goncharov concluded that Turgenev had received reports to this effect from his treacherous correspondents and had then ascribed everything to Flaubert, thereby only increasing the similarity between the two (to Goncharov's disadvantage of course).

Even the very mediocre novel by a F. Romer *The Dilettantes* which appeared in issues four, five, and six of the *Messenger of Europe* for 1872, fanned Goncharov's jealousy. He took it for a poorly camouflaged work of Turgenev's, a retelling of the sixth part of *The Precipice* in the form in which he had told it to Stasjulevich, who then, fancies Goncharov, must have passed it on to Turgenev: Returning from abroad, Rajskij looks up Sof'ja Belovodova and brings the relationship he had begun with her in Part One to an end. He then goes to the country and finds Granny sur-

---

1) Cf. N. I., pp. 84–89.
2) *ibid.*, pp. 90–91.

rounded by Marfen'ka's children. The existence of the Belovodova scene substantiates Goncharov's claim that he had been thinking along these lines, but Romer's novel has hardly anything to do with it. [1]

Goncharov finally came to suspect that Stasjulevich besides handing over to Turgenev a theme he had hinted at as a possible contribution to *Pooling Resources* (a sketch of a man of the people who reads poetry, an early sketch perhaps for Valentin in *Old-Time Servants*), had himself added a plot line to it and then tricked Turgenev into believing that the outline for the entire story had come from Goncharov. He did so, says Goncharov, to prove to Turgenev how faithfully he was carrying out his watchdog duties and the result of this double duplicity was Turgenev's "Punin and Baburin." When Stasjulevich did not respond to his accusations, Goncharov felt his worst suspicions confirmed. It is absolutely clear, however, that Stasjulevich remained silent to spare his already ailing friend new pain. [2]

Turgenev's behavior can be explained in the same way. On the occasions when the two got together, Goncharov, as he himself reports, would set traps for his adversary. Turgenev's reactions, again as reported by Goncharov, show an obvious attempt to avoid anything that might upset him. But no matter what he said, Goncharov interpreted it in an unfavorable light. It is no wonder that even when Goncharov would make as harmless a remark as "You remember how in my novel ∴ . . " Turgenev would break in with "No, I remember nothing, absolutely nothing." [3] Of course this sort of outburst could mean nothing to Goncharov but a clear admission of guilt.

Yet the more objectively wrong he is, the more pitiful he becomes. No one who reads his pamphlet can doubt that his *idèe fixe* caused him no end of suffering. He was unshakeable in his belief that Turgenev deprived him of his place in Russian literature. To dismiss the feeling as envy or megalomania would be an oversimplification ignoring the complex pathological aspect of Goncharov's condition. His obsession with harping on the same string, his constant denunciations of Turgenev as a jealous,

---

1) N. I., p. 98.
2) *ibid.*, pp. 100–101.
3) *ibid.*, p. 33.

ambitious genius of prevarication, his repeated assertion of being concerned only with vindicating himself from future charges of having
stolen material himself (and he felt certain such charges would be made
against him), not with proving that he had been robbed — all this has
the ring of authenticity to it, and this authenticity makes it gripping.
His was a persecution complex which, while subjecting its opponent's
actions to minute analysis, also inflicted martyrdom on the mind and
heart of the sufferer and turned his life into a hell. "And I came to
realise," says Goncharov at one of the climaxes of his exposition, "that
there was some sort of alliance bound by oath to plot against me . . .
For what guilt? Who? Life began to cause me pain, I felt afraid of it." [1]

Clearly Goncharov wrote the work under the influence of a severe
bout of depression, and as he wrote he got more and more carried away
with the accusations. His letters to Stasjulevich, for example, are perhaps
a bit less frequent and a bit cooler than before, but they are in no way
unfriendly. Moreover their tone soon returns to its former degree of
cordiality, which is sincere beyond all doubt.

Goncharov was apparently aware of his condition. In a letter to Stasjulevich dated December 10, 1874 he notes that with the years his
hypochondria has taken on a complicated character: "I always have the
feeling, especially on overcast days, that everywhere I go people would
like to hurt me, injure me, etc." [2] But apart from those "overcast" days
he was far from being a hypochondriac. His correspondence with Stasjulevich affords ample proof; right up until his death (the last letter is
dated July 27, 1891) they are playful — even in their plaints — warm,
and full of felicitous turns of phrase.

Above and beyond the polemics, *An Uncommon Story* contains a
synthesis of Goncharov's views on life, politics, and art. While adding
little to what he says elsewhere, it does yield a collection of well formulated aphorisms. Its curious interplay of wisdom and pathology gives
the work a unique sort of appeal.

----

1) N. I., p. 70.
2) Stasjulevich, IV, p. 134.

"A Literary Soirée"

During the summer of 1877 Goncharov undertook a more gratifying project, a sketch (ocherk) called "A Literary Soirée," which appeared on January 1, 1880 in *The Russian Language*. The action of the sketch — the reading of a literary work and the discussion that ensues — is clearly taken from a real life situation: now and again, Goncharov, a skillful performer, agreed to read at literary salons. [1] The work dealt with in "A Literary Soirée" is *Lorin,* a novel written by Goncharov's former superior, Petr Valuev (who held several ministerial positions during the course of his career), with whom Goncharov had kept up a detailed correspondence on literary matters. Given the high position of *Lorin*'s author a certain caution had to be exercised in dealing with the work. [2]

"Everything said in favor of your work is my own, everything against it relates to the criticism to come, the criticism I assume will make its way into print," [3] he wrote in a very long letter to Valuev, that contains a careful, clever, yet very candid criticism of this middling work. As is so often the case in his letters, Goncharov writes here with obvious relish. He explains his enthusiasm and "loquacity" by the fact that as a writer he has been sentenced to silence (another hint at Turgenev's "spy ring") and goes on to supplement his original theme with a profusion of insights on literature as such. Goncharov is one of those writers and poets who give much thought to literary theory but never try to formulate a unified system, perhaps fearing that in the attempt to avoid contradictions, systematization would turn truths into lies.

Goncharov opens his letter to Valuev by bidding him beware his future critics, who would be constantly on the lookout for "ideas" and sure to find fault with his treatment of love (or as they put it — sexual relations). Even Tolstoj did not escape them, he points out. For Goncharov, love in all its forms represented the motive force of all existence. He could not

---

1) Cf. Alekseev, p. 223.
2) The content of "Lorin, a Novel From High Society Life" (Lorin, roman iz veli-kosvetskoj zhizni) by Count P. A. Valuev, I–II, 1882, is retold by E. Ljackij in his "Goncharov", Stockholm 1920, pp. 151–164.
3) Alekseev, p. 224.

understand how an author could replace it with other passions and
emotions, when it played such a major role in every man's life, serving
as motivation, content, and goal of almost every endeavor and activity,
of almost all ambition and *amour propre*. By "other passions and
emotions" Goncharov means the "social" and "humanitarian" causes,
which he hated so much.

In connection with the praise — slightly tinged with irony — that
Goncharov lavishes on the description of a military parade in *Lorin,* he
discusses the various forms under which literature dealt with war —.

According to Goncharov the ideals of the age of chivalry — conquer,
capture and destroy — have given way to a new motto: protect the life,
property, honor and rights of the nation. And with the increasing mechan-
ical perfection of weaponry and general conscription, the exclusive position of the privileged military caste has been greatly undermined. All
this must necessarily leave its traces on modern attitudes to war, and
Goncharov expresses the fear that Valuev's attitude might seem a trifle
out of date. Yet he has no illusions as to the possibility of an "inter-
national court of arbitration" that would make war an impossibility;
these are hopes of "thinking theoreticians"; both the "practical thinker"
and the "warrior" he says, must realize that as long as men are made of
flesh and blood, they will continue to be made of passions and therefore
wage wars.

In matters of social import too Goncharov is the "practical pessimist."
Neither the ultraconservative nor the radical formulates his principles in
all their cynisism when writing fiction or plays. The former never says,
" 'You must revere name, rank, and position *quand même,* even though
the individual bearing them is not worth it; order demands you to act
thus.' Nor will the latter despite all his shamelessness go so far as to
announce, 'You have an ancient name, a title, and a high position, and
you are therefore a good for nothing, even though you do in fact deserve
them. But such are the needs of progress and the *Zeitgeist.'* These theses
are dealt with theoretically in tracts by scholars and politicians, in count-
less volumes and administrative principles, but it is not the tracts that
make decisions . . Decisions are made by conspiracies and revolutions
on the one hand and police agents and bayonets on the other. That's

the way things have been and will continue to be — i. e. struggle and struggle." [1]

This exposition gives Goncharov an opportunity to expostulate on the significance of thesis in novels in general. As an abstract statement a thesis is meaningless and never convinces anyone of anything. Every thesis can be argued, the logic of its ideas destroyed by a simple paradox or sophism. However, art — images, portraits, scenes — which sets forth its theses objectively, *sine ira* and rests firmly and majestically on the immovable foundation of truth, good, and honor, is as invulnerable as an impregnable fortress. Thus, Tolstoj's novels are strong when he thinks and speculates in images, but weak when he consciously takes up a philosophical position and leaves off describing. "Thinking in images," one of Goncharov's pet theories, is clearly delineated in this letter.

Goncharov does not advocate indifference in literature, but he feels that the writer should present his ideas objectively and without refering to the theses of his opponent. If ignored they will lose force by themselves. Democracy has successfully applied this method to rid itself of elements that harrassed it: aristocrats, militarism, various principles of rank and station, etc. All these problems have their place in the novel — everything that has place in life deserves a place in the novel — but only under the condition that they will be portrayed accurately and with talent. [2]

For Goncharov the most important element in any work of art is the skill with which it is wrought. Art has its own laws, laws that do not correspond to the laws of reality. Even events and reactions copied minutely from life may seem to lack authenticity, because the infinite number of psychological quirks that contributed to one or another reaction cannot be included in the novel. The artist must not reproduce the event. He must attempt to mirror it in his creative imagination, that is, "he must create probabilities that vindicate the events in his work. Reality is not too much of his concern." [3]

It is amazing how closely Goncharov approaches formalist doctrine in these reflections. Since absolute primacy in art belongs to the skill with

1) Literaturno-kriticheskie stat'i, p. 305.
2) *ibid.*, p. 306
3) *ibid.*, p. 310.

which it is wrought, Goncharov cannot stress strongly enough the importance of polishing a text, of final touches. "It is said that final touches make up half of the work. In my opinion they are everything, not only in art, but in thought too. There are no new theses. Everything depends on the way you group and state your thoughts, the fervor with which you defend them, the new light you throw on them, the skill you exhibit in formulating them . . . " [1]

Doubtless Goncharov is speaking *pro domo* when he continues: "Works that are written in too great a hurry sometimes suffer even in those areas where the author is so strong and invincible, for example somewhere in the gravity and exactitude of his ideas (pensées) or aphorisms, especially at the beginning (about experience and perhaps elsewhere, or about immutable principles at the end). He tosses such ideas about nonchalantly, en passant — obviously in haste — whereas judging by their gravity and significance they should be carefully delineated and set like diamonds." [2]

Goncharov's remarks on language in *Lorin* are also quite informative. Monotony and lack of *abandon* are his principle complaints. He proposes realism, i.e. individual characterization especially in conversational passages and gives a pertinent description of Plato's dialogue to make the negative point: "First Socrates puts forth his thesis, then one pupil objects, another asks a question, a third answers it, and so on. But all the reader can hear is one voice, one mind and one variety of speech — Plato's!" [3]

He applies the same criticism to the inserted letters and to Valuev's fear of using "low" words (like *krjakat'* 'to grunt'). The result, he finds, is an excess of propriety together with a certain frigidity of style. Following his own advice, Goncharov calls the representative of leftist radicalism in his "Literary Soirée" Krjakov (that is, Grunter).

Clearly Valuev encouraged Goncharov quite energetically to put down his critical remarks in literary form. Otherwise it seems scarcely likely that the highly timorous Goncharov would have dared to make the noted

1) Literaturno-kriticheskie stat'i, p. 312.
2) ibid., pp. 312–313.
3) ibid., p. 315.

statesman quite transparently the object of a literary discussion that was at times less than flattering to him.

In December 1877 he read the work aloud to Valuev. The impression it made on him was not entirely favorable; his pride must have been injured in quite a few passages, and he did not even hear the piece through. The result was another long and instructive letter to Valuev, in which he repeats that he had originally had no idea of publishing the essay; otherwise he would never have permitted himself to draw portraits bearing the slightest similarity to real persons (giving as an example the portrait of the deceased F.I.T. — obviously the poet Fedor Ivanovich Tjutchev) particularly not that of the author. He admits he will have to introduce some basic changes. "Above all, everything personal will have to be removed. All the portraits will be replaced by types. The milieu will be different etc." [1] He claims he will have no trouble with these charges and that much more work will be involved in generalizing the essay's main theses and treating the issues of the day in an objective manner. But even these obstacles can be overcome, he assures Valuev. And yet . . .

At this point he breaks off, only to lay bare his persecution complex in its most acute form to this date. The rest of the letter — more than half of it — is devoted to a bitter lament concerning the organized gang that is out to rob him of his literary projects and thereby forestall anything he might write. Somehow he connects this fear with the fear of being pigeonholed among the politically "red," a fear that can in no sense be logically connected with what precedes it, and he interprets the most harmless political questions posed by the most harmless people as attempts at provoking him into compromising himself.

Together with all this Goncharov includes a striking characterization of himself as an artist. Though colored by selfconfessed modesty and lack of confidence, it contains much that is to the point: " . . . if my thirty or forty years of living here in Petersburg has not told people enough about my way of thinking, my likes and dislikes, and my goals, then the most accurate source to turn to is my works in print. But do so with the critics, not with the police. Only criticism can pinpoint unerringly with what and whom my sympathies belong. — The first thing

---

1) Literaturno-kriticheskie stat'i, p. 319.

criticism would reveal is that I am one of those not great but mediocre artists who, like a garden pond, can faithfully reflect only what an artist sees, knows, and experiences, that is, only what peers into the pond – be it trees, a nearby hill, a snatch of sky and the like – and is later reworked in his imagination. As a result, he must neither take up any subject matter nor deal with any image or event that is not suggested to him by his artistic instinct. And even if he were to take it into his head for one reason or another to give in to an outside theme, nothing would come of it: he could not force his imagination to give in, and his art would betray him. – This sort of artist needs his own sort of independence, and independence that has nothing in common with other types of independence. This would seem to be why the arts used to be called *liberal*. But all this is forgotten now. – Criticism would also find that I as an artist have long since rendered to society the services required of me. But some people have been prevented from realizing this because others refused to acknowledge my merits and still others did their best to hush them up." [1]

Using these arguments as a backdrop Goncharov continues with an apologia for his *Precipice,* which may best be characterized as a preliminary study to "Better Late Than Never." It climaxes in a critique of modern attitudes toward art, which according to Goncharov either deny the place of art in contemporary society altogehter or force it into too practical, executive a role, despotically requiring it to serve a given cause and ignoring its basic attributes. The generation gap has made objective art criticism impossible. Still, Goncharov declares, he can't very well become his own critic and exegete and go about explaining to his readers that his three novels mirror – no matter how dimly – three aspects of Russian life: sleep, awakening, and the first rays of the dawn of a new life. Yet this is precisely what he does – to a greater and greater extent as time goes on.

"A Literary Soirée" is a sketch dramatizing the ideas set forth in Goncharov's correspondence with Valuev. Goncharov provided the first and second editions (1880 and 1881) with a forword that he omitted in the two subsequent editions (1884 and 1886). It tells of the soirées he had

---

1) Literaturno-kriticheskie stat'i, p. 322.

attended in the winter of 1876 and spring of 1877 and the works he
had heard there, novels of aristocratic life written by authors who had
not yet made their way into print (a slight exaggeration, since he was
concerned with a single novel only: the same *Lorin*, though it is not
named of course, written and read aloud by Valuev, who was prime
minister at the time). Having composed the sketch as a consequence of
his impressions from the readings and having read it before a circle of
intimates, he claims to have been requested to publish the work —
something he had not originally had in mind — on the grounds that
its observations pertain to more than one specific work, to an entire
genre — that of the high society Gsellschaftsroman (velikosvetskij roman) — and therefore had general significance. This statement is hardly
a pose, as Cejtlin thinks. [1] Goncharov needed a push from outside   in
order to publish; otherwise he would leave his works unfinished. The
forword continues with the claim that the sketch does not reflect his
own views on the novel in question, nor on literature in general, or on
current events, but that he intended his characters to express their own
ideas, each according to his own literary culture. He closes by assuring
his readers that the plot of the novel being read aloud and discussed
as well as the external circumstances of the reading are products of his
own imagination. It is certainly true that in the plot of the novel Goncharov wanted to give an overall idea of the character of such works,
but the atmosphere of the soirée doubtlessly corresponds to reality;
some of the characters may be read as portraits of actual people,
Cheshnev, for example, who is still endowed with many of the traits
of the poet Fedor Tjutchev and whose views, as well as those of the
Professor (perhaps Nikitenko), coincide almost completely with the views
of Goncharov himself.

The sketch, which is still nearly a hundred pages long is divided into two parts. The first part, "The Reading", sets the scene, introduces
the characters, and provides a summary of the part of the novel being
read. Part Two, "The Dinner," reproduces the discussion of the novel,
though the sharply divided opinions constantly diverge from it, to
touch upon issues of literature as such or even non-literary topics. The

---

1) Cejtlin, p. 294.

epigraph, from Ivan Krylov's fable "The Swan, the Pike, and the Crab," gives a foretaste of the irreconcilability of the views to be put forth and the resulting standstill in the discussion.

The author of the novel, Lev Ivanych Bebikov, is a highly placed government official. He has composed the work pretty much in secret, never talking about it and only rarely reading excerpts to his friends. One of his colleagues, Grigorij Petrovich Uranov, has no interest in literature and was not let in on the secret, but when Bebikov discovers how genuinely hurt he is by this lack of faith, he agrees to read an extended excerpt in Uranov's home before a selected group of the *haut monde*. Uranov is overjoyed: hosting a literary soirée is just the way for a rich bachelor and a *bon-vivant* to gain importance in society.

Goncharov's portraits of the guests show him at the peak of his talent: types and individuals fuse into lifelike unity. First there are the Princess Teckaja, a prudish *grande dame* suffering from "nerve trouble" and her young daughter, whose gaze would have expressed perfect indifference and who could have been compared to a marble image, had not she promptly switched to an expression of uncomprehending innocence each time love was mentioned in the novel. Later a young man of her acquaintance whispers to her that on her request he has slipped a copy of Zola's *La curée* – a far from innocent work – into her coat pocket.

The Countess Sinjavskaja, who though of an entirely different nature, is also accompanied by a young daughter, has been added to the list according to the express desire of the author, and Goncharov skillfully weaves their budding love into the plot.

Deaf, decrepit Count Peskov, "a fossil of the *haut monde*," is compared with Tugoukhovskij from Griboedov's comedy *Woe from Wit:* he is the incarnation of helpless old age in both its comic and tragic aspects. Among the host of brilliantly executed miniatures – all of whom probably had their prototypes in real life – we find Sukhov, a middle-age society hound who is quite bored, fat, and short of breath; a stalwart General who looks on literature "from a somewhat military point of view"; Kal'janov, a non-literary-inclined cohort of Bebikov from the office who trembles at the prospect of having to pass judgment on Bebikov's literary efforts (though he daily discusses his official documents and projects); the respectable and intelligent Professor who listens with "official attentiveness"; the old official Krasnoperov, who the host thought — rightly as it turns out — would be interested in literature because he had been friendly with the conservative journalists Bulgarin and Grech; the publisher of a journal (Kraevskij?) who was "of middle height and middle age, a well filled-out, blond-haired respectable-looking gentleman in evening dress with an opera hat in his hands who listened to the reading with a look of polite indifference on his face." [1]

Two characters stand out above the rest, however: Krjakov, a newspaper critic, and Skudel'nikov, an elderly novelist. Krjakov owes his presence at the soirèe to the host's young nephew, a student, who wanted a representative of the leftists and liberals to be invited. From the beginning he behaves strangely, and Goncharov places special stress on his thick beard "in which the entire lower part of his face and part of his nose lay hidden." [2]

Skudel'nikov, the novelist, immediately settles down into an armchair and gives the impression of having fallen asleep. "Every once in a while he would lift his apathetic eyes, look up at the author, and drop them again. He appeared indifferent both to the reading and to literature and to everything around him in general!" [3] In sum, Goncharov draws his self-portrait, playing cleverly around with the names: both *gonchar* and *skudel'nik* mean 'potter', but the adjective *skudel'nyj*, derived from the latter, denotes 'frail' and 'fragile' as well. In the end it turns out that Skudel'nikov has not been asleep at all and that he has been keeping close tabs on the proceedings.

The plot of the novel being read at the soirèe, as presented by Goncharov, is a masterpiece of subtle irony, a banal story of love and jealousy with delicately interwoven intrigues. Virtue and nobility of character prevail; evil remains no more than surface deep; unjust verdicts by the *haut monde* which lead to conflicts and confusion are easily set right because of the protagonist's high decency.Straddling

---

1) VII, p. 107.
2) *ibid.*, p. 112.
3) *ibid.*, p. 107.

the fence between seriousness and ridicule, Goncharov succeeds in putting across the plot as the author wrote it as well as his own attitude toward it. A passionate reunion scene between the heroes, for example, after an argument that led to separation goes like this: "I've been waiting for you, I knew you'd come!" she whispered in answer to his kiss. 'If you hadn't come, I would never have forgiven you . . . ' 'Oh paradise! Oh heaven!' he repeated, etc. etc. etc." [1]

In the midst of very amusing comments on the reactions of the audience during the reading, Goncharov sums up his own view of the work: "The author meanwhile introduced character after character and sketched out a number of artful scenes and landscapes. Noble, exalted ideas flow one faster than the next. Sparks of wit flash again and again. Tender feelings take free rein, and touches of keen observation abound. All this fits together freely and extremely smoothly and obediently expresses the main goals or theses of the author. . . . There is nothing vulgar, no bleak, everyday side to existence within the framework of this life; everything is as neat, clean, polished and ornamented as in the radiantly elegant reception rooms of a rich house. Antechambres, kitchens, courtyards in all their natural externals — none of this penetrates this novel; only the pure surfaces of life, like snowy Alpine peaks shine through." [2]

After the reading Goncharov describes — in what might be called a humorous intermezzo — how the guests deliver their judgments to the author. In so doing he cleverly develops those features touched upon in his sketches of their attitudes before and during the reading.

To everyone's surprise the host invites the entire company to a magnificent dinner. The ladies, with one exception, decline the invitation. The novel's author pleads fatigue — and accompanies the Countess Sinjavskaja to her coach. Many do remain behind, however, and an animated conversation about the novel begins over dinner.

From the very beginning two poles emerge: conservative vs. radical, the older generation vs. the younger. The conservatives are represented by Krasnoperov, "the friend of Grech and Bulgarin"; starting from a

1) VII, p. 120.
2) *ibid.*, pp. 125-126.

condemnation of neologisms, he soon turns to a sharp criticism of freedom of the press and finally of the entire young, nihilist generation. Not
only the younger generation comes under fire, however; Krasnoperov is
equally incensed at the middle generation — which, he feels made the
youth's radicalism possible by continually yielding to their vagaries —
and he tells it so in no uncertain terms. Though much of what Krasnoperov says, may be accurate, his exaggerations and the way he makes his
points — he familiarly calls all the older poets by their first name and
patronymic (Faddej Venediktovich for Bulgarin, Aleksandr Sergeevich
for Pushkin, and so on), thereby making the good old times seem almost
belong to the present — lead him into error and make him sound ridiculous.

The radicals are represented by Krjakov, who gradually becomes the
hero of the day. He is the uncompromising leftist, the "progressive," the
nihilist, who defends his basically untenable, one-sided, and primitive
views on what he thinks to be aesthetics, socialism and politics in general
(which from the standpoint he has chosen form a logical system) with a
certain coarseness, and yet with great clarity and outspokenness.

Whereas Krasnoperov soon talks himself out (without giving up his conservative, government-oriented position, however), Krjakov displays a
steadily increasing desire to attack even the moderate and quite logic-
tight views of his opponents, maintaining with great energy that a novel's
artistic merit lies in its progressive, revolutionary content. Consequently
he lends his placet to the novel *Histoire d'un paysan* by Erckmann and
Chatrian, which was widely read by the revolutionary youth of the seventies. In the first handwritten version of "A Literary Soirée" the novel
Krjakov backs was Chernyshevskij's *What Is To Be Done?*, which Goncharov himself thought very little of. [1] The discussion of the Chernyshevskij
novel was not allowed into print, however, because its author was at the
time in forced Siberian exile.

After Krjakov's "crystal clear" language and Krasnoperov's rigid stand
provide the conversation with several amusing turns of phrase, it returns
to the novel the guests have just heard. The professor proffers a definition
of the novel as such, and all agree that it must be a work of art. The pro-

[1] Cf. Zvezda, 1926, Nr. 5, p. 192 and VIII, pp. 501–505.

blem is what sort and what degree of art a novel offers, which inevitably brings up the concomittant problem of the sort and degree of talent its author exhibits. The professor contends that "some writers treasure their idea, their inner proposition, so to speak, more than anything else. Their main preoccupation is with *what* they wish to put across; for them art is a means rather than an end. A second group of writers, on the other hand, become infatuated with form and are more interested in *how* they put across their ideas. And finally a third group, comprising the truly first-rate talents, creates a happy combination of form and content, but how few of these there are. A Dickens, a Thackeray, a Balzac, Pushkin, Lermontov, or Gogol' — they do not grow on trees." [1]

Any novel with a clear message of whatever kind belongs to the first category. When the *what* takes prominence, the *how* is neglected. The professor is especially outspoken against the exaggerations of such works that portray only the bad, the filthy side of life. The examples he gives of works in which art serves as both a means and an end corroborate Goncharov's own preferences: Dickens' *David Copperfield* and *The Pickwick Papers*, Balzac's *Père Goriot* and *Eugènie Grandet*, Pushkin's *The Captain's Daughter*, and Lermontov's *A Hero of Our Time*. It is not wrong, the professor continues, for art to take upon itself a part of the younger generation's campaign for a progressive ideology; it *is* wrong, however for the politically committed progressive literature of our time to claim a monopoly and persecute all other points of view as idle, vain and "not useful."

At this point the conversation turns to the problem of defining realism, a problem dear to Goncharov's heart. Once again he allows the professor to propound his views. Realism is not only the representation of life as it is, maintains the professor. It entails a certain degree of imagination. The author's imagination has the power of inducing other men to experience his images as he expresses them, and this imagination is every bit as real as what normally goes by the name of reality.

To Krjakov's great indignation the professor declares Pushkin's poem "At the Gates of Eden" (V dverjakh Edema) to be completely and utterly real, even though its protagonists, angel and demon, are unreal. Pushkin

---

[1] VII, p. 150.

saw them as real in his imagination, and real they are for everyone who can see them as such by the force of his art. Krjakov's response: "Where did Pushkin find his devil over the abyss anyway? In life? Did he really see that angel?" [1] — clearly begs the question. Imagination can be truth; objective reality must first undergo the interpretation of the poet, and the poet's subjective self is an inevitable corrolary of truth in art. Objectivity should not be carried too far. "Of course the artist would be wrong to thrust his person into the picture, fill it with a 'that's the way I am' — this is true! On the other hand, his spirit, his imagination, thoughts, and feelings should be diffused throughout the work to make it a body created of a living spirit and not a faithful outline of a corpse, the creation of some colorless sorcerer! A vital link between the artist and his work must be felt by the spectator or reader. With the help of the author's emotions, so to speak, they can enjoy a scene, just as for example we enjoy sitting here tranquil, warm, and comfortable . . . but if all of a sudden our good host were to disappear, the room would stop radiating his hospitality and we would think ourselves in a tavern . . . " [2]

Again Krjakov finds himself up a tree, and he tries to get down by using quite a coarse behavior. Unshaken, the professor pursues his argument, pointing out that while genuine artistic creation, creation that involves the imagination and inner vision, is not accessible to everyone, realism and technique are doors that open to all knockers. What is more accessible naturally becomes the fashion.

When the conversation returns to the concrete, to the novel under discussion, the points that come up — and are often bandied about quite playfully — correspond closely to some of Goncharov's own concerns, and he is clearly defending his own point of view in them.

The problem of what constitutes a "boring" novel leads the conversation to a discussion of the relativity of boredom. Then because the novel deals entirely with the upper echelons of the aristocracy, it takes a more political and finally social tack. The consensus is that there is no reason to censure an author for limiting himself to the social sphere with which he is acquainted. Cheshnev now comes to the fore with the following

1) VII, p. 157.
2) *ibid.*

emphatic question: "What right do you have to condemn an author for what he failed to write? The critic should take into account only what the author has in fact written. Calame paints marshes; Le Lorrain, orderly, well-cleared patches of woods and sparkling brooks. And it never occurs to anyone to demand gardens of Calame or to take Le Lorrain to task for never having painted a marsh. Well, the same applies to literature." [1]

There can be no doubt that Goncharov meant this argument to cut the ground out from under the accusations that were so often brought against him. The objection that the upper classes could not exist without the lower classes (though the lower classes could exist without the upper) remains unrefuted; the novel does in fact concentrate too greatly on a single class and is therefore too "dainty" and not always convincing.

By this point social issues have monopolized the conversation. The climax comes when despite Krjakov's rather standoffish protests Cheshnev declares that Russia has social classes only in times of peace and that as soon as danger threatens, any sort of danger, the entire population fuses together in a single emotion, a single idea, a single will. What liberals call "the people," claims Cheshnev, is nothing more than a component part of a larger whole: the nation. And the idea of the nation tends to disappear as a result of the class hate fanned by the revolutionary Left.

When Krjakov accuses him of chauvinism, Cheshnev parries skillfully with a counteraccusation of pseudoliberalism. "This pseudoliberalism wears away the roots of true liberalism, which alone leads to progress. As its motto it has chosen the destruction of the civil state and civilization. It shrinks from no means, even arson and murder. And it doesn't even know what it's after or where it's rushing to." [2]

Krjakov's position becomes weaker and weaker. Like his attacks on the aristocracy, so his campaign against the military (brought on by the virtuoso description of a military parade in the novel) is rebuffed, and again it is Cheshnev, who draws up the balance sheet: ". . . it seems to me that anyone who tries to shake off his people's religion and its unanimous acceptance of the state and the social order removes himself

1) VII, p. 162.
2) *ibid.*, p. 175.

much farther from them than someone who studies foreign languages and serves his own tastes and habits." [1]

Russian culture's strain of negation — which calls for destruction as a preliminary step to alleged reconstruction comes under attack for the self-contradiction inherent in its recognition of a law of heredity in nature that is denied to the spiritual goods: "If we observe in the successive generations of living organisms," the professor argues, "a striking tendency toward the inheritance of distinctive signs, moral and physical features running from parent to child, then how can we deny the transferral of mental, spiritual, or aesthetic endowments? This would be tantamount to denying civilization — and starting over from scratch. What for?" [2]

Next Goncharov has the professor take up the cause for the sort of classical education he approved of (and set forth in a lengthy excursion in "At the University." [3]

For the last time Krjakov takes the floor; after a short discourse on the treatment of love in the novel, during which he again represents the forces of outspoken clarity, making the present lady blush, he rises to go. As he takes leave, he comes across again as a clever, quick-witted and basically benevolent person, who even displays a certain elegance and sense of style. His departure is followed by a real coup: Krjakov, it turns out, is no nihilist at all; he is a famous actor, who agreed to take on the role of the "modern man" as a practical joke, produced and staged by his friend the student.

The reason why Goncharov felt the need for this "disguise" (the beard, which had its part to play at the beginning of the work, returns toward the end when the terrified doorman rushes in to tell his master how the guest who had just left had peeled off his beard and moustache in front of the mirror before going out into the street) has occupied critics to this day, yet it is not difficult to uncover: Goncharov needed an intelligent, fluent, witty, and fundamentally good-natured man who for all his necessary bile could take a joke and skillfully repay in kind the attacks made

---

1) VII, p. 179.
2) *ibid.*, p. 181.
3) Cf. *ibid.*, pp. 200–202.

against him within the nihilist framework of the times. To Goncharov's mind, a real nihilist would definitely not have been up to the job. If nothing else, merely the brute sobriety of the typical nihilist would have precluded him from it. Introducing the typical nihilist into his story might mean even taking sides with nihilism, and that was something Goncharov refused to do. The result was this clever twist, which is in fact quite effective and surprises at the first reading.

The part played by the "middle-aged belle-lettrist" Skudel'nikov is also very important. Though he makes not a sound throughout the evening and indeed seems to be asleep, he does look up or even stare at one of the opponents when the argument produces a particularly felicitous formulation antagonistic to nihilism. When he is finally asked by the host to express his opinion, he replies: 'I've been wanting to tell you for quite some time now, but nobody gave me the chance.' 'Well, now you have it. What do you think? Tell us.' 'You've forgotten the melon, and you've forgotten the pineapple. They haven't even been cut open yet,' [1] he said. Everybody laughed. 'You're right! Just a moment!' cried the host. 'But why are you talking about the melon and don't say anything about the novel.' 'I've listened carefully' . . 'Well, then, say something.' 'I will tell everything.' 'Go ahead. We're all ears.' 'But I'm not going to tell you. I'm going to tell the author.' 'And what will you tell him?' 'Everything that went on here and that was said about his novel.' 'But you mustn't. So many things were said. He will take offense.' 'You call yourself his friends, and you don't even know him. I'll tell him everything that was said and done . . . ' 'Everything?' 'Everything. I won't even forget about the melon and the pineapple.'" [2] This retort is reminiscent of the last word of *Oblomov*. The genuine artist, though seemingly impassible, sees and hears everything and is able to put it all into words and even make a work of art out of it, just as Goncharov has succeeded in doing in this sketch.

The conversation in the second part moves forward not only because of its ideas, but also because of Goncharov's talent for characterization; he excells at conveying the uniqueness of each of his characters, especially in their sparkling dialogue. Realizing that long speeches tend to sound

---

1) A melon and a pineapple, it is suggested earlier in the work, are the goals of his furtive glances. Cf. VII, p. 164.
2) VII, pp. 186–187.

unnatural, Goncharov portrays the exchange of ideas as a continuous ebb and flow of expressions characteristic of first one, then the other character. The general, for example, is annoyed by the foreign words that pepper the discussion and that he does not always understand. Cheshnev speaks the elegant, polished language of the sensitive and highly educated; Krasnoperov speaks a Russian that is somewhat archaic, yet highly expressive. And Krjakov spices up his speech with the jargon then current, while adding just enough ironic overtones to foreshadow his later demasking.

Comic release is never far off. Civil Service Official Trukhin, a somewhat too soft-spoken conservative, is addressed as Mr. Blueye (Sineokov) by Krjakov, who does not know him, because he is wearing blue eyeglasses. Here, an example of the general tone of the piece, which comes very near to a brilliant comedy style: " 'Who's that?' the general asked Sukhov under his breath about the blue eyeglasses. 'I don't know,' said Sukhov. 'You'll have to ask Grigorij Petrovich.' 'A sycophant. Can't you see that yourself?' snapped Krjakov, having heard the general's question. Cheshnev even gave a slight start. 'What's that? His last name?' asked the general, and when several of the guests began to laugh and even Cheshnev smiled, he lost a bit of his composure. 'It's the name given him at his baptism,' Krjakov added. They all tried to keep from laughing. The guest in the blue eyeglasses had apparently not heard the exchange." [1]

Interludes like this continually break up the serious discussion. Far from taking away from the discussion's weight, they serve to point it up. The combination of sparkling wit, light irony, and deep meditation are extremely effective. In this sketch Goncharov is firmly in his element.

———————

While working on "A Literary Soirée," Goncharov was also carrying on a correspondence with a certain Peter Hansen. Like the "Soirée" his letters to Hansen yield many interesting insights into his ideas on literature, and like all his letters they provide a portrait of the man himself.

Peter Hansen, a Dane by birth, worked for the Northern Telegraph Company in Siberia (Omsk and Irkutsk) from 1871 to 1881. He was

1) VII, p. 141.

very interested in literature and apparently extraordinarily gifted in languages. In 1877 his translation of *A Common Story* was published in Copenhagen, and in February of the following year he sent Goncharov a copy of the book together with a letter in which he expressed his great admiration for Goncharov's work. Goncharov was quite touched by the tribute and wrote such a friendly reply that the two began a year-and-half long correspondence. In 1881 Hansen moved to Petersburg.

In his letters to Hansen Goncharov doubts the validity of putting his works into another language, claiming that all his characters and their personalities, the entire environment, the atmosphere were too national, too Russian to be understood by foreigners lacking the slightest inkling of what Russian life was like. Hansen, of course, contests this viewpoint and pleads his case with quite eloquent counterarguments. But even more characteristic of Goncharov's attitude toward his work is his reaction to the reissuing of his works in Russian. He maintains that he has become a writer of the past and adds that since literary taste and the demands literature and the public make on the writer have changed, he would do better to refrain from authorizing new editions of his works.

Once again Hansen does an eloquent job of refuting Goncharov's arguments with the result that Goncharov makes his case more concrete. He reveals how hurt he was by the reception of *The Precipice* and accuses the younger generation of either misusing art as a means of manipulating current events, or rejecting it out of hand, labeling it "the gentry's plaything" and turning exclusively to utilitarian pursuits. "There are of course true friends of sane principles and taste in both art and science, but for the time being they constitute a minority. Ideas about art, criticism, and taste have undergone so many changes with these new times that not only my *Precipice* but almost all works by older authors which lack a tendentious objective and remain true to artistic ideals are received coldly — to say the best! Perhaps this is natural, consonant with the *Zeitgeist,* the way things ought to be!" [1]

His plaint climaxes with the following statement: "If I do have any friends, they are of course to be found among the old, not the new generation! That is why I have no intention of making another appearance

----

1) Literaturnyj arkhiv, VI, p. 64.

to the tune of sideways glances and maybe even ironical and unkind remarks. They are difficult for an old man to take." [1]

Hansen's objections are at times quite inventive and well formulated: "If an artist were to try to keep up with the demands of the times, he would most certainly never get anything accomplished, for no sooner would he complete his work, than he would discover that the demands of the times had changed. The true artist, therefore, never tries to keep up with the times. He writes the way the tree turns green. If someone enjoys the results, so much the better; he has received an unexpected reward. For him the act of creation itself provides the highest degree of satisfaction, and if he has followed your laws of art, he can rest assured that the fate of his creation is secure. He has erected a sturdy edifice, and even though the wind play through its entire repertory on it, it will suffer little damage; it will stand firm through the ages and long serve as a model for others." [2] But despite Hansen's eloquence — bolstered by references to Søren Kierkegaard, whom he greatly admired — Goncharov continued to lament being an old man with no prospects among the young. He also hinted at other grounds for keeping his peace, but did not mention Turgenev by now. These letters state many times over that the attitude of the critics was what kept him from starting new works or reissuing these already published.

In ready response to Hansen's comments on his novels, he repeats that the three together are in fact one: the history or reflection of several successive periods of Russian life "in miniature, of course, and in a sphere with which the author is familiar." [3]

He also takes pains to set right some of Hansen's interpretations. Here is an example of a Hansen passage Goncharov calls into question: "In the three types: Aleksandr Fedorovich, Oblomov and Rajskij I see not only types of three periods of *Russian* society; I see them at the same time as depicting *man in general* at three different stages of his life. Each of us has gone through stages of roaming, flaring up — getting extinguished and agonizing in search of an ideal. This is why I am not alone

---

1) Literaturnyj arkhiv, VI, p. 65.
2) *ibid.,* p. 72.
3) *ibid.,* p. 51.

among the foreigners who have been and will be affected by Aleksandr's roamings, Oblomov's getting extinguished, and Rajskij's agonies. Because all these types are the fruit of a rich human soul with a profound understanding of the poetry of life and the skill necessary to voice this poetry as few mortals before him have done, for all times and in all places they will strike a resonant chord in every soul open to such poetry." [1] Goncharov replied: "Concerning your opinion about my three heroes, permit me to make the following change: take the *roaming* from *Aduev* and ascribe it to *Rajskij* and transfer *Rajskij's agonies* to *Aduev.* — Aduev represents precisely the *agonies* of youth, which constitute the *common story* of all young people, and then, following the path of the majority turns into a sedate adult (like his uncle). — The Germans call the first group *Burschen* and the second *Philister.* — *Rajskij,* on the other hand, represents the *roamings* of the Russian intellectuals (of the forties and fifties), who (for lack of serious interests or even any basis for them) did not know how to channel their energies. All they had was a consciousness, the urge to act. The reforms brought with them raw material to be acted upon — and awoke Russian society from its Oblomov-like sleep." [2]

Quite apart from these attempts at self vindication, Goncharov advises Hansen on what ought to be translated and in the process gives a good picture of his literary favorites. He lavishes great praise on Lev Tolstoj, singling out *War and Peace* for a special encomium. He also praises two of the three plays in Aleksej Tolstoj's historical trilogy (omitting *Tsar Boris)* and justifies his praise in a short but penetrating analysis. He finds much positive to say about Dostoevskij's *Notes from the Dead House* and also recommends *Crime and Punishment* with one qualification: "You must be amazed at my Oblomovian laziness and even more my old age and my indifference to everything," [3] he wrote: he had not read the novel himself. Though he recommends *A Huntsman's Sketches,* he includes no other works by Turgenev in the list. He suggests, however, that Hansen peruse the playwright Ostrovskij down to the last comma. He sums up as follows: "Tolstoj is a true creator and a great *artist,* a worthy representative of our literature. Dostoevskij is more of a psychologist and

---

1) *Literaturnyj arkhiv,* VI, p. 85.
2) *ibid.,* p. 87.
3) *ibid.,* p. 81.

pathologist; artistry is of secondary importance to him. Turgenev is brilliant, but he lacks depth. There's no denying that Count Tolstoj stands head and shoulders above all of us writers." [1]

In 1878 Goncharov's servant Karl Ludwig Treugut died. As a direct result of this sad event, however, Goncharov's daily life took a turn for the better. Treugut left a wife, two daughters and a son, all of whom lived with Goncharov, and after his death Goncharov took it upon himself to look after them. The widow took over her husband's duties, and the children so fell under his spell that he continued to minister to them for the rest of his life and derived much pleasure from seeing them grow up.

The older girl, seven-year-old Aleksandra, became his declared favorite, but he showed equal kindness to five-year-old Vasilij and three-year-old Elena, and he mentions all of them frequently in his letters. He undertook to prepare them for school himself and then made sure each one received an appropriate education. He clearly did everything he could for their welfare and even bequeathed his entire fortune to them (much to the displeasure of some of his relatives, who took revenge in their memoirs [2]).

Aleksandra Ivanovna, the children's mother, was a faithful servant who knew how to cope with Goncharov's ever increasing idiosyncrasies and cared for him in his old age with real devotion. With children constantly underfoot Goncharov came to think of himself as a sort of *pater familias,* and so there is no reason to give credence to scholars who make a great point of his loneliness as an old man. He seems to have been very fussy with his position as head of a household. The joy he experienced at being able to help the otherwise destitute Treugut children is reflected in a passage from one of his letters dating from this period: "It is as though God Himself had entrusted this family to me." [3]

1) Literaturnyj arkhiv. VI, p. 104.
2) Obvious untruths and vidicative bias characterize the "Reminiscences" of Goncharov's nephew Aleksandr Goncharov and his wife Elizaveta. Cf. Vestnik Evropy, 1908, Nr. 11, pp. 5–48, and Nr. 12, pp. 417–421.
3) Alekseev, p. 237.

In 1878 Goncharov decided in favor of rereleasing *The Frigate Pallada*.
One of the motives behind the move was to provide for Vasilij's education
from start to finish. This edition, the third, came out in April 1879. The
text incorporated only a few insignificant changes, but boasted a new forword by the author in which, though he once again feels the necessity
for apologizing for the unproportionately large part his own person plays
in the sketches — his pride in the work is manifest. It also included as a
new concluding chapter, his article from the charity collection *Skladchina*.[1]

The new edition of the *Frigate* provided a pleasant counterbalance to
the ongoing tribulations of work on the wicked *An Uncommon Story*
and such miscellaneous annoyances as an unauthorized translation into
French of the first part of *Oblomov*. That the translation incident enraged Goncharov in clear from this passage from a letter to Hansen:
"The translator is a French novelist, Charles Deulin. Last spring he sent
me this printed version of his work, informing me that *eighteen years
ago* he and a friend of his, M. De La Fite (the pseudonym of a Russian
whose real name is Petr Artamov) wrote me a letter asking for my
authorization *(autorisation)* that *he doesn't know one word of Russian*
and translated from literal translations made by his friend and other
Russians in Paris at the time, and that they translated only the first
part because Artamov died shortly after they had completed it. Without obtaining my consent, he published the first part by itself with a
ridiculous preface to boot — and *all this eighteen years after the fact.—*
If this had happened in Russia, I might suspect some sort of intrigue
or ill will, but since it happened abroad, it remains a mystery to me! —
I answered this impudent declaration by informing the translator that
he had no right to publish without my consent only the first part (and
weakest, in fact), which serves as a prologue or introduction to the
novel, and even more important that he had no right to impose his rash
veto on possible translations by others of the entire novel, and that even
if I did give him *une autorisation,* it was for publishing a translation of
the entire novel, not just bits and pieces, etc. — Later I read in the papers
that this Charles Deulin has died too, yet I hear that Didier, his publisher,
is still putting out the first part alone! They are correct in assuming that

---

1) Cf. p. 256.

I won't bring a case against them, and they go on doing as they please! All this seems to me a rather shady story!" [1]

In this account Goncharov lays out the facts of the matter exactly as they stood. There is every reason to believe that the last sentence refers to Turgenev.

To make matters worse, rumors began to spread as to how *The Precipice* had been made into a play without the knowledge of the author and that it would soon see the boards in Moscow. The adaptation did in fact exist, but the lithograph copy has been lost, and the play was never put on. [2]

Work on the apologia for *The Precipice* must also have been quite harrowing for Goncharov. As already mentioned, the psychological tension under which it was written is in evidence throughout.

———— · ————

In a letter to his wife dated September 9, 1878 Stasjulevich wrote the following about a meeting with Goncharov: "I found him . . . looking rather pitiful. He's aged terribly and gone way downhill. When he complains of an inflammation in his chest, he does so with reason. What is more, his suspicion of intrigues on the part of his enemies has returned, and he is sure they are setting all sorts of traps for him." [3]

During the summer of 1879 Goncharov took a cure at Dubbeln, near Riga, where he met with the author Nikolaj Leskov. In the biography Leskov's son Andrej wrote of his father [4], the two are described as having a polite, respectful regard for one another. The following, from the same work, is an account of the impression Goncharov made on Andrej Leskov's half brother: "He gave the appearance of a well brought up merchant or of an important, but slightly rundown provincial official in retirement. His face was puffy and grayish with a touch of yellow and almost completely lifeless, motionless. It was framed by gray, rounded-off

1) Literaturnyj arkhiv, VI, p. 63.
2) Alekseev, p. 238.
3) Stasjulevich, IV, p. 143.
4) Andrej Leskov, Zhizn' Nikolaja Leskova, Moscow, 1954, pp. 376–377.

side-whiskers on his cheeks. He had no moustache or beard. He sat motionless as if unaware we were moving in his direction." [1] Leskov himself
remarked on Goncharov's fear of acquaintances, characterizing him with
the phrase "Don't disturb me." This lethargy seems to have developed
largely as a result of the batings of the liberal camp. At any rate he never
recovered from the shock caused by the reception of *The Precipice*.

The publication of "A Literary Soirée" early in 1880 provided more
grist for the "liberals'" mill. [2] Their polemics brought Goncharov closer
and closer to the conservatives and consequently to court and government
circles.

That summer he returned to Dubbeln (a spa he became quite fond of,
enjoying the sea there every summer until 1886). A. F. Koni who happened to be there at the time, describes him to Stasjulevich in the following
terms: "Our old friend is much less exclusive and suspicious than in Petersburg. He is talkative and quite good-natured and at times he reminis-
ces in benignant tranquility. The way he carries on with the children, who
are all staying with him, is sometimes touching." [3]

In December several of his shorter works appeared in book form under
the title *Four Sketches*. The works chosen for this collection were "A
Literary Soirée," "A Million Torments," "Remarks on Belinskij's Personality" (published here for the first time), and "Better Late than Never."
This time reviews were mostly positive, and even Skabichevskij had some
good things to say about Goncharov.

———— · ————

Goncharov's attitude toward Belinskij was always somewhat equivocal.
On the one hand he admired in him the enthusiastic "tribune," who
would propagate and defend with might and mane any truth that won
him over or — as was sometimes the case — blinded him. He realized that
Belinskij knew how to use his undauntable spirit and highly developed
imagination to further the causes he supported and how to keep them

1) op. cit. p. 377.
2) For a typical example of their reaction, see A. Skabichevskij's "The Frivolity
   Epidemy" (Epidemija legkomyslija) in "Russian Wealth (Russkoe bogatstvo),1880,Nr.2.
3) Stasjulevich, IV, p. 426.

under the control of his powerful intellect. It was this controlled incandescence that had the power to charm and convince large numbers of people. Goncharov saw in Belinskij a creative personality who with perfect honesty, conviction, and originality stood up for whatever happened to seem true and genuine to him at the moment. The result was "streams of his more or less fervent improvisations, in print or by word of mouth," which succeeded in producing "an entire sphere of creative activity." [1] Belinskij's unceasing devotion to the ideals of freedom, truth, goodness, and humanity — which, as Goncharov often stresses, he often demonstrates with references to the Gospel — formed the fixed axes of his world outlook. These ideals represent his leading principles; they are not the result of sudden passion, and he never allowed himself or anyone else to depart from them.

On the other hand, Goncharov felt that his ardent belief in these ideals often led Belinskij to build up a "religion" from nothing more than the "germ of a hypothesis," [2] to put faith in an "ideal in swaddling clothes" [3] without ever suspecting the possibility of willful deception or masked lies, As an example Goncharov cites "the hazy and at that time here in Russia still novel rumors and reports about communism," [3] and laments that Belinskij wanted to contribute millions to it before having a clear idea of what it actually was or who would receive the millions.

It was Goncharov's opinion that Belinskij's eminently honest tendency to lose his head was particularly harmful to his perception as a literary critic. He never calls in question Belinskij's love for art, his feeling for what is true in art, or the power that "art in all its breadth and strength" had over him, [4] and he was certain that Belinskij would never have gone as far as "the all too exclusive champions of utilitarianism" [5] of his day.. But he understood that in the name of his ideals Belinskij believed in the necessity of tendentious art and that this belief together with the vagaries of his temperament had made him inconsistent, intolerant, and one-sided in his judgments. According to Goncharov's analysis Belinskij saw his

---

1) Cf. VIII, pp. 41–42.
2) *ibid.*, p. 43.
3) *ibid.*, p. 43.
4) *ibid.*, p. 51.
5) *ibid.*, p. 51.

"constant, much loved, and mostly unattainable goals" [1] at the germination stage in many a work of art and would praise one or another work to the skies only to discover that the germination stage was not potent enough or even that in the heat of his initial enthusiasm he had interpreted the work incorrectly. Tearing down idols he had just worshipped and setting out in search of new ones did not seem to bother him. In his absolute honesty he did not notice what he was talking about, says Goncharov, and to prove his point he gives a delightful account of how he himself once made Belinskij aware of it. When Belinskij went into raptures over *A Common Story*, Goncharov told him he would be lucky if in five years Belinskij would repeat only a tenth of what he was now saying. Goncharov responded to Belinskij's astonished "Why?" by pointing to his about-face with respect to the writer Sollogub. Belinskij was completely nonplussed; he had in all honesty diametrically altered his position vis- à -vis this author.

Goncharov compares Belinskij's attitude toward his ideals with that of Don Juan toward his ladies fair. Both idols and the beauties follow close on the heels of one another and are as easily tossed aside as they were raised onto their pedestals. Goncharov feels that Belinskij's enthusiasm for him was tempered by the fact that he had just undergone a severe disappointment: Dostoevskij, whom he had declared a genius after the appearance of his *Poor People,* had shattered his expectations with *The Double.*

Goncharov's record of Belinskij's short-lived love for the mediocre poet Aleksej Kol'cov takes the form of an amusing anecdote. According to his paraphrase Belinskij's initial reaction was: "Besides Kol'cov and except for Kol'cov there are no poets in the world, nor have there ever been." Then his enthusiasm cooled, and all that remained was the small portion of truth he had once sought, which had now reached the dregs. [2]

In many instances, felt Goncharov, Belinskij's tendency to be carried away caused him to make stiff-necked judgments, judgments based on personal animosities that no amount of argumentation could break down: he always detracted Nestor Kukol'nik and Vladimir Benediktov and

---

1) VIII, p. 46.
2) *ibid.,* p. 51.

always praised Ivan Panaev and Petr Kudrjavcev. In Goncharov's eyes these pronouncements were onesided and unjust.

To illustrate Belinskij's compulsion "to acquire any new sort of freedom or to broaden an old one," [1] Goncharov cites his attitude to George Sand, once again in highly amusing anecdotal form. The freedom in question here is the emancipation of women, the novel in question *Lucrezia Floriani*. When Belinskij pronounced the heroine "a goddess," Goncharov objected that a woman who had so little control over herself as to run through five lovers one right after the other (one of whom, it might be added, was of very doubtful provenance) could scarcely be called a goddess. Belinskij's reaction was to call him "a German and a philistine," and "the Germans he added, are the seminarians of mankind." [2]

Once Belinskij insisted that an artist had to immerse himself in a morass of debauchery to be able to find the right "colors for his palette." Goncharov describes this position as "a crude paradox" [3] in spite of the fact that his own attitude was very similar, even if on a much more harmless level.

The last part of the essay deals with the often expressed view that Belinskij's education left much to be desired. But even though he never finished his university studies, says Goncharov, he read so voluminously and was in such constant contact with his highly educated friends that his knowledge far surpassed the level that would normally constitute an adequate education. This knowledge plus his innate talent, acumen, and wit account in great measure for the enormous influence Belinskij exercised on his generation.

Goncharov's remarks are very objective; he neither belittles Belinskij's merits nor exaggerates their importance. He plainly gives the reader to understand that Belinskij never did believe in tendentious art, but that he never dared to admit it to himself and therefore often gave his reviews too biting a tonality.

The essence of the essay is contained in Goncharov's attitude toward literary criticism as such. Praising above all Belinskij's "passionate empathy

---

1) VII, p. 56.
2) *ibid.*, p. 59.
3) *ibid.*

with works of art" [1] leads Goncharov to make the following policy statement: "There have been and still are a number of more or less remarkable minds and pens among critics, but very few of them approach a work by the shortest and most direct route, that is, the candid impression the work makes on them. They examine it from a distance, allow their cold cerebral views to bring in all sorts of critical debris, and use their minds where they should be feeling and lighting the way for their minds with the light of emotion to a true evaluation of the work's virtues and faults." [2]

This call for subjective literary criticism is in perfect harmony with Goncharov's theory of creativity; this theory requires reality to pass through the artist's emotional and spiritual system before it can acquire validity as art; his theory of criticism requires that the critic allow his nervous system and intellect to be excited by a work before he can express his final opinion of it. To Goncharov's mind objectivity was neither to be sought after, nor could it be attained. [3]

The next few years passed uneventfully. Goncharov did his utmost to shelter himself from all official obligations and public appearances. At his express desire and contrary to Russian tradition the celebration commemorating his fiftieth year of literary activity (his first translation had appeared in 1832) took place with a minimum of both guests and publicity. He was presented by his literary colleagues with a marble desk-clock with a bust of Marfen'ka (from *The Precipice*), and if Marfen'ka seems a rather odd choice for the honor, the donors were scarcely committing themselves: the marble figure has no distinguishing characteristics, no individuality whatsoever, except the hint to the famous poultry feeding scene.

Despite all Goncharov's pains to avoid publicity, news of the anniversary celebration did leak out. The gratification he experienced as a result of the relative failure of his anti-publicity campaign was counter-

---

1) VII, p. 52.
2) *ibid.*, p. 53.
3) Cf. also Goncharov's remarks about Belinskij in "At Home," VII, p. 249–251, where he gives a different account of Belinskij's attitude to Nestor Kukol'nik.

balanced by growing health problems. His sight was troubling him most of all. The long hours of concentrated reading required of him as a censor had begun to take their toll; in 1882 an eye ailment that had developed during his days on the board of censors caused his right eye to go completely blind.

Turgenev's death in Bougival in August 1883 did little to reconcile Goncharov with his enemy. Although put off by the big to-do over the funeral preparations in September, he did attend the funeral, a bacchanalia, in his capsule description. Pleading eye trouble, he declined to take part in a commemorative literary evening. His letter of refusal contains no personal barbs, but is nonetheless distinctly cool in tone. [1)]

In the following year Goncharov began a correspondence with the Grand Duke Konstantin Konstantinovich, a mediocre poet who regularly sent Goncharov his works and valued his criticisms. He also took to visiting the Grand Duke. As was mentioned before, his relations with the Court were steadily growing.

When evaluating the work of the highly-placed poet, Goncharov exercised the same tact that had guided his dealings with Valuev. He makes his points quite forcefully, but camouflages them in a flurry of general aperçus about poetry and poets and of remarks about his own literary experience and views.

It is noteworthy that his letters to the Grand Duke constantly stress the central position of hard work in literary creation. Goncharov gives us a pregnant description of his own literary development at the very inception of the correspondence in a letter dating from January 1884: "Let me turn now to *the desire to express oneself, the desire to write* as a sign of talent. From the age of fourteen or fifteen, though not suspecting myself of having any talent, *I read everything I could get my hands on and wrote continuously*. Neither games nor — later on while I was a student or official — get-togethers with friends and conversations were able to pry me away from books. Novels, travelogues, history, but especially novels, and sometimes old novels, silly novels (works by Radcliffe, Cottin, and the like) — I devoured them all with

---

1) Ogonek, VIII, p. 482.

unbelievable speed and rapacity. — Then I began to translate great quantities — of Goethe, for instance, though not the poems (which I never did try my hands at), but many of his prose works, and Schiller, Winckelmann, and others. I had no practical goal in mind; *I just felt drawn to writing,* learning, and studying in the dim hope that something would come of it. Then I would keep the furnace going with stacks of scribbled-over paper. — All this reading and writing, however, served to sharpen my pen and provided an unconscious source of literary devices and tricks of the trade. Reading was my school, the literary circles of the time provided me with the tricks of the trade, that is, I attentively watched views, tendencies, etc. Only in these circles, not in solitary reading or on the student's bench, did I come to see, and not without a certain sorrow, what a limitless, fathomless sea literature was, and to realize, to my horror, that any man of letters who claims to merit serious attention, to be more than a dilettant had to devote practically his entire self, his entire life to the cause! . . . " [1]

To a politely negative discussion of the Grand Duke's miracle play *Manfred Reborn* (Vozrozhdennyj Manfred), Goncharov appendixed some more general comments concerning the type of the constantly belabored hero and its treatment in literature. They are cited below as an example of Goncharov's capacity for irony and aloofness in literary matters: "With us, ordinary people, we had no trouble being completely satisfied by the way in which heroes like Manfred, Don Juan, and the rest attain salvation. The one philosophized, concentrated in himself the very pith of earthly wisdom, spat on heavens and did not want to learn anything, rejected all strength and wisdom but his own, — i.e. perhaps the all-human wisdom, — and thought himself — God. The other debauched his life away, amusing his perverse imagination and satisfying his lusts, — and then bam! The one goes in for a little praying and an occasional fast toward the end of his life, the other starts repenting after his death — and look, an angel, usually a lady angel, appears from heaven (your *Manfred Reborn* too has its Astarta) — and the *Accursed Reprobate* is already pardoned, he rises up to heaven, and God himself talks to him in a friendly

---

[1] Literaturno-kriticheskie stat'i, pp. 337–338.

way, etc.! Really, so called salvation and absolvation comes cheaply to these gentlemen!" [1]

Other letters to the Grand Duke contain Goncharov's views on lyrical poetry and the poets of the time: "Our literature (and, it would seem, all literatures) still has an entire phalanx of agile, nimble-witted, self-assured poets who can sometimes even manage a beautiful, finely wrought verse and who write about anything at all, whatever is in demand, whatever they have buyers for. These are our *Vejnbergs, Frugs, Nadsons, Minskijs, Merezhkovskijs* and so on. – They can write a poem about anything, but they write *with indifference,* though often with *brilliancy,* and therefore *without sincerity.* – No matter how brilliantly they write, they'll never approximate or even successfully imitate such sincere, sensitive poets like e.g. Polonskij, Majkov, Fet, or, of from latest group of Russian poets – Count Kutuzov." [2]

Sincerity, then, is what Goncharov values most in a lyric poet: "There may be a good many sincere poets, but the sincerity most of them practice is insincere; sometimes they imitate quite artistically, powerfully (Pushkin, Lermontov and several others) sincerity, but indifference often lurks beneath the surface. Turgenev, for example, was as indifferent to everything and everybody as he could possibly be, yet as an artist he was a keen observer who could find sparks of poetry in everything, especially in nature. He placed his talent and selfesteem above everything. Many others exhibit this sort of showcase sincerity and talent. True feelings came naturally only to Pushkin and Lermontov, and even they are sometimes wanting in them. Among more recent poets I find Fet, Polonskij, Count Kutuzov, and several others the most sincere . . . " [3]

The jab at Turgenev, scarcely justifiable in this connection, gives an idea of Goncharov's mood. It is interesting to note that even Pushkin and Lermontov are not being considered to be always genuinely sincere. By placing special emphasis on Arsenij Golenishchev-Kutuzov he is showing sympathy for a subject matter, presumably dear to his heart: Kutuzov's intelligent brand of quietism (which later led Kutuzov to lean toward Buddhism).

1) Literaturno-kriticheskie stat'i, pp. 339– 340.
2) *ibid.,* p. 341.
3) *ibid.,* pp. 342–343.

Despite the quibbling in the above quotation Pushkin remains Goncharov's idol. "Almost all the writers of the new school — Lermontov, Gogol', Turgenev, Majkov, Fet, Polonskij, and I too by the way — followed and continue to follow the path laid by Pushkin. We followed him instead of turning off onto side roads because his is the only well trod, legitimate, classical way of art and artistic creation." [1)]

For all his interest in literature Goncharov never forsook art. Paintings and painters are mentioned in his letters again and again. Here an example from an unpublished letter to the Grand Duke: "Raphael was of course a genius . . . But although Titian, Guido Reni, Murillo, Rubens and Rembrandt were all geniuses too, they did not scale the heights of creative power inherent in Raphael's ' Sistine Madonna ' (more than anywhere else) and later in his other Madonnas, in the mothers and their infants. No one (in my opinion or rather on the basis of my personal aesthetic impression) has matched his perfection in portraying the mother's beauty or the charm of infancy, starting with the infant Jesus and the other children, among others the angels at the feet of the 'Sistine Madonna '." [2)]

Goncharov also kept up with music and St. Petersburg's musical life, exhibiting a particular fondness for the opera (which he seems to have attended regularly for many years). The following letter (of Februar 1886) to the great pianist and less important composer Anton Rubinstein bears eloquent testimony to his commitment: "*Thank you.* Whose lone voice dares deliver its *thank you* across an ocean of sounds to the ear of a great musician who 'with untold strength' embodies for the world aghast, the creations of his renowned colleagues and serves up a sumptuous feast of music to the entire world? — He receives a worthy reply from another ocean, a throng many thousand strong, with an intense feeling of wonderment and ecstasy and with passionate ovations! — Stunned by the titanic power of a genius, I lose myself in this throng and timidly whisper my 'thank you!' " [3)]

1) Alekseev, p. 284.
2) *ibid.*
3) Ogonek, VIII, p. 489.

After a long period of indecision Goncharov finally came over to the idea of issuing a collection of his works. For years his friends hat tried hard to persuade him to undertake the project, but he had put them off with two excuses: that everything he had written had grown obsolete in the meantime and would therefore attract no new readers and that the work involved in reading proof and making the necessary emendations would be too strenuous. The first doubt was easily allayed by the clearly discernible rise in demand for his long unavailable novels, the second by the assurance that the publishers would take on themselves the main burden of preparing the texts for reedition.

The actual reasons for the procrastination were probably first that Goncharov feared renewed attacks on the part of liberal critics, from whom he had taken enough of a beating as his works came out one by one, the second, once again his *idèe fixe*. A. F. Koni says in his memoirs: "In Dubbeln during the summer of 1880 I tried to convince him (Goncharov, V. S.) to publish an edition of his collected works by pointing out to him how difficult and expensive it had become to obtain a copy of *Oblomov*, which was by then in short supply. 'That kind of advice,' said Goncharov looking gloomily at the ground, 'could come only from an enemy. Can you really want them to start accusing me of having stolen everything from Turgenev? ' I realized that his *idèe fixe* had come full circle . . ." [1]

Only an impulse from above could break Goncharov's resistance. It came during an audience with Tsar Alexander III when the Tsar asked whether he would be republishing his works. Clearly flattered, Goncharov interpreted this query as a summons to do so and signed a contract with the publisher Ivan Glazunov in November 1882. [2] Preparation and printing proceeded without any major setbacks, and in December 1883 (the title page reads 1884) the first complete eight-volume edition of Goncharov's works came off the press. In January 1889 it was followed up by a ninth volume.

The edition's success measured up to the publisher's expectations, and there were no overly crusty reviews. Goncharov sent a copy to the Tsar and received in return a magnificent desk set. He was evidently quite

---

1) Utevskij, p. 239.
2) *ibid.*

pleased that the Tsar had seen fit to reward him. He also gave copies of
his novels to some members of the Tsar's family and to many of his
friends.

Some of them he provided with witty but at the same time very
melancholic dedications. The inscription he wrote in the copy of *The
Precipice* he gave to his servant Aleksandra Treugut is especially noteworthy, because it shows her to have been much more than a mere
servant to Goncharov: "To Aleksandra Ivanovna Treugut, solicitous
nurse of my eyes, my money, and my linen; executor of my affairs;
stern guardian of order in my house; skillful pourer of tea, etc. etc.
etc. that she may think back kindly on a sickly old author who is grateful for her care." [1]) Clearly he thought of her as a faithful helpmate
genuinely devoted to him who was at the same time capable of recognizing his intellectual significance.

Now more than ever he was in need of attendance, for his eye troubles
were growing steadily more serious. He even began dictating many of his
letters to Mrs. Treugut or her children. An acute danger developed when
once while undressing he filliped a trouser button into his bad eye, and
the infection thus produced caused him renewed pain. Goncharov's
propensity for mixing pain with humor once again makes itself felt in
this description of the trouser episode in a letter to Stasjulevich of June
1884: "Another few words about the trousers: instead of doing more
damage to my eye — which, as it is, has suffered enough blows of ill
fate — I might have turned my trousers to good use by supplying them
with a sufficient number of metal buttons to take care of all sorts of
enemies among others those of the fatherland. Tailors haven't the faint-
est idea that they deal in mortal weapons! — Whenever I look at my six
pairs of trousers hanging in the wardrobe, I feel the same sort of terror
and respect an old warrior feels looking over the panoply in his arms
chamber . . . — For the present, thank God, I am spending my days
in blissful sleep; there is nothing more I can do. I'm forbidden to read,
and anyway nothing appeals to me but the papers (local news and the
telegrams). My spirit and mind are beginning to go as fast as my sight

---

1) Alekseev, p. 267.

and hearing, and soon I'll be 'poor in spirit' though I can't say whether I'll be 'blessed.' " [1]

Another unauthorized translation, this time of *The Precipice*, gave rise to new aggravations. It appeared under the title *La faute de la grand-mère* in the Brussels newspaper *Indèpendance Belge*. The translator was journalist Mikhail Ashkinazi, who wrote under the name of Michel Dè-lines. Enraged at the news, Goncharov wrote to Dmitrij Certelev, at the time a quite noted poet and philosopher: "It is not a translation, but a so called *adaptation* of the novel with the title *La faute de la grand-mère*, a muddle of scenes with many cuts and abridgments, an insolent, ungifted, inane rehash that thoroughly deforms my work." [2] A year later yet another *adaptation* of *The Precipice*, this one entitled *Mark, le nihiliste*, was published, but we have no record of Goncharov's opinion of it. He wrote several letters to Ashkinazi in which he made no bones about his feelings on the matter. The following generalization summarizes these feelings: "A writer appearing in a foreign literature cannot mark out for himself even half the territory he occupies in his own country because of the difference in customs and living conditions." [3] Although Goncharov received frequent requests for permission to translate his works, his reaction was always one or indifference of rather recalcitrance.

Goncharov's letters from this period corroborate the following passage from A. Koni's memoirs: "From the mid-eighties Goncharov's life began to go noticeable downhill — especially after he became blind in one eye, the result of a hemmorrhage that made him suffer so much it brought tears to his eyes. He turned pale and lost weight. His handwriting grew larger and larger, but less and less legible. For weeks he refused to set foot outside the rather poorly lit and cheerless apartment on Mokhovaja he'd lived in for thirty years. Instead of spending his summers at Dubbeln, which he loved, but which was quite far away, he went to nearby Ust'-Narova and then to Petergof." [4]

---

1) Utevskij, p. 249.
2) Alekseev, p. 273.
3) *ibid.*, p. 281.
4) Utevskij, p. 251.

The letters from this period show Goncharov in low spirits, depressed. He continually expresses the wish to be alone, to return undisturbed to hiw own self. To A. Koni he wrote in June 1886: "You write that people like me. Well, you're wrong. No one can stand the sight of me. And I deserve this completely because of my unsociable ways and lack of patience. Now at age seventy-five I've become a confirmed grump. I simply wave my hand, at times a stick to my acquaintances, that they should go away." [1] Mrs. Treugut, the housekeeper, had strict instructions to dismiss — with very few exceptions — prospective callers and she saw to her duty diligently. Because by now the children spent most of the year away at school, they provided him with little diversion.

Nevertheless Goncharov did not abandon his literary endeavors entirely. He wrote the lively "From University Reminiscenses," [2] which appeared in the April 1887 issue of *The Messenger of Europe,* the "Old-Time Servants" sketches, and "Back Home". The latter two were quite well received, but their success did more than gratify him; it made him aware at the same time of how weak he had grown. "I didn't expect the article or especially the "Servants" to raise such a rumpus," he wrote to Dar'ja Kirmalova, his nephew's wife. "No sooner had they appeared in print than I was deluged with visitors and overwhelmed with letters requesting the rights to translate them into various languages etc. I'm not at all up to it. My health is bad and I'm weak. Every other day I catch cold from this freezing weather. I lock myself up and don't let anyone in to see me. It's bad to live for an old man. When the German kaiser died yesterday, he showed the way to all us old men." [3]

---

1) Utevskij, p. 253.
2) Published later under the title "At the University." Cf. the discussion on p.9.
3) Utevskij, p. 255.

"Old-Time Servants"

Goncharov completed his "Old-Time Servants" cycle (the original title was "Servants") in May 1887 and published the sketches separately in the journal *The Field* (Niva) in 1888. "Valentin," "Anton," and "Matvej" appeared in issues one, two, and three respectively, and the fourth and last, "Stepan and his Familiy" (which Goncharov had at first intended to withdraw entirely), in issue eighteen. All four appeared again in the ninth volume of his collected works (1889), but in a different order ("Stepan and his Family" and "Matvej" changed places) and with the new title "Old-Time Servants (From the Domestic Archive)."

The foreword Goncharov wrote for the sketches merits attention because he set great store by it. He recommended it emphatically to Lev Tolstoj [1] and mentioned it in a letter tò critic Viktor Ostrogorskij, who had devoted the first chapter of his *Studies of Russian Writers* (Moscow 1887) to Goncharov.[2]

Goncharov used the foreword to reply to the accusation often raised against him by "liberal" critics that he never treated peasant life or portrayed peasant types in his novels. At the time the peasantry was the favorite of all progressives, and they regarded all writers who ignored it as malevolent reactionaries. Goncharov says one might answer quite a lot to this reproach, but he chooses an argument that he proclaims will obviate the need for all others: he claims ignorance. He points out that he has no knowledge of peasant character or customs, of village life, or of agriculture, or rather whatever he does know is gleaned from the descriptions of other writers. That he never came in contact with peasants, he continues, is merely a fact of his biography; so how should he know and love them?

As far as house servants and single types of servants are concerned, he claims competency and asserts that even critics who charge him with a lack of interest in the people must admit he has devoted "many hues of the palette" to this class of the people. He then introduces the work at hand: sketches he had once copied from life and then consigned to the

1) Cf. p. 317 and VIII, pp. 494–499.
2) Alekseev, p. 291.

desk drawer. He talks again about reading them to a group of "knowlege-able people," who will judge about what is good, and this he will print, the rest will be fed to the fire.

And in fact Goncharov did read the sketches — just as he read most of his works — aloud to his friends. Here is A. Koni's report: "Old man Goncharov has me completely under his power. He demands I lend a critical ear to his new works, grabs me down by the shore (literally takes me by the hand and refuses to let go all evening), and then to keep me during the day tempts me with crabs and lampreys. He combines an old man's egotism with what can be a very touching warmth." [1]

The sketches prove that Goncharov was just as much the skillful por-traitist and wiley storyteller he had ever been, that he had suffered no decline whatsoever in surety of touch. "Valentin," the first sketch, tells of a servant who enjoys reading poetry he cannot understand, *because* he cannot understand it. Goncharov comments: "I now became convinced of what I had observed before: the simple Russian is not always wont to understand what he reads. I have seen simple people reading themselves to tears out of holy books in Church Slavic without understanding a thing or understanding only "a word here and there," like my Valentin. I remember watching sailors on ship as they listened to some such book. They would stare into the mouth of the reader for hours on end as long as he read with a full voice and with feeling. Simple people are not fond of simplicity." [2]

Valentin's simplicity (prostota), to be sure, shades into stupidity, and Goncharov is aware of this deficiency from the beginning of their relation-ship. Here is his portrait: "He had a nose that was so small as to be al-most negligible, the size and color of a cherry; blue eyes without any shade; and a clear, ruddy old-man complexion. Blue eyes without shade are to my mind an almost definite sign of naiveté that borders on stupidity, or more often stupidity plain and simple." [3] Eyes are often the decisive factor in Goncharov's character descriptions.

---

1) Alekseev, p. 285.
2) VII, p. 329. Because Goncharov brings sailors into this passage we may place Valentin's stint with Goncharov in the late fifties (contrary to the assertion in VII, p. 523, which would relate the action of the sketches to the forties).
3) VII, p. 320.

The colloquies on literature between master and servant are quite comic, but they soon come to an end; Valentin fancies the ladies as much as unintelligible poetry and the awkward situations his philandering gets him into — Goncharov sets them down with great verve — finally make his presence undesirable.

"Anton," the second sketch, deals with Valentin's successor, a strapping peasant giant whose main job back at the village was clubbing the ever rampant wolves to death. He is quite feebleminded (again Goncharov concentrates on the eyes: "He looked at me humbly, almost fearfully, with eyes so dull, so apathetic that they show not the slightest spark, to say nothing of a needle or ray of light," [1]) yet quite friendly and competent. His main fault lies in a hopeless attachment to the bottle; one day Goncharov just escapes being robbed of almost all his property while Anton, easy prey to specially commissioned big-city "wolves" who ply him with drink, is out cold.

By skillfully introducing all manner of variations on the "wolf" theme, Goncharov provides the sketch with artistic unity. Even a somewhat abrupt divagation in which he complains of feeling "alone" in the company of an unconscious servant and a ransacked apartment does not disturb it.

His loneliness brings to his mind a lady of his acquaintance who kept repeating to him: Get married! Anna Petrovna's greatest joy in life (she seems to have been modeled after Evgenija Majkova on this point) came from arranging marriages. Her answer to the author's objection that marriage might well spawn other "wolves" is an enigmatic smile and an enigmatic look, the latter of which serves as the motivation for a subtle psychological excursus into woman's gaze, and we have again the eye-motif, which plays an important role in cementing all four sketches.

Once again the proceedings may be dated by internal evidence. Since thirty large fascicles of *Oblomov* ready for print are strewn about the room, we may conclude the action takes place in or around 1858.

"Stepan and His Family," the third short sketch (and one Goncharov had originally thought of dropping), has to do with three servants, who follow one another in quick succession. All three are let go for the same

---

1) VII, p. 337.

reason as Anton: they cannot keep away from the bottle. Their antics
are both comical and pitiful: Petr becomes insolent when drunk, Maksim
steals, and Stepan, the sketch's climatic character, suffers fits or rage.

Stepan is hired together with his family because despairing Goncharov
hits upon the idea that a family man is more likely to be abstemious. It
soon becomes clear, however, that he now has not one but three drunkards on his hands: the otherwise friendly and hardworking Stepan, his
otherwise godfearing wife Matrena, and their seventeen-year-old son
Petrusha. The sketch closes with a scene that Goncharov compares to
a Teniers canvas: a vivid depiction of the family roaring drunk. The end
of Stepan and his wife is told with great skill. Several years after the main
part of the action takes place, Stepan's wife returns, a beggar, and relates
the story of her husband's death: " 'Quietly, gently, after he had just
taken Holy Unction and was about to die, he said, 'Cursed be he who
invented drinking vodka!' " [1]

The fourth sketch, "Matvej," takes place before Goncharov's voyage
around the world, and for this reason he presumably isolated it from the
others — which followed a certain sequence — in the collected works.
Matvej's real name was Filipp, and he worked for Goncharov from 1846
to 1852 as well as the year following his return from the voyage. At the
beginning of the sketch Goncharov is guilty of a slight anachronism —
easily to be explained by the fact that he wrote all sketches many years
after the related events — referring to his experiences with Anton, who
did not come to work for him until several years after Matvej.

Matvej's portrait is quite unusual and very well done, a typically Goncharovian mixture of the comic and the pitiful. The serf of a Polish gentleman who badly mistreated him, his "walking corpse" appearance is due
to the terrible beatings he had to endure. "He was about forty-five, quite
tall and thin, even emaciated. He looked as if he had just arisen from his
death bed — all skin and bones. His head was rather small, his eyes deeply
set and whitish — like the eyes of a Finn, completely expressionless. He
had large lips that always hung open — he was apparently too weak to
keep them shut — and a face riddled with deep drooping wrinkles, like
kid leather yellowed with age. His thinning hair was the color of old

1) VII, p. 357.

matting. Ne wore a long gray, threadbare frockcoat with a faded velvet collar and had a knitted scarf round his neck." [1] Despite his inauspicious appearance, however, Matvej does not drink, and it is for this reason he is hired.

Matvej is guided by one and only one thought: buying freedom from his master (who has released him temporarily on quitrent). Not only does he stay away from drink; he scarcely touches a morsel of food. He will do anything to add to his savings, including, as it turns out, a little illegal pawnbroking on the side. Although he loses all his money several times, by silly accidents, he is quite undaunted, and finally (just before the abolition of serfdom) he reaches his goal.

Goncharov skillfully contrasts Matvej's hard lot and corpselike mien with his ridiculous, monkeyish antics and his obstinacy his manic fear of thieves, and other idiosyncrasies made comic by his fastidious attachment to them. There is a great deal of love in this mélange of genuine honesty, propriety, misery, and comedy; by the end of the sketch Goncharov has raised his protagonist to the level of a Don Quixote in miniature. [2]

Structurally and stylistically all the sketches are extremely well conceived. Almost any line could be cited as proof of Goncharov's great power of expression. His similes, for example, are very striking; they seem to crop up almost incidentally and maintain a certain ironic incongruity between the object being compared and the object it is being compared to. The same sort of incongruity characterizes the servants' speech. Here, for example, is Matvej's diatribe against thieves: "Many are the times that beaming and so sparkling with life as a newly opened flower he would report to me how a thief had been caught in the attic or cellar of a house, sometimes a nearby apartment, or shop. 'Well, did they take him to the police?' I asked unperturbed. 'Oh no, sir. How could they? The police would have let him go tomorrow. No, we gave it to him by ourselves, something he won't forget.' 'We? You mean you were there too?' 'Of course I was, sir!' he spit out with great animation and display of gums. 'As soon as the janitors caught hold of him, I was

1) VII, p. 360.
2) *ibid.*, p. 380.

the first to run up and help them hold him. We gave him a real good
beating. His face was all smeared with blood.' 'Did *you* beat him too?'
I asked, fearing the answer. 'Hardly at all, sir. I mostly held him by the
neck, by his tie, like this, so he wouldn't get away!' 'Aren't you ashamed
of yourself? Isn't it a sin? ' I asked, trying to get through to him. 'Why
did he take what doesn't belong to him, sir? Think of how much the
man he robbed, would've been out! Serves him right!' he answered with
gusto." [1]

In terms of structure. Goncharov treats the preparation for Matvej's
first entrance à la Tartuffe. The reader hears a great deal about him before he actually appears and is consequently anxious to meet him. When
he appears one is certainly not disappointed. Goncharov is also quite clever
at dropping off-handed hints of events to come. At one point, for example,
he asks about Matvej's drinking habits: " 'Don't worry about me on that
account, sir!' said Matvej showing both gums. 'On that account,' I thought.
'And on what account will I have to worry?' " [2] The gum showing is one
instance for many of Goncharov's well-considered use of another structural
device, that of the returning characteristic detail.

On the whole these minature masterpieces make up a well-meaning somewhat melancholic, but sprightly and harmless album of his servants. They
are not servant *types,* however, and only the brutish humorlessness of the
"progressive" critics could interpret the work as a satirical invective against
the poor domestics. [3] Even Cejtlin comes to Goncharov's defense: "With
no idea of writing a satire, and certainly not thinking of a satire on the
scale of Saltykov-Shchedrin at any rate, he created 'sketches' out of his
daily life, fully aware of their limited significance." [4]

---

1) VII, p. 360.
2) *ibid.*, p. 364.
3) Cf. the review in "Russian Thought" (Russkaja Mysl'), 1888, Nr. 6 by the obdurate
   Shelgunov.
4) Cejtlin, p. 298.

"Back Home"

Goncharov wrote the reminiscences "Back Home" in the summer of 1887 in Hungerburg. They were published the following year in the first and second issues of the *Messenger of Europe*. Writing to Dar'ja Kirmalova Goncharov speaks of how he feels such a work should be put together: "It is impossible to write from nature and nature alone. Nothing can come of it, nothing effective. It's like putting raw beef out on the dinner table. In other words, the artist must polish, spruce up, sweep up and put everything in order. There are no lies; characters like godfather Jakubov, the governor, and others, whole conversations and scenes, I took faithfully, straight from nature. All I did was touch them up a bit and add a coat of varnish. This is what is known as artistic polish."[1]

This statement, which Goncharov included in much the same form in a short introduction dated August 1887, speaks entirely for itself. The validity of the work as biographical material has been discussed. [2]

In "Back Home" Goncharov is more concerned with what used to be *(byvalo)* than with what was *(bylo)*, that is, his main concern is generalization. But he does not stop there. As he puts it, generalization leads to typicalization, and typicalization with him is not a habit, but it is his nature. [3]

The work consists of fifteen chapters or rather sketches, containing a portrait gallery in which typicality alternates with strongly marked individual traits. Its fast-moving anecdotes and witty dialogues read much like a fragment from an absorbing novel. The monotonous, stupefying atmosphere of provincial city life and the questionable conventions and proprieties of the local — highly venal — officials are clearly meant to seem typical. It was here, Goncharov notes, face to face with people whose carefree lives consisted of nothing but lolling and lazing, that he had his first vague premonition of what would later be dubbed "oblomovism." That he was far from unhappy or out of place in this atmosphere

---

1) Ogonek, VIII, p. 504.
2) Cf. pp. 11–12.
3) VII, p. 226.

(with the exception of his distaste for outright dishonesty of course) is also quite indicative of his later position.

Remarkable and characteristic is Goncharov's attack on the critics of his time who made a habit of reviling former serf owners, claiming that their station had been incompatible with that of a gentleman. Through his portrait of Jakubov (Tregubov) — unmistakably a labor of love and a distant forerunner of Oblomov — he points out that the problem must be viewed in the proper historical perspective. Condemning a person outside the context of his times, he says, is like condemning an exquisite old portrait for failing to match contemporary fashion without taking into account the relationship it bears to its own period — the prevailing usages, mentality, educational goals etc.

There can be no doubt that the most striking portrait is that of Governor Uglickij (Zagrjazhskij), who in spite of all his negative traits comes across as a disarmingly charming, easygoing, and therefore highly attractive person. Nor does Goncharov deny him dignity and sometimes even kindness. This sympathetic treatment reflects a friendship that lasted long after Goncharov's stay in Simbirsk as it seems.

The governor's wife — long-suffering (as a result of her husband's infidelities), sentimental, and somewhat slow-witted — and her attractive fifteen-year-old daughter — wavering on the border between childhood and coquettery — are in their own way individualized, yet at the same time highly typical portraits. Much more individualistic are the figures of Lina and Chucha, poor orphaned sisters of noble lineage and uncertain age ("not less than twenty-five nor more than thirty" as Goncharov says) and indispensable to the governor's household. Malicious, sly, energetic Lina contrasts perfectly with her kind, gauche, passive sister Chucha. The scenes featuring the latter are among Goncharov's most successful attempts at comic description and dialogue.

The last two chapters narrate about the sad end of an overly light-hearted reign of office: the recall of the governor and his travel back to St. Petersburg in which Goncharov decided to join the censured official.

The last two chapters also see the introduction of a new character, the special duty official Andrej Petrovich Prokhin. Although subject to periodic fits of heavy drinking, Prokhin has an excellent chancery style when sober. Goncharov's virtuosity — in the person of Prokhin he is describing a character he finds very unsympathetic, as we know, one who enjoys spending his leisure *"dans les vignes du Seigneur"* [1] — reaches one of its high points in the scene in which Prokhin nearly gives up the ghost during an attack of *delirium tremens*, on the way from Moscow to Petersburg. The entire work comes to a close as he begins to recover shortly before arriving in Petersburg.

Throughout "Back Home" Goncharov keeps himself in the background; he is never more than an intelligent, ironical observer. Whenever he inserts one of his often self ironizing reactions or thoughts, however, he brightens up the narrative with his special brand of charm.

During 1887 and 1888 Goncharov wrote several touching letters to Lev Tolstoj in which he gave full expression to his admiration for him. Yet he also plainly asks him to give up his infatuation with tales for the people and return to the mainstream of literature. "You are right: one should write for the people — the way you have been writing; but are there many, who can do this? Anyway I regret seeing you sacrifice another group of readers, the educated audience, for this sort of writing. You yourself would be sorry, if Michelangelo had given up building the cathedral to build peasant huts that could be built by others. You also would be sorry if Dickens had written only the *Christmas Stories* and given up writing his great life pictures for everyone." [2]

When Tolstoj challenged him to follow in his footsteps and write for the people, Goncharov backed his claims of inaptitude with the foreword to "Old-Time Servants," which he sent to Tolstoj at the same time.

In his response to Tolstoj's favorable lines concerning "Back Home," Goncharov is as jocular as ever: "I can't figure out whether they are doing it (praising "Old-Time Servants,"V.S.) to be kind or to humor an old man . . . I was a little wary about showing myself in print with such pale

1) VII, p. 301.
2) Ogonek, VIII, p. 498.

empty stories. And what do you know, everything turned out all right. The wole business has somewhat the flavor of old age to it; as if an old fogey had sat and sat in one spot watching young people dance, and suddenly recalling the old days could keep his seat no longer and up and danced the grossvater. Of course he is applauded." [1]

As time went on, Goncharov tried harder and harder to withdraw from the spotlight. When Fet wrote him for permission to publish a letter he had written him long before, Goncharov responded with a long letter. It begins *"Et tu, Brute,"* continues by elaborating his long since established policy of opposing publication of private letters no matter how important the correspondents, and ends with the exclamation: "O eyes! O nerves! O back! O old age! Farewell! I shall never write anyone again! Don't touch me. Let an old man die in peace. I embrace you and Tolstoj *in absentia* and take my leave!" [2]

Goncharov spent the summer of 1887 at Hungerburg. In 1888 he went back to Dubbeln, but because he found the trip quite arduous, he rented cottages in Pavlovsk the following year and in Staryj Petergof the two years after that.

Up until his death he continued writing bittersweet letters, sketches, and toward the very end, a short story. He also prepared an essay on Aleksandr Nikitenko, which the historian Mikhail Semevskij, to whom Goncharov read it aloud, characterized as a "veritable artistic tableau," but it unfortunately never made its way into print and the manuscript has apparently been lost. [3]

————— ·—————

On March 1, 1889 the *Messenger of Europe* published Goncharov's essay "Last Will Disregarded." It promptly became the topic of lively press controversy. The essay reiterates Goncharov's aversion to the publication of the private correspondence of public personalities, he had expressed at the same time in the letter to Fet quoted above. In January

1) Ogonek, VIII, p. 503.
2) Utevskij, p. 257.
3) Alekseev, p. 295.

1891 his sketch "Through Eastern Siberia" appeared in *The Russian Review*. [1] In the same period he completed "May in Petersburg" and "A Trick of Fate," and wrote the first draft of an anecdote called "Fish Soup." These three works came out posthumously.

"Last Will Disregarded" is written in the style of an emotional plea *pro domo sua* and as such somewhat resembles *An Uncommon Story*. Goncharov's main point is that the sentence that a letter writer, whoever he may be, passes on his fellowmen and his fellowmen's works and deeds is all too often colored by spur-of-the-moment emotions and nervous reactions and that an artist's correspondence is therefore the least reliable source of his true thoughts and feelings. Goncharov resents literary historians, who peruse a writer's letters for his opinions, note the contradictions, and then draw all sorts of conclusions from them. He finds these conclusions worthless: in one instance the writer was in one frame of mind and in another — in just the opposite; in both instances his so-called opinions are far from binding.

Taking his position one step further, Goncharov rails against critics' passion for "digging" into a writer's biography; the work itself should suffice both public and critics. He is also very vocal in his protestations against the practice of "unearthing" sketches, outlines, and first drafts from a writer's "workshop." Such waste is being swept out of workshops. Any attempt at collecting it, at using it for research is both wrongheaded and fruitless; all it can do is damage the writer's image. The writer wants to appear in the raiments of his artistic maturity, and the public is being shown his diapers, small jackets and first scrawlings at the same time.

The climax of the piece is Goncharov's plea to his own correspondents to destroy his letters to them, to renounce all intention of making them public. When he claims that the letters have none of the polish and wit that characterize the correspondence of Pushkin or Turgenev (he was as much opposed, incidentally, to a complete edition of their letters as to one of his own), he is being unjustly hard on himself. He even goes so far as to maintain that they contain almost no reference to literature.

---

1) Cf. p. 94.

Fortunately, not all his correspondents did his bidding. The letters that have been gathered together show how groundless his self indictment was. But the extant letters are doubtless a mere fraction of the number he actually wrote. It is also a pity that he himself destroyed or had others destroy all the letters that were sent to him. If the obscure passages in his replies could have been deciphered, they would certainly have yielded many new insights into his complex psyche. This scarcity of correspondence places many obstacles in the way of the biographer and requires him to be extremely cautious in his generalizations.

"May in Petersburg" the first work, was completed in July 1891 and first published in the February 1892 issue of *The Cornfield* (Niva). The "hero" of the sketch — for it is a sketch in the style of "Christmas Time" or the "physiological sketches" of the forties — is a large apartment house in St. Petersburg. A.F. Koni claims it is the house on Mokhovaja Street that Goncharov lived in for so many years.

The reader makes the acquaintance of many of its tenants — the elegant Count and Countess Reshetilov with family and servants; Val'nev, a highly placed but incompetent official; a trio of lower officials — Bragin, Jukhnev, and Ponjushkin — and their cook Malan'ja; Chikhanov and his spouse, whose activities are not quite on the up-and-up; a pair of spinster sisters who are both idolized by Gruzdev, the wine-cellar owner downstairs; Ivan Ivanovich Khokhlov, the worldly wise superintendent; doorkeepers and janitors, and even/the cats, pigeons, and sparrows. Each character has a trait all his own, a living, telling keenly observed detail. Each goes about his own business, each strives for his own well-being, each cultivates his own goals, using whatever means he can.

From one May to the next the house stands firm, but inside everything is in motion. Though it may sometimes look as if life in it is standing still, everything is in fact changing. Only the slowness of the change makes it seem otherwise.

"Life is still life; everything keeps moving forward little by little. Onward and onward, somewhere, like everything in the world, on earth and in heaven." [1)]With this concluding philosophical remark Goncharov points

1) VII, p. 426.

up the action that has gone before: men of all kinds, resources, and convictions chasing after ephemeral pleasures. His style is new: instead of concentrating on long dialogues he strings together short, laconic sentences, effective images, expressive verbal interplay. Muted melancholy, a subdued humor, and a *vanitas vanitatum* spirit pervade this old man's message to the world that will survive him.

It is difficult to determine when the novella "Fish Soup" (the second "article") was written, but the handwriting [1] and the style would seem to place it toward the very end of his life. The fact that he gave it to Elena Treugut along with two late sketches lends credence to the internal evidence. Elena chose not to publish "Fish Soup," probably because of its somewhat frivolous content; the work did not appear until 1923 [2], and even then the text, taken from a rough copy, was riddled with errors. It made its second appearance in the 1952 collected works edition somewhat but apparently not completely purged of them. [3]

Quite scabrous for Goncharov, this anecdote is thematically reminiscent of Boccaccio's *novelle*. In its laconic style too it recalls the Italian Renaissance novella. It is supposedly based on a "half-true story" Goncharov had heard in Simbirsk, the story's locale, as it seems.

Two carts with three couples are on their way to the Volga for a picnic meal that is to consist of a fish soup made from fish caught on the spot. The wives occupy the first cart and their husbands — a bailiff, a deacon, and a small businessman — the second.

The first cart is being driven by Erema, a sexton and quiet God-fearing man who would gladly have married if he could have found someone to have him. But he was too poor and had such "a long back and short legs" that none of the robes in church would fit him.

Urged by their husbands, the women chide Erema and poke him in the back with their parasols. But Erema puts up with the pranks good-naturedly and takes care to say prayer every time they pass by a church.

---

1) Ogonek, VII, p. 502.
2) Engel'gardt, pp. 67–74.
3) Ogonek, VII, p. 490 sq.

As soon as they arrive, the men set off for the river and the women begin setting the table. Erema's duties consist only of caring first for the horses and later the samovar, and he immediately puts up a tent in a considerable distance to shield himself from the sun and lays down to sleep.

While the men are off fishing, one woman after the other goes over to make sure he is not sleeping on the job. Each one stays nearly an hour and emerges nervously, putting her hair and clothes in order.

All three women are quite still for the rest of the day. Their quiescence irritates the men, who continue to make fun of the equally quiet Erema when he appears with the samovar and while he sitting aside partakes plentifully of the soup. Nor do the women loosen their tongues on the way back; there is no teasing, no parasol prodding this time. But the men keep up their remarks from behind, and Erema once again says a prayer before every church. "Allholy Trinity, have mercy on us sinners," he intones as they pass the last one, the Church of Trinity. Silent Erema has made proper fools of three men and three women.

Although the narration is quite graphic and realistic details plentiful, anything the least bit suggestive remains unsaid. This opposition is as piquant as the opposition between Erema's piety and his actions or the husbands' self-assured jollity and their actual position. Doubtless the story would have been even more pointed and polished had Goncharov not dropped it before he had given it the finishing touches.

"A Trick of Fate," the third story, was completed on August 20, 1891, shortly before his death. It shows him in what seems to be an attempt at following Tolstoj's advice and writing a "tale for the people" in clear, universally understandable yet expressive language. As he himself notes at the story's end, the very simple plot derives from a story he heard from Uglickij (in fact, Zagrjazhskij), the governor of Simbirsk.

Leontij Khabarov, a poor but capable officer, cuts such a fine figure during a parade in Poland that the Grand Duke Konstantin Pavlovich (the action takes place around 1820) orders that he be transferred from his village regiment to Warsaw. Because his means do not allow him to remain in the city living in accordance to his rank, however, he is forced to ask for a discharge. His superiors write him such an excellent certificate that he feels assured of a fine Civil Service post. At first his wish seems to come true, but the procedures that must be followed before he is appointed drag on, and he soon finds himself destitute. After several ill-fated attempts to pull himself up by himself, without the State's assistance, he settles for a hard job as an unskilled laborer, with horny hands and half starved.

One day he gets by chance into the park of the Tsar's summer residence and meets Alexander I in person. He tells the Tsar his story and shows him his highly honorable discharge as proof. His fortune immediately takes an about face, and as soon as he recovers from the severe fever, caused by the physical and mental thrills he had been subjected to he receives a handsome sum from the Tsar and a position that relieves him from all future financial cares.

This last sketch suffers somewhat from the obvious pains Goncharov is taking to write "simply." What is more, the very material is not particularly fertile, though it is quite characteristic of his general conciliatory attitude and his feelings about monarchy.

On August 25, 1891 Stasjulevich visited Goncharov in Petergof and found him in such good health that he even had the strength to read aloud one of his recently completed sketches. Two days later he came down with an acute case of pneumonia that quickly sapped all his extra strength. For a while he seemed to be getting better, and on September 6th he was taken back to his apartment in Petersburg. But the sudden loss of energy proved too much for him; he had begun to feel the approach of death. Koni writes in his memoirs: "I visited him two days before his death. When I expressed the hope he would recover, he stared at me with his good eye, which was still twinkling and flickering with life, and said in a firm voice, 'No! I shall die . . . I saw Christ during the night, and He has pardoned me . . .'" [1] This is one of the very few vocalizations of the genuine religious feeling Goncharov always possessed, but had never gone out of his way to proclaim. [2]

---

1) Utevskij, p. 260.
2) It is interesting to note that N. Piksanov, the Soviet literary historian expressly states that Goncharov was a "religious man"; cf. "Roman Goncharova Obryv v svete social'noj istorii", Leningrad, 1968, p. 51.

At about noon after a visit from his doctor on September 15th Goncharov fell asleep never to awaken.

According to the newspapers' reports the crowd that gathered for the office for the dead on the next day was so large it filled the courtyard of the house out to the entrance gates. The funeral on the nineteenth turned into a major event. Mountains of wreaths followed the catafalque, and hundreds of people lined the streets from his house to the Aleksandr Nevskij Monastery where the last rites took place and where he was buried. Almost all the literary world was present, and the Grand Duke Konstantin Konstantinovich was charged with representing the Tsar and his family. Large scale participation by the greater public showed clearly that despite his seclusion Goncharov had not been forgotten.

When in 1956 the cemetery was closed, Goncharov's remains were re-interred in the literary section of the Volkov Cemetery.

Bibliographical Remarks

A near complete Goncharov-Bibliography exists now:

A. D. Alekseev: Bibliografija I.A. Goncharova. Goncharov v pechati. Pechat' o Goncharove. (1832–1964). Leningrad 1968. (Referred to in the notes as "Bibliografija".)

The two most complete editions of Goncharov's works are:

Sobranie sochinenij, tt. I–VIII. Komm. A.G. Cejtlina, Moskva, "Pravda", 1952 (B–ka "Ogonek").(Referred to as "Ogonek and volume number.")
Sobranie sochinenij, tt. I–VIII. Moskva, Goslitizdat, 1952–1955. (Referred to by volume number.)

Not included in any edition (Ogonek has short excerpts):

Neobyknovennaja istorija. (Istinnye sobytija). Redakcija i primechanija D.I. Abramovicha. – Sbornik Rossijskoj Publichnoj Biblioteki, t. II. Materialy i issledovanija, vyp. 1. Petrograd, 1924. (Referred to as "N. I.".)

Goncharov's letters from his voyage were published with an excellent introduction by B.M. Èngel'gardt:

Putevye pis'ma I.A. Goncharova iz krugosvetnogo plavanja (29). Publikacija i komm. B.M. Engel'gardta. – Literaturnoe nasledstvo, Moskva, 1935, t. 22–24, s. 344–427. (Referred to as "Literaturnoe nasledstvo".)

Interesting material will be found in:

I.A. Goncharov. Literaturno-kriticheskie stat'i i pis'ma, Redakcija vstupitel'naja stat'ja i primechanija A.P. Rybasova. Leningrad, 1938. (Referred to as "Literaturno-kriticheskie stat'ji".)

The most important monographs dealing with Goncharov in chronological order are:

1) E.A.Ljackij: I.A.Goncharov. Kriticheskie ocherki. St.Petersburg, 1904.

2) André Mazon: Un maître du roman russe Ivan Goncharov, Paris, 1914. (Referred to as "Mazon".)

3) E.A. Ljackij: Goncharov. Zhizn', lichnost', tvorchestvo. Kritiko-biograficheskie ocherki. Stokgol'm, 1920.

4) I.A.Goncharov i I.S.Turgenev. Po neizdannym materialam Pushkinskogo doma. S predisloviem i primechanijami B.M. Èngel'gardta. Petrograd, 1923. (Referred to as "Èngel'gardt".)

5) E.A. Ljackij: Roman i zhizn'. Razvitie tvorcheskoj lichnosti I.A. Goncharova. Zhizn' i byt. 1812–1857. Praga, 1925. (Referred to as "Ljackij".)

6) L.S. Utevskij: Zhizn' Goncharova. Moskva 1931. (Referred to as "Utevskij".)

7) A.G. Cejtlin: I.A.Goncharov. Moskva, 1950. (Referred to as "Cejtlin".)

8) A.D.Alekseev: Letopis' zhizni i tvorchestva I.A.Goncharova. Moskva-Leningrad, 1960. (Referred to as "Alekseev".)

9) N. I.Pruckov: Masterstvo Goncharova-romanista. Moskva-Leningrad, 1962. (Referred to as "Pruckov".)

10) Walther Rehm: Gontscharow und Jacobsen oder Langeweile und Schwermut. Göttingen, 1963. (Referred to as " Rehm".)

11) O.M. Chemena: Sozdanie dvukh romanov. Goncharov i shestidesjatnica E.P. Majkova. Moskva, 1966. (Referred to as "Chemena".)

12) I.A.Goncharov v vospominanijakh sovremennikov. Podgotovka teksta i primechanija A.D. Alekseeva i O.A.Demikhovskoj. Leningrad, 1969. (Referred to as "Vosp.sovr.".)

Most valuable information about Goncharov contain:

E.A.Shtakenshnejder: Dnevnik i zapiski (1854–1886). Moskva-Leningrad, 1934.(Referred to as "Shtakenshnejder".)

A.V. Nikitenko: Dnevnik, tt. I–III, Moskva, 1955–1956. (Referred to as "Nikitenko".)

Two stimulating and original articles were not included in "Bibliografija":

Leon Stillman: Oblomovka Revisited. The American Slavic and East European Review, 1948, v. VII, Nr.1, pp. 46–77.

N. Narokov: Opravdanie Oblomova. (K 100- letiju romana).
Novyj Zhurnal, 1960. Kn. 59, pp. 95–108.

Published in 1969: François de Labriolle: Oblomov n'est-il
qu'un paresseux? Cahiers du Monde russe et sovietique, v. X,
pp. 38–51.

Volumes 3, 4 and 6 of Literaturnyj arkhiv, Materialy po istorii
literatury i obshchestvennogo dvizhenija. Pod redakciej M.P. Alekseeva, 1951, 1953 and 1961 contain drafts and letters by Goncharov with valuable commentaries. (Referred to as "Literaturnayj
archiv".)

Index of Goncharov's Works

For a discussion of Goncharov's four poems see pp. 14–16

Index of Proper Names

If no nationality is indicated the personalities mentioned are Russian.

Genlis, Stéphanie-Félicité (1746–1830), French writer, 3, 132
Gercen, see Herzen
Gessner, Salomon (1730–1788), Swiss poet and painter, 109
Glazunov, Ivan (1826–1889), publisher and bookseller in Petersburg, 305
Godunov, Boris (ca. 1552–1605), Tsar of Russia (1598–1605), 263
Godwin, William (1756–1836), English writer, 135 n.
Goethe, Johann Wolfgang (1749–1832), German poet, dramatist and writer, 69,
          132, 170, 207, 265, 302
Gogol', Nikolaj (1809–1852), writer and dramatist, 17, 19, 20, 21, 25–27, 29, 32,
          33, 55, 63, 71, 156, 159, 177, 193, 204, 263, 284, 304
Golenishchev-Kutuzov, Arsenij (1848–1913), poet, 303
Golikov, Ivan (1735–1801), historian, 3
Goncharov, Aleksandr (1754–1819), father of the writer, 1
Goncharov, Aleksandr (1843–1907), nephew of the writer, 239, 293 n.
Goncharov, Nikolaj (1808), brother of the writer, 1, 4
Goncharova, Aleksandra, see Kirmalova
Goncharova, Anna, see Muzalevskaja
Goncharova, Avdot'ja (1785–1851), mother of the writer, 1, 2, 79, 234
Goncharova, Elizaveta (? –1883), wife of the writer's brother, 111
Goncharova, Elizaveta, wife of the writer's nephew Aleksandr, 293 n.
Grech, Nikolaj (1787–1867), journalist, writer and philologist, 281, 282
Griboedov, Aleksandr (1795–1829), dramatist, poet and writer, 31, 32, 69, 204,
          252, 253–255, 263, 280
Grigor'ev, Konstantin (1799–1871), governor of Yakutsk 1850–1856, 94, 96
Grigorovich, Dmitrij (1822–1899), writer, 13
Grimm, Avgust (1805–1878), educator of Grand Duke Nikolaj, 122
Grot, Jakov (1812–1893), literary historian, slavist, 122, 178

Hall, Basil (1788–1842), English traveller, 90
Haller, Albrecht (1708–1777), Swiss poet and scientist, 90
Hansen, Peter (1846–1930), Danish translator, 289–292, 294
Heine, Heinrich (1797–1856), German poet and writer, 233
Herzen, Aleksandr (1812–1870), writer and journalist, 119, 166, 167, 255
Hesiod (8th century B.C.?), Greek poet, 128
Hoffmann, Ernst Theodor Amadeus (1776–1822), German writer, 26
Homer (ca. 8th century B.C.), Greek epic poet, 7, 77

Innokentij (Ivan Pavlov-Veniaminov) (1797–1879), Archbishop in Siberia (since
          1848), Metropolitan of Moscow (since 1868); ethnographer, missionary,
          94, 97

Ivan IV, „the Terrible" (1530-1584), Tsar of Russia (1544-1584), 263
Ivanov, Aleksandr (1806-1858), painter, 212
Ivashkovskij, Semen (1775-1850), Professor of Greek at Moscow University, 6, 10

Janin, Jules (1804-1874), French writer, 8
Jazykov, Mikhail (1811-1885), close friend of Goncharov, so as his wife Ekaterina
     (? - 1896), 41, 87-90, 97

Kachenovskij, Mikhail (1775-1842), historian, 10
Kameneckij, Tit (1790-1844), headmaster of Moscow Commercial Academy, 4
Karamzin, Nikolaj (1766-1826), writer, poet, historian, 3, 5, 68, 84, 195
Khalezov, Aleksandr, senior navigation officer of the frigate "Pallada", 82
Kheraskov, Mikhail (1733-1807), poet, dramatist, writer, 3, 5
Kierkegaard, Sören (1813-1855), Danish philosopher, 149, 203, 291
Kirmalov, Mikhail (? - 1850), landowner; husband of Goncharov's sister Alek-
     sandra, 112
Kirmalov, Viktor (1834-1912), Goncharov's nephew, 180, 181, 185, 236
Kirmalov, Vladimir, Goncharov's nephew, 239
Kirmalova, Aleksandra (1815-1896), Goncharov's sister, 1, 79, 112, 180
Kirmalova, Dar'ja (1841-1918), wife of Goncharov's nephew Viktor, 185, 308, 315
Klopstock, Friedrich Gottlieb (1742-1803), German poet, 7
Kol'cov, Aleksej (1809-1842), poet, 298
Kolzakova, Avdot'ja, an acquaintance of Goncharov in the fifties, 112
Koni, Anatolij (1844-1927), lawyer, academician, 23, 24 n., 110, 296, 305, 307,
     308, 310, 320, 323
Koni, Fedor (1809-1879), poet, writer, journalist, 9
Konstantin Konstantinovich, Grand Duke (1858-1915), poet writing under the
     pseudonym K.R., 263, 301-304, 324
Konstantin Nikolaevich, Grand Duke (1827-1892), statesman, high military of-
     ficer, 116, 256
Konstantin Pavlovich, Grand Duke (1779-1831), Cesarevich of Russia, 322
Korenev, Andrej (1821-1891), Goncharov's colleague at the Ministry of Finances,
     121
Kovalevskij, Evgraf (1790? -1867), geologist; Minister of Education 1858-1861,
     167
Kraevskij, Andrej (1810-1889), journalist, 78, 79, 167, 266, 281
Kramskoj, Ivan (1837-1887), painter, 258, 261
Krashennikov, Stepan (1711-1755), explorer of Kamchatka, 3
Kridener, Nikolaj, lieutenant on the frigate "Pallada", 82
Krylov, Ivan (1768-1844), poet, 69, 103, 280

Margaret Dalton

Andrei Siniavskii and Julii Daniel'
Two Soviet "Heretical" Writers

1973. 190 pages. DM 26.—   ISBN 3 7778 0082 1
(= colloquium slavicum, Band 1)

Marina Ledkovsky

The Other Turgenev: From Romanticism to Symbolism

1973. 170 pages. DM 24.—   ISBN 3 7778 0085 6
(= colloquium slavicum, Band 2)

Joan Delaney Grossman

Edgar Allan Poe in Russia
A Study in Legend and Literary Influence

1973. 245 pages. DM 30.—   ISBN 3 7778 0084 8
(= colloquium slavicum, Band 3)